ICWMC 2017

The Thirteenth International Conference on Wireless and Mobile Communications

July 23 - 27, 2017

Nice, France

ICWMC 2017 Editors

Carlos Becker Westphall, University of Santa Catarina, Brazil

Khalil El-Khatib, University of Ontario, Canada

Dragana Krstic, University of Nis, Serbia

Hamid Menouar, Qatar Mobility Innovations Center, Qatar

Printed from e-media with permission by:

Curran Associates, Inc.
57 Morehouse Lane
Red Hook, NY 12571

Some format issues inherent in the e-media version may also appear in this print version.

Printed by Curran Associates, Inc. (2017)

International Academy, Research, and Industry Association (IARIA)
412 Derby Way
Wilmington, DE 19810

Phone: (408) 893-6407
Fax: (408) 527-6351

petre@iaria.org

Additional copies of this publication are available from:

Curran Associates, Inc.
57 Morehouse Lane
Red Hook, NY 12571 USA
Phone: 845-758-0400
Fax: 845-758-2633
Email: curran@proceedings.com
Web: www.proceedings.com

Table of Contents

Systematic Review: Techniques and Methods of Urban Monitoring in Intelligent Transport Systems 1
Sergio F Lima, Sergio A. A. Barbosa, Priscila C Palmeira, Lucas Matos, Ingrid Secundo, and Rogerio Nascimento

Performance Evaluation of User Class Based Call Admission Control Techniques in Next Generation Wireless Networks 6
Mahesh Gangathimmappa, Gowrishankar Subramanian, and Rameshbabu H Siddamallaiah

Throughput Evaluation Approach for GSM Networks 12
Ismail Yildiz and Sena Aydeniz

Multicriteria QoS-aware Solution in Wireless Multi-hop Networks 17
Jean Nunes R. Araujo, Claudio de Castro Monteiro, and Lucas de Souza Batista

Performance Enhancement of MTC in LTE Networks by Maximizing Random Access Procedure Throughput 24
Ibraheem Fayed and Eman S. El-Din

Level Crossing Rate of Macrodiversity in the Presence of Short Term Fading and Long Term Fading with Different Average Powers 29
Dragana Krstic, Mihajlo Stefanovic, Vladeta Milenkovic, and Sinisa Minic

Behavior Analysis for WebRTC Peer-to-Peer Streaming with Dynamic Topology 35
Khalid Kahloot, Patrik J. Braun, and Peter Ekler

A WSN Testbed to Enhance Irrigation Techniques Using a Novel Event-Based Routing Protocol 41
Maher Al Rantisi, Glenford Mapp, and Orhan Gemikonakli

Locating Multiple Camera Sensors and Wireless Access Points for a Generalized Indoor Positioning System 51
Jaime Duque Domingo, Carlos Cerrada, Enrique Valero, and Jose Antonio Cerrada

Delay-Aware Network Optimization in LTE Based High-Speed Railway Wireless Networks 57
Ali Huseyin Rustem, Selcuk Cevher, and Hakan Ali Cirpan

Battery-less Near Field Communication Sensor Tag Energy Study with ContactLess Simulator 63
David Navarro, Guilherme Migliato-Marega, and Laurent Carrel

Residential Wireless Interfaces Virtualization: a Feasibility Study 67
Antonio da Silva Farina, Ana B. Garcia Hernando, and Mary L. Mouronte Lopez

Towards a Mobile Enhancement of Glocal Heritage? Developing user experiences in relation to mobile technologies, geo-localisation and culture 73

Laurent Antonczak and Catherine Papetti

Monetizing IoT: Enabled via LTE Broadcast 78
Rajat Kochhar and Nipun Sharma

Blockchain for Enterprise: Overview, Opportunities and Challenges 83
Elyes Ben Hamida, Kei Leo Brousmiche, Hugo Levard, and Eric Thea

Roadside-Assisted V2V Messaging for Connected Autonomous Vehicle 89
Manabu Tsukada

A Robust Distributed Notch Filtering Algorithm for Frequency Estimation Over Sensor Networks 95
Wael Bazzi, Amir Rastegarnia, Azam Khalili, and Mahtab Bahrami

An Optimal Design of Multiplexer Based Conservative Gate in Quantum-Dot Cellular Automata 100
Jeon Jun-Cheol and Nuriddin Safoev

Design of QCA Full Adder for Multiplier Circuit 102
Jeon Jun-Cheol and You Young-Won

A Sensor Networking Architecture for ENTROPY - Energy-Aware Information and Communication Technologies Infrastructure Enabling Smart Building Solutions 104
Aristotelis Agianniotis, Vincent Schule, Antonio Jara, Mariam Barque, and Dominique Genoud

Accurate Localization Using Augmented UHF RFID System for Internet-of-Things 107
Jing Wang and Miodrag Bolic

Channel Estimation and Equalization Algorithm for OFDM-Based Underwater Acoustic Communications Systems 113
Mhd Tahssin Altabbaa and Erdal Panayirci

Trust-Based Defence Model Against MAC Unfairness Attacks for IoT 119
Nabil Djedjig, Djamel Tandjaoui, Imed Romdhani, and Faiza Medjek

Distributed Upstream Data Cleaning in VANET 123
Mohamed Ben Brahim and Hamid Menouar

ICWMC 2017

Foreword

The Thirteenth International Conference on Wireless and Mobile Communications (ICWMC 2017), held between July 23 - 27, 2017 - Nice, France, followed on the previous events on advanced wireless technologies, wireless networking, and wireless applications.

ICWMC 2017 addressed wireless related topics concerning integration of latest technological advances to realize mobile and ubiquitous service environments for advanced applications and services in wireless networks. Mobility and wireless, special services and lessons learnt from particular deployment complemented the traditional wireless topics.

We take here the opportunity to warmly thank all the members of the ICWMC 2017 Technical Program Committee, as well as the numerous reviewers. The creation of such a high quality conference program would not have been possible without their involvement. We also kindly thank all the authors who dedicated much of their time and efforts to contribute to ICWMC 2017. We truly believe that, thanks to all these efforts, the final conference program consisted of top quality contributions.

Also, this event could not have been a reality without the support of many individuals, organizations, and sponsors. We are grateful to the members of the ICWMC 2017 organizing committee for their help in handling the logistics and for their work to make this professional meeting a success.

We hope that ICWMC 2017 was a successful international forum for the exchange of ideas and results between academia and industry and for the promotion of progress in the area of wireless and mobile communications.

We are convinced that the participants found the event useful and communications very open. We also hope that Nice provided a pleasant environment during the conference and everyone saved some time for exploring this beautiful city.

ICWMC 2017 Chairs:

ICWMC Steering Committee

Carlos Becker Westphall, Universidade Federal de Santa Catarina, Brazil
Brian M. Sadler, Army Research Laboratory, USA
Magnus Jonsson, Halmstad University, Sweden
Afrand Agah, West Chester University of Pennsylvania, USA
Pradipta De, Georgia Southern University, USA
David Sanchez, University of Las Palmas de Gran Canaria, Spain
David Navarro, Ecole Centrale de Lyon, France
Carl James Debono, University of Malta, Malta
Xiang Gui, Massey University, New Zealand
Zdenek Becvar, Czech Technical University in Prague, Czech Republic
Dragana Krstic, University of Niš, Serbia

ICWMC Industry/Research Advisory Committee

ICWMC 2017

Committee

ICWMC Steering Committee

Carlos Becker Westphall, Universidade Federal de Santa Catarina, Brazil
Brian M. Sadler, Army Research Laboratory, USA
Magnus Jonsson, Halmstad University, Sweden
Afrand Agah, West Chester University of Pennsylvania, USA
Pradipta De, Georgia Southern University, USA
David Sanchez, University of Las Palmas de Gran Canaria, Spain
David Navarro, Ecole Centrale de Lyon, France
Carl James Debono, University of Malta, Malta
Xiang Gui, Massey University, New Zealand
Zdenek Becvar, Czech Technical University in Prague, Czech Republic
Dragana Krstic, University of Niš, Serbia

ICWMC Industry/Research Advisory Committee

Augusto Morales, Check Point Software Technologies, Spain
Hua Zhou, Fujitsu R&D Center Ltd - Beijing, China
Sivakumar Sivaramakrishnan, vToggle Ltd., New Zealand
Christian Makaya, IBM T.J. Watson Research Center, USA
Cheng Bo, Huawei Technologies, USA
Kostas Katsalis, Eurecom, France
Christopher Nguyen, Intel Corp., USA

ICWMC 2017 Technical Program Committee

Afrand Agah, West Chester University of Pennsylvania, USA
Hamed Al-Raweshidy, Brunel University London, UK
Hanan Al-Tous, United Arab Emirates University, AlAin, UAE
Radu Arsinte, Technical University of Cluj-Napoca, Romania
Stylianos Basagiannis, United Technologies Research Centre, USA
Carlos Becker Westphall, Universidade Federal de Santa Catarina, Brazil
Zdenek Becvar, Czech Technical University in Prague, Czech Republic
Luca Bedogni, University of Bologna, Italy
Chafika Benzaid, University of Sciences and Technology Houari Boumediene (USTHB), Algeria
Vincent Beroulle, Univ. Grenoble Alpes LCIS, France
Robert Bestak, Czech Technical University in Prague, Czech Republic
Cheng Bo, Huawei Technologies, USA
Jean-Marie Bonnin, Institut Mines Télécom / IMT Atlantique - Inria IRISA, France
David Boyle, Imperial College London, UK
Maurizio Bozzi, University of Pavia, Italy

Carlos Enrique Palau Salvador, Universidad Politecnica de Valencia, Spain
Erdal Panayirci, Kadir Has University, Turkey
Jung-Min Park, Korea Institute of Science and Technology (KIST), Korea
Salvatore F. Pileggi, The University of Queensland, Brisbane, Australia
Iwona Pozniak-Koszalka, Wroclaw University of Science and Technology, Poland
Yue Qiao, Ohio State University, USA
Piotr Remlein, Poznan University of Technology, Poland
Éric Renault, Institut Mines-Télécom | Télécom SudParis, France
Dushantha Nalin K. Jayakody, National Research Tomsk Polytechnic University, Russia
Imed Romdhani, Edinburgh Napier University, UK
Brian M. Sadler, Army Research Laboratory, USA
David Sánchez Rodríguez, University of Las Palmas de Gran Canaria (ULPGC), Spain
José Santa Lozano, University of Murcia, Spain
Hossein Sarrafzadeh, Unitec Institute of Technology, Auckland, New Zealand
Kuei-Ping Shih, Tamkang University, Taiwan
Mohammad Shojafar, CNIT | University of Rome Tor Vergata, Italy
Sivakumar Sivaramakrishnan, vToggle Ltd., New Zealand
Wojciech Siwicki, Gdansk University of Technology, Poland
Kuo-Feng Ssu, National Cheng Kung University, Taiwan
Álvaro Suárez Sarmiento, Universidad de Las Palmas de Gran Canaria, Spain
Young-Joo Suh, Postech (Pohang University of Science & Technology), Korea
Li Sun, University at Buffalo, The State University of New York, USA
Fatma Tansu Hocanın, Eastern Mediterranean University, Northern Cyprus
Necmi Taspinar, Erciyes University, Turkey
Rui Teng, Advanced Telecommunications Research Institute International, Japan
Angelo Trotta, University of Bologna, Italy
Guodong Wang, South Dakota School of Mines and Technology, USA
You-Chiun Wang, National Sun Yat-sen University, Taiwan
Wei Wei, Xi'an University of Technology, China
Ouri Wolfson, University of Illinois at Chicago, USA
Pei Xiao, University of Surrey, UK
Ping Yang, State University of New York at Binghamton, USA
Tiguiane Yelemou, Polytechnic University of Bobo-Dioulasso, Burkina Faso
M. Erkan Yuksel, Mehmet Akif Ersoy University, Turkey
Sherali Zeadally, University of Kentucky, USA
Junqing Zhang, Queen's University Belfast, UK
Yan Zhang, Imec-NL, Netherlands
Bo Zhou, Shanghai Jiao Tong University, China
Hua Zhou, Fujitsu R&D Center Ltd - Beijing, China
Yuxun Zhou, University of California, Berkeley, USA

Copyright Information

Systematic Review: Techniques and Methods of Urban Monitoring in Intelligent Transport Systems

Lima, S. F., Barbosa, S. A. A., Palmeira, P. C., Matos, L., Secundo, I., Nascimento, R.
Department of Post-Graduation in Computer Science
Federal University of Sergipe - UFS
Sergipe, Brazil
email: sergio@acad.unit.br; saabarbosa@gmail.com; priscilacopeland@gmail.com; lucas.matos.cc@gmail.com; ingrid.secundoo@gmail.com; rogerio@ufs.br.

Abstract— **The process of urbanization and the formation of large urban complexes influence the increasing complexity for the planning, management and operation of urban mobility. Everyday problems related to urban mobility, such as congestion, quality of urban roads and inefficiency of public transport are evident, and can only be solved by the increase of technology and intelligence. Studies in Intelligent Transport Systems (ITS) act as an efficient solution to improve the functioning and performance of traffic systems, reducing congestion and increasing safety for citizens. With the objective of identifying and analyzing urban monitoring techniques, this article presents a systematic review of the monitoring techniques, in order to extract traffic behavior on the road in real time, making it possible to detect congestion, avoid accidents, among others Improvements to urban traffic. The significant benefit of this article includes a bibliographical research, based on the analysis of the problems related to ITS in function of the evolution, the variety and the complexity of technologies existing in the last years.**

Keywords- ***ITS; Urban Monitoring; Open Data; Smart Cities***.

I. INTRODUCTION

With the growth of urban centers and the need for agility and efficiency in access to services and information, connectivity plays a key and essential role in this global and digital interaction. In this context, the "Digital Cities" gain space and present themselves as a viable path, as can be observed in studies that point to the use of technologies in an urban context [1].

One of the main problems of urban centers today is mobility. The connectivity inherent to the "Digital Cities" opens a very promising frontier with regard to the control of access to information, as can be seen in the works related to ITS in China [2][3] and the distributed ITS architectures [4].

An ITS represents "the application of advanced sensors, computers, electronic devices and communication technologies and integrated strategic management, aiming to improve the safety and efficiency of the traffic management system" [5]. This interconnectedness of the "Intelligent Cities", when applied to the control of urban mobility, aims at the search of the efficiency in the displacement and fluidity of traffic and, consequently, an improvement of quality for the people that interact in this system and depend, directly, of the efficiency and Quality of this environment. According to Kim [6], "the speed of traffic is an important part in communicating the data. For engineers, this data complements other traffic information that reflects on road network performance and alerts of possible road traffic incidents. For drivers, the speed information reflects in the drivability. This is easily achieved, unlike other traffic data such as volume and density that are harder to relate to. "

However, these sources of Information and Communication Technologies (TIC) form complex structures and generate a large volume of data, which present great challenges and opportunities, making it difficult to offer programs that integrate sensor information and capture the physical space In real time. It is worth mentioning that open data initiatives are being carried out by governments at all levels in order to increase transparency, empower citizens, foster innovations and reform public services [2]. These initiatives converge with "Smart Cities" and different solutions are already in place in cities such as New York, Amsterdam, Helsinki, Chicago, Barcelona, Quebec City, Rio, Dublin, Nairobi and Manchester at different rates and scales.

In this context, the present article presents monitoring techniques with the objective of contributing to a better understanding and enrichment for the state of the art in ITS. It is worth mentioning that using these techniques, urban monitoring, has been extremely efficient, allowing a rigth and fast response for the community's needs, especially on intervention in traffic flow and safety. The most types of equipment and technological monitoring solutions are available for the safety and well-being of society. Some related works cited in this review, address several techniques, whether they are carried out in a simulated environment or real-time environment, but most of them do not follow policies of effective urban control, formalized by laws, norms and monitoring, that allows the coexistence and harmony between citizens, respecting the space of all.

The structure of the article is organized as follows. In section II, we consider the application of a systematic review to identify the techniques and methods of urban monitoring in ITS. In section III, a literature review to confront authors addressing the subject proposed. In section IV, an analysis and summary of selected papers about the subject researched. And section V, show the research findings.

II. Systematic Review Protocol

This section contains the protocol based on [7], which was used to apply the systematic review, whose focus of the searches, focused on the identification of the researches that present proposals related to techniques and methods of urban monitoring in ITS.

A. *Formulations of questions*

Question: What are the techniques and methods of urban monitoring in ITS that use/not Open Data?

B. *Source Selection Criteria*

Availability of query of articles in databases through the web (IEEE Xplorer, ACM Digital Library, DPLP Computer Science Bibliography), using the search field Title. The following search string used:

- (intelligent <and> transport <and> system) <and> (open <and> data) <and> (urban <and> monitoring)

C. *Criteria for inclusion of articles*

- Articles should be available for download on the web;
- The articles found must present complete texts of the studies in electronic format;
- Articles should be described in English or Portuguese;
- Articles that have been published in the last 5 years (between 2011 and 2016);

D. *Preliminary screening process for primary studies*

The search strategy will be applied for the identification of potential primary studies. With the studies researched, the title and summaries will be read. Given the relevance of a study, already highlighted in the abstract, it will be selected to be read in its entirety.

E. *Final selection process of primary studies*

It consists of the complete reading of the selected studies in the preliminary selection stage. The reviewers will be responsible for making a general summary and considerations on the results observed in the selected studies.

III. Literature Review

The ITS, aim to support the various everyday situations related to urban mobility, through the use of technologies and interoperability between communication systems, data transmission and connectivity.

Its efficiency in monitoring and agility in the distribution of information is essential so that the results regarding the optimization of transportation systems are felt by the general population that are included in this scenario, allowing a better management of the transportation system Urban [17][18].

The work of Nasim and Kassler [18] can be subdivided into six advanced management areas: Advanced Traffic Management System, Advanced Traveler Information Systems, Advanced Public Transport Systems, Commercial Vehicle Operating Systems, Advanced Vehicle Control Systems, Electronic Toll Collection. All these subsystems have the objective of acting in a specific and targeted manner on subareas of transportation management, seeking to guarantee the efficiency and quality of urban mobility.

According to the Open Definition [19], open data is data that can be freely used, reused and redistributed by anyone - subject to at most the requirement of original source allocation and sharing by the same licenses in which the information was presented. In other words, the opening of data is interested in avoiding a mechanism of control and restrictions on the data that are published, allowing both individuals and corporations, to exploit this data freely. From this perspective, the definition of the term open data presents three fundamental norms [20]: availability and access, reuse and redistribution and universal participation (areas of action and people / groups).

From the moment that there is a movement to make data available, where the three fundamental norms mentioned above are respected, it is possible that different organizations and systems can work in a collaborative way. This is due to the ability of these organizations and systems to interoperate the data that have been opened, thus increasing communication and enhancing the efficient development of complex systems [21].

IV. Analysis and Summary of Selected Work

After the implementation of the Systematic Review Protocol (PRS), 83 scientific articles were initially identified (36 articles in the IEEE Xplorer, 28 in the ACM Digital Library and 19 in the DPLP Computer Science Bibliography), from the keywords used in the three databases. Data consulted. When the inclusion and exclusion criteria were applied in the reading of the title and abstracts of the articles, 6 articles were selected and analyzed in order to answer the two questions proposed in the PRS. The following is an overview of the work.

Jérôme et al. [8] show a platform that models and simulates applications within the scope of ITS. In the work is pointed out an open source framework, called iTETRIS, where it is formed by a set of other tools, each one having its specificities. These tools are: the Simulation of Urban Mobility (SUMO) framework that is responsible for simulating vehicle traffic; And a network simulator called the NS-3. In addition to these tools, there is a layer of control that does all management, keeping the data of each application synchronized. According to [8], the methodology used resources to analyze and manage applications, such as bus lane management, emergency vehicles, dynamic route planning, and the study of speed adaptation. This article also highlights the benefits that the framework can bring, such as reducing travel time, fuel economy or reducing pollutant emissions. Also mentioned are the characteristics that stand out over other works in the literature, where among these particularities mentioned in it, is the possibility of extending functionalities, precisely because it is an open source source. Despite the benefits mentioned in the article, it was not necessary to evaluate the studies in real environments, which would imply in the more loyal dimensioning of the results.

Ilya et al. [9] have an approach for monitoring traffic in large urban areas using drone technology. The authors state that the use of this technology offers innumerable advantages, such as: ease of access to irregular areas due to their small dimensions, coupling of several sensors to estimate general conditions of traffic in real time, independent monitoring of climatic factors, monitoring of offenders The creation of cartographic models of road traffic structures, among others. According to [9], Global Positioning System (GPS) technologies, although with high open-pit accuracy, may be inefficient with respect to the signal in areas of dense urban shading. Thus, in the absence of GPS signals, an analysis was proposed on the drone control system using a bimodal structure. The bimodal scheme allows the performance in safe mode of navigation. In case of a malfunction, the system allows the equipment to remain or return to the point of origin, thus avoiding possible accidents on public roads. This prototype was successfully tested for the monitoring of the transport infrastructure of the city of Orel (Russia).

Zan et al. [10] present an application was installed in the users' smartphone, where the personal data, the travel profile (origin, destination, purpose, location and time) and sensor data (GPS, time, and Accelerometer). During application operation, if your smartphone is connected to a power source and the connection is available, the data is automatically transmitted to the server. These collected data are analyzed for events such as congestion of frequent braking activities, speed and travel time variation. With this one can notify the drivers of the traffic condition and send driving recommendation so that they will be able to make informed decisions. Due to the smartphones used by the users of different brands and models, it resulted in the inconsistency of the data collected. This issue has to be resolved in future implementations.

The results of Fayazi et al. [11] are based on data from bus movements in the city of San Francisco. Data bus power is provided by NextBus to a number of cities in North America in XML. The attributes of interest are the position and speed of each vehicle along with its weather identifier and the bus identification number. In addition, bus route data and bus location locations were extracted from the same data stream. Fayazi et al. [11] also demonstrated the feasibility of timing estimation of fixed-time traffic lights, for example, at intersections in the city of San Francisco the feasibility of estimating cycle time, red signal time, green signal start, Change of signal programming. The extensive use of filtering / preprocessing data is elementary to the successes found in [11]. It is noted that the influence of heavy traffic conditions on the prediction is not investigated in this work neither the adaptive signals were considered.

Shi et al. [12] used the Bayesian Logic model to predict in real time. The probability of an accident occurring, logistic regression models were evaluated under Bayesian conditions. Therefore, this statistical method is able to handle information from different sources. With the rapid development in Big Data, it is expected that new data sources can be incorporated into this modeling framework in the future.

Unlike other previous real-time traffic safety studies, Shi et al. [12] incorporate a reliability analysis to determine the conditions under which it is appropriate to trigger safety warnings on the expressway. The First-Order Reliability Method (FORM) model was constructed based on the real-time fall forecast model and based on the critical point of the CI system, where volume and velocity were obtained. It was found that the average peak IC for failures per hour was equal to the congestion threshold, which suggested that when congestion is detected at a specific location, both congestion and safety warnings should be sent to drivers. Also in [12], a method of combined real-time congestion and safety monitoring in urban expressways was proposed through the Multipoint Video Distribution System (MVDS) system.

Wang et al. [13] designed a monitor urban traffic using the Markov model to measure the estimated traffic accuracy according to vehicle position and speed. This model takes into account the mean, variance, and correlation of the traffic in a particular stretch of road being mapped over a given period with the impact of granularity on the accuracy of traffic estimation so that we can measure the quality of service in the system through Granularity function.

Santos et al. [14] method can be conceptualized as: rule, norm, search for truth, detection of errors in the attempt to achieve a desired goal. Some authors, in defining method, emphasize intelligence and talent in the way they perform tasks. Others focus on the aspects of order, path, security and economy in the accomplishment of an activity.

Lakatos et al. [15] show that among various concepts of methods we can mention: Method is the "path by which a certain result is arrived at, although that path has not been fixed in advance in a reflected and deliberate way".

Method is a way of selecting techniques for evaluating alternatives to scientific action. So, while the techniques used by a scientist are the fruit of their decisions, the way in which such decisions are made depends on their decision rules. Methods are rules of choice; techniques are their own choices " [15].

Method is also the way to proceed along a path. In science, methods are the basic tools that order the thought of systems in the first place, and in an orderly way the scientist's way of proceeding along a path to achieve an objective.

The term method already existed in classical Greek (méthodos), having been used by Plato and Aristotle in the sense of "ordered study of a philosophical or scientific question". The word can be decomposed into the prefix metá + hodós, which means path, path, route. In the generic sense, therefore, it is the "way by which a certain result is arrived at". In scientific terminology, method can be defined as a set of data and rules to proceed, allowing to reach a predetermined end.

Marconi et al. [16] technique is a set of precepts or processes that serve a science or art; this technique allow him to bring the teorical norms to the practice. Marconi's technique defines the way of proceeding in its smallest details, the operationalization of the method according to standards. It is a result of experience and requires skill in its execution. The same method may involve more than one technique. The semantic difference between method and technique can be compared to that between gender and species.

In order to discover and analyze the techniques and methods most used in the selected articles, the techniques and the monitoring methods present in each article, set out in Table 1 and 2, were identified where the symbol "✓" indicates the existence of the observed characteristic:

TABLE I. MONITORING METHODS

Methods	[8]	[9]	[10]	[11]	[12]	[13]
Traffic Management				✓	✓	
GPS monitoring		✓	✓			
Drone Monitoring		✓				
Camera Monitoring		✓				
Combined Real Time Monitoring					✓	

According to Table 1, it is possible to note that the most used methods are: "Traffic Management", with two articles; And "GPS monitoring", also with two articles. It is assumed that these characteristics were the most used, as they are responsible for managing the traffic and obtaining the location of the transport, respectively.

TABLE II. MONITORING TECHNIQUES

Techniques	[8]	[9]	[10]	[11]	[12]	[13]
Framework for simulating vehicle traffic	✓					
Markov model						✓
Open Data Approach	✓			✓	✓	
Use of Monitoring Software		✓	✓	✓	✓	✓
Data Mining			✓	✓		✓
Bayesian Inference					✓	
MVDS					✓	
PHP Web Interface Monitoring				✓		

With regard to the most used techniques shown in Table 2, we have: "Open Data", with three articles; The "Monitoring Software", with five articles; And the "Data Mining Technique", with three articles. It is assumed that these techniques were the most used for being responsible for obtaining traffic data in order to analyze and perform urban monitoring to find a better solution.

The author of [22] presented some techniques of traffic analysis focusing on urban environments. As an example, we have the automatic monitoring by video, through urban surveillance cameras, aiming to observe congestion, interaction of vehicles and check violations of traffic rules. Because of these problems, different classifying algorithms were presented in Buch et al. [22], that the authors created in order to classify the vehicles and increase the capacity of detection level and tracking. The use of these cameras became feasible because of the reduction of the cost (hardware), causing a great ascendancy in the implantation of these cameras, making possible and facilitating the analysis of the urban traffic. This area is of great interest to ITS and offers several future challenges, such as some assessments in challenging weather conditions, among others.

Through the methods and techniques of urban monitoring in ITS we can demonstrate that there are several advantages related to our suggested approach. The innumerable advantages using technologies are increasingly improving the way in which we can use these techniques and methods for the development of field research. The advantages are monitoring traffic offenses, weather factors, locating vehicles by GPS, improving traffic congestion through traffic lights, etc.

We propose that ITS, along with these methods and techniques described in this article, bring a better development in vehicle traffic monitoring so that we can differentiate alternative routes from vehicles in congested areas. ITS is increasingly improving through existing technologies in order to provide better distribution of vehicles on a given route. Monitoring methods and techniques are conducive to better tracking of alternative routes through applications that can assist vehicle drivers through these routes and demonstrate the estimated time of their commuting from one location to another.

V. CONCLUSION AND FUTURE WORK

In this article, work related to the area of intelligent transport systems was considered. With the purpose of identifying and evaluating urban monitoring techniques. A systematic review was presented on the monitoring techniques, in order to extract traffic behavior on highways, making it possible to detect congestion, avoid accidents, among other improvements for urban traffic.

Due to the investigation, it was noticed how small a number of articles correlated with the search theme, this shows that the research area is relatively new and at the same time shows a research path to be explored.

ACKNOWLEDGMENT

We would like to thank the Post-Graduation Department of Computer Science at UFS, for the support and encouragement of research and investigation with new technologies.

REFERENCES

[1] K. Kuikkaniemi, G. Jacucci, M. Turpeinen, E. Hoggan, and J. Müller. From space to stage: how interactive screens will change urban life. IEEE Computer Society, pp.40-47, 2011.

[2] C. Li, Travel Information Service System for Public Travel Based on SOA. Beijing Jiaotong University, China, pp.321-324, 2010.

[3] T. Zhu, and Z. Liu, Intelligent Transport Systems in China: Past, Present and Future. IEEE ICMTMA, pp. 581-584, 2015.

[4] National ITS Architecture team, "Regional ITS architecture guidance", U.S. department of transportation, 2001.

[5] R. Nasim, and A. Kassler, "Distributed Architectures for Intelligent Transport Systems: A Survey", NCCA, pp. 130-136, 2012.

[6] K. K. Chin, and C. W. Lee, Trafficscan —Bringing Real-time Travel Information to Motorists, Land Transport Authority, Singapore, pp.7-14, 2009.

[7] S. N. Mafra, "Protocolo de Revisão Sistemática" Grupo de Engenharia de Software Experimental, Programa de Engenharia de Sistemas e Computação (COPPE/UFRJ), 2005.

[8] H. Jérôme, et al. 2011. Modeling and simulating ITS applications with iTETRIS. In Proceedings of the 6th ACM workshop on Performance monitoring and measurement of heterogeneous wireless and wired networks (PM2HW2N '11). ACM, New York, NY, USA, pp. 33-40, 2011.

[9] B. Ilya, V. Vlasov, A. Demidov, and N. Kanatnikov, The Use of Multicopters for Traffic Monitoring in Dense Urban Areas. In Proceedings of the 2014 Conference on Electronic Governance and Open Society: Challenges in Eurasia (EGOSE '14). ACM, New York, NY, USA, pp. 42-44, 2014.

[10] T. Zan, L. Gueta, and T. Okochi, "Enabling Technology for Smart City Transportation in Developing Countries". Conference Paper IEEE Smart City December 2015, pp.170-174.

[11] A. S. Fayazi, A. Vahidi, G. Mahler, and A. Winckler, "Traffic Signal Phase amd Timing Estimation from Low-Frequency Transit Bus Data". IEEE Trasactions on Intelligent Transportation Systems, vol. 16, no. 1, pp. 19 - 28, 2015.

[12] Q. Shi, and M. Abdel-Aty, "Big Data applications in real-time traffic operation and safety monitoring and improvement on urban expressways". Elsevier, Transportation Research part C, vol. 58, pp. 380 - 394, 2015.

[13] C. Wang, H. Liu, K. L. Wright, B. Krishnamachari, and M. Annavaram, "A Privacy mechanism for mobile-based urban traffic monitoring". Elsevier, Pervasive and Mobile Computing, vol. 20, pp. 1 - 12, 2015.

[14] I. E. dos Santos, Textos selecionados de métodos e técnicas de pesquisa científica. 4. ed., rev., ampl. e atual. Rio de Janeiro: Impetus, 2003. 363 p.

[15] E. M. Lakatos, and M. A. Marconi, Metodologia científica: ciência e conhecimento científico, métodos científicos .... São Paulo: Atlas, 1989. 231 p.

[16] M. A. Marconi, and E. M. Lakatos, Técnicas de pesquisa: planejamento e execução de pesquisa: amostragens e técnicas de pesquisa .... 2. tiragem. São Paulo: Atlas, 1982. 205 p.

[17] T. Zhu and Z. Liu, "Intelligent transport systems in china: Past, present and future," in Measuring Technology and Mechatronics Automation (ICMTMA), 2015 Seventh International Conference on. IEEE, 2015, pp. 581–584.

[18] R. Nasim and A. Kassler, "Distributed architectures for intelligent transport systems: A survey," in Network Cloud Computing and Applications (NCCA), 2012 Second Symposium on. IEEE, 2012, pp. 130–136.

[19] O. Definition. The open definition. http://opendefinition.org/. Accessado: 11/11/2015. [Online]. Available: http://opendefinition.org/

[20] Open Data. K. Foundation. Open data handbook. http://opendatahandbook.org/guide/en/. Accessado: 18/11/2015. [Online]. Available: http://opendatahandbook.org/guide/en/

[21] S. Isotani and I. I. Bittencourt, Dados Abertos Conectados. Novatec Editora, 2015.

[22] N. Buch, S. A. Velastin and J. Orwell. "A Review of Computer Vision Techniques for the Analysis of Urban Traffic". IEEE Transactions on intelligent transportation systems, Vol. 12. Nº 3, pp. 920-939, september 2011.

Performance Evaluation of User Class Based Call Admission Control Techniques in Next Generation Wireless Networks

Mahesh G, Gowrishankar S
Department of Computer Science and Engineering,
B M S College of Engineering,
Bengaluru, Karnataka, India.
Email: maheshg@acharya.ac.in, gowrishankar@bmsce.ac.in

RameshBabu H S
Department of Computer Science and Engineering,
Sai Vidya Institute of Technology,
Bengaluru, Karnataka, India.
Email: rameshbabu.hs@saividya.ac.in

Abstract— **The users in the next generation wireless networks will be offered with abundant services by the network operators. The objective of the network operators would be to enhance revenue by accommodating maximum number of users, while at the same time they need to ensure that the users are given with the quality of service promised. Call admission control is the process of accepting or rejecting the call in the system and has a direct control on the number of users in the system. The design of call admission controller will be of utmost importance to the network operators as increase in the number of users in the system will increase the revenue generated. In this paper, the working of five different user class based models for call admission control are explained and evaluated. The simulation results for system call blocking probability versus utilization rate of different models are presented.**

Keywords-Partitioning; Queuing; Threshold; Reservation; Differential Access.

I. INTRODUCTION

The network operators in the Next Generation Wireless Networks (NGWN) come up with wide array of services to their users thus increasing the customer base of the network operators. The users in NGWN demand for Quality of Service (QoS) requirements of varied types, as they may not be willing to use all the services provided by the network operator. Hence, user differentiation plays a vital role in NGWN and providing QoS guarantee to users in NGWN will become a challenging problem [1]. In this paper, we categorize the users into three classes namely, ClassP, ClassG and ClassS representing platinum class users, gold class users and silver class users, respectively.

Accepting a user call or rejecting a call is totally determined by Call Admission Control (CAC) and hence, the number of users in the system is also directly controlled by CAC [2]. CAC is a prominent radio resource management technique that plays influential role in ensuring the desired QoS to the users and applications in NGWN [3][4]. General metrics used for CAC is Call Blocking Probability (CBP), call dropping probability and call rejection percentage [5]. This paper uses CBP as an appropriate parameter for evaluating the user class based CAC models.

The paper is organized as follows: Section II surveys the related work. Section III provides the intricacies of partition, queuing, threshold, reservation and differential access techniques for admission control. The simulation results are presented in Section IV. Insight to further research and conclusion are provided in Section V.

II. RELATED WORK

Wide spectrum of CAC mechanisms are proposed in literature to guarantee QoS, primarily focusing on the application types, such as real time and non real time applications. The majority of work related to CAC, as reported by surveys on CAC [5] - [9] is carried out under two major headings namely, number of users based CAC and interference based CAC. However, few works of CAC based on type of users are also reported.

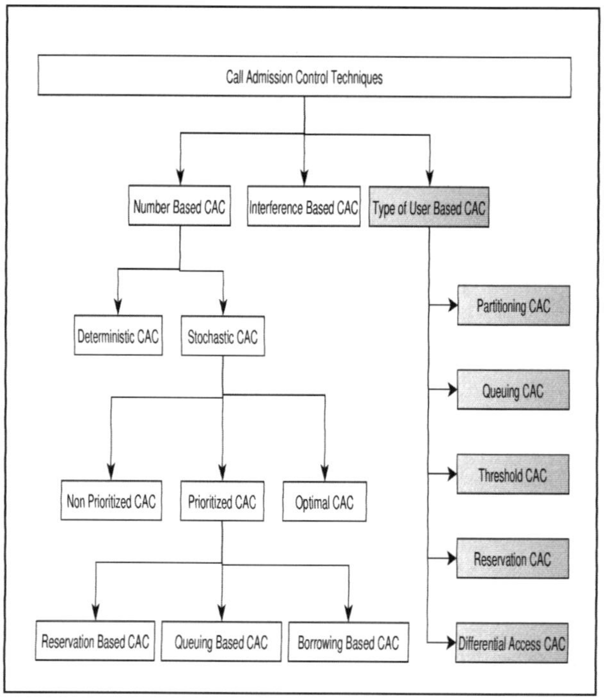

Figure 1. Classification of CAC Techniques.

Pal et al. [10] have proposed a QoS framework based on traffic class and user satisfaction. Kumar et al. [11] have proposed a user based bandwidth allocation technique for WiMAX named Differentiated Bandwidth Allocation Mechanism (DBAM). Algur et al. [12] have proposed a graded priority based admission control algorithm for LTE and WiMAX. AlQahtani [13] has proposed a user classification based CAC technique for LTE Advanced networks. Hosein [14] has proposed a QoS framework that allows an operator to provide class based connection admissions. Ozianyi et al. [15] have proposed a pricing approach that introduces three classes of user profiles platinum, gold and silver. Abraham et al. [16] have proposed a method and apparatus for adjustable QoS based admission control and scheduling in WLANs. Mahesh et al. [17] - [20] have proposed Partition Model (PM), Partition with Queuing Model (PQM), Reservation Model (RM) and Differential Access Model (DAM) for user class based CAC. A new classification of CAC techniques by adding "type of user" as an additional vertical to the existing classification is as shown in Figure 1. In this paper, the details of PM, PQM, RM and DAM are provided. The Threshold Model (TM) for user class based CAC is proposed and performance evaluation of PM, PQM, RM, DAM and TM is done.

III. USER CLASS BASED CAC MODELS

In this paper, we consider five user class based admission control models for performance evaluation namely, PM, PQM, TM, RM and DAM. For all the five models, three classes of users are considered namely, ClassP (Platinum Class Users), ClassG (Gold Class Users) and ClassS (Silver Class Users). This classification is done based on users varying QoS requirement and their willingness to pay the extra cost for the opted priority class of service. It is assumed that the ClassP user calls are of highest priority, ClassS user calls are of lowest priority and ClassG user calls are in between ClassP and ClassS. The arrival rates of ClassS, ClassG and ClassP user calls are denoted by λ_S, λ_G, and λ_P, respectively and are assumed to follow Poisson process. The mean service time of calls for all classes of users is assumed to follow a negative exponential distribution with a mean rate of $1/\mu$. The total number of virtual channels in the system is assumed to be equal to N.

A. *Partition Model*

The channel partition model is proposed in [17]. In this model, the entire set of N channels is divided and grouped into three disjoint sets P_1, P_2 and P_3. The first set of channels P_1 is to be used only by ClassS user calls, the second set of channels P_2 is to be used only by ClassG user calls and the third set of channels P_3 is to be used by only ClassP user calls. It is assumed that the number of channels in the third set P_3 is very much greater than the other two sets P_1 and P_2. Also, the number of channels in the second set P_2 is very much greater than the first set P_1.

Upon arrival of a call, the admission controller will first determine the class of call and based on availability of channels for the arrived calls' class, the call gets accepted or rejected. If the arrived call is of ClassP and if there are no free channels available between 1 to P_3, then the ClassP call gets rejected. The ClassP call gets accepted only if there are any free channels available between 1 to P_3. Similarly, ClassG and ClassS call gets accepted only if there are free channels available between 1 to P_2 and 1 to P_1, respectively, else the calls get rejected.

In [17], the expressions for call blocking probability for all the three classes of users namely ClassS, ClassG and ClassP are derived for partition model. The expressions for call blocking probability of ClassS, ClassG and ClassP users are denoted by B_{PS}, B_{PG} and B_{PP}. (1), (2) and (3) represents the CBP of ClassS, ClassG and ClassP users, respectively.

$$B_{PS} = \frac{\frac{1}{P_1!}\left(\frac{\lambda_S}{\mu}\right)^{P_1}}{\sum_{j=0}^{P_1}\frac{1}{j!}\left(\frac{\lambda_S}{\mu}\right)^{j}} \tag{1}$$

$$B_{PG} = \frac{\frac{1}{P_2!}\left(\frac{\lambda_G}{\mu}\right)^{P_2}}{\sum_{j=0}^{P_2}\frac{1}{j!}\left(\frac{\lambda_G}{\mu}\right)^{j}} \tag{2}$$

$$B_{PP} = \frac{\frac{1}{P_3!}\left(\frac{\lambda_P}{\mu}\right)^{P_3}}{\sum_{j=0}^{P_3}\frac{1}{j!}\left(\frac{\lambda_P}{\mu}\right)^{j}} \tag{3}$$

B. *Partition With Queuing Model*

The channel partition with queuing model is proposed in [18]. In this model, the entire set of N channels is divided into three disjoint groups P_1, P_2 and P_3. The first set of channels P_1 is to be used only by ClassS user calls, the second set of channels P_2 is to be used only by ClassG user calls and the third set of channels P_3 is to be used by only ClassP user calls. It is assumed that the number of channels in the third set P_3 is very much greater than the other two sets P_1 and P_2. Also, the number of channels in the second set P_2 is very much greater than the first set P_1.

The model is built with an idea that a small amount of delay in providing the service is better than not providing the service at all and the major objective is to minimize the denial service to all classes of users. Hence, in this model, if a class of users finds that all channels belonging to its class are occupied, then instead of dropping the call they are queued in appropriate queue class. When a channel of a particular class is released and if the queue of that particular class is not empty then the released channel is assigned to the user call in front of the queue.

In [18], the expressions for call blocking probability for all the three classes of users namely ClassS, ClassG and ClassP are derived for partition with queuing model. The expressions for call blocking probability of ClassS, ClassG and ClassP users are denoted by B_{QS}, B_{QG} and B_{QP}. (4), (5) and (6) represents the CBP of ClassS, ClassG and ClassP users, respectively. In (4), (5) and (6), Q_S, Q_G and Q_P represents the queue size for ClassS, ClassG and ClassP, respectively.

$$B_{QS}=\frac{(P_1\rho_S)^{P_1}\rho_S^{Q_S}}{P_1!}*\frac{1}{\sum_{k=0}^{P_1-1}\frac{(P_1\rho_S)^k}{k!}+\frac{(P_1\rho_S)^{P_1}}{P_1!}\left(\frac{1-\rho_S^{Q_S+1}}{1-\rho_S}\right)} \quad (4)$$

$$B_{QG}=\frac{(P_2\rho_G)^{P_2}\rho_G^{Q_G}}{P_2!}*\frac{1}{\sum_{k=0}^{P_2-1}\frac{(P_2\rho_G)^k}{k!}+\frac{(P_2\rho_G)^{P_2}}{P_2!}\left(\frac{1-\rho_G^{Q_G+1}}{1-\rho_G}\right)} \quad (5)$$

$$B_{QP}=\frac{(P_3\rho_P)^{P_3}\rho_P^{Q_P}}{P_3!}*\frac{1}{\sum_{k=0}^{P_3-1}\frac{(P_3\rho_P)^k}{k!}+\frac{(P_3\rho_P)^{P_1}}{P_3!}\left(\frac{1-\rho_P^{Q_P+1}}{1-\rho_P}\right)} \quad (6)$$

C. Threshold Model

In this model, the entire set of N channels is divided into two disjoint groups, P_1 and P_2. The first set of channels P_1 is to be used by ClassS and ClassP user calls and the second set of channels P_2 is to be used by ClassG and ClassP user calls. It is assumed that the number of channels in the second set P_2 is much greater than the number of channels in the first set P_1. T_S and T_G are the thresholds for ClassS and ClassG, respectively.

Upon arrival of a call, the admission controller will first determine the class of call and based on availability of channels for the arrived calls' class, the call gets accepted or rejected. If the arrived call is of ClassP and if there are no free channels available between 1 to P_1 and 1 to P_2, then the ClassP call gets rejected. The ClassP call gets accepted as long as there are any free channels available in the system. A ClassG user call gets accepted only if there are free channels available between 1 to P_2 and its utilization threshold is less than T_G else it gets rejected. Similarly, a ClassS user call gets accepted only if there are free channels available between 1 to P_1 and its utilization threshold is less than T_S else it gets rejected.

The expressions for call blocking probability of ClassS, ClassG and ClassP users are denoted by B_{TS}, B_{TG} and B_{TP}. (7), (8) and (9) represents the CBP of ClassS, ClassG and ClassP users, respectively.

$$B_{TS}=\frac{\sum_{b=0}^{P_1-T_S}\frac{1}{T_S!}\left(\frac{\lambda_S}{\mu}\right)^{T_S}*\frac{1}{b!}\left(\frac{\lambda_P}{\mu}\right)^{b}+\sum_{a=0}^{T_S-1}\frac{1}{a!}\left(\frac{\lambda_S}{\mu}\right)^{a}\frac{1}{(P_1-a)!}\left(\frac{\lambda_P}{\mu}\right)^{P_1-a}}{\sum_{a=0}^{T_S}\frac{1}{a!}\left(\frac{\lambda_S}{\mu}\right)^{a}\sum_{b=0}^{P_1-a}\frac{1}{b!}\left(\frac{\lambda_P}{\mu}\right)^{b}} \quad (7)$$

$$B_{TG}=\frac{\sum_{d=0}^{P_2-T_G}\frac{1}{T_G!}\left(\frac{\lambda_G}{\mu}\right)^{T_G}*\frac{1}{d!}\left(\frac{\lambda_P}{\mu}\right)^{d}+\sum_{c=0}^{T_G-1}\frac{1}{c!}\left(\frac{\lambda_G}{\mu}\right)^{c}\frac{1}{(P_2-c)!}\left(\frac{\lambda_P}{\mu}\right)^{P_2-c}}{\sum_{c=0}^{T_G}\frac{1}{c!}\left(\frac{\lambda_G}{\mu}\right)^{c}\sum_{d=0}^{P_2-c}\frac{1}{d!}\left(\frac{\lambda_P}{\mu}\right)^{d}} \quad (8)$$

$$B_{TP}=\left[\frac{\sum_{a=0}^{T_S}\frac{1}{a!}\left(\frac{\lambda_S}{\mu}\right)^{a}\frac{1}{(P_1-a)!}\left(\frac{\lambda_P}{\mu}\right)^{P_1-a}}{\sum_{a=0}^{T_S}\frac{1}{a!}\left(\frac{\lambda_S}{\mu}\right)^{a}\sum_{b=0}^{P_1-a}\frac{1}{b!}\left(\frac{\lambda_P}{\mu}\right)^{b}}*\frac{\sum_{c=0}^{T_G}\frac{1}{c!}\left(\frac{\lambda_G}{\mu}\right)^{c}\frac{1}{(P_2-c)!}\left(\frac{\lambda_P}{\mu}\right)^{P_2-c}}{\sum_{c=0}^{T_G}\frac{1}{c!}\left(\frac{\lambda_G}{\mu}\right)^{c}\sum_{d=0}^{P_2-c}\frac{1}{d!}\left(\frac{\lambda_P}{\mu}\right)^{d}}\right] \quad (9)$$

D. Reservation Model

The reservation model is proposed in [19]. In this model, exclusive reservation of channels is done for high priority users. ClassP users have an exclusive reservation of R_1 channels out of the N channels. Amongst the remaining $C_2=N-R_1$channels, ClassP and ClassG users have prioritized access to R_2 channels. The remaining channels $C_1=C_2-R_2$ can be used by all the three classes of users.

Upon arrival of a call, the admission controller will first determine the class of call and based on availability of channels for the arrived calls' class, the call gets accepted or rejected. If the arrived call is of ClassP and if there are no free channels available in the system, then the ClassP call gets rejected. The ClassP call gets accepted as long as there are any free channels available in the system. A ClassG user call gets accepted only if there are free channels available between 1 to C_2 else it gets rejected. Similarly, A ClassS user call gets accepted only if there are free channels available between 1 to C_1 else it gets rejected.

In [19], the expressions for call blocking probability for all the three classes of users namely ClassS, ClassG and ClassP are derived for reservation model. The expressions for call blocking probability of ClassS, ClassG and ClassP users are denoted by B_{RS}, B_{RG} and B_{RP}. (10), (11) and (12) represents the CBP of ClassS, ClassG and ClassP users, respectively.

$$B_{RS}=\frac{\sum_{i=c1}^{c2}\frac{1}{i!}\left(\frac{\lambda_1}{\mu}\right)^{c1}\left(\frac{\lambda_2}{\mu}\right)^{i-c1}+\sum_{i=c2+1}^{N}\frac{1}{i!}\left(\frac{\lambda_1}{\mu}\right)^{c1}\left(\frac{\lambda_2}{\mu}\right)^{c2}\left(\frac{\lambda_3}{\mu}\right)^{i-c2}}{\sum_{i=0}^{c1}\frac{1}{i!}\left(\frac{\lambda_1}{\mu}\right)^{i}+\sum_{i=c1+1}^{c2}\frac{1}{i!}\left(\frac{\lambda_1}{\mu}\right)^{c1}\left(\frac{\lambda_2}{\mu}\right)^{i-c1}+\sum_{i=c2+1}^{N}\frac{1}{i!}\left(\frac{\lambda_1}{\mu}\right)^{c1}\left(\frac{\lambda_2}{\mu}\right)^{c2}\left(\frac{\lambda_3}{\mu}\right)^{i-c2}} \quad (10)$$

$$B_{RG}=\frac{\sum_{i=c2}^{N}\frac{1}{i!}\left(\frac{\lambda_1}{\mu}\right)^{c1}\left(\frac{\lambda_2}{\mu}\right)^{c2}\left(\frac{\lambda_3}{\mu}\right)^{i-c2)}}{\sum_{i=0}^{c1}\frac{1}{i!}\left(\frac{\lambda_1}{\mu}\right)^{i}+\sum_{i=c1+1}^{c2}\frac{1}{i!}\left(\frac{\lambda_1}{\mu}\right)^{c1}\left(\frac{\lambda_2}{\mu}\right)^{i-c1}+\sum_{i=c2+1}^{N}\frac{1}{i!}\left(\frac{\lambda_1}{\mu}\right)^{c1}\left(\frac{\lambda_2}{\mu}\right)^{c2}\left(\frac{\lambda_3}{\mu}\right)^{i-c2}} \quad (11)$$

$$B_{RP}=\frac{\frac{1}{N!}\left(\frac{\lambda_1}{\mu}\right)^{c1}\left(\frac{\lambda_2}{\mu}\right)^{c2}\left(\frac{\lambda_3}{\mu}\right)^{N-c2}}{\sum_{i=0}^{c1}\frac{1}{i!}\left(\frac{\lambda_1}{\mu}\right)^{i}+\sum_{i=c1+1}^{c2}\frac{1}{i!}\left(\frac{\lambda_1}{\mu}\right)^{c1}\left(\frac{\lambda_2}{\mu}\right)^{i-c1}+\sum_{i=c2+1}^{N}\frac{1}{i!}\left(\frac{\lambda_1}{\mu}\right)^{c1}\left(\frac{\lambda_2}{\mu}\right)^{c2}\left(\frac{\lambda_3}{\mu}\right)^{i-c2}} \quad (12)$$

E. *Differential Access Model*

The differential access model is proposed in [20]. In this model, priority to users is given by allocating more number of channels for high priority user calls. It is assumed that ClassP user calls require 3 channels, ClassG user calls require 2 channels and ClassS user call requires 1 channel. BP, BG, and BS are the call blocking probabilities of ClassP, ClassG and ClassS users, respectively. When a user call requests for channels, the admission controller accepts the user call request if and only if there are free channels available to accommodate that particular user class (3 channels for ClassP, 2 channels for ClassG and 1 channel for ClassS) else rejects the user call requests.

In [20], the expressions for call blocking probability for all the three classes of users namely ClassS, ClassG and ClassP are derived for differential model. The expressions for call blocking probability of ClassS, ClassG and ClassP users are denoted by B_{DS}, B_{DG} and B_{DP}. (13), (14) and (15) represents the CBP of ClassS, ClassG and ClassP users, respectively.

$$B_{DS}=\frac{\lambda}{3\mu}\left(P(n-1)+P(n-2)+P(n-3)\right) \quad (13)$$

$$B_{DG}=\frac{\lambda}{3\mu}\left(P(n-2)+P(n-3)+P(n-4)\right) \quad (14)$$

$$B_{DP}=\frac{\lambda}{3\mu}\left(P(n-3)+P(n-4)+P(n-5)\right) \quad (15)$$

IV. RESULTS

In this section, we present the numerical results and compare the system call blocking probability of different models. Logarithmic scale bar graphs are used to interpret the results obtained. The bars in the graph represent the system CBP. It is to be noted that smaller the size of the bar, larger is the value and vice versa.

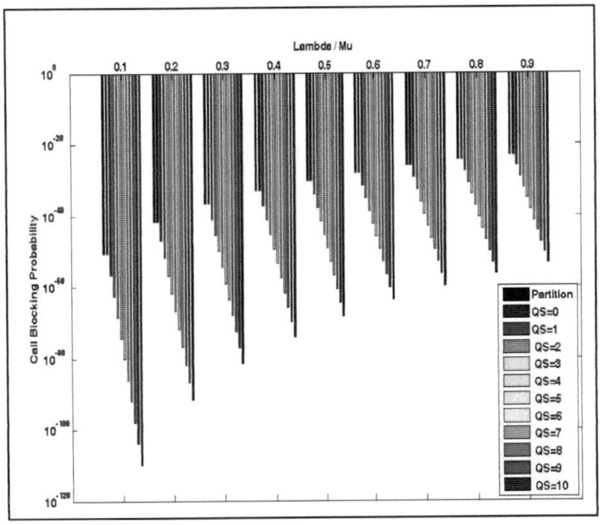

Figure 2. PM versus PQM (Ratio 2:3:5 and N=30)

It is assumed that the total number of virtual channels available in the system is 30. Figure 2 shows the graph of system CBP versus utilization rate of partition model and partition with queuing model for partition ratio 2:3:5, N=30 and queue size ranging from 0 to 10.

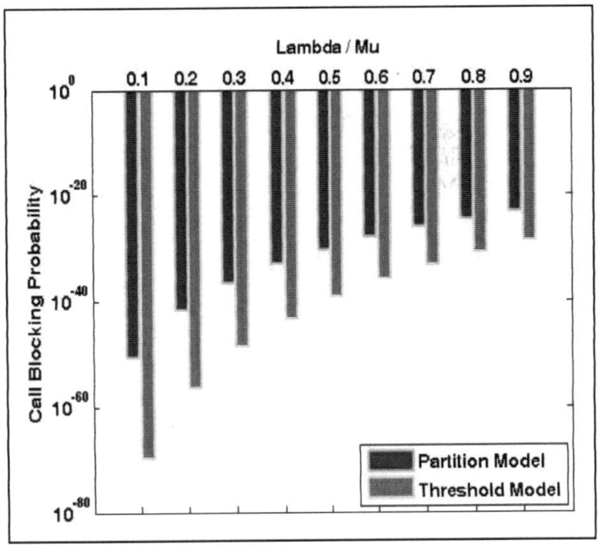

Figure 3. PM versus TM (Ratio 2:3:5, T_S=6, T_G=9 and N=30)

It can be seen that when queue size is zero, partition model and partition with queuing behave alike i.e., their CBP is same. Also, it is observed that with increase in queue size, the CBP decreases. Figure 3 shows the graph of system CBP versus utilization rate of partition model and threshold model for N= 30. It can be seen that threshold model exhibits lower CBP when compared to partition model in all cases.

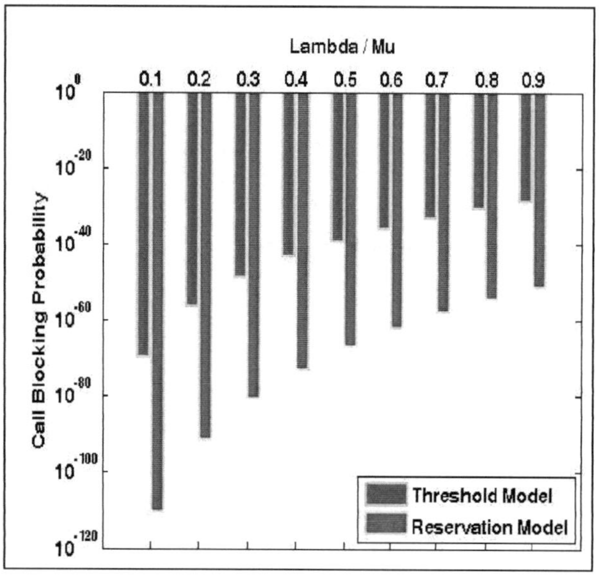

Figure 4. TM versus RM (Ratio 2:3:5, R_1=6, R_2=15 and N=30)

Figure 4 shows the graph of system CBP versus utilization rate of threshold model and reservation model for N= 30. It can be seen that reservation model exhibits lower CBP when compared to threshold model in all cases.

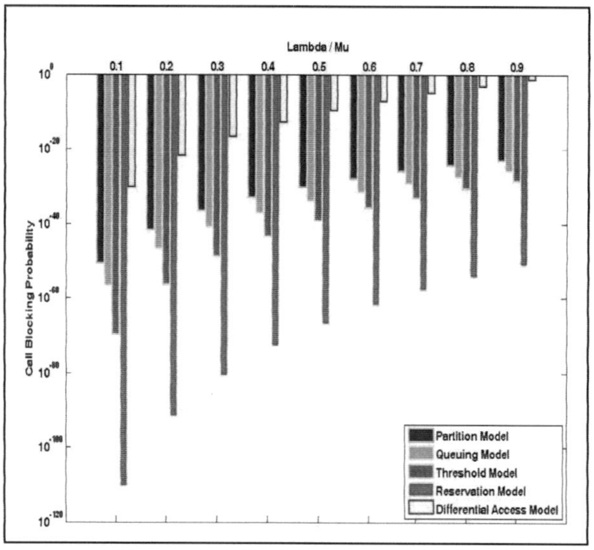

Figure 5. CBP of all 5 Models (N=30)

Figure 5 shows the graph of system CBP versus utilization rate of all the five models for N= 30 and partitioning ratios 2:3:5. It can be seen that reservation model exhibits the lowest CBP in all cases when compared to all other models.

The simulation study was conducted by considering different partition ratios with varied number of channels in the system; however the same observations were reported.

V. CONCLUSION

In this paper, we have evaluated performance of five different models for user class based CAC in NGWN. The models are simulated using Matlab and the simulation results are as shown in Figure 2 to Figure 5. The results clearly indicate that reservation model outperforms other models interms of CBP. Second in line is the threshold model, followed by partition with queuing model, partition model and finally differential access model. The CBP of partition with queuing improves with increase in queue size. The reason for differential access model to have greater CBP is that it allocates more than one channel for prioritized users and hence will be able to accommodate less number of users in the system. The pricing plays important role in commercialization of any experimental studies. NGWN is no exception and it has to primarily address pricing factor. Models of this nature are very essential to realize an optimal pricing model. The models evaluated in this paper are expected to bring delight to users and optimal revenue to service providers - ‘a win-win scenario’. Future work is to integrate pricing strategies of various players with the proposed CAC models. The proposed models are envisioned to realize optimal resource utilization, greater user flexibility and satisfaction.

REFERENCES

[1] X. F. Mao, X. Y. Li and G. J. Dai, "Flow admission control for multi-channel multi-radio wireless networks," Springer’s Journal of Wireless Networks, vol. 17, no. 3, April 2011, pp. 779 – 796.

[2] Y. Ishikawa and N. Umeda, "Capacity design and performance of call admission control in cellular CDMA systems, IEEE Journal on Communications," vol. 15, no. 8, August 2002, pp. 1627 – 1635.

[3] H. S. Rameshbabu, S. Gowrishankar and P. S. Satyanarayana, "A QoS Provisioning Recurrent Neural Network based Call Admission Control for beyond 3G Networks," International Journal of Computer Science Issues, vol. 7, no. 2, March 2010, pp. 7 –15.

[4] Y. Fang and Y. Zhang, "Call Admission Control Schemes and Performance Analysis in Wireless Mobile Networks," IEEE Transactions on Vehicular Technology, vol. 51, no. 2, March 2002, pp. 371–382.

[5] M. Ghaderi and R. Boutaba, "Call Admission Control in Mobile Cellular Networks: A Comprehensive Survey," Wireless Communications and Mobile Computing, vol. 6, no. 1, February 2006, pp. 69–93

[6] M. H. Ahmed, "Call Admission Control in Wireless Networks: A Comprehensive Survey," IEEE Communications, vol. 7, no. 1, 2005, pp. 50–69.

[7] H. Beigy and M. R. Meybodi, "User Based Call Admission Control Policies for Cellular Mobile Systems: A Survey," CSI Journal on Computer Science and Engineering, vol. 1, 2003, pp. 27–40.

[8] P. Saravanaselvi and P. Latha, "A Survey on Call Admission Control and Bandwidth Allocation for WiMAX,"International Journal of Innovative Research in Computer and

Communication Engineering, vol. 1, no. 9, November 2013, pp. 2185–2193.

[9] D. E. Asuquo, E. E. Williams and E. O. Nwachukwu, "A Survey of Call Admission Control Schemes in Wireless Cellular Networks," International Journal of Scientific & Engineering Research, vol. 5, no. 2, February 2014, pp. 111–120.

[10] S. Pal, S. K. Das and M. Chatterjee, "User-Satisfaction Based Differentiated Services for Wireless Data Networks," IEEE International Conferences on Communications, May 2005, pp. 1174–1178.

[11] N. Kumar, K. N. B. Murthy and A. M. Lagare, "DBAM: Novel User Based Bandwidth Allocation Mechanism in WiMAX," 2nd International Conference on Recent Trends in Information, Telecommunication and Computing, March 2011, pp. 229–236.

[12] S. P. Algur and N. Kumar, "Novel, graded, priority-oriented admission control in mobile networks," Turkish Journal of Electrical Engineering & Computer Sciences, November 2014, pp. 2696–2716.

[13] S. A. AlQahtani, "Users' classification-based call admission control with adaptive resource reservation for LTE-A networks," Journal of King Saud University - Computer and Information Sciences, vol. 29, no. 1, January 2017, pp. 103–115.

[14] P. Hosein, "A Class-Based Admission Control Algorithm For Shared Wireless Channels Supporting Qos Services," Proceedings of Fifth International Conference on Mobile and Wireless Communications Networks, Singapore, October 2003, pp. 81–85.

[15] V. G. Ozianyi and N. Ventura, "Dynamic Pricing for 3G Networks Using Admission Control and Traffic Differentiation," 13th IEEE International Conference on Networks, November 2005, pp. 838–843.

[16] S. P. Abraham, M. C. Chuah and T. Liu, United States Patent Application Publication, Publication No: US 2005/0048983 A1, March 3, 2005, pp. 1–5.

[17] G. Mahesh, Gowrishankar and H. S. RameshBabu, "Channel Partitioning Model for User Class Based Call Admission Control In Next Generation Wireless Networks," Elixir International journal on Network Engineering, May 2012, pp. 8451–8453.

[18] G. Mahesh, Gowrishankar and H. S. RameshBabu, " Channel Partitioning with Queuing Model for User Class based Call Admission Control in Next Generation Wireless Networks", International Journal of Computer Applications, vol. 45, no.12, May 2012, pp. 40–44.

[19] G. Mahesh, Gowrishankar and H. S. RameshBabu,"Channel Reservation Model for User Class Based Admission Control in Next Generation Wireless Networks," International Journal of Computer Science Issues, vol. 9, no. 3, May 2012, pp. 109–112.

[20] G. Mahesh, Gowrishankar and H. S. RameshBabu, "Differential Access Model for User Class based Call Admission Control Mechanism in Next Generation Wireless Networks," CIIT International Journal of Wireless Communication, May 2012, pp. 351–354.

Throughput Evaluation Approach for GSM Networks

İsmail Yıldız
Business Intelligence Solutions – Network Analytics
TURKCELL TEKNOLOJI
Istanbul, Turkey
e-mail: ismail.yildiz@turkcell.com.tr

Sena Aydeniz
Statistical Quality Assurance
TURKCELL
Istanbul, Turkey
e-mail: sena.aydeniz@turkcell.com.tr

***Abstract* — Data Usage in GSM networks has increasingly become more important compared to voice calls. Smartphone usage grew rapidly in the last few years and Internet access via mobile devices is ever increasing. Experienced speed while using data, often called throughput, is a vital part of GSM service quality. Although throughput itself is a straightforward concept, evaluation of the values for throughput is complex. Experienced throughput value depends on many factors. Determining factors and their significance is central to measuring and improving perceived throughput. This papers deals with the evaluation problem and proposes a new approach to evaluate GSM network throughput experienced by subscribers.**

Keywords—Throughput evaluation; expected throughput; GSM network; data usage; evalution approach; smartphone; mobile network; mobile throughput evaluation.

I. Introduction

It is believed that communication between people far away started with smoke. Many years later telegraph was invented, which was a crucial invention. In the following decades, telephone, radio, computer, internet and cell phone were invented. Finally, smartphones have become widespread which was the sign of a different era. In this era, people increasingly tend to access Internet with their mobile devices predominantly using GSM network.

In the smartphone era, almost every person acquires a smartphone in order to increase life quality. Some people use it for its original purpose, which is connectivity, but now the phone became more than that; it can be used for social media, navigation, gaming, business, and even health. People also customized their smartphones according to their needs.

Intensive smartphone and mobile application usage led to intensive data download and upload volumes. So speed of data, which is called throughput, has become the most crucial service quality indicator in mobile communication business.

Since definition and measurement of throughput is performed easily, evaluation of measured values is not easy for GSM companies because there is not any globally accepted standard or reference point.

In this paper, the problem of throughput evaluation is discussed in detail. Previous market experience and measured values are combined in order to propose a modern approach to solve this problem. Finally, expected throughput approach is devised and success of this approach is tested, which lead to excellent results.

II. Problem Definition

Data experience of subscriber is one the hottest and most complex topics in GSM world. Since data experience has become more and more important for the smartphone era, companies tend to focus much on this topic.

Throughput, which is the measured data speed, is one of the most vital performance indicators of subscriber data experience and widely used by GSM companies while monitoring network health and data service quality. Although it is easy to define and calculate throughput, it is not so easy to evaluate measured throughput values. It is a complicated issue to make inferences from measured throughput values. As example, measured experience of 5 Mbps data download speed is acceptable and a good speed for many people. But for some people who are used to much higher speeds, 5 Mbps data speed is definitely not acceptable and means a poor quality of service.

In order to clarify the situation, we can look closer to a similar problem from daily life. Assume that one is driving a vehicle and it reached the speed of 110 km/h. Is it possible to accept that speed as good, or bad? Of course, that depends on some factors. If one is driving on a highway, we can say that it is a slow speed. What about if one is driving a heavy-duty truck? Then the speed is fair enough. As we can see, the type of car is another factor used to evaluate the speed. Some other factors such as condition of the vehicle, top speed and engine type of vehicle, and driver's past experience can be added.

Similar to driving example, throughput in GSM network depends on many factors. Measuring the actual values and simple mathematical operation like average may not result in the correct evaluation.

Figure 1 shows the average throughput values measured in mobile network in the first quarter of 2015. Because of market competition and commercial limitations, exact throughput values cannot be revealed, instead values are multiplied by a private multiplier and general trend is depicted. The unit of multiplied throughput values is defined as "T" in the remaining part of this paper. Regarding Figure 1, throughput values vary daily and it is difficult to interpret this figure in terms of experience evaluation.

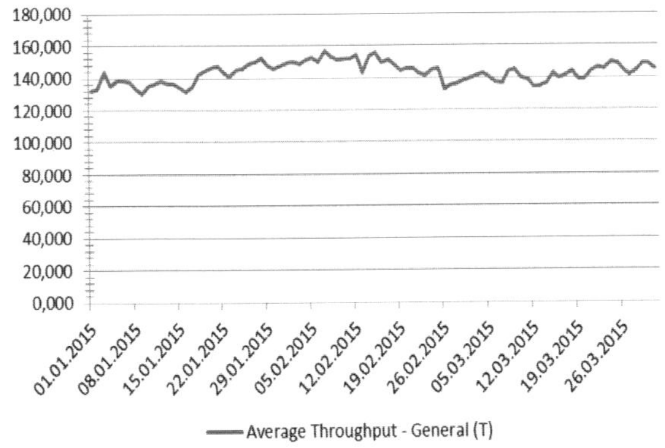

Fig. 1. Average Throughput values of whole GSM network

To better understand the variation, two cities of Turkey were selected for sampling. Because of the data security rules and market competition, we do not name the cities explicitly. Instead we call them as City A and City B.

Figure 2 shows the throughput trend of City A versus whole network in the first quarter of 2015. 2015 Q1 time period is used in the whole study. Throughput average values of City A are fluctuating more than the whole network and have different characteristics compared to the whole network. For some of the days, throughput average value of City A is higher than the whole network's throughput average. But for some of the days, throughput average value of City A is lower than the whole network's throughput average.

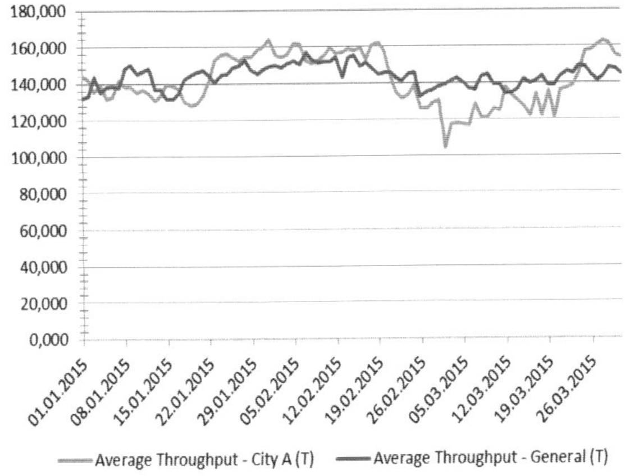

Fig. 2. Average Throughput values of City A vs whole GSM network

Figure 3 shows the throughput trend of City B in the first quarter of 2015. For most of the days, throughput average of City B is lower than the whole network's average values.

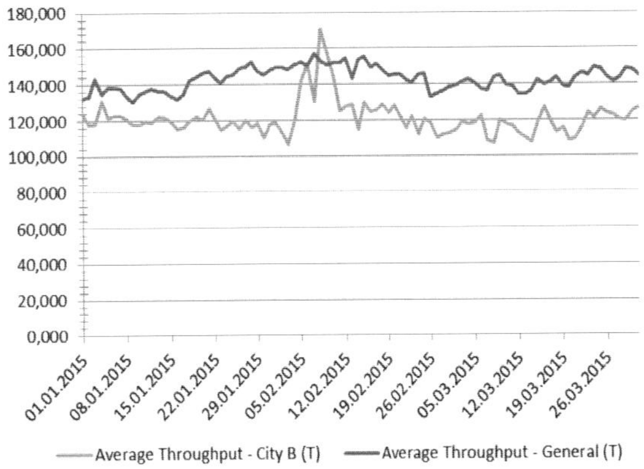

Fig. 3. Average Throughput values of City B vs whole GSM network

Only two cities are given as example for this article, but during the study nearly 30 cities were analyzed. Increasing number of city analysis, even smaller regions called districts, did not change the fact that there is no correlation between average throughput trends of cities and whole network.

If we come back to throughput evaluation problem for data experience, one common methodology is comparing individual subscriber's throughput figures with the whole network's throughput average. Another common methodology is location based throughput comparison. Individual subscriber's throughput figures are compared to his/her city or district's throughput average. As we mentioned previously, these methodologies may result in wrong interpretations. Data experience should be evaluated session by session and generalizations will lead to incorrect results.

In the remaining part of the study, factors affecting experienced throughput by GSM subscribers are analyzed in detail and a modern approach is devised.

III. Investigation of Factors

In this section of the article, investigations of various factors that are assumed to affect experienced throughput of subscriber are performed.

First, type network or GSM technology must be the dominant factor affecting experienced throughput. By nature, detail specifications and methods are different for each network type. By the mid of 2015 2G and 3G network technologies were in use in Turkey. Figure 4 shows the average throughput trend for 2G and 3G network technologies for the first quarter of 2015. As expected, average throughput of 3G network type is obviously higher than 2G network type. So, it is proved that network type is a major factor affecting experienced throughput.

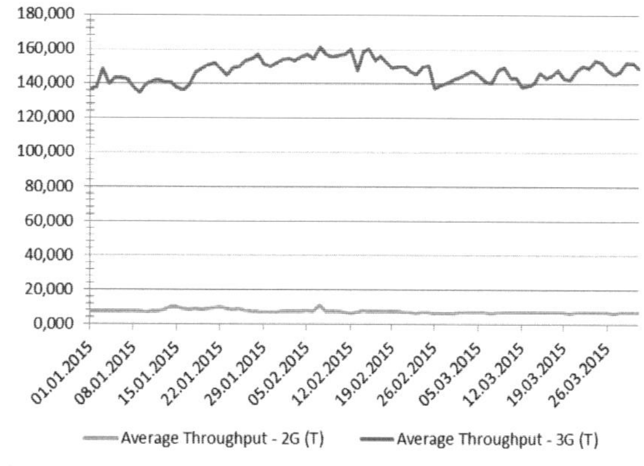

Fig. 4. Effect of network type

Second, data traffic direction may be another important factor affecting experienced throughput. Figure 5 shows the average throughput trend of downlink and uplink data traffic directions in the first quarter of 2015. Not surprisingly, average throughput of downlink direction is clearly higher than uplink direction. Therefore, data traffic direction is another factor affecting experienced throughput.

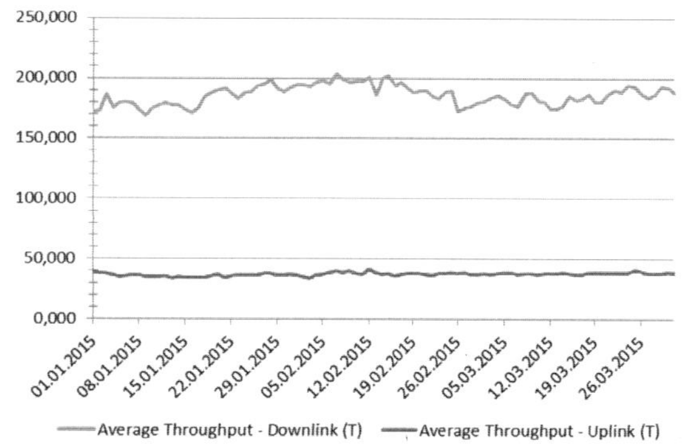

Fig. 5. Effect of traffic direction

Another factor may be the subscriber and mobile application behavior. Figure 6 shows the average throughput trend of selected popular applications in the first quarter of 2015. In this figure, the first finding is that video based applications, such as Youtube and Vine, have higher average throughputs. Messaging applications like Whatsapp and Turkcell Bip have comparably lower average throughputs. Facebook, which can be assumed having a mixed character (combination of text, image &video), has the lowest average throughput. Also, significant decrease in Vine's average throughput is detected towards the end of the quarter.

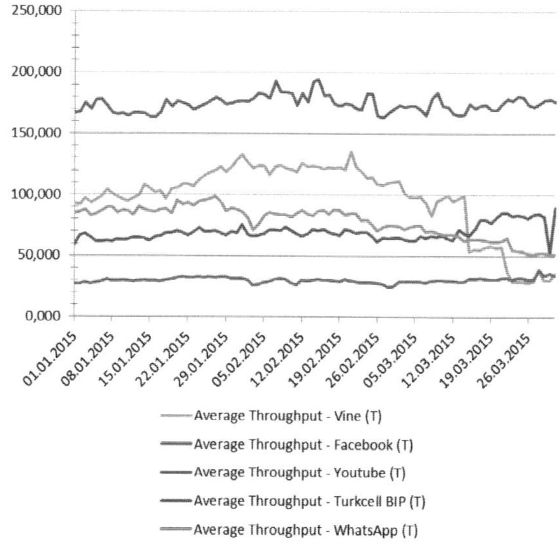

Fig. 6. Effect of mobile applications

Application based analysis gave us better understanding, but it is not sufficient to come to a result. It can be said that content type of data traffic that is called mime type (video, image, text, audio, web browsing) should be considered while analyzing application effect. Figure 7 shows the average throughput trend of mime types in the first quarter of 2015. As we see in the figure, mime type directly affects experienced throughput values.

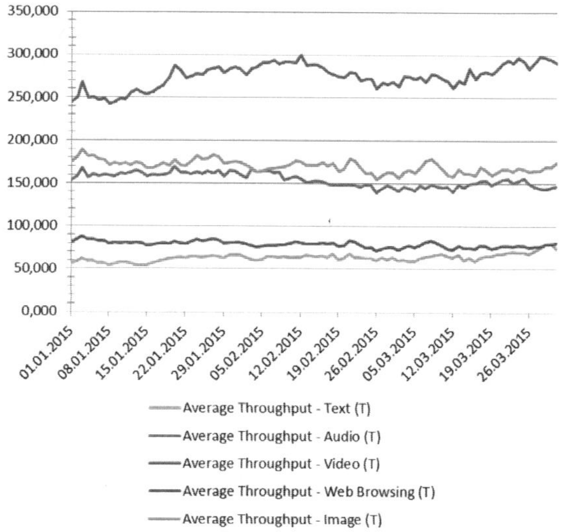

Fig. 7. Effect of mime type

Applications also vary in communication protocols used behind. Hypertext Transfer Protocol (HTTP) and Secure Hypertext Transfer Protocol (HTTPS) are two major protocols used by applications. Figure 8 shows the average throughput trend of communication protocols in the first quarter of 2015. As it is known, HTTPS is a secured version of HTTP protocol. Relevantly, HTTPS average throughput values are lower than HTTP protocol's average throughput values. It is clear that, impact of communication protocol on experienced throughput is significant.

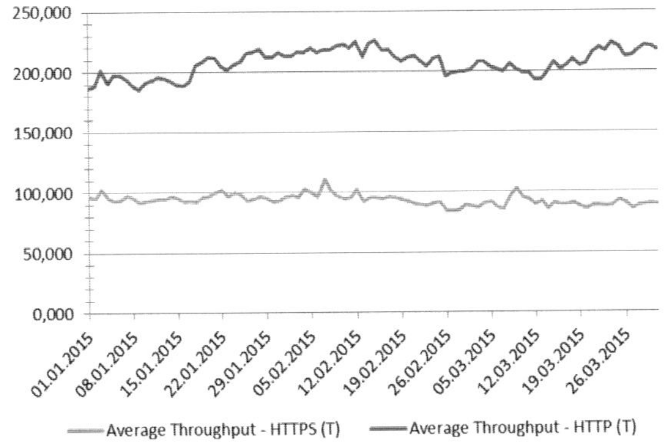

Fig. 8. Effect of application communication protocol

When we come back to driving example, the vehicle itself is a key factor for speed evaluation. In our case, the device used by the subscriber called terminal is another factor that may affect experienced throughput. Figure 9 shows the average throughput trend of terminal types in the first quarter of 2015. It is clear that, type and HDSPA support of terminal is another factor affecting experienced throughput.

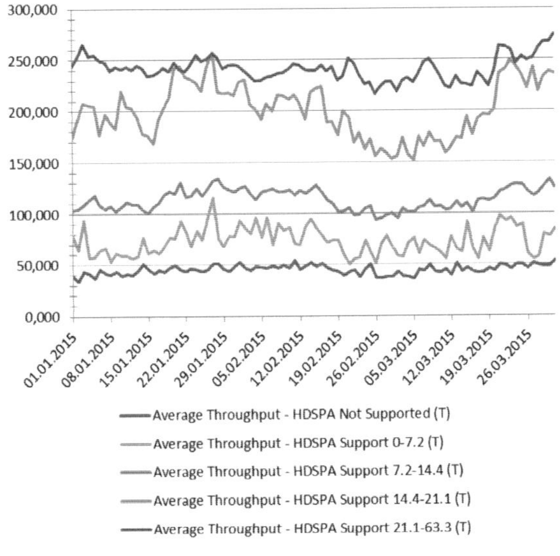

Fig. 9. Effect of terminal type

IV. Proposal of New Approach

In the previous section we have proved that experienced throughput depends on various factors which are:

- Network type (2G, 3G)
- Data traffic direction (downlink, uplink)
- Mime type (video, text, audio, web browsing, image)
- Communication protocol (HTTP, HTTPS)
- Terminal HDSPA Support (Not Supported, 0-7.2, 7.2-14.4, 14.4-21.1, 21.1-63.3)

When data traffic is simplified down to session level, each session has unique characteristics of 5 major factors mentioned above. In other words, a session is either 2G session or 3G session (4G was not launched in Turkey yet by mid of 2015). Similarly, a session is either established by HTTP or HTTPS.

TABLE I. SAMPLE SESSION CHARACTERISTICS

Sessions	Major Factors				
	Network Type	*Data Traffic Direction*	*Mime Type*	*Communication Protocol*	*Terminal HDSPA Support*
Session 1	2G	Uplink	Video	HTTP	21.1-63.3
Session 2	2G	Downlink	Video	HTTPS	14.4-21.1
Session 3	2G	Downlink	Image	HTTP	Not Supported
Session 4	2G	Uplink	Image	HTTPS	0-7.2
Session 5	2G	Downlink	Audio	HTTPS	7.2-14.4
Session 6	3G	Downlink	Text	HTTP	7.2-14.4
Session 7	3G	Uplink	.Text	HTTPS	21.1-63.3
Session 8	3G	Downlink	Web Browsing	HTTPS	Not Supported
Session 9	3G	Uplink	Image	HTTPS	0-7.2

Table I shows 9 different session characteristics as an example. Since characteristic of a session is formed by 5 major factors, we reach 200 (2x2x5x2x5) possible combinations, therefore 200 distinct session characteristics.

Each of the 200 distinct session characteristics has its own requirements and story. We have come up with the concept of **Expected Throughput** that is ideal throughput value of a session. Formula for expected throughput is devised as follows:

*Expected Throughput = C * Square Root (Net Data Volume)*

where C is a constant value for related session characteristic. Net Data Volume is measured total data volume; the packet header and footer are not included. For each session characteristic, detailed statistical analysis are performed and constant C values are calculated. So 200 different C values are formed.

For any subscriber session, Expected Throughput is calculated by measuring net data volume, square rooting and then multiplying by related constant C value.

In order to test the success of proposed Throughput Evaluation Approach, which is Expected Throughput concept, subscriber complaints are correlated with expected throughput values. All sessions of subscribers who made a complaint about data speed are taken into account. In order to make a correct matching, only sessions before actual complaint time are included in the analysis set. During the analysis, it is found that 97.7% of individual subscribers who complained about bad data experience or low data speed fall below expected throughput values within complaint period. As a result, it can be said that the proposed Expected Throughput Approach is successful in evaluating subscriber data experience.

V. Conclusion and Future Work

This paper presented a detailed analysis on experienced throughput values and the problem of evaluation. Depending on analysis results, a new concept of expected throughput was formed and a formula was created.

The solution was easy to use and very applicable in subscriber data experience evaluation. Success rate of the expected throughput concept and formula to reflect real subscriber data experience was very high.

Currently, the solution is in use in Turkcell and feedbacks from our colleagues are very positive.

Acknowledgment

Firstly, many thanks to our Turkcell as a visionary company that heavily supports research & development activities. Also, thanks to network technologies teams for their contribution in building signalization knowledge base and application operations team for providing detailed measurements of mobile network. Finally special thanks to our managers for their encouragement for writing this article.

References

[1] J. Laiho, A. Wacker, and T. Novosad, "Radio Network Planning and Optimization for UMTS", Wiley & Sons, 2006.

[2] B. Ballard, "Designing the Mobile User Experience", Wiley & Sons, 2006.

[3] O. Krecjar, "Problem solving of low data throughput on mobile devices by artefacts prebuffering", EURASIP Journal on Wireless Communications and Networking - Special issue on enabling Wireless Technologies for Green Pervasive Computing, vol.2009, 2009, Article No. 8.

[4] IEEE, "A novel mechanism for data streaming across multiple IP links for improving throughput and reliability in mobile environments", Twenty-First Annual Joint Conference of the IEEE Computer and Communications Societies, vol.2, 2002, pp.773-781.

[5] M. Mouly and M. B. Pautet, "The GSM System for Mobile Communications", Telecom Publishing, 1992.

[6] M. J. Dixon and F. J. Massey, "Introduction to Statistical Analysis", McGraw Hill, 1957.

[7] N. R. Draper and H. Smith, "Applied Regression Analysis", Wiley & Sons, 1998.

Multicriteria QoS-aware Solution in Wireless Multi-hop Networks

Jean Nunes R. Araujo
Graduate Program in Electrical Engineering
Federal University of Minas Gerais
Belo Horizonte, MG, Brazil
Email: jeannra@ufmg.br

Claudio de Castro Monteiro
Federal Institute of Education, Science and Technology of Tocantins
Network Computer Group - GREDES
Email: ccm@ifto.edu.br

Lucas de Souza Batista
Operations Research and Complex Systems Laboratory
Department of Electrical Engineering
Federal University of Minas Gerais
Email: lusoba@ufmg.br

***Abstract*—Ad-hoc Wireless Networks provide a major base for ubiquitous computing development. In such networks, the communication occurs by multiple hops in a shared medium. In order to meet the different requirements of the applications, routing solutions aware of Quality of Service (QoS) have been developing. However, single-criterion strategies are unable to cope with conflicting objectives that commonly appear in these networks. This work proposes a multicriteria approach that considers End-to-End Delay (E2ED) and Packet Delivery Probability (PDP) as vital criteria in the route discovery process. For this purpose, Optimized Link State Routing Protocol (OLSR) with a modified Dijkstra algorithm is applied, wherein the bi-objective problem is transformed into a mono-objective problem through the epsilon-constraint technique. Extensive simulations have demonstrated that the multicriteria method can provide efficient routing in mobile environments, and it has outperformed the best results of single-criterion methods in terms of Packet Loss Ratio (PLR) by nearly 5 - 35 %. The results also have shown the potential of the model in finding a proper trade-off in relation to the number of hops and End-to-End Delay.**

Keywords–Multicriteria optimization; Mobile Ad-Hoc Networks; Quality of Service.

I. INTRODUCTION

The spread of mobile services has boosted the advance of wireless networks. Such growth has demanded endeavors to provide Quality of Service (QoS) and to ensure that the network resources are spent as fairly as possible. In fact, the proper provision of quality enables the wireless technology to be used when limited or no infrastructure is available [1]. In this context, Mobile Ad-Hoc Networks (MANETs) are representative as they have particularly worthwhile features. First, mobile wireless devices are able to communicate each other without relying on a fixed infrastructure. Second, messages can be exchanged collaboratively provided that devices are able to operate as both router and host. Third, the varying mobility patterns and the low deployment cost are factors that can promote the emergence of new applications [2].

Among several relevant problems in MANETs, routing issue is one of the most challenging. In recent years, efforts have been directed at proposing new or reformed protocols to address varied scenarios, from mesh networks to underwater networks [1]. Up to now, there is no routing protocol that provides a proper performance in any scenario [3].

Furthermore, applications can have conflicting quality requirements, which indicates the need to optimize opposing objectives. For example, elastic applications, as file transfer programs, demand reliable and stable links. On the other hand, real-time applications, as voice over IP, are extremely sensitive to delay. As a glimpse, regarding the elastic applications, it would make sense to minimize the Packet Loss Ratio (PLR), while for real-time applications, it would be fitting to minimize the End-to-End Delay (E2ED) [3][4]. Future standardized routing mechanisms will possibly follow the trend towards more flexible support to the multiple QoS requirements [3]. Hence, it becomes vital to take into account the performance trade-offs in the route discovery process [5][6][7][8].

The aim of this paper is twofold. First, the need to take decisions bearing in mind multiple criteria in ad-hoc networks is demonstrated. For that, two traditional QoS-aware metrics were considered, wherein one is applied to minimize E2ED and the other one is utilized to maximize the reliability of packet delivery. Second, in order to arrange both metrics in the route discovery process, the employment of the well-known scalar epsilon-constraint method [9][10][11] is proposed. The idea is to turn one of the metrics into a constraint in the optimization model. As such, the route discovery problem was modeled as a Constrained Shortest Path Problem (CSPP) [12]. A modified Dijkstra's algorithm was used as the solver. The routing protocol utilized was the OLSR [13]. In addition, the selection process of the MultiPoint Relays (MPR) was adjusted in order to consider both metrics. The hypothesis is that the multicriteria approach can achieve better results when recognizing the trade-off between E2ED and PLR.

The proposal was compared to single-criterion solutions in a Wireless Multi-hop Network with different node speeds via OMNET++ simulator. Summarily, our solution has reached consistent reductions in PLR. Moreover, when comparing to the single-criterion Minimum Packet Loss (MPL) metric, our solution has obtained routes with a lower average number of hops, which also has promoted a decrease in E2ED. Accordingly, our proposal improves the link reliability, without generating prohibitive delays.

The remainder of this paper is organized as follows. Section II presents the related works and the motivation. Section III introduces the multicriteria optimization problem and presents the suggested mathematical model. Section IV provides the simulation parameters and investigates the results by comparing the single-criterion OLSR implementation with the multicriteria one. Section VI shows the conclusions and future works.

II. RELATED WORK AND MOTIVATION

A MANET network is composed of self-organized and self-manageable devices distributed in a given area [1]. In addition, messages can be transmitted by multiple hops, that is, the nodes provide support to the network, playing the role of relays. Therefore, whenever nodes want to "talk" each other, routes must be established. Routing protocols are in charge of defining rules and procedures to provide such routes [2]. However, because of shared medium, interferences and mobility, links can be constantly broken and frequently rebuilt. Due to these instabilities, typical from a wireless environment, it has been a challenge to make feasible the use of applications which are sensitive to high delay, limited bandwidth, and recurrent packet losses [3]. In order to address these issues and, furthermore, meeting the requirements of new applications and kinds of MANET networks, QoS-aware routing solutions have emerged [4].

Table I shows distinct quality requirements related to the main applications that can be made available in a network. Indeed, forthcoming MANETs will have to deal with a particular set of constraints in view of the current exigencies of performance. Therefore, providing QoS guarantees for different services is essential to the development and deployment of future wireless multi-hop networks [4][14].

TABLE I. QoS REQUIREMENTS OF MAIN APPLICATIONS. ADAPTED FROM [14]

Applications	*Bandwidth*	*Sensibility to Delay*	*Packet Delivery Ratio*
Elastic (FTP, Email)	Low	Low	High
Voice over IP	Low	High	Medium
Videoconference	High	High	Medium
Streaming audio	Low	Medium	Medium
Streaming VoD	High	Medium	Medium

Standardized protocols, such as OLSR (Optimized Link State Routing) and AODV (Ad-hoc On-demand Distance Vector), do not resort to any QoS parameter when building the routes. Both work with an elementary *hop-count* metric. While OLSR uses *hop-count* to evaluate the shortest path [13], AODV verifies *hop-count* to update routing table entries [15]. Given the need, there is a move in the direction of proposing new and reformed protocols that are QoS-aware [2][4].

Nevertheless, just including a single QoS metric in the routing protocol is not enough to offer solutions that cover each scenario, precisely because the QoS provision changes according to the application or the network status. Furthermore, one application may need the guarantee of several metrics simultaneously. If these metrics are conflicting, it is necessary to yield solutions that reach a trade-off between them [3].

The authors in [16] identify a diversity of possible requirements to be addressed in a MANET, such as: minimizing hop-count, minimizing delay, maximizing data delivery, minimizing energy consumption, minimizing computational overhead, maximizing route stability, balancing traffic load, among others. The work also relates these requirements to the main link evaluation metrics and points out the associated performance trade-offs. In [17], the authors advance in the analysis by demonstrating the conflicting performances between some QoS-aware metrics as: Minimum Delay (MD) and Minimum Packet Loss (MPL). However, in both works, multiple metrics are not employed.

The reason of satisfying conflicting requirements has been deeply studied in fields as decision theory and operations research. The goal is to make effective decisions by pondering the criteria through an optimization process [11]. Recently, multicriteria optimization on ad-hoc networks has been drawing attention as a tool to design routing protocols that deal with more than one QoS parameter. Although it is still an open-field, multicriteria optimization can be a valuable alternative in search for robust and adaptive solutions that fit in distinct scenarios [4].

In spite of the diverse multicriteria optimization techniques available, varying from sophisticated evolutionary algorithms to outranking methods, the applicability in ad-hoc networks is restricted to simple approaches [11]. Indeed, since mobile devices have limited processing and power resources, the method needs to run as fast as possible [9].

Considering an opportunistic route discovery process in Mobile Ad-hoc Networks, the authors in [18] propose to incorporate some context criteria, such as signal quality, geographic progress, and node residual energy, when evaluating the link quality. A weight is assigned to each criterion, composing the measure called Dynamic Forwarding Delay (DFD). In [19], the weighted sum method is used in order to minimize the delay and maximize the throughput in Static Wireless Mesh Networks.

The research presented in [5] proposes, for proactive routing in MANETs, a composite-additive utility function that employs normalized weights for two metrics: delay and energy. Likewise, in [6] is introduced a solution driven by battery and queue metrics, taking a normalized weighted additive utility function as QoS metric. Both solutions utilize OLSR as the base protocol.

In [7], two metrics for route selection in Multi-hop Wireless Ad-hoc Networks are derived, namely, Secrecy Outage Probability (SOP) and Connection Outage Probability (COP). The former is concerned with to meet security requirements and the latter seeks to address the different QoS requirements. The route selection algorithm uses a control parameter β to adjust the weights in terms of priority of each metric.

The authors in [8] investigate the trade-off between energy consumption and end-to-end delay when selecting clusterheads in Wireless Sensor Networks. The choice of clusterhead is made by means of a weighted metric where the weights α and β indicate the importance of energy consumption and end-to-end delay, respectively. In addition, a Depth-First Search (DFS) algorithm is proposed to calculate the number of probable routes from clusterhead nodes to the sink node considering an end-to-end delay constraint Δ.

As one can see, the weighted sum method is the most used approach for dealing with more than one criteria in the optimization process related to Wireless Multi-hop Ad-hoc Networks. Although it is easy to implement, this method has some drawbacks. First, fine-tuning of weights is by itself an optimization problem that implies generating and evaluating several weight distributions in order to model each scenario. It means that when one does not have *a priori* preferences, an excessive computational processing can be required to obtain a representative weights distribution [9][11]. Second, distributed uniformly weights do not ensure a uniform distribution of points on the Pareto front. Third, these methods are unable to reach points in non-convex regions of the Pareto front [3].

In [20] is proposed a hybrid routing algorithm which combines Cellular Automata (CA) with Genetic Algorithm (GA) in Mobile Ad-Hoc Networks, wherein energy and delay are considered restrictions in the model rather than metrics to be weighted. Although the deployment of metaheuristics for

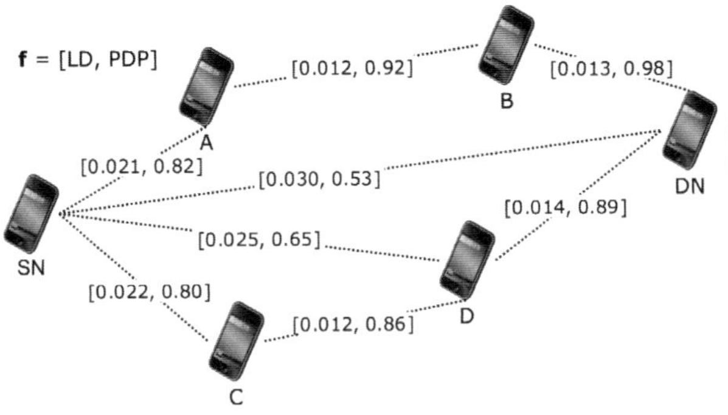

	Route	E2ED (s) Σ	PDP (%) Π
1	SN -> A -> B -> DN	0.046	75
2	SN -> DN	0.027	53
3	SN -> D -> DN	0.039	58
4	SN -> C -> D -> DN	0.041	61

Figure 1. Multicriteria ad-hoc wireless network

solving the MANET routing problem has gained remarkable relevance in the last years [21][22], its viability is still unclear when applying in very dynamic environments. That is because such stochastic methods can spend much time to reach a satisfactory solution since the optimization process depends on an iterative search which involves repeated execution of the algorithm [3]. Hence, research works have given preference to scalar techniques.

This paper develops a mathematical model that applies the epsilon-constraint scalar technique in order to minimize the E2ED, transforming the PDP into a link constraint. This strategy, besides being able to reach non-convex regions of the Pareto front, can generate points in specific regions that meet the demand of underlying network [9][10][11]. That is, when we have a reasonable clarity about the level of quality to be reached regarding a given metric, this technique can be more effective in achieving such point. Even though the model foresees more than two metrics, one can work with a single metric as the objective function and the remaining ones as restrictions. However, these constraints need to be defined accurately, otherwise, there is the risk of rendering the model unfeasible. In fact, when this is uncertain, finding proper constraint for one metric can be as difficult as to find well-suited weights for several path selection metrics. In this case, one can resort to the underlying layers to define such constraints [3], as summarized in Table I.

Apart from demonstrating the associated trade-off between the two QoS-aware metrics, our proposal presents a feasible alternative to achieve a better compromise related to conflicting metrics in a mobile network.

III. QoS MULTICRITERIA SUPPORT IN MANETs WITH THE EPSILON-CONSTRAINT METHOD

In this section, the mathematical formulation and the description of the proposed multicriteria routing optimization method are presented.

A. *Mathematical modeling*

An Ad-hoc Wireless Network can be defined as a directed graph $G(V, E)$, where the vertices $V = \{v_1, v_2, \ldots, v_n\}$ describe a finite set of nodes, and the edges $E = \{e_1, e_2, \ldots, e_m\}$ yield a finite set of links that connect these nodes. A node subset $N_{(v_i)} \subset V$ is established within the coverage area of each node v_i, producing a neighborhood that draws the network topology. In transmission context, there is also a destination node $DN \subset V$ and a source node $SN \subset V$. Each link e_k, $k = [1, \ldots, m]$, has an associated cost of packet transmission w_{e_k} from v_i to v_j. If necessary, a subset F of relay nodes are elected from the neighborhood based on the cost, in order to build a route $R_{SN,DN} = (SN, F_1, \ldots, F_n, DN) \subset V$ that connects SN to DN. Figure 1 can be considered a handy and simple example of a Wireless Multi-hop Ad-hoc Network drawn by means of the OLSR protocol.

In this paper, the cost is not composed of only one value. Thereby, as a multiobjective problem, it must be represented by a vector $\mathbf{f} : \mathbb{B}^m \to \mathbb{R}^k$, wherein each item denotes a function to be optimized. In general, a minimization problem with multiple objectives can be defined as

$$\begin{aligned} \min_{\mathbf{x}} \quad & [f_1(\mathbf{x}), f_2(\mathbf{x}), ..., f_k(\mathbf{x})] \\ \text{s.t.} \quad & \mathbf{x} \in S, \end{aligned} \tag{1}$$

where k is the number of objectives, S is the feasible decision space, $\mathbf{x}$ is the decision variable vector, and $f_i(\mathbf{x})$ describes the scalar value of the i-th objective. A decision vector $\hat{\mathbf{x}} \in S$ belongs to the Pareto-optimal set if there is no other decision vector $\mathbf{x} \in S$ such that $f_i(\mathbf{x}) \leq f_i(\hat{\mathbf{x}})$, for all i; and $f_i(\mathbf{x}) \neq f_i(\hat{\mathbf{x}})$ for at least one $i = \{1, \ldots, k\}$ [11].

As can be seen in Figure 1, two criteria are pondered to optimize the path considering the following objectives: I) minimize the E2ED and, II) maximize the reliability of packet delivery. The latter can be seen as: minimize the PLR. Thus, link QoS is represented by a vector $\mathbf{f}$ containing two metrics: Link Delay (LD) and Packet Delivery Probability (PDP). The objective functions are given as follow:

$$\begin{aligned} f_1 = f_{E2ED} &= \sum_{(v_i, v_j) \in E} LD_{(i,j)} \times x_{i,j} \\ f_2 = f_{PDP} &= \prod_{(v_i, v_j) \in E} PDP_{(i,j)} \times x_{i,j} \end{aligned} \tag{2}$$

The decision variable $x_{i,j}$ is 1 when the node $j \in N(v_i)$ belongs to the route. Otherwise, $x_{i,j}$ is 0. The Link Delay measurement is estimated using the AdHoc Probe algorithm [23]. This algorithm uses a pair of packets to measure the dispersion between them. Thus, in a route from SN to DN, having D as the relay node, f_{E2ED} is given by:

$$E2ED_{(SN \to DN)} = LD_{(SN \to D)} + LD_{(D \to DN)} \tag{3}$$

Details of calculating the LD metric can be found in [17][23][24]. In Figure 1, if only LD was employed in the optimization, the route 2 ($SN \rightarrow DN$) would be chosen, in spite of lower PDP.

The second function aims to maximize reliability in packet delivery and, consequently, reducing the PLR. This function is given below

$$PDP_{AB} = d_f \times d_r \tag{4}$$

where d_f and d_r are the forward and the reverse delivery ratios, respectively. The product between them is the probability of successful transmission from A to B. In a route from SN to DN, having D as relay node, the end-to-end f_{PDP} is the product of probabilities related to each link, as follow:

$$PDP_{(SN \rightarrow DN)} = PDP_{(SN \rightarrow D)} \times PDP_{(D \rightarrow DN)} \tag{5}$$

In a time window w, each node computes the delivery ratio by dividing the number of OLSR HELLO messages that should have been received by the number of OLSR HELLO messages actually received. Every t seconds, HELLO packets are sent. Delivery ratio of 100% means all messages were fully received in period w. More details of calculating the PDP metric can be found in [17][23][25]. In Figure 1, if only PDP metric was employed, the route 1 ($SN \rightarrow A \rightarrow B \rightarrow DN$) would be chosen, in spite of the larger E2ED and number of hops.

Our proposal aims to minimize E2ED and maintain the PDP of link equal or above an acceptable threshold. This threshold will depend on the application requirements or even network current condition. For this purpose, the bi-objective problem was modeled as a mono-objective problem applying the epsilon-constraint method, where the PDP of link was turned in a constraint into [9]. Therefore, the routes are created based on a Constrained Shortest Path Problem model (CSPP). Herein, instead of treating the PDP as an end-to-end metric, it is evaluated locally along the route. The model is proposed as follow,

$$\text{minimize } f_{E2ED} = \sum_{(v_i,v_j)\in E} LD_{(i,j)} \times x_{i,j}$$

s.t.

$$PDP_{(i,k)} \times x_{i,k} > \epsilon_b, \quad k \in N(v_i),$$

$$\sum_{(v_i,v_j)\in E} x_{i,j} - \sum_{(v_j,v_i)\in E} x_{j,i} = 0, \quad \forall v_i \in V \backslash \{SN, DN\},$$

$$\sum_{(SN,v_j)} x_{SN,j} = 1,$$

$$\sum_{(v_j,DN)} x_{j,DN} = 1,$$

$$x_{i,j} \in \{0,1\}, \quad \forall (v_i,v_j) \in E$$

where ϵ_b is the minimum PDP that a link must guarantee to be part of the route. Thus, ϵ_b represents the link reliability, whose value can be defined *a priori* or it can be changed iteratively during network operation. The former option is employed in this paper, while the latter is an improvement that relies on probabilistic models, which will be studied in future researches.

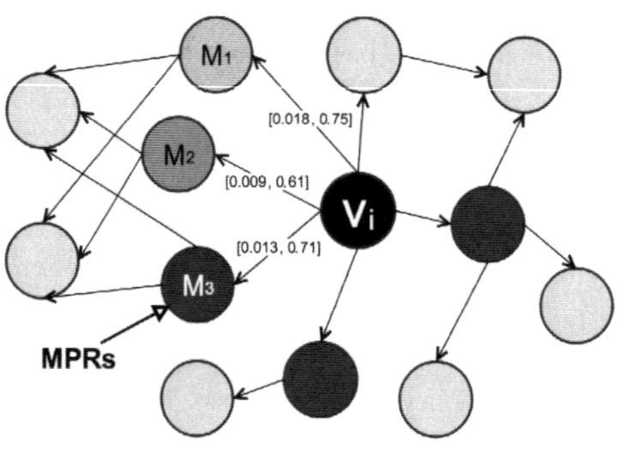

Figure 2. MPRs selection with reliability constraint

The remaining constraints ensure flow conservation and establish that the first node will be the source (SN) and the last node will be the destination (DN). Finally, decision variables must have binary values, which describes whether or not a link belongs to the route.

In Figure 1, if $\epsilon_b = 0.6$ (60%), the route 3 ($SN \rightarrow D \rightarrow DN$) would be chosen since it presents the lowest delay among routes that do not violate the PDP constraint. If $\epsilon_b = 0.7$ (70%), the route 4 ($SN \rightarrow C \rightarrow D \rightarrow DN$) would be created. Note that these promising solutions would be lost in the case of a single-criterion optimization problem.

As a step towards bi-objective optimization in routing, a modified Dijkstra's algorithm was employed to solve the CSPP model. The goal is to find lower delay paths while simultaneously bounding the PDP of link for a lower limit. In short, after comparing the cumulative delay in deciding between paths, as in common Dijkstra's algorithm, the PDP of link is compared to the ϵ constraint. If the PDP is lower than ϵ, this path is pruned off.

Furthermore, a change in the OLSR protocol was proposed to bear the desired minimum reliability constraint when building the Multipoint Relay (MPR) set of a node. When there are more than one 1-hop neighbors covering the same number of uncovered 2-hop neighbors, the one with the lowest link delay and that does not violate the reliability constraint ϵ to the current node is selected as MPR. Figure 2 illustrates such procedure. Let us consider ϵ equal to 0.7. Note that the node M_2 has the lowest delay (0.009s), however, the PDP (0.61) violates the constraint ϵ. Since both $M1$ and $M3$ do not violate ϵ, the one with the lowest delay is selected to be part of the MPR set.

IV. Simulation Results

Extensive simulations were conducted in OMNET++ 5.0 simulation tool. A sample size of 10 topologies was defined for each method in order to obtain a confidence level of 95%. The comparison between the methods was performed using Analysis of Variance (ANOVA) test and Honestly Significant Difference (HSD) test [26]. All the assumptions required to carry out the ANOVA test were analyzed and the results are provided in a support information file [27].

A. Experimental design

The physical layer is implemented using the log-distance path loss model, where the path loss $P_l = P_t - P_r$ in dB over a distance d is simply defined $P_l = 10log(c/4\pi f)^2 + 10log(1/d^{\lambda})$, where c is the speed of light, f is the carrier frequency of 802.11g (2.4 GHz), d is the distance between the transmitter and receiver and $\lambda = 2$ is the path loss exponent. The interference is modeled using the SNIR (Signal-to-interference-plus-noise ratio), where the power of other transmissions is considered as interference for the signal power. There is a MAC protocol which deals with the media contention and ensures that, among the neighbors, only the addressed receiver will retain the message, while the other neighbors will discard it. Table II summarizes the remaining parameters.

TABLE II. SIMULATION PARAMETERS

Parameter	*Configuration*
Simulation area	1500 m x 300 m
Simulation duration	500 seconds
Traffic flow	Constant bit rate with UDP transport
Number of flows	10 IP unidirectional flows
Connection rate	5 packets/s
Packet size	1000 bytes
Number of nodes	50 nodes
Mobility pattern	Random Waypoint Mobility
Moving speeds	2, 5 and 10 mps
Pause time between node movements	10 seconds

In addition to the static scenario, moving speeds of 2, 5, and 10 mps were tried. All the hosts communicate on the same shared wireless channel and each node has a unique identifier with at least one transmitter and one receiver. It is assumed that the effective transmission distance between every node is equal. Nodes are neighbors when they are in the transmission range of one another. The OLSR protocol is in charge of discovering neighborhood. The fixed specific parameters for OLSR include: HELLO message interval of 2 seconds, TC message interval of 5 seconds and time window for PDP calculation of 20 seconds.

The Mobile Ad-hoc Network has 50 mobile wireless devices distributed in a given geographic region with two-dimensional (2D). Routing performances are measured in terms of PLR, average E2ED, average number of hops, and Packet Error Ratio (PER).

B. Trade-off analysis

At the beginning, the associated trade-off between E2ED and PLR was evaluated. The method that applies the LD metric is called Minimum Delay (MD) [24]. Herein, the method that applies the PDP metric is called Minimum Packet Loss (MPL) [25]. In an independent batch of 10 simulations of each method configured according to Table II, a straightforward compromise between the quality measures in all mobility scenarios was identified. Figure 3 highlights the non-dominated points.

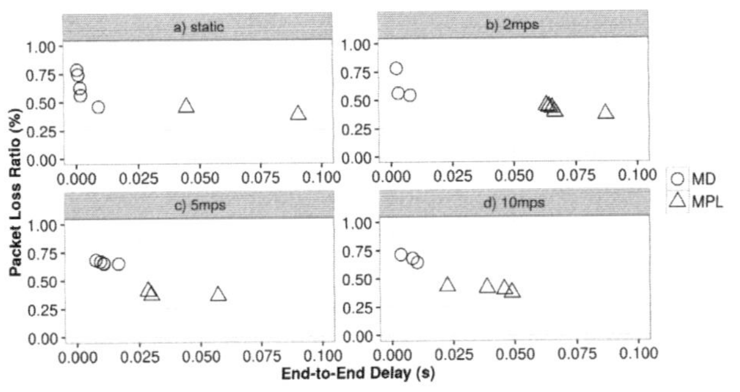

Figure 3. Packet Loss Ratio and End-to-End Delay trade-off

The MD generates straighter routes, which minimizes the E2ED. However, packet drops can overly enlarge due to the increased probability of choosing slower links. On the other hand, the MPL generates routes with more hops, regardless of the latency. That decreases the PLR but provokes larger E2ED. As can be seen in Figure 3, the trade-off is sharp. Furthermore, as mobility increases, this compromise narrows.

C. Comparison of multicriteria and single-criterion methods

Our method is labeled of EC (Epsilon-constraint) plus the corresponding minimum PDP constraint. Thereby, four settings were simulated according to such constraints: $\epsilon_b = (50\%, 60\%, 70\%, 80\%)$.

1) Minimum Delay (MD): MD remarkably achieves less E2ED than MPL and ECs methods, which is depicted in Figure 4. In fact, the source node usually sends packets directly to the destination node, if they are in the range area from one another. Figure 6 indicates such reality when displaying the average number of hops equal to 1 for all the node speed set. MD measures the one-way delay through ad-hoc probe packets. Thus, paths with less Round Trip Time (RTT) are selected. On the one hand, this reduces the latency in transmission, but on the other hand, increases the probability of handling poor quality links. Figures 4a. and 4b. show that the reduced mobility favors the stability of E2ED. Figures 4c. and

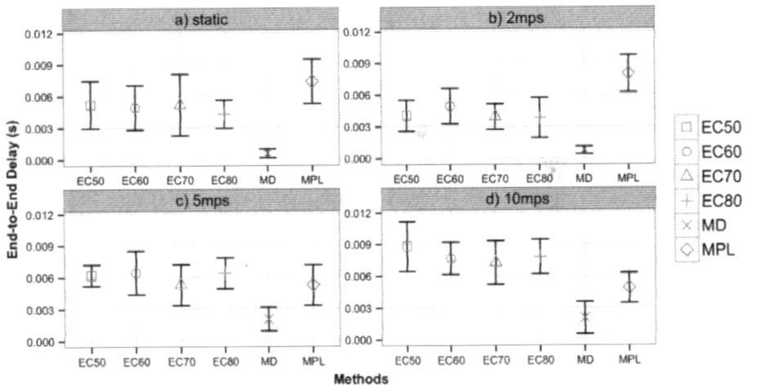

Figure 4. End-to-End Delay to such mobility scenarios: a) static, b) 2mps, c) 5mps, and d) 10mps.

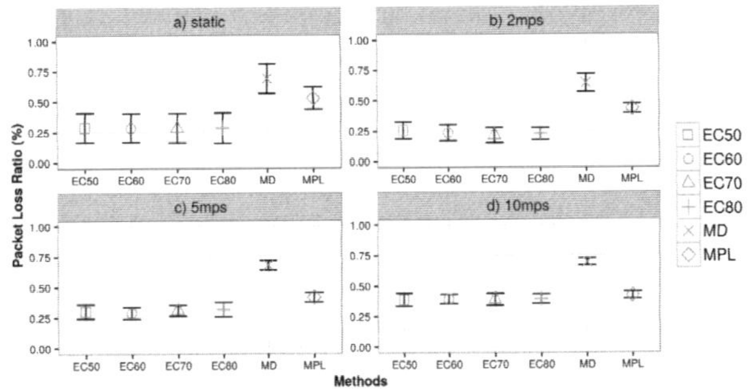

Figure 5. Packet Loss Ratio to such mobility scenarios: a) static, b) 2mps, c) 5mps, and d) 10mps.

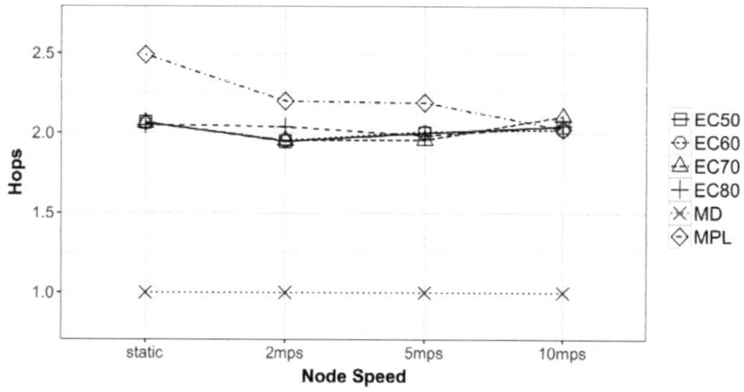

Figure 6. Average number of hops

4d. present larger variations, precisely because of additional mobility.

Figure 5 shows that PLR always has values above 50% in all mobility scenarios. Such poor performance can be justified by the distance between nodes of the route, which promotes the formation of slow and direct links. As nodes speed increases, drops are even more constant, since the source and destination are distancing and approaching speedily, which generates nonstop packet loss due to disconnections, collisions, and interferences.

If a delay-sensitive traffic is being transmitted, delay-aware routing protocols can be useful. However, in the simulated scenarios, E2ED as a single criterion does not reach a proper trade-off, as the small delay is followed by excessive loss rate.

2) Minimum Packet Loss: MPL selects paths with less PLR, i.e., those routes with high successful delivery are preferred, even though it means longer paths, as shown in Figure 6. Meanwhile, Figure 4 displays that longer routes augment the E2ED compared to MD. In terms of PLR, Figure 5 reveals that MPL overcomes MD in all mobility scenarios, having mean values below 50%. The high loss rate identified in Figures 5a. and 5b. is due to the fact that in a dense environment, MPL selects closer nodes, which implies routes with an additional number of hops, as shown in Figure 6. This fact naturally contributes to a higher incidence of packet drops and interferences in the shared medium. Interestingly, more mobility may shorten the length of path, since a given relay node can be moving closer to the destination. Note that, in Figures 5c. and 5d., there was some reduction in drops.

Reliability-aware routing protocols are well-suited to provide QoS when the application is delay-tolerant, but requires high delivery rate. Likewise, they also be feasible for multimedia applications as long as the delay requirements are met.

3) Epsilon-Constraints: As shown in Figure 1, in terms of PLR, the EC multicriteria methods get better results than single-criterion methods. This is because our model seeks to minimize the E2ED as long as the PDP requirement is satisfied. Such result is corroborated by the constant average number of hops displayed in Figure 6. The variability in Figure 5a. (static scenario) is because of fixed density, which leads to a high need for contention. In Figure 5d., ECs and MPL obtained equivalent results. Actually, the high mobility impacts on the efficiency of the Dijkstra's algorithm when dealing with the imposed constraint. Upon constant and strong mobility, it is difficult to find links that do not violate the reliability requirement. This condition further generates an increase in the E2ED, as displayed in Figure 4d. In addition, it is relevant to record that the OLSR protocol is not suitable for highly mobile networks due to its proactive characteristic. In this context, the routes become outdated quickly and the protocol is not able to rebuild them timely.

In Figure 4, although not achieving the best latency results, the multicriteria method can be suited to multimedia traffic, since there was a significant decrease in the PLR and the E2ED remained at a reasonable threshold. In summary, as speed increases, the delay also increases. However, the PLR remains stable.

Looking at the underlying layer, the errors caused by collisions and interferences were analyzed. Packet Error Rate (PER) is the number of incorrectly received data packets divided by the total number of packets received. A packet is declared incorrect if at least one bit is corrupted. Figure 7 demonstrates that delay-aware methods (MD and ECs) have higher estimated PER. This is due to some factors. In general, the delay calculation is made through the ad-hoc probes, which increases the overhead, causing more collisions. In MPL, this addition of packets is not necessary since, as aforementioned, the metric calculation is done using short HELLO messages. Specifically, MD obtains routes with few hops, generating less reliable connections, whereas EC methods obtain routes with more hops than MD, generating additional need of contention, which adds errors by interferences and collisions. In short, it is possible to correlate the number of hops to the PER. Mostly, the PER values of the EC methods are slightly larger compared to the MD because of the additional hops. This condition is also evident for the MPL, since, inasmuch as the number of hops decreases, the PER also decreases.

In terms of PLR compared to the best result of single-criterion methods, our multicriteria model obtained, in each scenario, better results of about: 34% in static, 28% in 2mps, 18% in 5mps, and 6% in 10mps. Such results show that multicriteria optimization in ad-hoc networks can be a valuable strategy since it encourages the design of intelligent, adaptive and robust protocols that fit into the dynamic nature of MANETs.

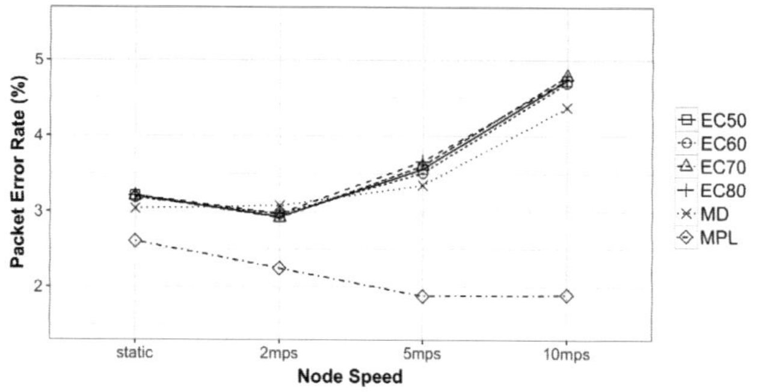

Figure 7. Average Packet Error Rate

V. CONCLUSION

Routing plays a key role in the development and spread of mobile ad-hoc networking. The multi-hop wireless network technology has gained commercial attention and new applications have emerged. However, in this context, there exists a crescent demand by QoS levels that are compatible with these new applications. As MANETs are dynamic networks, such expectations are difficult to achieve. Now, it is not only necessary to provide properly and timely routes, but also manage the scarce resources available. That means conflicting requirements can be found when trying to satisfy such demands, which implies in need to find a trade-off solution. The compromise between delay and reliability exemplifies such challenge.

This work has demonstrated such a trade-off through two link quality metrics. While MD metric seeks to minimize the E2ED, MPL metric aims to maximize the reliability of packet delivery. The introductory contribution of this paper was to present a multicriteria mathematical model that copes with both metrics in route optimization process. From our results, it was concluded that by dealing with the reliability metric as a constraint, an expressive decrease in PLR can be achieved. Besides, a handy trade-off can be earned.

In future works, new criteria that consider node residual energy and link stability will be added. Other mobility models, such as Gauss-markov, and different network density will be applied as well. Moreover, it is intended to compare the proposal to the weighted sum and existing works that take into account more than one QoS metric. The main target is to create a flexible and robust model where QoS constraints can be dynamically adapted to the network conditions and the type of application, for example. For this purpose, probabilistic models should be proposed and implemented in an optimization and decision-making support module that can be used by different routing protocols. Another relevant challenge is to eliminate or at least reduce the need for probes to compute the delay. Time series forecasting methods can be tested, therefore.

ACKNOWLEDGMENT

The authors would like to thank the Brazilian agencies CAPES (PROEX), CNPq and FAPEMIG for the financial support.

REFERENCES

[1] J. Loo, J. L. Mauri, and J. H. Ortiz, Mobile ad hoc networks: current status and future trends. CRC Press, 2016.

[2] N. Chakchouk, "A survey on opportunistic routing in wireless communication networks," IEEE Communications Surveys & Tutorials, vol. 17, no. 4, 2015, pp. 2214–2241.

[3] B. B. Jauregui and F. L. Malaina, "New approaches to mobile ad hoc network routing: application of intelligent optimization techniques to multicriteria routing," Mobile Ad Hoc Networks: Current Status and Future Trends, 2016, pp. 171–200.

[4] L. Khoukhi, A. El Masri, and D. Gaiti, "Quality-of-service state information-based solutions in wireless mobile ad hoc networks: A survey and a proposal," Mobile Ad Hoc Networks: Current Status and Future Trends, 2016, p. 279.

[5] Z. Guo, S. Malakooti, S. Sheikh, C. Al-Najjar, and B. Malakooti, "Multi-objective OLSR for proactive routing in MANET with delay, energy, and link lifetime predictions," Applied Mathematical Modelling, vol. 35, no. 3, 2011, pp. 1413–1426.

[6] W. A. Jabbar, M. Ismail, and R. Nordin, "Multi-criteria based multipath OLSR for battery and queue-aware routing in multi-hop ad hoc wireless networks," Wireless Networks, vol. 21, no. 4, 2015, pp. 1309–1326.

[7] Y. Xu, J. Liu, Y. Shen, X. Jiang, and T. Taleb, "Security/QoS-aware route selection in multi-hop wireless ad hoc networks," in Communications (ICC), 2016 IEEE International Conference on. IEEE, 2016, pp. 1–6.

[8] T.-T. Huynh, A.-V. Dinh-Duc, and C.-H. Tran, "Delay-constrained energy-efficient cluster-based multi-hop routing in wireless sensor networks," Journal of Communications and Networks, vol. 18, no. 4, 2016, pp. 580–588.

[9] A. L. Jaimes, S. Z. Martınez, and C. A. C. Coello, "An introduction to multiobjective optimization techniques," Optimization in Polymer Processing, 2009, pp. 29–57.

[10] M. Emmerich and A. Deutz, "Multicriteria optimization and decision making," LIACS. Leiden university, NL, 2006.

[11] Y. Collette and P. Siarry, Multiobjective optimization: principles and case studies. Springer Science & Business Media, 2013.

[12] M. Ziegelmann, Constrained Shortest Paths and Related Problems-Constrained Network Optimization. VDM Verlag, 2007.

[13] T. Clausen and P. Jacquet, "Optimized link state routing protocol (OLSR)," Tech. Rep., 2003.

[14] J. F. Kurose and K. W. Ross, Computer networking: a top-down approach. Pearson, 2013, vol. 6.

[15] C. Perkins, E. Belding-Royer, and S. Das, "Ad hoc on-demand distance vector (AODV) routing," Tech. Rep., 2003.

[16] N. Javaid, M. Ullah, and K. Djouani, "Identifying design requirements for wireless routing link metrics," in Global Telecommunications Conference (GLOBECOM 2011), 2011 IEEE. IEEE, 2011, pp. 1–5.

[17] N. Javaid et al., "Investigating quality routing link metrics in wireless multi-hop networks," annals of telecommunications-annales des télécommunications, vol. 69, no. 3-4, 2014, pp. 209–217.

[18] Z. Zhao, D. Rosário, T. Braun, and E. Cerqueira, "Context-aware opportunistic routing in mobile ad-hoc networks incorporating node mobility," in 2014 IEEE Wireless Communications and Networking Conference (WCNC). IEEE, 2014, pp. 2138–2143.

[19] N. A. Alwan, "Performance analysis of Dijkstra-based weighted sum minimization routing algorithm for wireless mesh networks," Modelling and Simulation in Engineering, vol. 2014, 2014, p. 32.

[20] M. Ahmadi, M. Shojafar, A. Khademzadeh, K. Badie, and R. Tavoli, "A hybrid algorithm for preserving energy and delay routing in mobile ad-hoc networks," Wireless Personal Communications, vol. 85, no. 4, 2015, pp. 2485–2505.

[21] Y.-S. Yen, H.-C. Chao, R.-S. Chang, and A. Vasilakos, "Flooding-limited and multi-constrained QoS multicast routing based on the genetic algorithm for MANETs," Mathematical and Computer Modelling, vol. 53, no. 11, 2011, pp. 2238–2250.

[22] B. Nancharaiah and B. C. Mohan, "The performance of a hybrid routing intelligent algorithm in a mobile ad hoc network," Computers & Electrical Engineering, vol. 40, no. 4, 2014, pp. 1255–1264.

[23] L. Shi, A. Fapojuwo, N. Viberg, W. Hoople, and N. Chan, "Methods for calculating bandwidth, delay, and packet loss metrics in multi-hop IEEE802.11 ad hoc networks," in Vehicular Technology Conference, 2008. VTC Spring 2008. IEEE. IEEE, 2008, pp. 103–107.

[24] W. Cordeiro, E. Aguiar, W. M. Junior, A. Abelem, and M. Stanton, "Providing quality of service for mesh networks using link delay measurements," in Computer Communications and Networks, 2007. ICCCN 2007. Proceedings of 16th International Conference on. IEEE, 2007, pp. 991–996.

[25] D. Passos, D. V. Teixeira, D. C. Muchaluat-Saade, L. C. S. Magalhães, and C. Albuquerque, "Mesh network performance measurements," in International Information and Telecommunicatios Technologies Symposium (I2TS), 2006, pp. 48–55.

[26] D. C. Montgomery, Design and analysis of experiments. John Wiley & Sons, 2008.

[27] J. Araujo. Design and analysis of experiments: Multicriteria QoS-aware solution in wireless multi-hop networks. [retrieved: 06, 2017]. [Online]. Available: http://rpubs.com/jeannra/dae-anova-multicriteria-qos-aware (2017)

Performance Enhancement of MTC in LTE Networks by Maximizing Random Access Procedure Throughput

Ibraheem M. Fayed

Eman S. El-Din

Network Planning Department, National Telecommunication Institute (NTI)
Cairo, Egypt.

Email: ibrahim.fayed@nti.sci.eg

Email: emanserag@gmail.com

***Abstract*—A fundamental requirement for any cellular system is the possibility for the device to request a connection setup, commonly referred to as random access procedure. In Long Term Evolution (LTE) networks, the distribution of a limited number of radio resources among Human-to-Human (H2H) users and increasing number of Machine-Type-Communication (MTC) devices in Machine-to-Machine (M2M) communications is one of the main problems. An analytical model is conducted to compute the throughput for message 1 and message 2 using a Markov chain model for the four messages signaling flow with buffering for message 4 in LTE Third-Generation Partnership Project (3GPP) random access. The network performance will be enhanced by determining a dedicated arrival rate corresponding to maximum throughput of message 2 that will assist the network planner to optimize the network performance.**

Keywords-Machine Type Communication (MTC) ; Machine to Machine (M2M); LTE network; Random Access Procedure throughput.

I. INTRODUCTION

In the last decades, mobile communication has evolved from being an expensive technology for a few selected individuals to today's ubiquitous systems used by a majority of the world's population [1]. Modern wireless communication schemes like 3GPP LTE network, do not allow serving effectively M2M connections between a huge numbers of interacting MTC devices. A good background of this issue "when a huge number of machines request access" was explained in [2]. Increasing the network performance is not possible due to the finance approach. One possible solution of the problem is based on the use of random access procedure (RACH) procedure [3].

Increasing network capacity is the major objectives of LTE network. This increasing will provide high data rates for end users with low latency, ensure high Quality of Service (QoS), and reduce the cost. For channel access and ensuring the Quality of Service (QoS), there are two attributes of random access procedures in LTE: contention-free and contention-based random access.

In contention-free random access, the e-NodeB signals a reserved preamble for the mobile station, thus avoiding the contention. In contention-based random access, all mobile stations need to participate in contention for the resources [4].

A very huge number of machines, such as user equipment (UE) may dwell in coverage area of cell, which may request to access the network periodically or sporadically. They also have a small power that must be used as efficiently as possible. The 3GPP has carried in different studies [5] [6] that try to address the issues related to M2M communications in the present systems, as well as in the future releases of LTE. A detailed study and analysis of physical downlink control channel (PDCCH) performance for M2M traffic in LTE was introduced in [7].

The main aim of this paper is to obtain the upper band of the request arrival rate in order to sustain the network performance metric such as the throughput for MTC in LTE network. An explicit analysis for evaluation of throughput for message 1 and message 2 using a Markov chain model for the four messages signaling flow with buffering for message 4 in LTE 3GPP random access is presented.

This paper is organized as follows: random access procedure using four messages in LTE network is explained in Section 2. Markov chain model for transient states for the four messages with queuing buffer for message 4 and model assumptions and analysis is introduced in Section 3. In Section 4, results and verification are shown. Section 5 is devoted to conclusion.

II. RANDOM ACCESS PROCEDURE

A brief description of the contention-based random access procedure utilized, for example, by the MTC traffic, is explained as follow.

Step 1: The MTC device (UE) requests to initiate the RACH procedure by selecting one of the available RACH preambles randomly and then sending the preamble in Message 1 over the physical random access channel (PRACH) in the uplink. A collision occurs when two or more machines (UEs) get the same preamble in the same subframe. However, after preamble sending the UE waits for a random access response (RAR) (Message 2) from the e-NodeB within the time interval called a response window [3], i.e., even if two or more UEs use the same preamble for Message 1 and a collision occurs, the e- NodeB will detect this event and will not send reply to UE. The transmission of a random access preamble is restricted to certain subframes. Let b denote their periodicity, i.e., random access is possible in every b^{th} subframe. In addition, let K denote the total number of available preambles.

Step 2: e-NodeB replies with Message 2, which is also known as the RAR and it includes UL grant for Step 3. Message 2 is sent over the physical downlink shared channel (PDSCH). So, schedule the user is needed [7], i.e., send a downlink assignment control message over the PDCCH. There may be at most one RAR message in each subframe, but each may have more than one UL grant (each referring to a different preamble). Let c is defined as the maximum number of UL grants per RAR per subframe. Note that in this model, an UL grant is given for every uncollided preamble.

Step 3: In the case of successful preamble transmission after receiving Message 2 from the e-NodeB and RAR processing time, the UE sends a RRC connection request (Message 3) to the e-NodeB over Physical Uplink Shared Channel (PUSCH).

Step 4: RACH procedure is completed after the UE receiving a contention resolution message (Message 4) from the e-NodeB. Hybrid Automatic Repeat request (HARQ) procedure guarantees a successful transmission of Message 3/ Message 4. HARQ procedure provides a limit in Message 3/ Message 4 sequential transmission attempts. If the limit is reached UE should start a new RACH procedure by sending a preamble.

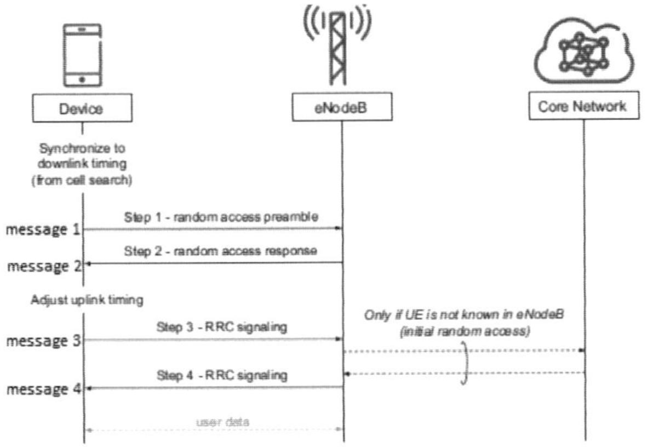

Figure 1. Four messages control signaling flow sequence in LTE random access. [1]

Let N be defined as the PDCCH resource size (in control channel elements CCEs), N^{Msg2} and N^{Msg4} are the number of CCEs used to send a Message 2 and a Message 4, respectively. So, a maximum of $M = N/N^{Msg4}$ Message 4's can be sent in one subframe if Message 2 is not present in that subframe [7]. When a Message 2 is sent in a subframe, then at most $m = (N - N^{Msg2})/N^{Msg4}$ Message 4's can be sent in that subframe. Although the parameters N, N^{Msg2}, and N^{Msg4} are closely connected from the system point of view, our model is greatly simplified when we use the derived parameters M and m. This messaging scheme is demonstrated in Figure 1.

III. MODEL PARAMETERS AND ASSUMPTIONS

In LTE there are K parallel Aloha channels used, and each time a UE makes a request of retransmission, the preamble is selected in random. By this random selection, the fresh random access requests and the retransmission attempts will be mixed. In addition, the input parameter of the model will be a, which is the aggregate rate of all requests (arrival of new requests and retransmission requests) not λ, which is the rate of fresh requests per sub-frame.

Let θ be defined as the throughput of successful requests. When the system is stable, it can be determined from the model as a function of a. The system is stable if the average input rate is the same as the average output rate, which means that the arrival rate λ of fresh requests is equal to the throughput θ of successful requests whenever the system is stable. This is how we get the functional relationship between the aggregate request rate a and the arrival rate λ of fresh requests.

Now, let A_{nk} represent the total number of random access requests with preamble k (including both the new requests and the retransmissions) in time slot n. Since the aggregate stream of requests (including the fresh ones and the retransmissions) is assumed to obey a Poisson process and the preambles are independently chosen from the uniform distribution, A_{nk} are independent and identically distributed random variables obeying a Poisson distribution with mean ab/K and point probabilities, i.e.,

$$P_i(a) = P_r\{A_{nk}=i\} = \frac{\left(\frac{ab}{k}\right)^i}{i!} e^{-ab/K} \tag{1}$$

The probability of failure can be calculated as follow:

P_r\{failure\} = P_r\{collision occurs in Step 1\} +P_r\{no collision occurs in Step 1, loss occurs in Step 2\} +P_r\{no failure occurs in Steps 1 and 2, delay occurs in Step 4\}.

A call flow for successful and unsuccessful session setup establishment based on RACH procedure is shown in Figure 2.

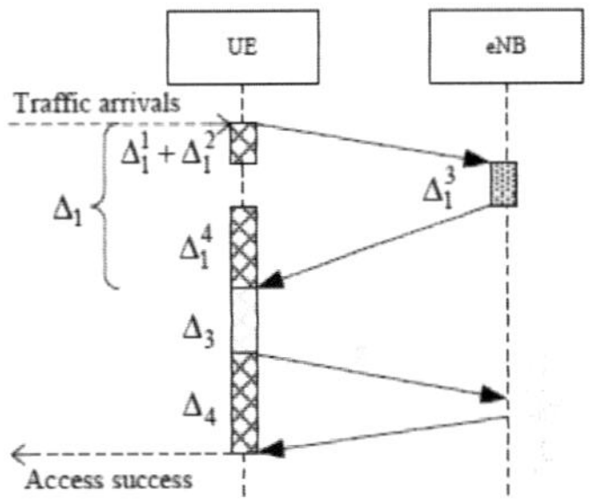

Figure 2. A request access success without collision

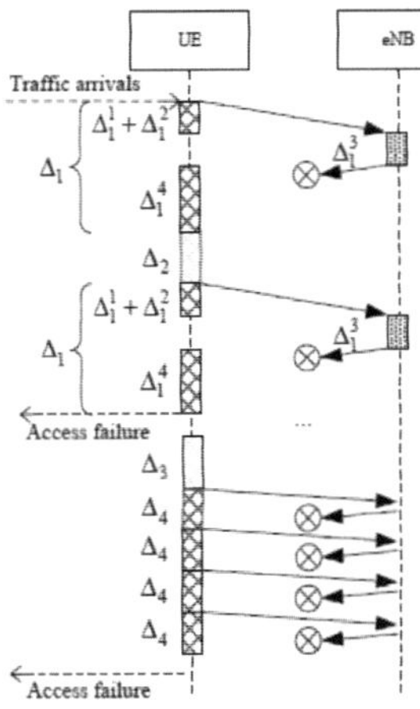

Figure 2b. request access failure

Figure 2. Four messages control signaling flow sequence to transmit data with retransmissions in LTE random access [3]

A mathematical model is proposed in the form of discrete Markov chain that follows the steps of RACH procedure and describes the evolution of Message 4 buffer and determines the number of preamble attempt collisions and the number of sequential Message 3/ Message 4 transmission attempts. With this model the access delay for each state of the Markov chain can be calculated by summing up the corresponding time intervals introduced as follow:

• Δ_{11}, Δ_{21}, Δ_{31}, and Δ_{41} are defined respectively as: waiting time for a RACH opportunity to transmit a preamble, preamble transmission time, preamble processing time at the e-NodeB, and RAR response window. Then $\Delta_1 = \Delta_{11} + \Delta_{21} + \Delta_{31} + \Delta_{41}$ is the time interval from the beginning of RACH procedure until sending message 3 or resending a preamble.

The back off window is defined as Δ_2 , the RAR processing time as Δ_3, and time for Message 3 transmission, waiting for Message 4, and Message 4 processing is Δ_4.

Let us consider inhomogeneous discrete Markov chain $\{\xi\}$ over the state space

$\iota=\{(0), (1), (2), (n,m), 0\leq n\leq N, 0\leq m\leq M)$ which determines the process of transitions between states. We assume that state (0) is the start point of RACH procedure, state (1) is the absorbing state denoting access success, state (2) is another absorbing state denoting access failure, the pair of (n,m) denotes the state when n Message 1 retransmissions and m Message 3/ Message 4 retransmissions occurred. The maximum number of retransmission for message 1equals (N-1) and the maximum number of retransmission of message (2) (M-1). The values of (N,M) will be taken from [9].

The start of transmission or retransmission of message 3 must be done after success in sending message 1. The two events are independent.

Let g denote the HARQ retransmission probability for Message 3/ Message 4. And p is the probability of retransmission failure for message 1 expressed in equation (1).

The probability of success P in state (n, m) will be:

$$P(n,m) = (1-p)(1-g)p^n g^m \tag{2}$$

$P(n,m)$ will be shown and calculated as a future work.

Now, define

$$Y_n(1) := \#\{k : A_{nk} = 1, k = 1, \ldots, K\} \tag{3}$$

$$\hat{Y}_n(1) := \#\{k : A_{nk} \geq 1, k = 1, \ldots, K\} \tag{4}$$

where $\hat{Y}_n(1)$ and $Y_n(1)$ are referring to the total number of preambles chosen in time slot n, and the number of successful (uncolliding) Message 1's respectively. The joint distribution of the random variables $Y_n(1)$ and $\hat{Y}_n(1)$ is calculated as follows:

$$q_{ij}^{(1)}(a) := \Pr\{Y_n^{(1)} = i, Y_n^{\sim(2)} = j\} \tag{5}$$

$$= \binom{K}{i\ j-i} p_o^{K-j} p_1^i (1-p_o-p_1)^{j-i}$$

$$0 \leq i \leq j \leq K$$

There is at most b Message 2's and so at most bc UL grants per time slot. Message 2's in time slot n are generated by Message 1's of the previous time slot. Let $\hat{Y}_n(2)$ and $Y_n(2)$ denote the total number of UL grants included in Message 2 in time slot n and the number of successful (uncolliding) UL grants respectively. No losses appear in this step, i.e., $\hat{Y}_n(2) = \hat{Y}_{n-1}(1)$ and $Y_n(2) = Y_{n-1}(1)$, if the total number of preambles chosen in the previous time slot is sufficiently small, i.e., $\hat{Y}_{n-1}(1) \leq bc$, which is trivially true if $K \leq bc$. However, if $\hat{Y}_{n-1}(1) > bc$, then losses occur so that $\hat{Y}_n(2) = bc$. Let the preambles that are given a UL grant in the latter case are chosen in random by e-NodeB. Thus, we have (for the nontrivial case $K > bc$

$$q_{ij}^{(2)}(a) := Pr\{Y_n^{(2)}=i, \hat{Y}_n=j\} \tag{6}$$

$$\begin{cases} q_{ij}^{(1)}(a) & 0 \leq i \leq j \leq bc \\ \displaystyle\sum_{k=bc}^{K} \sum_{l=i}^{k} q_{lk}^{(1)}(a) \frac{\binom{l}{i}\binom{k-l}{bc-i}}{\binom{k}{bc}}, & 0 \leq i \leq j = bc \end{cases}$$

With the following marginal distributions:

$$q_i^{(2)}(a) := \Pr\{Y_n^{(2)}=i\} = \sum_{j=i}^{bc} q_{ij}^{(2)}(a) \tag{7}$$

$$0 \leq i \leq bc$$

$$\tilde{q}_j^{(2)}(a) := \Pr\{\tilde{Y}_n^{(2)}=j\} = \sum_{i=0}^{j} q_{ij}^{(2)}(a)$$

$$0 \leq j \leq bc$$

Utilizing the definition of $q_{ij}^{(2)}(a)$, we find that

$$\tilde{q}_j^{(2)}(a) = \begin{cases} \binom{K}{j} p_0(a)^{K-j}(1-p_0(a))^j, & 0 \leq j < bc \\ \displaystyle\sum_{l=bc}^{K} \binom{k}{l} p_0(a)^{K-l}(1-p_0(a))^l, & j = bc \end{cases} \tag{8}$$

So, $\tilde{Y}_n^{(2)} = min\{B(a), bc\}$

where $B(a)$ is a binomially distributed random variable with parameters K and $1 - p_0(a)$.

For throughput analysis, the throughput θ of successful requests must be equal to the arrival rate λ of fresh requests.

This proposal finds conditions for stability in terms of the total traffic a and then to determine the throughput of successful requests $\theta(a)$ as a function of a, as well as the maximum throughput $\theta^* = max_a\ \theta(a)$. To simplify the notation, we assume here that $K > bc$. The generalization to the case $K \leq bc$ is straightforward.

By using the Slotted Aloha model in [8] for the RACH used in Step 1the throughput (per subframe) of successful Message 1's as a function of a, which is the arrival rate of all random access requests per subframe, can be calculated as follows:

$$\theta^{(1)}(a) = \frac{E\left[Y_n^{(1)}\right]}{b} = ae^{-\frac{ab}{K}} \tag{9}$$

To calculate the throughput in Step 2, Since $K > bc$, the throughput is then reduced by the limited number of UL grants in Message 2. The throughput (per subframe) of successful UL grants as a function of a is distinctly

$$\theta^{(2)}(a) = \frac{E\left[Y_n^{(2)}\right]}{b} = \frac{1}{b}\sum_{i=1}^{bc} i q_i^{(2)}(a) \tag{10}$$

Equations (9) and (10) can be solved using MATLAB software to show the throughput of message 1 and throughput of message 2

IV. RESULTS ANALYSIS AND VERIFICATION

A typical values for the model parameters are taken from [7] [9] and summarized in Table 1.

TABLE I TYPICAL VALUES FOR THE MODEL PARAMETERS

Notion	Definition	Typical Values
K	Number of preambles	54
B	RACH Periodicity	5
C	Maximum number of UL grants per subframe	3

Using the above values in equations (1:10) and solving using MATLAB program which explained by the flowing flowchart in Figure 3, we get the results shown in Figures 4-6.

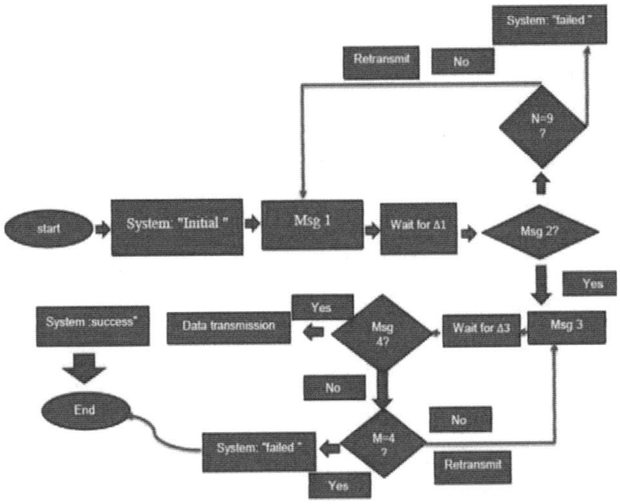

Figure 3. Flow chart explains the steps used in MATLAP program

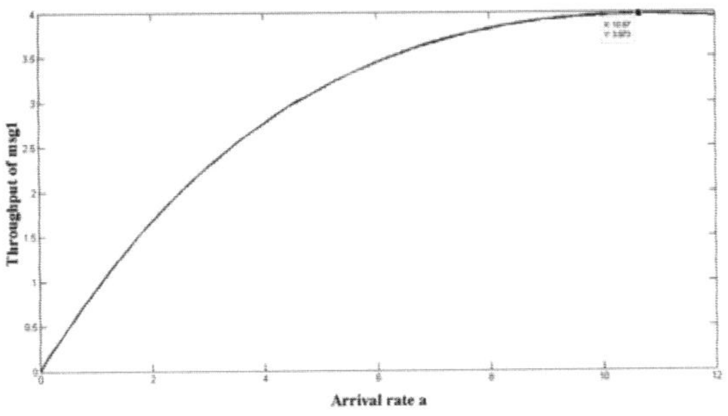

Figure 4. The throughput of message 1 with the increasing the aggregate arrival rate a

As shown in Figure 4 as the arrival rate for requests increases the throughput of message 1 increases till a certain value ($\theta^{(1)}(a) = 3.973$) at arrival rate $a = 10.67$ $requests/ms$. Then the throughput approximately sets at this value because of the UE will know after a certain window time that the collision is occurred and retransmits message 1 again directly with new preamble in the uplink.

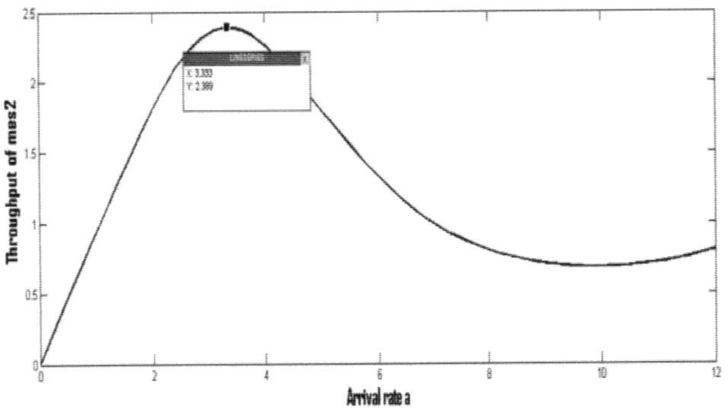

Figure 5. The throughput of message 2 with the increasing the aggregate arrival rate *a*

As shown in Figure 5, as the arrival rate for requests increases the throughput of message 1 increases till a certain value ($\theta^{(2)}(a) = 2.377$) at arrival rate $a = 3.333$ $requests/ms$ and then throughput decreases because the message 2 contains information for more than one user up to 8 users and in case of collision lose downlink for message 2 the all users in this control channel will retransmit (requests) message 1 again directly and may be have the same preamble and collision in message 1 dose again.

The failure in message 2 affects directly in message 1 so to get the maximum throughput of message 1 and message 2, the intersection between throughput curve of message 2 and message 1 (which is the maximum throughput for message 2) will be considered as shown in Figure 6.

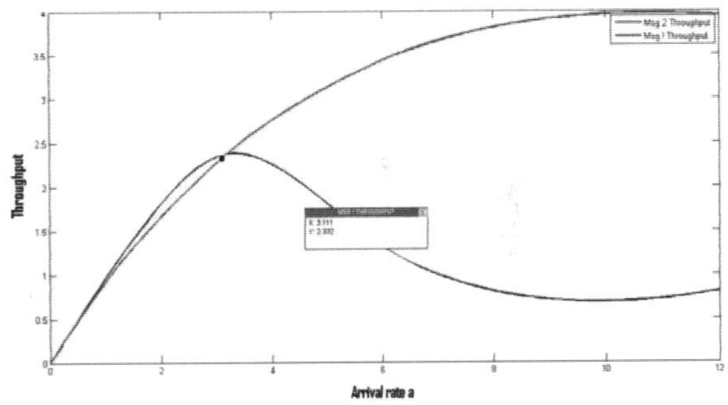

Figure 6. The intersection between throughput of message 1and throughput of message 2 with the increasing the aggregate arrival rate a

As shown in Figure 6, the maximum throughput is equal 2.332 at arrival rate a equals $a = 3.333$ $requests/ms$ and this results is agree with [7].

V. CONCLUSION

The main aim of this paper is to obtain the upper band of the arrival request rate in order to sustain the network performance metric such as the throughput for MTC in LTE network. Explicit analysis for evaluation of throughput for message 1 and message 2 using a Markov chain model for the four messages signaling flow with buffering for message 4 in LTE 3GPP random access was presented.

In LTE planning, it is important to take into consideration the requests arrival rate (as forecasting plan) and the planner must select the network parameters (such as the base station locations, antennas height, etc.) to achieve the maximum throughput. So in this paper, it was found that, the planner has to design the system with arrival rate less than 3.333 $requests/ms$ to maximize network throughput. If the arrival rate increases above this value, the collisions in message 1 will increase, causing a degradation of the network throughput and also a decrease of the network performance.

The proposed analytical model will be assigned as a future work to calculate the state probability by using the Markov chain model explained in the proposed model.

REFERENCES

[1] E. Dahlman, S. Parkvall, and J. Skold, 4G, LTE-Advanced Pro and The Road to 5G. 3rd Edition, London, United Kingdom, Academic Press, Elsevier, 2016.

[2] S. Y. Lien, K C. Chen, and Y. Lin, "Toward ubiquitous massive accesses in 3GPP machine-to-machine communications," IEEE Commun. Mag., vol. 49, no. 4, pp. 66–74, Apr. 2011.

[3] V. Y. Borodakiy, K. E. Samouylov, Y. V. Gaidamaka, P. O. Abaev, I. A. Buturlin, and S. A. Etezov, " Modelling a Random Access Channel with collisions for M2M Traffic in LTE Networks ", The reported study was partially supported by the RFBR, research projects No. 13-07-00953, 14-07-00090, 2014.

[4] A. N. Khan, J. Khalid, H. K. Qureshi, " Performance Analysis of Contention-Based Random Access Procedure in Clustered LTE Networks ", Seventh International Conference on Next Generation Mobile Apps, Services and Technologies,pp 203-209, 2013.

[5] 3GPP R2 112863, "Backoff enhancements for RAN overload control," ZTE, Barcelona, Spain, May 2011.

[6] 3GPP TR 23.888 V1.6.0, Third-Generation Partnership Project; Technical Specification Group Services and System Aspects; System Improvements for Machine-Type Communications (MTC), Sophia-Antipolis, France, Nov. 2011.

[7] P. Osti, P. Lassila, S. Aalto, A. Larmo, and T. Tirronen, "Analysis of PDCCH Performance for M2M Traffic in LTE", IEEE Transactions on Vehicular Technology, Vol. 63, No. 9, pp. 4357– 4371, November 2014.

[8] D. Bertsekas and R. Gallager, Data Networks, 2nd ed. Upper Saddle River, NJ, USA: Prentice-Hall, 1992.

[9] 3GPP TR 37.868 – Study on RAN Improvements for Machine-type Communications. (Re-lease 11). 2011.

Level Crossing Rate of Macrodiversity in the Presence of Short Term Fading and Long Term Fading with Different Average Powers

Dragana Krstić, Mihajlo Stefanović, Vladeta Milenković
Faculty of Electronic Engineering, University of Niš
Aleksandra Medvedeva 14, 18000 Niš,
Serbia
e-mail: dragana.krstic@elfak.ni.ac.rs

Sinisa Minić
University of Pristina, Kosovska Mitrovica
Teachers' Training Faculty in Prizren,
Nemanjina Street, 38218 Leposavić
Serbia

Abstract—**The macrodiversity system reduces long term fading effects and short term fading effects on wireless system performances simultaneously. The received signal is subjected to Nakagami-m short term fading and Gamma correlated long term fading resulting in signal envelope and envelope average power variation, respectively. The macrodiversity considered in this paper has macrodiversity selection combining (SC) receiver and two microdiversity SC receivers. Signal envelope average power at inputs in microdiversity SC receivers have correlated Gamma distribution with different average values. Level crossing rate of macrodiversity SC receiver output signal envelope is evaluated for the case that the user is at different distances of microdiversity SC receivers.**

Keywords- Gamma correlated long term fading; Nakagami-m short term fading; level crossing rate; selection combining (SC).

I. INTRODUCTION

Gamma long term fading and Nakagami-*m* short term fading degrade the bit error probability and the outage probability of wireless mobile communication radio system [1]. Macrodiversity technique can be applied to mitigate small scale fading effects and large scale fading effects on the outage probability, average bit error probability, the level crossing rate and average fade duration [2].

There are several diversity techniques which reduce fading effects on the bit error probability, the outage probability and the channel capacity. Maximal ratio combining (MRC), equal gain combining (EGC) and selection combining (SC) are the most widely used diversity combining schemes. In the scenario where Gaussian noise power is equally distributed in each branch of MRC receiver, squared output signal can be calculated as a sum of squared signals from its inputs [3]. Signal envelope at the EGC receiver output is a sum of signal envelopes from its inputs [4]. The SC receiver selects the branch with the highest signal envelope from input to provide service to user [5]-[7]. MRC is the optimal combining scheme, but its price and complexity are the highest. MRC and EGC combiners require knowing of all or some of the fading channel information and separate receiver for each branch of the diversity system, which increase the complexity of the system.

The macrodiversity, considered in this paper, consists of macrodiversity SC reception and two microdiversity SC receptions. The macrodiversity SC reception selects the microdiversity with the highest signal envelope average power to enable transmission to the user and microdiversities select the branch with the highest signal envelope. Microdiversity receivers use antennas at one base station and macrodiversity receiver uses antennas at two or more base stations.

Nakagami-*m* distribution describes small scale signal envelope in non line of sight multipath fading channels. For the case when parameter *m* is 1, shadowed Nakagami-*m* fading channel becomes shadowed Rayleigh fading channel, and when *m* goes to infinity, shadowed Nakagami-*m* channel becomes shadowed fading channel. When Gamma long term fading severity parameter goes to infinity and Nakagami-*m* short term fading severity parameter goes to infinity, Gamma shadowed Nakagami-*m* multipath fading channel becomes no fading channel [8].

The first order performance measures of wireless mobile radio systems are average symbol error probability, the channel capacity and the outage probability, and the second order performance measures are the level crossing rate (LCR) and average fade duration (AFD). The level crossing rate can be evaluated as mean of the first order of random process and average fade duration can be calculated as the ratio of the outage probability and the level crossing rate.

There are more works considering LCR of wireless macrodiversity communication system operating over shadowed multipath fading channel. In [5], LCR and AFD of macrodiversity, with macrodiversity SC receiver and two microdiversity maximal ratio combining (MRC) receivers, operating over correlated Gamma long term fading and Nakagami-*m* short term fading channel are calculated. On the other side, the authors in [6] derived the infinite-series expressions for the second-order statistics (LCR and AFD) at the output of SC macrodiversity consisting of two microdiversity systems of MRC type with arbitrary number of branches, which is operating over Gamma shadowed Nakagami-m fading channel.

The macrodiversity system with macrodiversity SC receiver and three microdiversity SC receivers working over Gamma shadowed Nakagami-m multipath fading environment is studied in [7]. The level crossing rate of signals at outputs of microdiversity SC receivers are calculated and based on these formulas, the closed form expression for average LCR of macrodiversity SC receiver output signal is calculated.

The second order statistics of macrodiversity in Gamma shadowed Rician fading channel is analyzed in [3]. In paper [9], macrodiversity, with macrodiversity SC receiver and two microdiversity SC receivers, is studied and LCR of macrodiversity SC receiver output signal is calculated for the presence of Gamma shadowed k-μ multipath fading.

In this paper, macrodiversity, with macrodiversity SC receiver and two microdiversity SC receivers, in the presence of Nakagami-*m* small scale fading and correlated Gamma long term fading is considered. Average powers of Gamma distribution are different. The distances of user and microdiversity receivers are different. The closed form expression for LCR of proposed wireless macrodiversity system is calculated. The level crossing rate of macrodiversity, when distances of user from microdiversity receivers are different, is not considered in open technical literature.

This paper consists of five sections. After the first section, Introduction, where the topic is introduced and related papers analyzed, in the second section the system model is described. The expression for level crossing rate of macrodiversity SC receiver output signal is derived in the third section. In the forth section, numerical results are analyzed. Then, Conclusion is given with some final comments. In the Appendix, the integrals, which appear in the expressions for LCR, are solved.

II. Model of Macrodiversity System

The macrodiversity has macrodiversity SC receiver and two microdiversity SC receivers. Macrodiversity operates in the presence of Gamma long term fading and Nakagami-*m* short term fading. This macrodiversity SC receiver selects microdiversity with the highest signal envelope average power and microdiversity SC receiver selects the branch with the strongest signal envelope. Model of considered system is shown in Figure 1.

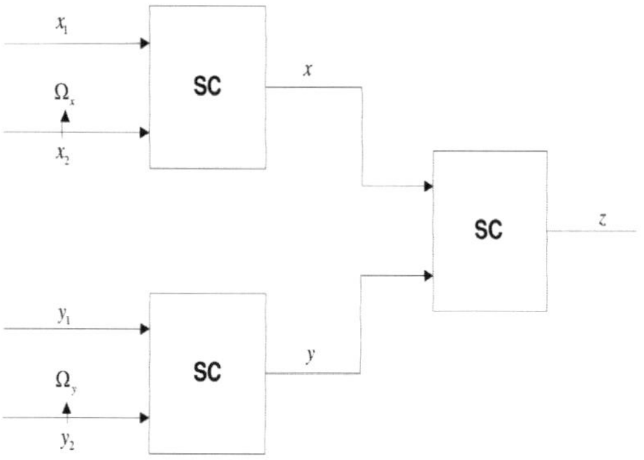

Figure 1. Model of considered system

Probability density function (PDF) of x_1 and x_2 is:

$$p_{x_i}(x_i)=\frac{2}{\Gamma(m)}\left(\frac{m}{\Omega_x}\right)^m x_i^{2m-1}e^{-\frac{m}{\Omega_x}x_i^2},\ x_i\ge 0,\quad i=1,2 \qquad (1)$$

Probability density function of y_1 and y_2 is:

$$p_{y_i}(y_i)=\frac{2}{\Gamma(m)}\left(\frac{m}{\Omega_y}\right)^m y_i^{2m-1}e^{-\frac{m}{\Omega_y}y_i^2},\ y_i\ge 0,\quad i=1,2. \qquad (2)$$

Cumulative distribution function (CDF) of x_i is:

$$F_{x_i}(x_i)=\frac{1}{\Gamma(m)}\gamma\left(m,\frac{m}{\Omega_x}x_i^2\right),\quad x_i\ge 0,\quad i=1,2, \qquad (3)$$

and cumulative distribution function of y_i is:

$$F_{y_i}(y_i)=\frac{1}{\Gamma(m)}\gamma\left(m,\frac{m}{\Omega_y}y_i^2\right),\quad y_i\ge 0,\quad i=1,2, \qquad (4)$$

where $\gamma(n,x)$ is incomplete Gamma function.

The level crossing rate of x_i random process is:

$$N_{x_1}=\frac{f_m\sqrt{2\pi}}{\Gamma(m)}\left(\frac{m}{\Omega_x}\right)^{m-1/2} x_1^{2m-1}e^{-\frac{m}{\Omega_x}x_i^2},\ x_i\ge 0;\ i=1,2. \qquad (5)$$

The level crossing rate of y_i is:

$$N_{y_1}=\frac{f_m\sqrt{2\pi}}{\Gamma(m)}\left(\frac{m}{\Omega_y}\right)^{m-1/2} y_1^{2m-1}e^{-\frac{m}{\Omega_y}y_i^2},\ y_i\ge 0;\ i=1,2. \qquad (6)$$

The LCR of x random process is:

$$N_x=2N_{x_1}F_{x_2}(x)=\frac{2\sqrt{2\pi}f_m}{\Gamma(m)}\left(\frac{m}{\Omega_x}\right)^{m-1/2} x^{2m-1}e^{-\frac{m}{\Omega_x}x^2}\cdot$$

$$\cdot\frac{1}{\Gamma(m)}\gamma\left(m,\frac{m}{\Omega_x}x^2\right),\quad x\ge 0. \qquad (7)$$

The LCR of y random process is:

$$N_y=2N_{y_1}F_{y_2}(y)=\frac{2\sqrt{2\pi}f_m}{\Gamma(m)}\left(\frac{m}{\Omega_y}\right)^{m-1/2} y^{2m-1}e^{-\frac{m}{\Omega_y}y^2}\cdot$$

$$\cdot\frac{1}{\Gamma(m)}\gamma\left(m,\frac{m}{\Omega_y}y^2\right),\quad y\ge 0. \qquad (8)$$

The powers Ω_x and Ω_y follow correlated Gamma distribution:

$$p_{\Omega_x\Omega_y}(\Omega_x\Omega_y)=\frac{m_1^{m_1+1}(\Omega_x\Omega_y)^{\frac{m_1-1}{2}}\rho^{\frac{1-m_1}{2}}}{\Gamma(m_1)(1-\rho)(\Omega_1\Omega_2)^{\frac{m_1+1}{2}}}\cdot$$

$$\cdot e^{-\frac{m_1}{(1-\rho)}\left(\frac{\Omega_x}{\Omega_1}+\frac{\Omega_y}{\Omega_2}\right)} I_{m_1-1}\left(\frac{2m_1\sqrt{\rho}}{(1-\rho)}\left(\frac{\Omega_x\Omega_y}{\Omega_1\Omega_2}\right)^{1/2}\right)=$$

$$=\frac{m_1^{m_1+1}\rho^{\frac{1-m_1}{2}}}{\Gamma(m_1)(1-\rho)(\Omega_1\Omega_2)^{\frac{m_1+1}{2}}}\cdot$$

$$\cdot\sum_{i_1=0}^{\infty}\left(\frac{m_1\sqrt{\rho}}{(1-\rho)(\Omega_1\Omega_2)^{1/2}}\right)^{2i_1+m_1-1}\frac{1}{i_1!\Gamma(i_1+m_1)}$$

$$\Omega_x^{i_1+m_1-1} e^{-\frac{m_1}{(1-\rho)\Omega_1}\Omega_x}\Omega_y^{i_1+m_1-1} e^{-\frac{m_1}{(1-\rho)\Omega_2}\Omega_y},\ \Omega_x\geq 0,\ \Omega_y\geq 0 \quad (9)$$

where ρ is Gamma long term fading correlation coefficient, m_1 is Gamma long term fading severity parameter and $\Omega_1=\overline{\Omega_x}$ and $\Omega_2=\overline{\Omega_y}$. In this paper, parameters Ω_1 and Ω_2 are different.

III. LEVEL CROSSING RATE OF MACRODIVERSITY SC RECEIVER OUTPUT SIGNAL

Macrodiversity SC receiver selects microdiversity SC receiver with higher signal envelope average power to provide service to user. For that reason, the level crossing rate of macrodiversity SC receiver output signal envelope is:

$$N_z=\int_0^{\infty}d\Omega_x\int_0^{\Omega_x}d\Omega_y N_{x/\Omega_x}p_{\Omega_x\Omega_y}(\Omega_x\Omega_y)+$$

$$+\int_0^{\infty}d\Omega_y\int_0^{\Omega_y}d\Omega_x N_{y/\Omega_y}p_{\Omega_x\Omega_y}(\Omega_x\Omega_y)=J_1+J_2. \quad (10)$$

Now, we need to solve the integrals J_1 and J_2. These integrals will be solved in Appendix.

Finally, the LCR of macrodiversity SC receiver output signal envelope is:

$$N_z=\frac{2\sqrt{2\pi}f_m}{\Gamma(m)^2}m^{m-1/2}z^{2m-1}\cdot$$

$$\cdot m^{m-1}z^{2m}\cdot\sum_{j_1=0}^{\infty}\frac{1}{(m+1)(j_1)}m^{j_1}z^{2j_1}\cdot\frac{m_1^{m_1+1}\rho^{\frac{1-m_1}{2}}}{\Gamma(m_1)(1-\rho)(\Omega_1\Omega_2)^{\frac{m_1+1}{2}}}\cdot$$

$$\cdot\sum_{i_1=0}^{\infty}\left(\frac{2m_1\sqrt{\rho}}{(1-\rho)(\Omega_1\Omega_2)^{1/2}}\right)^{2i_1+m_1-1}\frac{1}{i_1!\Gamma(i_1+m_1)}$$

$$\frac{1}{i_1+m_1}\cdot\sum_{j_2=0}^{\infty}\frac{1}{(i_1+m_1+1)(j_2)}\left(\frac{m_1}{\Omega_2(1-\rho)}\right)^{j_2}\cdot$$

$$\cdot\left(\frac{mz^2(1-\rho)\Omega_1}{m_1}\right)^{i_1+m_1-m+1/4-j_1/2+j_2/2}\cdot$$

$$\cdot K_{2i_1+2m_1-2m+1/2-j_1+j_2}\left(2\sqrt{\frac{4mz^2m_1}{(1-\rho)\Omega_1}}\right)+$$

$$+\frac{2\sqrt{2\pi}f_m}{\Gamma(m)^2}m^{m-1/2}z^{2m-1}\cdot$$

$$m^{m-1}z^{2m}\cdot\sum_{j_1=0}^{\infty}\frac{1}{(m+1)(j_1)}m^{j_1}z^{2j_1}\cdot\frac{m_1^{m_1+1}\rho^{\frac{1-m_1}{2}}}{\Gamma(m_1)(1-\rho)(\Omega_1\Omega_2)^{\frac{m_1+1}{2}}}\cdot$$

$$\cdot\sum_{i_1=0}^{\infty}\left(\frac{2m_1\sqrt{\rho}}{(1-\rho)(\Omega_1\Omega_2)^{1/2}}\right)^{2i_1+m_1-1}\frac{1}{i_1!\Gamma(i_1+m_1)}$$

$$\frac{1}{i_1+m_1}\cdot\sum_{j_2=0}^{\infty}\frac{1}{(i_1+m_1+1)(j_2)}\left(\frac{m_1}{\Omega_1(1-\rho)}\right)^{j_2}\cdot$$

$$\cdot\left(\frac{mz^2(1-\rho)\Omega_2}{m_1}\right)^{i_1+m_1-m+1/4-j_1/2+j_2/2}\cdot$$

$$\cdot K_{2i_1+2m_1-2m+1/2-j_1+j_2}\left(2\sqrt{\frac{4mz^2m_1}{(1-\rho)\Omega_2}}\right) \quad (11)$$

where $K_n(x)$ is the modified Bessel function of the second kind, n –th order and argument x [10].

IV. NUMERICAL RESULTS

The level crossing rate curves for the macrodiversity SC receiver output signal versus the SC receiver output signal envelope is presented in Figure 2, for power of Nakagami-*m* fading in branches: Ω_1= Ω_2=1, and variable Gamma fading parameter β_2.

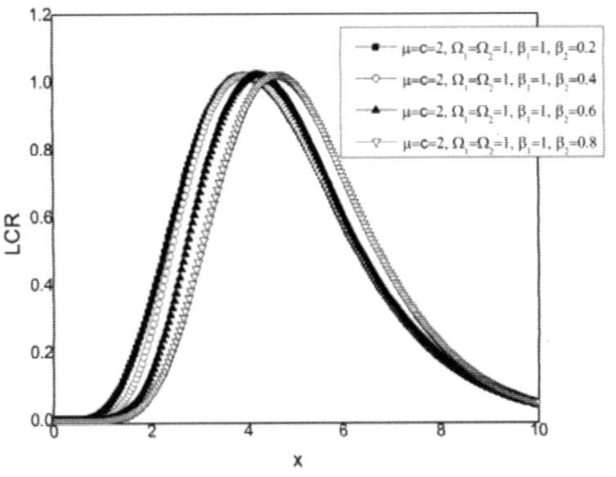

Figure 2. LCR versus macrodiversity SC receiver output signal envelope.

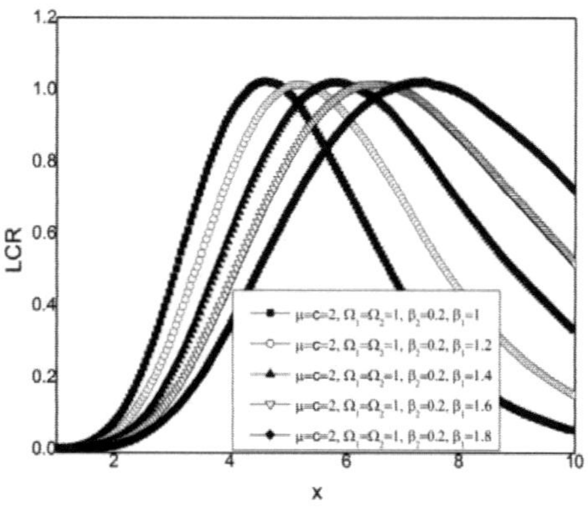

Figure 3. LCR versus macrodiversity SC receiver output signal envelope for variable Gamma fading severity parameter.

It is visible from Figure 2 that LCR is bigger for smaller values of Gamma fading parameter β_2 at low values of the signal envelopes. The system performances are better for lower values of the average level crossing rate.

All these curves have maximums. When the Gamma shadowing severity increases, the maximal values increase also, moving to higher values of the SC receiver output signal envelope.

The LCR takes greater values as the correlation coefficient increases. When the correlation coefficient goes to one, the least values of signal envelope occur at both microdiversity receivers and system has the worst performance.

In Figure 3, the level crossing rate, depending on microdiversity SC receiver output signal envelope, is plotted for a few values of Gamma fading severity parameter. The LCR increases as the parameter β_1 decreases at small values of the signal envelopes. Then, all curves achieve maximums and start to decline. The curves become wider at higher values of the parameter β_1.

V. Conclusion

In this paper, macrodiversity with macrodiversity SC receiver and two microdiversity SC receivers is studied. Received signal experiences correlated Gamma long term fading and Nakagami-m short term fading resulting in signal envelope variation and signal envelope average power variation. Performance of macrodiversity system is considered for the case when distances between user and microdiversity SC receivers are different. Macrodiversity SC receiver mitigates Gamma long term fading effects on the level crossing rate and microdiversity SC receivers reduce to Nakagami-m short term fading effects on the outage performance, simultaneously.

The closed form expression for LCR of macrodiversity SC receiver output signal is evaluated. The obtained expression can be used for calculation the level crossing rate at the output of macrodiversity operating over Gamma shadowed Rayleigh multipath fading. The influence of Gamma long term fading severity parameter, Nakagami-*m* short term fading severity and Gamma long term fading correlation coefficient is analyzed and discussed. Also, the influence of distances of the users from microdiversity SC receivers is studied.

The system performance is better for lower values of the level crossing rate. The level crossing rate decreases as Gamma long term fading severity parameter increases and when Nakagami-*m* short term fading severity parameter increases. When Gamma long term fading correlation coefficient goes to one, LCR increases and macrodiversity system has performance as simple microdiversity system.

LCR increases for lower values of the SC receiver output signal, and decreases for higher values of that signal. The influence of SC receiver output signal on the level crossing rate is more pronounced for lower values of this signal.

The biggest contribution of this paper is derivation of LCR of macrodiversity system with different distances between user and microdiversity receivers.

Appendix

The integral J_1 is equal to the first addend in the expression for the LCR defined in (10):

$$J_1 = \int_0^{\infty} d\Omega_x \int_0^{\Omega_x} d\Omega_y N_{x/\Omega_x} p_{\Omega_x\Omega_y}\left(\Omega_x\Omega_y\right) \qquad (12)$$

Let's solve this integral by putting N_{x/Ω_x} from (7) and $p_{\Omega_x\Omega_y}\left(\Omega_x\Omega_y\right)$ from (9) into (12) [11] [12]:

$$J_1 = \int_0^{\infty} d\Omega_x \int_0^{\Omega_x} d\Omega_y \frac{2\sqrt{2\pi} f_m}{\Gamma(m)} \left(\frac{m}{\Omega_x}\right)^{m-1/2} z^{2m-1} e^{-\frac{m}{\Omega_x} z^2} \cdot$$

$$\frac{1}{m} \frac{m^m}{\Omega_x^m} z^{2m} e^{-\frac{m}{\Omega_x} z^2} \cdot \sum_{j_1=0}^{\infty} \frac{1}{(m+1)(j_1)} \frac{m^{j_1}}{\Omega_x^{j_1}} z^{2j_1}$$

$$\cdot \frac{m_1^{m_1+1} \rho^{\frac{1-m_1}{2}}}{\Gamma(m_1)(1-\rho)(\Omega_1\Omega_2)^{\frac{m_1+1}{2}}} \cdot$$

$$\cdot \sum_{i_1=0}^{\infty} \left(\frac{m_1\sqrt{\rho}}{(1-\rho)(\Omega_1\Omega_2)^{1/2}}\right)^{2i_1+m_1-1} \frac{1}{i_1!\Gamma(i_1+m_1)}$$

$$\Omega_x^{i_1+m_1-1} e^{-\frac{m_1}{(1-\rho)\Omega_1}\Omega_x} \Omega_y^{i_1+m_1-1} e^{-\frac{m_1}{(1-\rho)\Omega_2}\Omega_y} =$$

$$= \frac{2\sqrt{2\pi} f_m}{\Gamma(m)} m^{m-1/2} z^{2m-1} \cdot \frac{1}{m} m^m z^{2m} \cdot \sum_{j_1=0}^{\infty} \frac{1}{(m+1)(j_1)} m^{j_1} z^{2j_1}$$

$$\cdot \frac{m_1^{m_1+1} \rho^{\frac{1-m_1}{2}}}{\Gamma(m_1)(1-\rho)(\Omega_1\Omega_2)^{\frac{m_1+1}{2}}} \cdot$$

$$\cdot\sum_{i_1=0}^{\infty}\left(\frac{m_1\sqrt{\rho}}{(1-\rho)(\Omega_1\Omega_2)^{1/2}}\right)^{2i_1+m_1-1}\frac{1}{i_1!\Gamma(i_1+m_1)}$$

$$\int_0^{\infty} d\Omega_x \Omega_x^{i_1+m_1-1-m+1/2-m-j_1} e^{-\frac{2m}{\Omega_x}z^2-\frac{m_1}{(1-\rho)\Omega_1}\Omega_x}$$

$$\int_0^{\Omega_x} d\Omega_y \Omega_y^{i_1+m_1-1} e^{-\frac{m_1}{(1-\rho)\Omega_2}\Omega_y} = \frac{2\sqrt{2\pi} f_m}{\Gamma(m)^2} m^{m-1/2} z^{2m-1}\cdot$$

$$m^{m-1}z^{2m}\cdot\sum_{j_1=0}^{\infty}\frac{1}{(m+1)(j_1)}m^{j_1}z^{2j_1}\cdot\frac{m_1^{m_1+1}\rho^{\frac{1-m_1}{2}}}{\Gamma(m_1)(1-\rho)(\Omega_1\Omega_2)^{\frac{m_1+1}{2}}}\cdot$$

$$\cdot\sum_{i_1=0}^{\infty}\left(\frac{2m_1\sqrt{\rho}}{(1-\rho)(\Omega_1\Omega_2)^{1/2}}\right)^{2i_1+m_1-1}\frac{1}{i_1!\Gamma(i_1+m_1)}$$

$$\int_0^{\infty} d\Omega_x \Omega_x^{i_1+m_1-2m-1+1/2-m-j_1} e^{-\frac{2m}{\Omega_x}z^2-\frac{m_1}{(1-\rho)\Omega_1}\Omega_x}$$

$$\cdot\left(\frac{(1-\rho)\Omega_2}{m_1}\right)^{i_1+m_1}\cdot\gamma\left(i_1+m_1,\frac{m_1\Omega_x}{\Omega_2(1-\rho)}\right)=$$

$$=\frac{2\sqrt{2\pi} f_m}{\Gamma(m)^2} m^{m-1/2} z^{2m-1}\cdot m^{m-1}z^{2m}\cdot\sum_{j_1=0}^{\infty}\frac{1}{(m+1)(j_1)}m^{j_1}z^{2j_1}$$

$$\cdot\frac{m_1^{m_1+1}\rho^{\frac{1-m_1}{2}}}{\Gamma(m_1)(1-\rho)(\Omega_1\Omega_2)^{\frac{m_1+1}{2}}}\cdot$$

$$\cdot\sum_{i_1=0}^{\infty}\left(\frac{2m_1\sqrt{\rho}}{(1-\rho)(\Omega_1\Omega_2)^{1/2}}\right)^{2i_1+m_1-1}\frac{1}{i_1!\Gamma(i_1+m_1)}$$

$$\int_0^{\infty} d\Omega_x \Omega_x^{i_1+m_1-2m-1/2-m-j_1} e^{-\frac{2m}{\Omega_x}z^2-\frac{m_1}{(1-\rho)\Omega_1}\Omega_x}$$

$$\cdot\left(\frac{(1-\rho)\Omega_2}{m_1}\right)^{i_1+m_1}\cdot\frac{1}{i_1+m_1}\cdot\left(\frac{m_1}{(1-\rho)\Omega_2}\right)^{i_1+m_1}\Omega_x^{i_1+m_1}e^{-\frac{m_1\Omega_x}{\Omega_1(1-\rho)}}.$$

$$\cdot\sum_{j_2=0}^{\infty}\frac{1}{(i_1+m_1+1)(j_2)}\left(\frac{m_1\Omega_x}{\Omega_2(1-\rho)}\right)^{j_2}=$$

$$=\frac{2\sqrt{2\pi} f_m}{\Gamma(m)^2} m^{m-1/2} z^{2m-1}\cdot m^{m-1}z^{2m}\cdot\sum_{j_1=0}^{\infty}\frac{1}{(m+1)(j_1)}m^{j_1}z^{2j_1}$$

$$\cdot\frac{m_1^{m_1+1}\rho^{\frac{1-m_1}{2}}}{\Gamma(m_1)(1-\rho)(\Omega_1\Omega_2)^{\frac{m_1+1}{2}}}\cdot$$

$$\cdot\sum_{i_1=0}^{\infty}\left(\frac{2m_1\sqrt{\rho}}{(1-\rho)(\Omega_1\Omega_2)^{1/2}}\right)^{2i_1+m_1-1}\frac{1}{i_1!\Gamma(i_1+m_1)}$$

$$\frac{1}{i_1+m_1}\cdot\sum_{j_2=0}^{\infty}\frac{1}{(i_1+m_1+1)(j_2)}\left(\frac{m_1}{\Omega_2(1-\rho)}\right)^{j_2}\cdot$$

$$\int_0^{\infty} d\Omega_x \Omega_x^{2i_1+2m_1-2m-1/2-m-j_1+j_2} e^{-\frac{2m}{\Omega_x}z^2-\frac{2m_1\Omega_x}{(1-\rho)\Omega_1}}=$$

$$=\frac{2\sqrt{2\pi} f_m}{\Gamma(m)^2} m^{m-1/2} z^{2m-1}\cdot m^{m-1}z^{2m}\cdot\sum_{j_1=0}^{\infty}\frac{1}{(m+1)(j_1)}m^{j_1}z^{2j_1}$$

$$\cdot\frac{m_1^{m_1+1}\rho^{\frac{1-m_1}{2}}}{\Gamma(m_1)(1-\rho)(\Omega_1\Omega_2)^{\frac{m_1+1}{2}}}\cdot$$

$$\cdot\sum_{i_1=0}^{\infty}\left(\frac{2m_1\sqrt{\rho}}{(1-\rho)(\Omega_1\Omega_2)^{1/2}}\right)^{2i_1+m_1-1}\frac{1}{i_1!\Gamma(i_1+m_1)}$$

$$\frac{1}{i_1+m_1}\cdot\sum_{j_2=0}^{\infty}\frac{1}{(i_1+m_1+1)(j_2)}\left(\frac{m_1}{\Omega_2(1-\rho)}\right)^{j_2}\cdot$$

$$\cdot\left(\frac{mz^2(1-\rho)\Omega_1}{m_1}\right)^{i_1+m_1-m+1/4-j_1/2+j_2/2}\cdot$$

$$\cdot K_{2i_1+2m_1-2m+1/2-j_1+j_2}\left(2\sqrt{\frac{4mz^2m_1}{(1-\rho)\Omega_1}}\right) \quad (13)$$

with $K_n(x)$ as modified Bessel function of the second kind, n –th order and argument x.

Integral J_2 is the second summand in the expression for the LCR in (10):

$$J_2=\int_0^{\infty} d\Omega_y \int_0^{\Omega_y} d\Omega_x N_{y/\Omega_y} p_{\Omega_x\Omega_y}(\Omega_x\Omega_y) \quad (14)$$

In the similar way, it is solved by introducing N_{y/Ω_y} from (8) and $p_{\Omega_x\Omega_y}(\Omega_x\Omega_y)$ from (9) in (14) [11] [13]:

$$J_2=\frac{2\sqrt{2\pi} f_m}{\Gamma(m)^2} m^{m-1/2} z^{2m-1}\cdot$$

$$m^{m-1} z^{2m} \cdot \sum_{j_1=0}^{\infty} \frac{1}{(m+1)(j_1)} m^{j_1} z^{2^{j_1}} \cdot \frac{m_1^{m_1+1} \rho^{\frac{1-m_1}{2}}}{\Gamma(m_1)(1-\rho)(\Omega_1\Omega_2)^{\frac{m_1+1}{2}}} \cdot$$

$$\cdot \sum_{i_1=0}^{\infty} \left(\frac{2m_1\sqrt{\rho}}{(1-\rho)(\Omega_1\Omega_2)^{1/2}} \right)^{2i_1+m_1-1} \frac{1}{i_1!\Gamma(i_1+m_1)}$$

$$\frac{1}{i_1+m_1} \cdot \sum_{j_2=0}^{\infty} \frac{1}{(i_1+m_1+1)(j_2)} \left(\frac{m_1}{\Omega_1(1-\rho)} \right)^{j_2} \cdot$$

$$\cdot \left(\frac{mz^2(1-\rho)\Omega_2}{m_1} \right)^{i_1+m_1-m+1/4-j_1/2+j_2/2} \cdot$$

$$\cdot K_{2i_1+2m_1-2m+1/2-j_1+j_2} \left(2\sqrt{\frac{4mz^2 m_1}{(1-\rho)\Omega_2}} \right). \tag{15}$$

where $K_n(x)$ is defined earlier.

ACKNOWLEDGMENT

This article is partly funded under the patronage of the projects TR-33035 and III-44006 by the Serbian Ministry of Education, Science and Technological Development.

REFERENCES

[1] M. K. Simon and M. S. Alouini, Digital Communication over Fading Channels, USA: John Wiley & Sons. 2000.

[2] P. M. Shankar, Fading and Shadowing in Wireless Systems, Springer, Dec 7, 2011. DOI 10.1007/978-1-4614-0367-8

[3] M. Bandjur, N. Sekulovic, M. Stefanovic, A. Golubovic, P. Spalevic, and D. Milic, "Second-order statistics of system with microdiversity and macrodiversity reception in Gamma-shadowed Rician fading channel", ETRI Journal, Vol. 35, No. 4, pp. 722-725, Aug. 2013.

[4] B. Milošević, P. Spalević, M. Petrović, D. Vučković, S. Milosavljević, "Statistics of Macro SC Diversity System with Two Micro EGC Diversity Systems and Fast Fading", Electronics and Electrical Engineering, No. 8(96), pp. 55–58, 2009.

[5] A. D. Cvetković, M. Č. Stefanović, N. M. Sekulović, D. N. Milić, D.M.Stefanović, and Z. J. Popović, "Second-order statistics of dual SC macrodiversity system over channels affected by Nakagami-m fading and correlated gamma shadowing", Przegląd Elektrotechniczny (Electrical Review), R. 87 NR 6, pp. 284-288, 2011.

[6] D. M. Stefanović, S. R. Panić, and P. Ć. Spalević, "Second-order statistics of SC macrodiversity system operating over Gamma shadowed Nakagami-*m* fading channels", AEU International Journal of Electronics and Communications, vol. 65, Issue 5, pp. 413-418, May 2011.

[7] G. Petković, S. Panić, and B. Jakšić, "Level crossing rate of macrodiversity with three microdiversity SC receivers over Gamma shadowed Nakagami-m channel", University Thought, Publication in Natural Sciences, Vol. 6, No 1, pp. 55-59, 2016, doi:10.5937/univtho6-9797

[8] S. Panic, M. Stefanovic, J. Anastasov, and P.Spalevic, Fading and Interference Mitigation in Wireless Communications. CRC Press, USA, 2013.

[9] D. Krstic, B. Jakšić, V. Doljak, and M. Stefanović, "Second order statistics of the macrodiversity SC receiver output signal over Gamma shadowed k-μ multipath fading channel", 1st International Conference on Broadband Communications for Next Generation Networks and Multimedia Applications, CoBCom'16, Graz, Austria, 14th – 16th of September, 2016, DOI: 10.1109/COBCOM.2016.7593496

[10] Modified Bessel function of the second kind, Available from: http://mathworld.wolfram.com/ModifiedBesselFunctionofthe SecondKind.html, retrieved: May, 2017.

[11] I. S. Gradshteyn and I. M. Ryzhik, Table of Integrals, Series and Products. Academic Press, USA San Diego, 2000.

[12] M. Abramowitz and I. A. Stegun, Handbook of Mathematical Functions, National Bureau of Standards, 1964; reprinted Dover Publications, 1965. Tenth Printing December 1972, with corrections

[13] A. P. Prudnikov, Y. A. Brychkov, and O. I. Marichev, Integrals and Series, Volume 3: More Special Functions. 1st ed., Gordon and Breach Science Publishers, New York, 1986.

Behavior Analysis for WebRTC Peer-to-Peer Streaming with Dynamic Topology

Khalid Kahloot, Patrik J. Braun & Peter Ekler
Automation and Applied Informatics Department (AUT)
Budapest University of Technology and Economics (BME)
Budapest, Hungary
{kahloot.khalid, braun.patrik, ekler.peter}@aut.bme.hu

Abstract— **Peer-to-Peer (P2P) data streaming in web browsers without the need of a third-party plugin is a preferable privacy-preserving option. However, the complexity of network is a challenge concerning theP2P topology and coding calculations. Despite the performance enhancing added by Web Real-Time Communication (WebRTC) over traditional P2P Communication, protocols overhead produce burst Traffic and the burstiness has a significant impact on the network performance. In this paper, we present a behavior analysis for burstiness and correlation for a WebRTC P2P file steaming. Then, we suggest a model of states like the Markovian chain. We evaluate some of the popular burstiness measures and present different kinds of traffic produced by two protocols WebPeer and CodedWebPeer based on P2P streaming. For modeling, we describe three main stochastic states of the peers regarding their position in the network and their stored data. We aim to contribute to better understanding of the behavior of traffic overhead caused by the protocols in static topology and dynamic joining topology. The results presented in this paper help to design P2P solutions based on WebRTC technologies.**

Keywords- Burstiness; Correlation; Peer-to-Peer (P2P); State Modeling; Markov chains.

I. INTRODUCTION

Video on demand (VoD) streaming is one of the P2P applications that consumes a big portion of the network resources and the computational power as well. In general, the P2P applications are overtaking the traffic share of the the Internet [13][14]. The concept of P2P sharing depends on chunking a file into slices, which are distributed over the peers. However, the functioning protocol should be able to adapt to the nature of the P2P system as individual peers join or leave the network stochastically. This feature of the protocol became very critical when serving time critical data, like videos.

In the recent years, there have been many notable studies concerning the performance of P2P protocol regarding video on demand streaming. For instance, many types of research perform system design, traffic measurement, performance analysis, and optimization over the BitTorrent. For example, Qiu et al. [13] provided a complete modeling and performance analysis of BitTorrent-like P2P Networks. Barbera et al. [5] standardized the processes of the BitTorrent system in the model of states to analyze the free rider phenomenon.

In our research, the key research area is to evaluate the performance of P2P WebRTC protocols. Moreover, we provide a suggestion for network performance enhancement, which shows how these protocols can evolve in the future. Studies concerning performance analysis help to understand the network traffic protocols such as WebPeer and CodedWebPeer [1]. A lot of efforts have been dedicated in this area, including real data measures, game-theoretic analysis and differential equation based macroscopic analysis. Through these efforts, it is clear now that piece and neighbor selection strategies are the two keys of efficient and scalable P2P systems. For each peer, piece and neighbor selection strategies decide which peers to upload to and which pieces to download from which service peers.

In this paper, we form a comprehensive basis for which we have a fundamental understanding of design parameters for WebPeer and CodedWebPeer protocols including performance analysis, burst and correlation measures. In addition, we reverse engineered the *WebPeer* protocol into a state modeling as Markov chain approximation. States and sub-states are modeled for CodedWebPeer and CodedWebPeer protocols. We present a comprehensive survey of analytical performance Modeling for video streaming. The results obtained not only will help to design better protocols, but also be useful for establishing a generally acceptable burstiness and correlation measures.

The layout of this paper is organized in seven sections. The following section reviews the previous related work on both modeling and performance measures. In Section 3, we introduce the *WebPeer* and *CodedWebPeer*. In addition, the components of the protocols are described to provide more understanding of their functionalities. The traffic measures are explained in Section 4. A state model is presented in Section 5. Finally, Section 6 concludes the paper and proposes further research areas.

II. RELATED WORK

In traffic analysis, a well-defined model is used study the behaviour of packet arrival and performance. Empirical or statistical studies calculate numerical approximations for network protocols. The WebPeer is a BitTorrent-like protocol, especially designed to work over WebRTC. Therefore, we first summarize previous P2P modeling studies. Then, we contrast traffic analysis, especially, burst and correlation measures.

Most of the empirical studies used modeling for simulations and data generation. Gerber et al. [16] report the behavior of Gorilla and its analysis of P2P traffic of two different regions. Sen and Wang [17] report measurement and analysis of three P2P systems, which include FastTrack, Gnutella, and DirectConnect. In both [4][16], Cisco Netflow is used to measure flow-based P2P traffic. Matei et al. in [18][19], modeled the Gnutella by using a crawler, which collected topology information and connectivity among peers. Multi-hop Carrier Sense Multiple Access (CSMA)-based was also considered for modeling. Stajkic et al. [2] proposed a novel approach based on a semi-Markov chain analysis, decoupling node and network levels. The state modlling is presented through a Semi-Markov Process.

Plenty of measures can investigate the performance of the traffic. Statistics from [24] can provide continuous measures and the analysis of Abilene network traffic. A weekly report is generated under the category of "File sharing" as it includes the majority of currently relevant P2P protocols. Cisco provides a NetFlow report as well [2]. To be more precise, we have chosen measures for burst and correlation of the traffic flow. Those measures are described in details in [20]-[22][24].

Izal et al. [8] and Pouwelse et al. [7] present measurement-based studies of BitTorrent based on tracker logs of different torrents. Gkantsidis and Rodriguez [6] present a simulation-based study of a BitTorrent-like system. They show results indicating that the download time of a BitTorrent-like system is not optimal. Other studies, e.g., [10]-[13], are concerned with the effective performance and the QoS issues of P2P systems. The key difference between previous research and our paper is that we started with traffic measures for network analysis. Then we modeled the process into functional states.

Some studies modeled the P2P traffic itself in a non-Markovian way. For instance, Gummadi et al. [15] model characteristics of P2P traffic in KaZaa as objects. They represent P2P processes as immutable, multi6media, large objects. On the other hand, Klemm et al. [9] use two Zipf distributions to model query popularity in Gnutella. We noticed that a few types of research applied Markov modeling approach over a P2P system such as Zhang et al. [3][4] who included an extended Markov chain model and insensitivity of count-down time. In addition, they provided an analysis on the trade-off between approximation gap and mixing time.

In this paper, we gathered the measures presented in P2P modeling studies [4], [15]-[17] due to the similarity of WebPeer and CodedWebPeer compared to BitTorrent. In addition, we followed the semi-Markov modeling apeared in [2] but we reverse engineered the already processes into states and substates.

III. System Environment

The functioning system is part of student research from the Automation and Applied Informatics Department (AUT) at the Budapest University of Technology and Economics (BME). Braun, Ekler and Fitzek [1] developed two versions of P2P protocol, which can establish direct browser to browser connections. Those protocols are designed to be efficient for browser-based P2P streaming. The first is called WebPeer protocol, which splits the original data into several equal sized pieces. Similar to BitTorrent's bitfield, however, it is a completely embedded in the web browser of the peer. The other protocol is called CodedWebPeer, extends the WebPeer protocol with network coding [24] capabilities. CodedWebPeer introduces new packet types for distributing Random Linear Network Coding (RLNC) coded data.

In both protocols, the P2P communication is implemented in JavaScript with WebRTC. In other words, WebRTC is still not officially standard, but several browsers already implement it. Moreover, storing huge amount of data at client-side or accessing file-system from browsers is not possible because of security reasons. In addition, the newly connected partner peer would have a higher probability of finding the missing packet, with a comparison to P2P communication using random packet dropping approach.

The target system uses network coding to enhance browser-based P2P streaming. In WebPeer and CodedWebPeer protocols, there are three kinds of entities: seeder, leecher, and tracker. The tracker is the active server, which is responsible for maintaining information about the peers and the available files for sharing. On the other hand, the leecher is a regular peer, which either sending or receiving files. Leecher carries out three basic operations; tracking, seeding and leeching.

The description above is quite similar to BitTorrent architecture. However, the tracker of WebPeer protocol does not keep track of the data amount stored at the individual peers [13].

We setup multi-variations for the selected measures. We choose to have 18 peers in the network in average, the peers could store 100%, 50%, 10% of the data. We carry out these measurements with WebPeer and CodedWebPeer protocols as well. In all cases, the peer can leech as;

- All slices of the file will be streamed from the server.
- Slices of the file will be streamed from randomly selected other peers in static topology.
- Slices of the file will be streamed for randomly selected other peers in dynamic topology, which means that peers can leave and join during the streaming.

IV. Burst and Correlation Measures

In this Section, we present a burst and correlation measuring for a collection of Ethernet traffic. We evaluated some of the popular burst and correlation measures and presented variant kinds of figures to describe traffic behavior. Our aim is to contribute to the understanding of the behavior of traffic overhead regardless of the used protocols in LAN and WAN.

The only data field we are considering is the timestamp, which represents the actual time in which current reading was recorded. First of all, we need to decide the amount of time ***t*** which we will carry out the measures over it. Obviously, the selected time is part of the total time, e.g., $t \subset T$. Therefore, if we decided to study the behavior of packet arrival for one hour of time then ***t*** will be 60. This period will be divided into sub-periods ***N***.

Define the $P_N = \{P_1, P_2, P_3, \ldots, P_N\}$, which is a set of period times for the selected ***t*** of study period. Then for each S_i, we will calculate t_i, which is the average arrival time for this period. Define the ***arrTime,*** arrival times corresponding to each period. In addition, define the set of inter-arrival times ***interArr*** to represent the amount of time separating the packet arrivals. Define the set of lags, which represent the cumulative time of inter-arrival packets for a set of periods from X_N and the tests are:

- Stationarity test: is used to indicate the arriving rate of packets during the study period. It is good that the arriving rate or packets are stationary.
- Intensity test: is used to count the number of arrivals per unit time.
- Probably Density function: is used to describe the distribution of data over time.
- Correlation: is used to indicate how the consecutive shifted inter-arrival time is correlated.
- IDI: the index of dispersion for intervals is used to the sequence of inter-arrivals
- IDC: the index of dispersion for counts is used to the sequence of counts of arrivals in consecutive time units.

Since we have only the time stamp and the traffic size in bytes, then the inter-arrival time and the number of packets should be calculated first. The inter-arrival time is defined as the time between the start of arrival two packets. Suppose that a dataset is acquired to recording packet arrival time for ***T*** amount of time. Bustiness cause interference because when the packets get queued this will make the departures less burst. Delay is caused by packet interference. If arrivals are regular or sufficiently spaced apart, no queuing delay occurs.

Other measures are used, some of which ignore the effect of second order properties of the traffic. A first measure is the ratio of peak rate to mean rate and has the drawback of being dependent upon the interval used to measure the rate. A second measure is the coefficient of variation of the inter-arrival times. A metric considering second order property of the traffic is the IDC. In particular, given an interval of time τ, Because of the relationship in IDC includes in the numerator the effects of the correlation between the inter-arrivals.

Measures based on the first-order properties are the Peak to mean ratio (PMR), SCV and Higher Moments. For the PMR, inter-arrival time and the number of packets are correlated then graphed. The peak to mean ratio can be found when the arrays of frequencies are used as input for d2 frequency offset and tune the offset frequency and the rate of data collection in Hz.

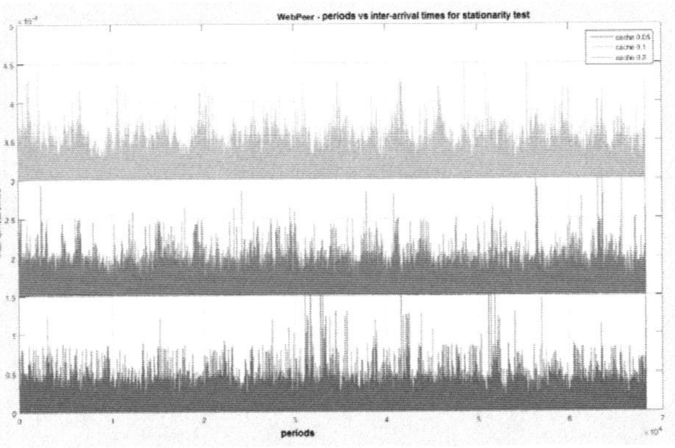

Figure 1. (a) WebPeer inter-arrival times for stationarity test

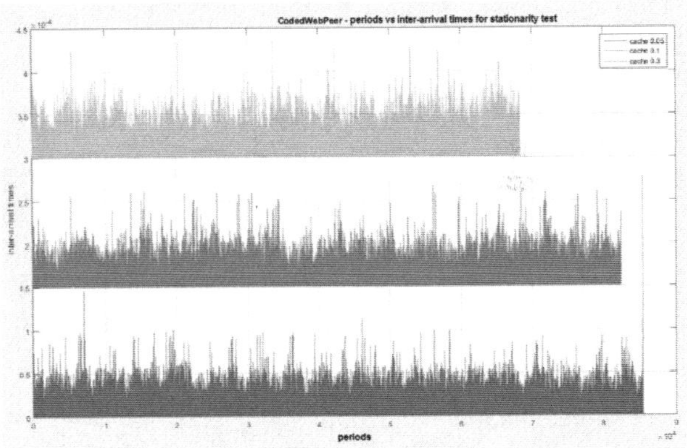

Figure 1. (b) CodedWebPeer inter-arrival times for stationarity test

Coefficient of Variation is the percentage variation in mean, standard deviation being considered as the total variation in the mean. For the the Squared coefficient of Variation (SCV), is considered more accurate to measure improved accuracy and it can be evaluated by visualization.

The moment represents the central sample moment of X specified by the positive integer order. For a given matrix, the moment characterizes the central moment of the specified order with respect to the elements of first, second, third, etc. As shown in Table I, the third moment of CodedWebPeer is much higher than the WebPeer, which indicates higher traffic.

TABLE I. FIRST ORDER MEASURES

	PMR	SCV	M3	M2	M1
WebPeer	8.8150	6.4187	1.0360	6.4053	0
CodedWebPeer	11.095	6.8053	7.34440	4.4415	0

Stationarity is time invariance of data, as shown in Fig. 1. For example, inter-arrival times in packet traffic undergoing reliability growth testing usually increases with time statistically and inter-arrival times in the network in service can be decreasing with time stationary.

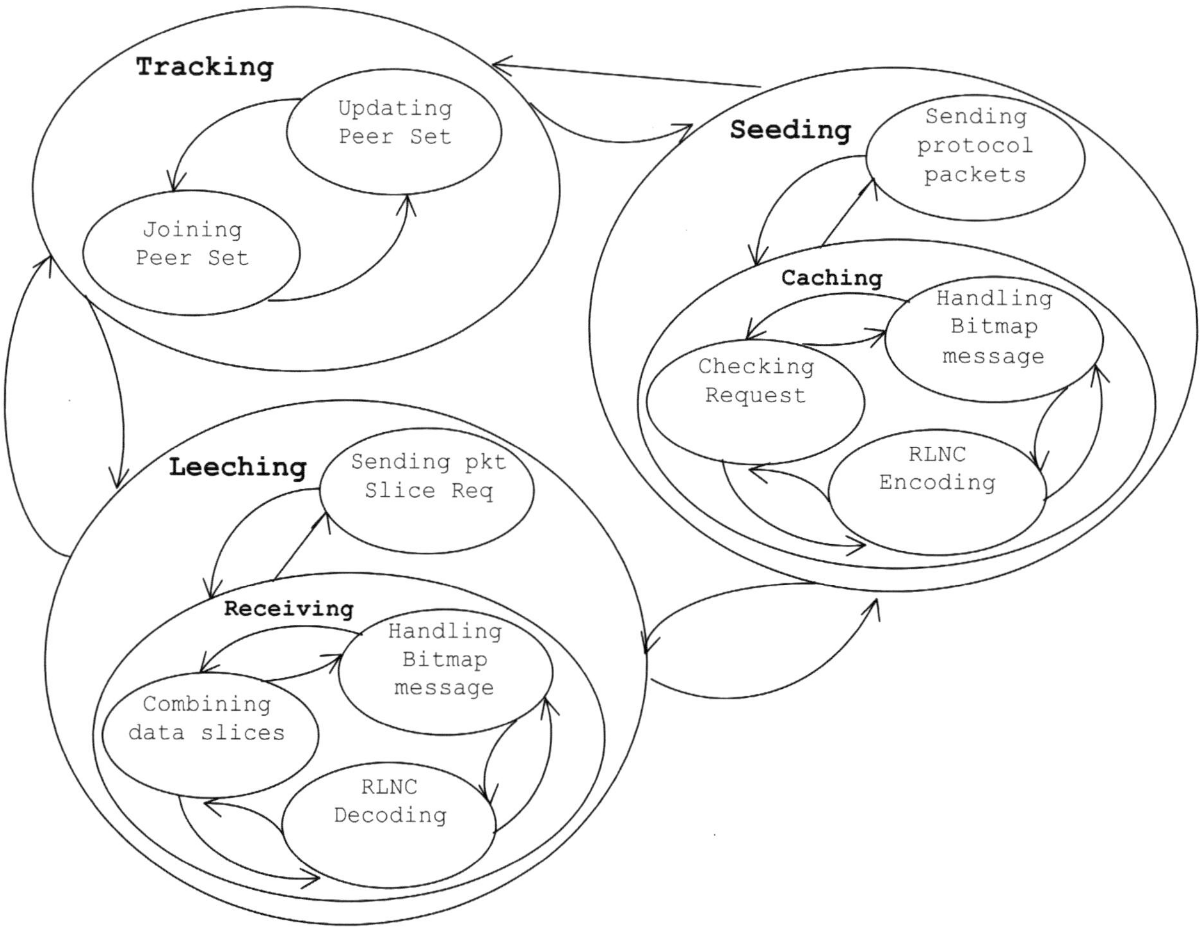

Figure 2. **State Modeling for CodedWebPeer and CodedWebPeer protocol**

If such trends do not exist, the arrival process of the traffic is stationary. The objective of stationarity tests is to determine whether the pattern of arrivals is significantly changing with time as to select appropriate models for modeling the data.

The intensity of packet arrival is the count of packet arrived in a particular point of time, as shown in Fig. 3. Using the average packet arrival count as observed by the test packets as an indicator, the intensity for active measurements is plotted.

The probability distribution function (PDF) of packet inter-arrival times should be viewed as a flat histogram to describe the scholastic process of packet traffic. The more we have independent sources of packets in the networks, the more it causes absolutely random inter-arrival times. As shown in Fig. 4, the PDF of inter-arrival times appears to be flat. When the PDF has different peak rates, this means that the capacity of connecting to the aggregate node gets lower many times. In other words, packets have been in queuing several before arriving at the aggregate node.

Correlation is used to measure the similarity of two types of traffic of different lengths. However, here we used it to measure the similarity between shifted inter-arrival times. The positive correlation will imply a low burst in the traffic. Mathematically, traffic burstiness is related to short-terms correlations between the inter-arrival times. However, there is accepted the notion of burstiness. A metric considering second order property of the traffic is the IDC. In particular, given an interval of time τ, it is an important measure of the correlation for a sequence arrival counts. The dependence among successive inter-arrival times can be expressed by means of the IDI. The IDI, also called the k-interval squared coefficient of variation sequence is defined as the sequence of indices. The limit of the IDI is an important measure to characterize the effect of an arrival process on the congestion of a queue in heavy traffic.

V. Protocol Modeling

The original functionalities of WebPeer and CodedWebPeer are explained in details in [1]. The purpose of the modeling is to represent and to reshape traffic behavior from grounds up for the system environment discussed in the previous section. We aim for a synthesized behavior of P2P peers, based on empirical observations of the WebRTC video streaming. Peers transfer 'request/message' among each other. Thus, transfers are to be modeled into a functional state. Packets can flow as traffic between the states in a hierarchical way. However, there are ten sub-states included as shown in Fig. 2 and details are listed in Table II.

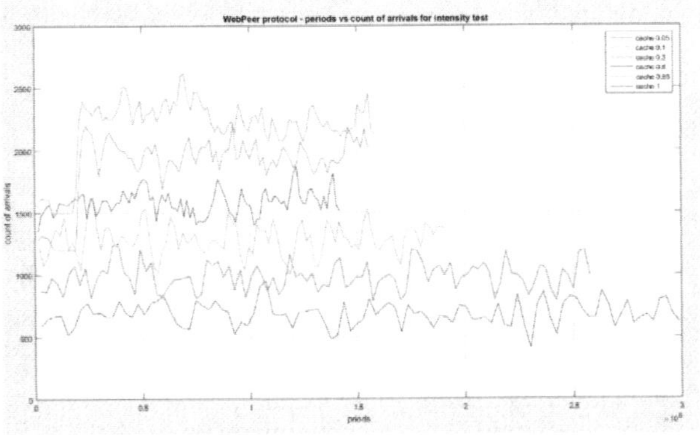

Figure.3. (a) WebPeer count of arrivals for intensity test

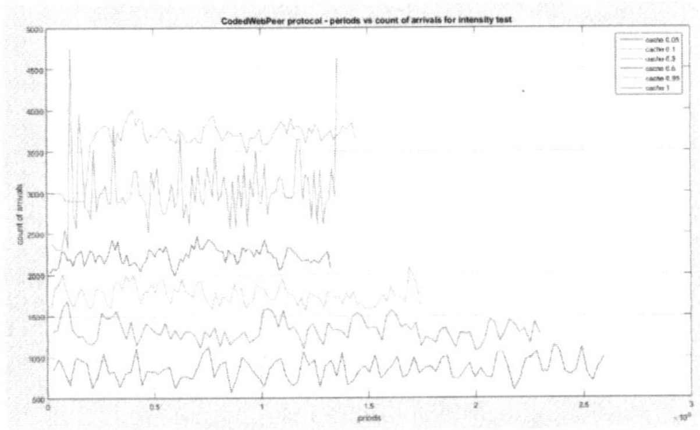

Figure 3. (b) CodedWebPeer count of arrivals for intensity test

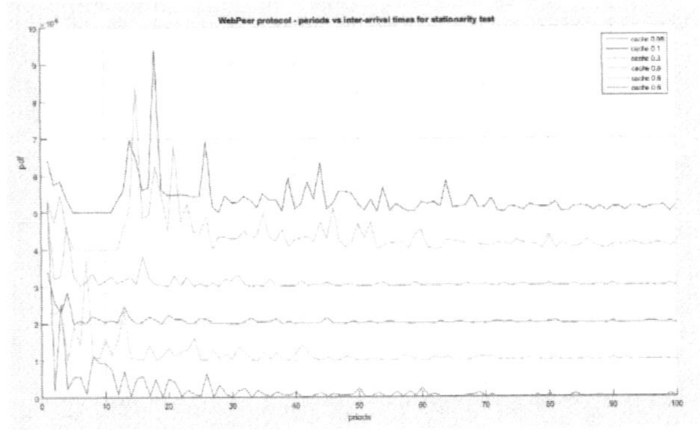

Figure 4. (a) WebPeer probability distribution function

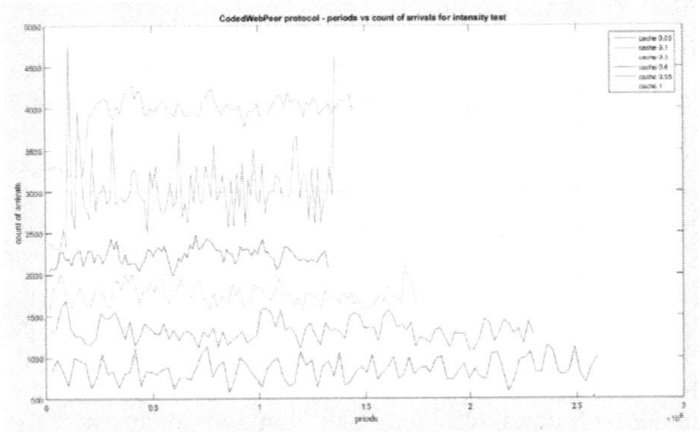

Figure 4. (b) CodedWebPeer probability distribution function

TABLE II STATES of WEBPEER & CODEDWEBPEER

State	Description
- Tracking	Describe the behavior of a Peer operates on P2P network topology
---- Updating Peer Set	Update the Set containing the Peers on the network
---- Joining Peer Set	Join a specific Set of Peers
- Seeding	Describe the behavior of a Peer seeding data
---- Sending protocol pkts	Send communication packets of peer protocols
---- Caching	Process Data to be sent on the P2P network topology
------- Handling Bitmap mg	Bitmap protocol message tells the Peer how to seed
------- Checking Request	Generating network coded packets for Slices of data
------- RLNC Encoding	Slice and encrypt data
- Leeching	Describe the behavior of a Peer performing actual video streaming
---- Sending pkt Slice Req	Send Slice of a requested packet
---- Receiving	Prepare the received data for the peer
------- Handling Bitmap mgs	Bitmap protocol message tells the Peer how to leech
------- Combining data Slices	Arrange the sliced data into real time stream
------- RLNC Decoding	Calculating and decrypting data

VI. Conclusion

We have reported a burst and correlation analysis study by investigating the most important candidate measures of burst to compare the characteristics of traffic flow and we can state that increasing the number of peers has a direct effect on the intensity and the probability density distribution of packet arrival. The IDC of the traffic of both protocols illustrates the effect the burstiness of the WebRTC streaming. IDI and IDC measures for the CodedWebPeer traffic show that RLNC can be highly inaccurate, even though it is affected by network performance as well. Both protocols are modeled into three hierarchal states with a total of ten sub-states. We concluded that both protocols have overhead, which produces burst traffic. Therefore, the numerical results of the used measures and the states in the supposed model can be used in a future work for optimization. The States will be reflected into parallel processes and the measures will be used to parametrized the algorithms.

Acknowledgment

This work was supported by the Janos Bolyai Research Fellowship of the Hungarian Academy of Sciences.

References

[1] P. J. Braun, P. Ekler and F. Fitzek, "Network coding enhanced browser based Peer-to-Peer streaming," 2016 IEEE International Conference on Systems, Man, and Cybernetics (SMC), Budapest, 2016, pp. 002104-002109. doi: 10.1109/SMC.2016.7844550

[2] A. Stajkic, C. Buratti and R. Verdone, "Modeling multi-hop CSMA-based networks through Semi-Markov chains," 2015 International Wireless Communications and Mobile Computing Conference (IWCMC), Dubrovnik, 2015, pp. 520-525. doi: 10.1109/IWCMC.2015.7289138

[3] H. Zhang, Z. Shao, M. Chen, and K. Ramchandran. 2011. Optimal neighbor selection in BitTorrent-like peer-to-peer networks. In Proceedings of the ACM SIGMETRICS joint international conference on Measurement and modeling of computer systems (SIGMETRICS '11). ACM, New York, NY, USA, 141-142. DOI:10.1145/1993744.1993796

[4] S. Zhang, Z. Shao, and M. Chen, "Optimal distributed p2p streaming under node degree bounds," in Proc. of IEEE ICNP 2010, 2010, pp. 253–262.

[5] M. Barbera, A. Lombardo, G. Schembra and M. Tribastone, "A Markov model of a freerider in a BitTorrent P2P network," GLOBECOM '05. IEEE Global Telecommunications Conference, 2005., 2005, pp. 5 pp.-. doi: 10.1109/GLOCOM.2005.1577784

[6] C. Gkantsidis and P. R. Rodriguez, "Network coding for large scale content distribution," Proceedings IEEE 24th Annual Joint Conference of the IEEE Computer and Communications Societies., 2005, pp. 2235-2245 vol. 4. doi: 10.1109/INFCOM.2005.1498511

[7] J.A. Pouwelse, P. Garbacki, D.H.J. Epema, and H.J. Sips, "A Measurement Study of the BitTorrent Peer-to-Peer File-Sharing System," Technical Report PDS-2004-003, Pages 205-216, Delft University of Technology, The Netherlands, April 2004.

[8] M. Izal, G. Urvoy-Keller, E.W. Biersack, P. Felber, A. Al Hamra, and L. Garc´ es-Erice, "Dissecting BitTorrent: Five Months in a Torrent's Lifetime," PAM, Apr. 2004.

[9] A. Klemm, C. Lindemann, M. K. Vernon, and O. P. Waldhorst, "Characterising the query behavior in peer-to-peer file sharing systems," in Proc. of ACM/SIGCOMM Internet Measurement Conference (IMC'04), Taormina, Sicily, Italy, Oct. 2004, pp. 55–67.

[10] M. Iguchi, M. Terada, K. Fujimura, "Managing Resource and Servent Reputation in P2P Networks", in Proc. 37th Annual Hawaii Int. Conf. on System Sciences (HICSS'04), 2004

[11] D. Hughes, I. Warren, G. Coulson, "Improving QoS for Peer-to-Peer Applications through Adaptation", in Proc. Of the 10th Int. Workshop on Future Trends in Distributed Computing Systems (FTDCS 2004), Suzhou, China, May 26-28, 2004.

[12] E. Kalyvianaki and I. Pratt, "Building adaptive peer-to-peer systems," Proceedings. Fourth International Conference on Peer-to-Peer Computing, 2004. Proceedings., 2004, pp. 268-269. doi: 10.1109/PTP.2004.1334959

[13] D. Qiu and R. Srikant, "Modeling and Performance Analysis of BitTorrent-Like Peer-to-Peer Networks", ACM SIGCOMM Computer Communication Review 34(4):367-378 · October 2004, Portland, Oregon, USA

[14] A. Gerber, J. Houle, H. Nguyen, M. Roughan, S. Sen, "P2P The Gorilla in the Cable", in National Cable & Telecommunications Association (NCTA) 2003 National Show, Chicago, IL, June 8-11, 2003.

[15] K. Gummadi, R. Dunn, S. Saroiu, S. Gribble, H. Levy, and J. Zahorjan, "Measurement, modeling, and analysis of a peer-to-peer file-sharing workload," in Proc. of the 19th ACM Symposium on Operating Systems Principles (SOSP'03), Bolton Landing, NY, USA, Oct. 2003, pp. 314–329.

[16] Alexandre Gerber, Joseph Houle, Han Nguyen, Matthew Roughan, and Subhabrata Sen, "P2P The Gorilla in the Cable", National Cable & Telecommunications Association (NCTA) 2003 National Show, Chicago, IL, June8-11,2003

[17] S. Sen and J. Wang, "Analysing peer-to-peer traffic across large networks", in Proc. of ACM SIGCOMM Internet Measurement Workshop, Marseilles, France, Nov. 2002.

[18] R. Matei, A. Iamnitchi and P. Foster, "Mapping the Gnutella network," in IEEE Internet Computing, vol. 6, no. 1, pp. 50-57, Jan/Feb 2002. doi: 10.1109/4236.978369

[19] R. Matei, I. Foster, and A. lamnitchi, "Mapping the Gnutella Network Properties of Large-scale Peer-to-Peer Systems and Implications for System Design", IEEE Internet Computing Journal, vol. 6(1), pp. 80-86, 2002.

[20] D. Kouvatsos, R. Fretwell, "Batch Renewal Process: Exact Model of Traffic Correlation", High-Speed Networking for Multimedia Application, Kluwer Academic Press, pp. 285-304, 1996.

[21] R. Gusella, "Characterizing the variability of arrival processes with indexes of dispersion," in IEEE Journal on Selected Areas in Communications, vol. 9, no. 2, pp. 203-211, Feb 1991. doi: 10.1109/49.68448

[22] S. Molnar, G. Miklos, "On Burst and Correlation Structure of Teletraffic Models", 5th IFIP Workshop on Performance Modeling and Evaluation of ATM Networks, 21-23 July 1997, West Yorkshire, U.K.

[23] D. R. Cox, P. A. W. Lewis, "The Statistical Analysis of Series of Events", Methuen & Co Ltd, 1966.

[24] Ahlswede, R., Ning Cai, Li, S.-Y.R., Yeung, R.W.: Network information flow, Information Theory, IEEE Transactions on (Volume:46, Issue: 4), pages: 1204-1216, ISSN: 0018-9448, 2000.

A WSN Testbed to Enhance Irrigation Techniques Using a Novel Event-Based Routing Protocol

Maher Ali Al Rantisi
Department of Communications
Middlesex University London,
London, UK
mr818@live.mdx.ac.uk

Glenford Mapp
Department of Communications
Middlesex University London,
London, UK
g.mapp@mdx.ac.uk

Orhan Gemikonakli
Department of Communications
Middlesex University London,
London, UK
o.gemikonakli@mdx.ac.uk

Abstract— **Due to rapid changes in climatic conditions worldwide, environmental monitoring has become one of the greatest concerns in the last few years. With the advancement in wireless sensing technology, it is now possible to monitor and track fine-grained changes in harsh outdoor environments. Wireless sensor networks (WSN) provide very high quality and accurate analysis for monitoring of both spatial and temporal data, thus providing the opportunity to monitor harsh outdoor environments. However, to deploy and maintain a WSN in such harsh environments is a great challenge for researchers and scientists. Several routing protocols exist for data dissemination and power management but they suffer from various disadvantages. In our case study, there are very limited water resources in the Middle East, hence soil moisture measurements must be taken into account to manage irrigation and agricultural projects. In order to meet these challenges, a WSN that supports a robust, reactive, event-based routing protocol is developed using Ad hoc On-Demand Multipath Distance Vector (AOMDV) as a starting point. A prototype WSN network of 5 nodes is built and a detailed simulation of 30 nodes is also developed to test the scalability of the new system.**

Keywords- wireless sensor networks; reactivity; reliability; soil moisture; rainfall

I. INTRODUCTION

Wireless sensor networks (WSN) are part of a growing technology that has been designed to support a wide range of applications in wireless environments [1][2]. Although sensor networks have been used in various different applications, environmental monitoring is a domain in which they have had a huge impact. Recent climate change-related catastrophes have illustrated the importance of a detailed understanding of the environment and its evolution for the wellbeing of human beings. The capacity of researchers to improve this knowledge is mainly limited by current data collection techniques, which are based on very expensive stations [3]. WSN's are particularly useful in remote or dangerous environments whose behaviors have rarely been studied due to their inaccessibility. Therefore, environmental monitoring is an important area for applying wireless sensor networks [4].

In our study we are using WSN testbed for such harsh environments in Middle East region where the sun is present for at least 12 h per day which makes the climate very dry and hot. One of the biggest problems in the Middle East is the limitation of water resources. We need to measure the soil moisture regularly and very accurately to allow targeted irrigation techniques to be implemented. We are deploying WSN to detect when and where it is raining so that necessary irrigation control measures can be applied.

Many research efforts have tried to deploy WSNs for such environments. But there are many issues with their solutions [3]. Hence in attempting to deploy a WSN successfully in these types of harsh environments and to ensure proper operation of sensor networks we need to resolve following issues.

In order to deal with the harsh environment, it is necessary to build a system which has two main proprieties, i.e., event-driven and robustness. The sensor network should be reactive so that it can detect different events correctly, for example, the presence and the absence of rainfall and hence the changes in degree of moisture in the soil. After the event is detected, the affected nodes need to sample the environment at a much faster rate for example if the system is set to sample after every few minutes when it is not raining then it should sample at few seconds when it is raining. Hence the available bandwidth should be more at nodes affected by rain. Hence the required information is sent across as fast as possible and also accurately to the monitoring center or base station.

Currently there is no such robust and event-based wireless routing protocol to react to such type of outdoor environments. Resource limitations of the sensor nodes and unreliability of low-power wireless links [5], in combination with various performance demands of different applications, impose many challenges in designing efficient communication protocols for wireless sensor networks [6].

In this paper, we discuss the shortcomings of popular routing protocols for our application and we exploit the advantages of the popular routing protocol "Ad hoc On-Demand Multipath Distance Vector" (AOMDV) and modify it to achieve the objectives. To achieve the robustness of wireless sensor network (WSN) this project will enhance the protocol to be an energy aware routing protocol to expand the life time of the nodes. We also discuss in detail the design of a WSN testbed network that can provide all necessary physical parameters to be used in soil moisture and rainfall monitoring algorithms. We implement an algorithm for monitoring and controlling soil moisture events and evaluate the network based on power used, throughput, etc. We deploy an outdoor WSN testbed for testing our algorithm. The rest of the paper is outlined as follows: Section 2 provides a literature review, Section 3 explores a solution approach. Section 4 looks at sensor network design and in Section 5 we provide testbed results and performance. Finally, we conclude in Section 6.

II. Literature Review

There are numerous routing protocols proposed by researchers in this area, to improve performance demands of different applications through the network layer of wireless sensor networks protocol stack [7, 8]. Most of the existing routing protocols in wireless sensor networks are designed based on the single-path routing strategy without considering the effects of various traffic load intensities [9, 10]. In this approach, each source node selects a single path, which can satisfy performance requirements of the intended applications for transmitting its traffic towards the sink node.

Although route discovery through single-path routing approach can be performed with minimum computational complexity and resource utilization, the limited capacity of a single path significantly reduces the achievable network throughput [11, 12]. Therefore, due to the resource constraints of sensor nodes and the unreliability of wireless links, single-path routing approaches cannot be considered effective to meet the performance demands of various applications. In order to cope with the limitations of single-path routing techniques, another type of routing strategy, known as multipath routing, has become a promising technique in wireless sensor and ad hoc networks. Dense deployment of the sensor nodes enables a multipath routing approach to construct several paths from individual sensor nodes towards the destination [13].

Discovered paths can be utilized concurrently to provide adequate network resources in intensive traffic conditions.

In the past decade, the multipath routing approach has been widely utilized for different network management purposes such as improving data transmission reliability, providing fault-tolerance routing, congestion control and Quality of Service (QoS) support in traditional wired and wireless networks.

However, the unique features of wireless sensor networks (e.g., constrained power supply, limited computational capability, and low-memory capacity) and the characteristics of short-range radio communications (e.g., fading and interference [14, 15]) introduce new challenges that should be addressed in the design of multipath routing protocols.

In [7], routing challenges and design issues in wireless sensor networks were discussed. In [16] the researchers provided a brief overview on the existing fault-tolerant routing protocols in wireless sensor networks and categorized these protocols into retransmission-based and replication-based protocols. The researchers in [17] and [18], classified the existing multipath routing protocols in ad hoc networks based on the primary criterion used in their design.

Many routing protocols have been proposed for Wireless Sensor and Ad Hoc Networks. Since we are interested in dynamic and event driven protocol, we studied the likes of AODV, which is a reactive protocol that discovers routes only on the basis of demand using a route discovery mechanism.

It uses traditional routing tables with one entry per destination. The main advantage of AODV [9,10] compared to other routing protocols is that less memory space is required as information of only active routes are maintained, in turn increasing the performance. While on the other side, the disadvantage is; this protocol is not expandable and in large networks, it does not perform well and is not capable to support asymmetric links.

Ad-hoc On-demand Multipath Distance Vector Routing (AOMDV) [19] protocol is an extension to the AODV protocol for computing multiple loop-free and link disjoint paths [20] which aims to remove the disadvantages and the limitation of AODV. The main idea in AOMDV is to compute multiple paths during route discovery. It is designed primarily for highly dynamic ad hoc networks where link failures and route breaks occur frequently. When single path on-demand routing protocol such as AODV is used in such networks, a new route discovery is needed in response to every route break. This inefficiency can be avoided by having multiple redundant paths available. Now, a new route discovery is needed only when all paths to the destination break. AOMDV can also be used to find node-disjoint or link-disjoint routes. But, AOMDV has more message overheads during route discovery due to increased flooding because it is a multipath routing protocol, the destination replies to the multiple RREQs which results in longer overheads.

In [21], researchers improved the performance of standard AOMDV in conditions like mobility or multi communication. They proposed link reliability in route choice. They modified the Route request process to enable reliable paths using Bit Error Rate (BER). They tested the effectiveness of new protocol by considering these improvements under realistic conditions and the result was compared to standard AOMDV and AODV protocols to show improved performance. Researchers in [22] modified AOMDV protocol by proposing a new fuzzy logic based scheme. The proposed protocol was shown to select better paths and increase network survivability. An AOMDV based method (E-AOMDV) was proposed by [23], to conserve energy, find shortest path and for load balancing. In [24], the authors proposed a modified AOMDV protocol called Network Coding-based AOMDV (NC-AOMDV) routing algorithm for MANET. The proposed method tried to increase data transmission reliability and ensure load balancing. An algorithm find maximal nodal remaining energy was proposed in [25], called Delay Remaining Energy for AOMDV (DRE-AOMDV) routing protocol. It claimed to get a solution for finding maximal nodal remaining energy for all routes in selecting a path for end-to-end requirement.

An extension to AOMDV routing protocol was proposed in reference [26]. It was channel adaptive routing protocol to accommodate channel fading. The proposed algorithm was called Channel-Aware AOMDV (CA-AOMDV). It used channel average nonfading duration as routing metric. Using this it selected stable links for path discovery by applying a pre-emptive handoff strategy. A Modified AOMDV (M-AOMDV) Routing Protocol for Maritime Inter-ship Communication [27] was proposed that provides routing recovery mechanism when a link breaks in an active route to reduce lost packets, this will reduce packet loss ratio and delay time.

Another modified version of AOMDV was proposed in [28], called ant-AOMDV or ant colony optimization modification for AOMDV in MANET, in this research the writers uses the modified AOMDV for multipath routing using ant colony for mobile ad hoc networks (MANETs).

Another researcher [29] published a paper about AOMDV-PAMAC, they started their paper explaining that power consumption of nodes in ad-hoc networks is a critical issue, because they operate on batteries, they suggested a new link layer algorithm knows as Power Aware medium Access Control (PAMAC) protocol is proposed which enables the network layer to select a route with minimum total power requirement among the possible routes between a source and a destination.

AOMDV modifications overcomes many limitations of AOMDV but it still has some limitations when used for a real time and robust routing scenario like we have. Thus, we modified AOMDV to suit our purpose and make it more robust, reactive, event driven, and energy aware.

III. Solution Approach

Figure 1 shows the wireless sensor network being deployed over a large geographical area. Each node is able to measure the amount of soil moisture through the soil moisture sensor in the ground as well as detect the presence of rain through the rainfall sensor. The latter is necessary as the amount of soil moisture may not be enough to detect the presence of rain. In addition, the system must quickly react in order to discover over which part of the sensor network is experiencing the event: in this case rain. When rain is detected as falling in a given part of the system, the data is sent from the relevant nodes to a central administrative server or base station through the PC-USB Gateway. We have to change the routing so that information on the change in the soil content in the affected area could be sent to the server as quickly as possible. Hence, this data is routed at a higher priority that other information being sent. Our modified AOMDV protocol works as follows in two schemes. Under the first scheme, the sensor data under normal events (no rainfall) are sampled after every 3h for 10s and sent to the server. During these 3h, the sensors are in sleep mode to save energy and after the data is sampled they again go to sleep mode for another 3h. If we have rainfall event we implement second scheme, in which the data sample is taken after every 1s for the sensor node experiencing the rainfall event, hence the affected nodes send data after every 1s, since the soil moisture may change very rapidly. In second scheme, we also increase the priority of this affected node to transfer data to the base station through the gateway. All the other sensor nodes where there is no rainfall still keep sampling after every 3h. In our previous work [30], we proposed a modified version of the AOMDV protocol. To accommodate these changes dynamically we made changes in the existing AOMDV protocol and proposed a dynamic and robust event driven routing protocol as described below.

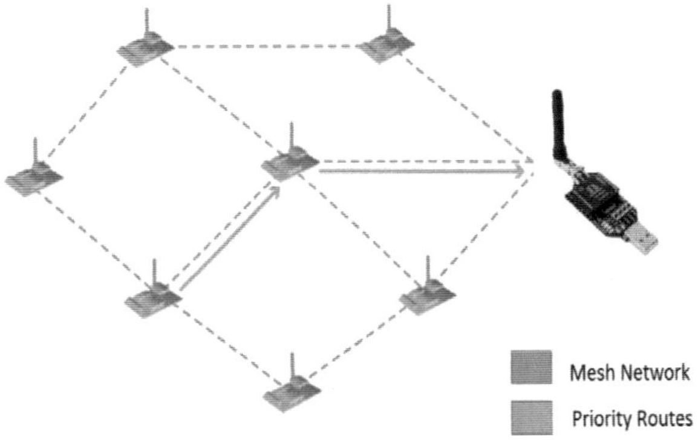

Figure 1. Sensor Network forming mesh.

A. *Proposed Changes to AOMDV*

The plan is therefore to enhance AOMDV to support a dynamic event-driven system as detailed in this paper. The first issue is that the routes may change due to the change in status of the individual nodes, it is necessary to allow HELLO messages, which are used to detect link changes, to not just monitor links but to fully indicate the status of the node at the other side of the link. So in this case, HELLO messages would also indicate whether or not it is raining on the other end, the network load as well as the power left in the system. A key piece of data is whether or not a node is able to route data on behalf of other nodes. As explained before, if a node is at the center of a downpour, its data is probably more important than the data of its neighboring nodes so it should not route data on behalf of other nodes. In such a situation, the node should also not respond to routing request (RREQ) messages, which are used to discover routes to individual destinations. In addition, though HELLO messages will be sent periodically, it is necessary to have another message type which can be sent immediately in response to sudden environmental, link, or node changes. These messages are called STATUS messages and are sent to neighboring nodes. For example, when a node first detects rain, it will send a STATUS message which is picked up by other nodes. By storing this information from various nodes, it would be possible to detect where the rain is falling in the sensor network.

STATUS messages will cause routes to the central server to be re-evaluated. Let us consider the case depicted in Figure 2. If node A that is not affected by rain, was using a route to the central server via node B and node A, now receives a STATUS message from node B saying that, it has detected rain; then node A, which is not rain-affected, should no longer send data through node B if possible, since, for irrigation purposes, the data being generated by node B is more important. Node A should look for another route back to the server using other non-affected nodes. This would suggest that routes may have priorities based on the importance of the data being routed relative to the data being generated. In this case, node A will downgrade its route through node B, resulting in other routes through non-affected nodes being favored. This is illustrated in Figure 2.

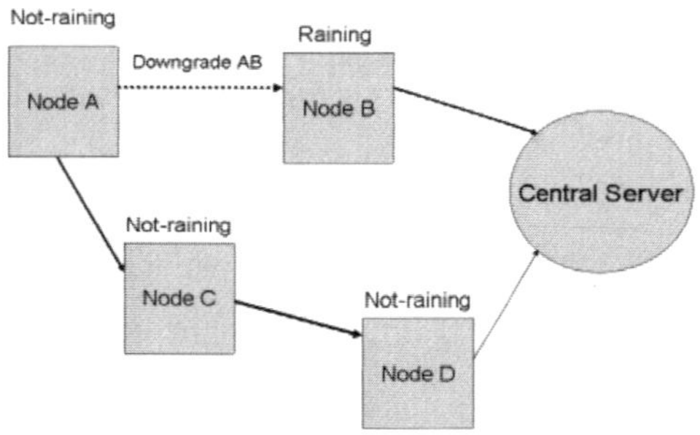

Figure 2. Routing decisions made based on external events.

If both nodes, A and B, detect rain both nodes will send each other their absolute measurements as well as relative changes in the soil moisture content. Nodes with less relative soil moisture content changes which indicate less rain will downgrade routes through regions with high relative soil moisture content changes. So data will be routed away from the most rain-affected areas towards the least rain-affected areas.

C++ language compiler has been used to modify the source code of AOMDV; this modification consists of several enhancements for the current AOMDV protocol. In the following, Algorithm 1, we describes the modification:

```
Algorithms 1
if(event == NO_RAIN)
 begin
     //use standard AOMDV
 end
else
if(event == RAIN)
begin
   sendBrodcastRainPacket(node_id);
   Disable_hello();
   limit_response();
   setPacketPriority(1);
end
else if(event == END_RAIN)
begin
   Enable_Hello();
   replyto_response();
   setPacketPriority(0);
end
```

In the above Algorithm 1, when we detect rain we broadcast "node_id", disable "hello" messages and set packet priority to 1 for the rain affected node.

When a node is affected by rain it will receive a rain event, this event triggers a rain STATUS broadcast message. Every node that is adjacent to this node will receive this packet. The affected nodes will still send HELLO messages but stop responding to RREQ messages, this will prevent the neighboring nodes from seeing it and sending their data through the affected node. Finally, we implemented a simple priority for the packets that are originated from the affected node; all packets that are sent from this node will have a greater value for its QoS value in the IP header.

If the event ends, the node will return to its normal activity, it will send HELLO packets normally and continue to respond on the RREQ packets and finally sets the QoS value to its normal value.

```
Algorithms 2

if(packet.type == RAIN_PACKET)
begin
   for each(r in routing_table)
   begin
      if(r.nextHop == packet.source)
         remove(packet.source);
   end
end
```

In the above Algorithm 2, when an adjacent node receives a rain packet it will immediately remove all the next hops that this node is involved in. This will prevent any node from sending any data through this node.

IV. Sensor Network Design

Sensor network design is clearly described in this section as bellow:

A. *Monitoring Goals*

Our proposed wireless sensor network will be used to monitor spatial variations in soil moisture as well as detect the presence of rainfall over time. Our experimental WSN testbed is set up in Jordan monitored surface soil moisture and presence of rainfall. Our long-term objective is to monitor soil moisture regularly so as to implement targeted irrigation techniques. The data we gather from our system will also be used for managing the irrigation resources throughout Jordan by providing improved guidelines for the Jordan irrigation management model.

The reactivity of the system should be also very high to detect the occurrence of the event as soon as possible, as in this case, rainfall. When such an event is detected the data or sensor readings should be sent to the base station reliably and quickly and for this reason we need to select the right routes. This data should be sent to the base station at a higher priority than all other data being sent [30].

Wireless systems are likely to face errors as the environment in which these sensors are deployed are harsh environments, which might have severely dry conditions and can affect their performance. Hence we need a very reliable system which ensures that information is correctly and accurately routed to the base station. The sensor network must also ensure heavy data flow in case of rainfall so that no routes or links are overwhelmed with data. We need to manage the information flow and to also reduce redundancy from data to reduce traffic.

Finally, since there are always energy crises in the case of wireless sensor networks, we need to carefully plan each activity to maximize battery life also take advantage of the high duration of sunlight available in the Middle East Region. Hence we make use of the solar-powered WSN nodes by which the problem is somewhat lessened. We still need power management as a lot of data will be sent when a wireless node is experiencing rainfall and it needs to send a lot of information and a lot of power will be required at this time. Hence, the sensor network needs to strike a perfect balance and trade-off between the power left and the information required to be sent.

We are using ZigBee medium range communication module standard, which is based on the IEEE 802.15.4 [31], which has a lot of advantages such as: consumes less power, also saves power as it has sleep mode, has a large capacity network, is more reliable and has low cost of related components [32,23]. The authors in [33] have proposed to reduce energy consumption by using a routing algorithm, which is a combination of Ad hoc On-Demand Distance Vector Routing Junior and the Cluster-Tree technique. However, there is no practical implementation for all these research initiatives. In our system, power is directly saved by using priority based routing algorithm hence reducing the data at times of raining event when many data is produced. However, even after raining data should be sampled more frequently in order to keep track of the soil moisture.

B. WSN Architecture

At each sensor nodes, we have a soil moisture sensor and rainfall sensor attached to it. Our sensor network is based on Libelium Waspmotes sensor nodes and ATmega1281rds Microcontroller [34]. It is connected to following components:

- Wireless Interface (Waspmote XBee based on IEEE 802.15.4 standard)
- Soil moisture sensor (Watermark 200SS)
- Rainfall sensor (Libelium Weather Station WS 3000)
- USB-PC Interface (Waspmote Gateway)
- Solar Panel (Waspmote rigid solar panel 7 V-500 mA)
- 6600 mA Li-Ion rechargeable batteries

The current network deployment has four sampling nodes, but more generally, the architecture supports many nodes [34].

Zigbee RF nodes are used as communication models to transmit the sampled data to the gateway; these can have the best average lifetime of 8 years using dual batteries 3 V, at 3000 mAh. Some studies like [31], show that ZigBee model based on IEEE 802.15.4 standard with correct topology can last up to 10 years. Hence, we are using ZigBee communication model for our research.

C. WSN Working Principle

The objective of our research is to provide a dynamic and robust event driven protocol for soil moisture monitoring so that the results can be used in the future to manage irrigation resources throughout Jordan. We use a mesh topology for network connectivity because of its advantages in our application scenario. Mesh topologies are able to route data and messages to the final gateway node through several different nodes. Even if the connection to any RF node is lost because of any environmental tragedy or loss of power, etc. still all the important data can reach to the gateway node and the base station due to the mesh topology.

D. Hardware Design

1) Sensor Nodes: We are using Waspmote WSN as shown in Figure 3, which is an open source wireless sensor platform the speciality of which is implementing sensor nodes having low power consumption capability [31]. Hence, our sensor nodes can work autonomously, working on battery power and having a maximum lifetime of 7–8 years [35] based on the cycle of operation, communication protocol and the communication module used.

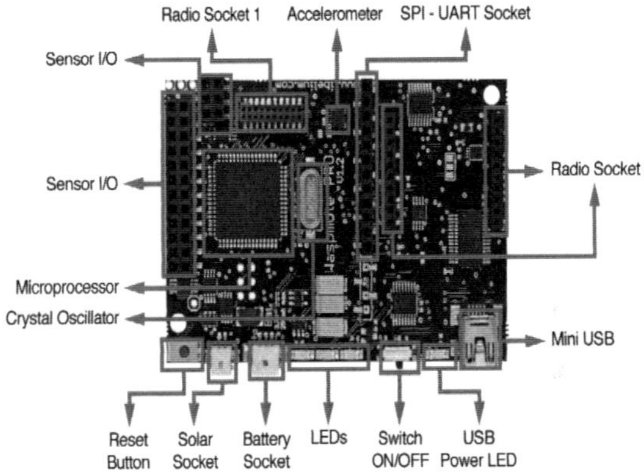

Figure 3. Waspmote Sensor Node.

This RF module has a long range of 7000 m but lower power consumption than Wi-Fi (802.11). It operates at a very low data rate of 250 kbps at 2.4 GHz [36,37]. These modules have mechanism to extend battery life by using sleep modes.

2) Soil Moisture Sensor: The Soil Moisture Sensor Watermark 200SS [38] developed by Irrometer, as shown in figure 5, is one of the most important component in our research. It has very satisfactory features like stable calibration, a measurement range from 0 to 239 cb (kPa), it has no soil dissolvability, can withstand freezing temperatures, and is low cost and low maintenance [38].

3) Rainfall Sensor: The rainfall sensor is a part of the Weather Station WS-3000, shown in Figure 5, which comprises of an anemometer, a wind vane, and a pluviometer [39]. The Weather Station is placed above ground on a pole and connected to the WSN sensor node. Our study is only concerned about pluviometer readings which provides a digital signal whose frequency is directly proportional to the intensity of rainfall.

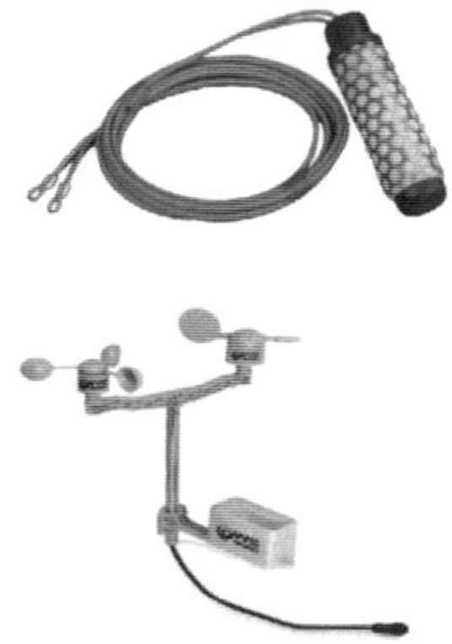

Figure 4. Watermark Soil Moisture Sensor and Weather Station having Rainfall Sensor.

V. TESTBED AND SIMULATION RESULTS

The primary goal for this section is to clarify testbed setup and result for simulation and testbed.

A. *WSN Testbed Setup*

We setup our testbed in a garden in Jordan. The current network deployment has five nodes, which are 5 m apart from each other, but more generally, the architecture supports many nodes [15].

The setup of this scenario consists of 5 wireless nodes from node 0 (N0) to node 3 (N3), as shown in Figure 6 and one gateway node (GW) which is connected to the server. We will have two constant bit rates (cbr) streams, one from node 0 and the other from node 2. The destination for both streams will be gateway node (GW). We will call them cbr0 and cbr2 respectively. According to AOMDV protocol, cbr2 traffic will go from node 2 to node 0 then node GW, and cbr0 traffic will go to node GW directly. Node 2 traffic, cbr2 will go through two paths, the primary one through node 0 and the secondary through node 1. After three hours during sending packets, node 0 is affected by RAIN (which is the event).

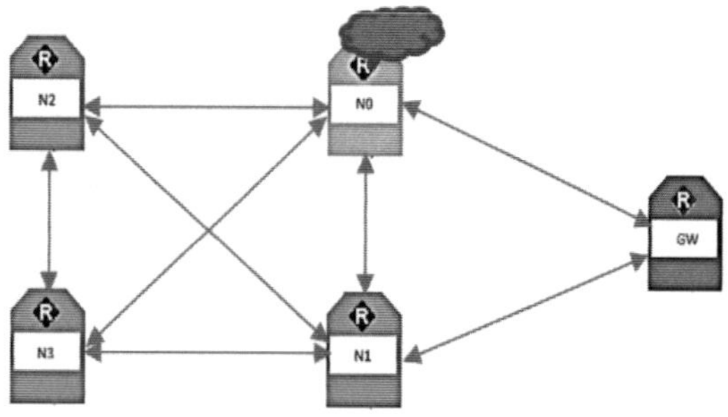

Figure 5. Five Node wireless sensor network (WSN) Test Bed Setup.

Tables I and Table II show the result of routing table before and after rain is detected at node 0, the routing table for node 2 and 3 has been changed which take another route through node 1 instead of the primary one through node 0 to send data to GW (destination) because node 0 is affected by RAIN. Hence, node 0 has very important data (soil moisture) and it has to send it first and should take the highest priority to send data.

TABLE I. TABLE BEFORE RAIN BEING DETECTED AT NODE 0

N0		
Dest No	**Nxt hop**	**Hop cnt**
3	3	1
GW	GW	1
1	1	1
2	2	1

N1		
Dest No	**Nxt hop**	**Hop cnt**
3	3	1
GW	GW	1
2	2	1
0	0	1

N2		
Dest No	**Nxt hop**	**Hop cnt**
3	3	1
1	1	1
0	0	1
GW	1	2
	0	2

N3		
Dest No	**Nxt hop**	**Hop cnt**
1	1	1
2	2	1
0	0	1
GW	1	2
	0	2

GW		
Dest No	**Nxt hop**	**Hop cnt**
0	0	1
1	1	1
2	0	2
	1	2
3	0	2
	1	2

TABLE I. ROUTING TABLE AFTER RAIN BEING DETECTED AT NODE 0

N0		
Dest No	**Nxt hop**	**Hop cnt**
3	3	1
GW	GW	1
1	1	1
2	2	1

N1		
Dest No	**Nxt hop**	**Hop cnt**
3	3	1
GW	GW	1
2	2	1
0	0	1

N2		
Dest No	**Nxt hop**	**Hop cnt**
3	3	1
1	1	1
0	0	1
GW	1	2

N3		
Dest No	**Nxt hop**	**Hop cnt**
1	1	1
2	2	1
0	0	1
GW	1	2

GW		
Dest No	**Nxt hop**	**Hop cnt**
0	0	1
1	1	1
2	1	2
3	1	2

B. Simulation Setup

To show that our proposed protocol is also expandable we used simulation tools for 5 nodes scenario and for a very large scenario consisting of 30 nodes. The source code of the simulation is written in TCL language and runs the simulation example on ns-2.35 Linux Ubuntu version 12.

For 5 node setup, we use standard AOMDV in first period from 0 to 900 in second one from 900 to 2000 we use the modified version of AOMDV.

An AWK script was built to calculate the average of Throughput and End to End Delay on node 0 and node 1 before and after node 1 is affected by raining. The highest priority data stream will grant to cbr1 coming from node 1 because it affected by rain and it has important data that should be send to the destination node 2. Rerouting cbr0 coming from node 0 traffic through node 4, which has data with low priority. In this way we reduce forwarding load on node 1 that means the throughput and end to end delay will be better on cbr1 after node 1 affected by rain.

For the complex scenario consisting of 30 nodes, we calculate that 5 out of 30 nodes were affected by rain and measure the performance and the energy consumption.

There are 30 wireless nodes from node 0 to node 29 distributed with fixed location across the testbed as shown in Figure 7. We will have two constant bit rates (cbr) streams one from node 0 and one from node 1 the destination for both streams will be node 29 (GW) we will call them cbr0 and cbr1 respectively. According to AOMDV, protocol cbr0 traffic will go through the path node 0 -> node 1 -> node 2 -> node 13 -> node 4 -> node 15 -> node 6 -> node 17 -> node 18 then node 29, and cbr1 traffic will go through the same path.

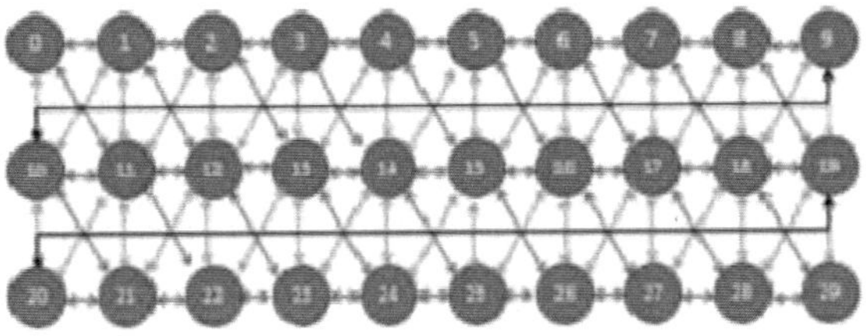

Figure 6. 30-Nodes Simulation Setup.

The five nodes which are affected by rain are 1, 12, 16, 21, 25. This means that node 0 or 1 will use secondary paths when any node in the primary path is affected by RAIN.

Simulation time is 2500 ms, we set up the constant bit rate (cbr) with variable rate values depending on rain level. For example, when it is raining lightly, the (cbr) rate will be 0.05 Mbps, when rain becomes heavier, the (cbr) rate changed to 0.1 Mbps and, finally, when flood occurs, the (cbr) rate changes to 0.5 Mbps. Packet size for all (cbr) is 1000 byte.

C. Performance Measurements

1) Performance Measurements for 5 Node Simulation Setup

The results listed in Table III clearly show improvement of Throughput and End to End Delay on cbr0 coming from node 0 which validate our assumptions and it showing that the event-driven approach does improve overall network efficiency.

TABLE II. PERFORMANCE MEASUREMENT BEFORE AND DURING THE TIME WHEN NODE 0 IS AFFECTED BY RAIN.

Type/protocol and Time	Standard AOMDV 3 hours Before Rain	Modified AOMDV 3 hours After Rain
Total Sent Size From cbr2	5000 kbit	3749 kbit
Total Sent Size From cbr0	4375 kbit	6874.7 kbit
End-to-End Delay (cbr2)	256910 ms	349410 ms
End-to-End Delay (cbr0)	16210 ms	5.67 ms
Throughput (cbr2)	2.65 kbps	3.70 kbps
Throughput (cbr0)	4.20 kbps	6.20 kbps

2) Performance Measurements for 30 Node Simulation Setup

Before rainfall, we used the standard AOMDV protocol and after the rainfall, we used our modified AOMDV protocol to compare its performance with the standard AOMDV. In this simulation scenario we divided the simulation period depending on raining level, for instance with no rain the period from 0 to 900 s, light rain period from 900 to 2000 s and heavy rain from 2000 to 2500 s.

Node 1 is affected by two levels of rain light rain and heavy rain, so we compared the Throughput and End to End Delay in two levels.

The results listed in Table IV clearly show improvement in Throughput and End to End Delay on cbr1 coming from node 1 which validates our assumptions and it shows that the event-driven approach does improve overall network efficiency.

TABLE III. PERFORMANCE MEASUREMENT BEFORE AND DURING THE TIME WHEN NODE 1 IS AFFECTED BY RAIN.

Type/Rain-Level (Time)	Light rain - 0.05Mbps (0 – 900) s	Heavy Rain - 0.1Mbps (900 – 2000) s	Very Heavy flood - 0.5 Mbps (2000 – 2500) s
Total Sent Size From cbr0	5000.1 kbit	6875.4 kbit	18746 kbit
Total Sent Size From cbr1	4375 kbit	13748.7 kbit	18750.2 kbit
End-to-End Delay (cbr0)	18.78 ms	18.79 ms	4465.59 s
End-to-End Delay (cbr1)	16.62 ms	16.50 s	16.42 ms
Throughput (cbr0)	5.56 kbps	6.25 kbps	3.75 kbps
Throughput (cbr1)	4.86 kbps	12.50 kbps	37.50 kbps

Figure 7 shows the throughput of Node 1, separately being affected by rain. The reason behind this increase in throughput is that at heavy and very heavy rain, we use the modified AOMDV protocol.

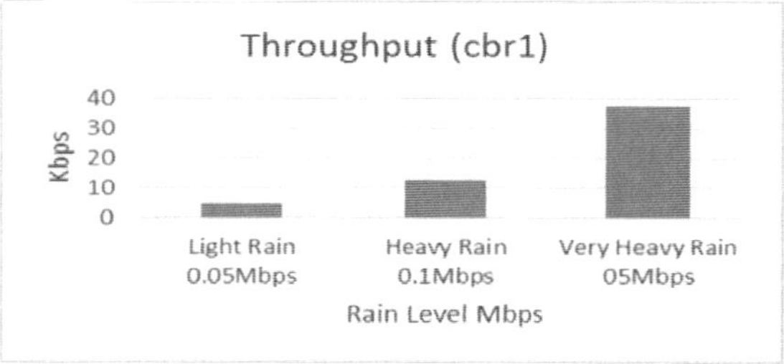

Figure 7. The throughput differences between light rain, heavy and very heavy rain, on node 1.

D. *Energy Consumption*

We measure the energy consumption in three modes for each sensor node, idle mode, receiving mode and transmitting mode. The energy consumed in idle mode is called idle energy (Idle Energy). The energy consumed by a node in transmission of data is called transmission energy (Trans Energy) and the energy consumed by a node to receive data is called receiving energy (Rec Energy).

When a node is affected by rain it will receive a rain event, this event triggers a special broadcast rain packet called STATUS message. Every node that is adjacent to this node will receive this packet. The affected nodes will still send HELLO messages but stop responding to RREQ messages, this will prevent the neighboring nodes from seeing it and sending their data through the affected node.

Hence, the nodes affected by rainfall will not receive any packets from other nodes and hence they will require very less receiving energy, on the other hand, they will just have their own data to transmit, hence the transmission energy also decreases.

1) *Energy Consumption for 5 Node WSN Testbed*

The Waspmotes consumes 15mA of energy per hour in switched on state and just consumes 55µA of energy per hour in sleep state [40]. We have designed our protocol to be energy-efficient. In our protocol sensor, data under normal events are sampled for 10s after every 3h and sent to the server. When we measured energy consumption for our protocol it was found that, it only consumes 0.004 mA of energy per hour. If we have a rainfall event, we implement second scheme under which we sample the data for 10s after every 10s, only for the sensor node experiencing the rainfall event, since the soil moisture may change very rapidly. In second scheme, when there is a rainfall our protocol consumes only 0.042 mA of energy per hour for the effected node, which is also very less than the default energy consumption of 15 mA per hour for the Waspmote [40]. Hence, our protocol is also energy efficient.

As shown in Tables V and VI the energy measurements in mA taken after rainfall when we use modified AOMDV, are less than those taken before rainfall when we use standard AOMDV, for both received energy (Rec Energy) as well as transmission energy (Trans Energy) because the nodes affected by rainfall will not receive any data from other nodes and hence they will require very less receiving energy, on the other hand they will just have their own data to transmit, hence the transmission energy also decreases. We also show these results in Figures 8 and 9.

TABLE V. ENERGY MEASUREMENT BEFORE NODE 0 AFFECTED BY (AOMDV).

Node No	Idle_Energy mili Ampere	Rec_Energy mili Ampere	Trans_Energy mili Ampere
GW	0.0275	3.75	3.75
0	0.0272	4.35	3.1
1	0.0271	4.33	3.3
2	0.0269	3.21	4.31
3	0.0270	3.31	4.35

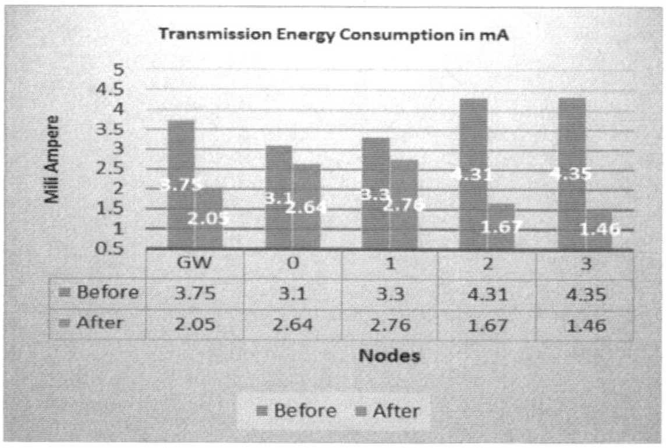

Figure 8. Transmission Energy Consumption in mA.

TABLE IV. ENERGY MEASUREMENTS DURING RAINFALL ON NODE 0 (MODIFIED AOMDV).

Node No	Idle_Energy mili Ampere	Rec_Energy mili Ampere	Trans_Energy mili Ampere
GW	0.0275	4.21	2.05
0	0.0265	1.02	2.64
1	0.0260	3.01	2.76
2	0.0245	1.82	1.67
3	0.0210	1.79	1.46

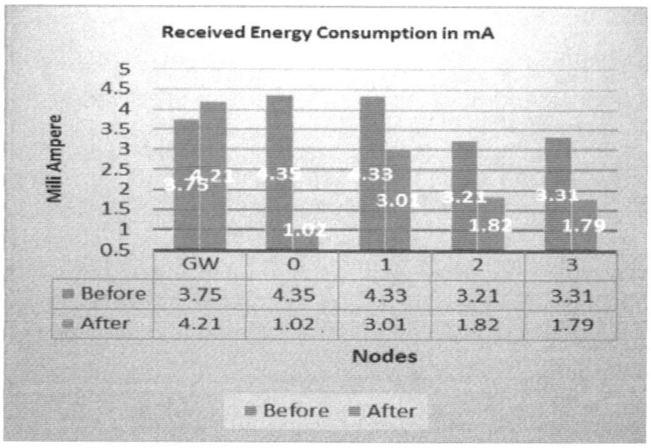

Figure 9. Received Energy Consumption in mA.

2) *Energy Consumption for 30 Node Simulation Setup*

This section of our paper is concerned about the energy, consumptions for all nodes before the nodes are affected by rain, when the nodes will use the standard version of AOMDV and after the nodes are affected by rain when they will use the modified version of AOMDV, the calculation of total energy has been done during the simulation periods for each cases before and after the nodes affected by rain.

The total energy consumed has been calculated for all nodes before and after the nodes were affected by rain for the three simulations. In addition, we calculated the rate of decrease in consumed energy before and after the nodes are affected by rain.

TABLE V. ENERGY MEASUREMENTS BEFORE NODE 1 IS AFFECTED BY RAIN.

Node No.	Total_Energy (joules)	Idle_Energy (joules)	Tran_Energy (joules)	Rec_Energy (joules)
1	218940000.00	191000000.00	4140000.00	23800000.00
12	35506380.00	30100000.00	26380.00	5380000.00
16	35726423.20	29300000.00	26423.20	6400000.00
21	23737540.90	20700000.00	17540.90	3020000.00
25	23817550.60	19100000.00	17550.60	4700000.00

Tables VII and VIII clearly show that of consumption energy for affected nodes before is greater than energy consumption after rainfall starts. As we can see from the 'Total' columns in both tables, the total energy consumed decreases for all the nodes and the decrease in energy is much greater for the nodes affected by rainfall. The idle energy, transmission energy as well received energy decreases for all the nodes. The largest decrease in total energy is due to the decrease in transmission energy.

TABLE VI. ENERGY MEASUREMENTS DURING RAINFALL ON NODE 1.

Node No.	Total_Energy (joules)	Idle_Energy (joules)	Tran_Energy (joules)	Rec_Energy (joules)
1	140710000.00	123000000.00	1310000.00	16400000.00
12	23851969.88	20300000.00	1969.88	3550000.00
16	27722152.14	22800000.00	2152.14	4920000.00
21	15771225.74	13800000	1225.74	1970000
25	16011241.87	12900000	1241.87	3110000.00

We calculate total energy consumed by all the nodes that are affected by rainfall.

The total energy for node (k) =

$$idle\_energy\ (k) + trans\_energy(k) + recv\_energy(k)$$

The total energy for all affected nodes =

$$\sum_{k=0}^{n} idle\_energy(k) + trans\_energy(k) + recv\_energy(k)$$

We calculated the total consumed energy for all affected nodes before rains as = T-energy-before = 337727894.70

And total consumed energy for all affected nodes after rains = T-energy-after = 224066589.63

Therefore the consumed energy decreasing rate = (T-energy-before/ T-energy-after) %

Rate of decrease in Consumed energy (affected nodes) = 51%

We can clearly observe that the energy consumptions for all nodes affected by rain has decreased sharply as shown in Figure 11, also the energy consumptions on all nodes has decreased.

The above figure is showing energy consumption by 5 nodes before and after they are affected by rain. Again our modified AOMDV clearly outperforms the standard AOMDV in terms of energy consumption.

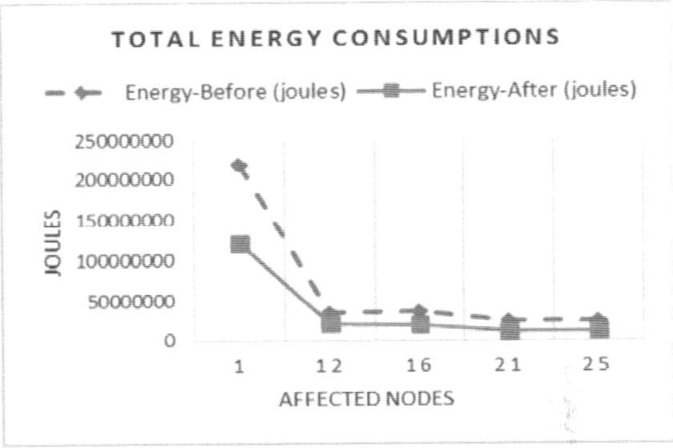

Figure 10. Energy consumed by nodes before and during rainfall.

VI. CONCLUSIONS

This paper outlined design, deployment and evaluation of our reactive, robust and enhanced version of AOMDV protocol. Our event driven enhancements mean that our protocol not only increases the performance but also makes it energy efficient as the energy consumption is considerably reduced for the nodes experiencing the rainfall and also in general because we use the sleep mode when it is not raining. We also successfully showed in simulation results that our enhanced AOMDV protocol is scalable. We compared its performance with prior AOMDV protocol. For our proposed protocol the results clearly show that it reduces average delay while at the same time increases the throughput of the nodes being affected by rain. The enhanced throughput and low delay clearly indicates that the proposed changes to AOMDV to support events such as rain would be a significant and meaningful addition to AOMDV, which can be used in several WSN applications.

REFERENCES

[1] M.A. Matin and M.M. Islam, Overview of Wireless Sensor Network, Wireless Sensor Networks - Technology and Protocols, Dr. Mohammad Matin (Ed.), InTech, DOI: 10.5772/49376, 2012.

[2] K. Martinez, J. K. Hart and R. Ong, "Environmental sensor networks," in Computer, vol. 37, no. 8, pp. 50-56, 2004.

[3] D. Steere, A. Baptista, D. McNamee, C. Pu, Walpole, J. Research challenges in environmental observation and forcasting systems. In Proceedings of the 6th International Conference on Mobile Computing and Networking (MOBICOM), Boston, MA, USA, 2000.

[4] R. Cardell-Oliver, K. Smettem, M. Kranz and K. Mayer, "Field testing a wireless sensor network for reactive environmental monitoring [soil moisture measurement]," Proceedings of the 2004

Intelligent Sensors, Sensor Networks and Information Processing Conference, 2004.

[5] D.S.J.D. Couto, D. Aguayo, J. Bicket, R. Morris, A High-Throughput Path Metric for Multi-Hop Wireless Routing. Wirel, 2010.

[6] D. Chen, P.K. Varshney, QoS Support in Wireless Sensor Networks: A Survey. In Proceedings of the International Conference on Wireless Networks, (ICWN), Las Vegas, NV, USA, 21–24 June 2004.

[7] J. N. Al-Karaki and A. E. Kamal, "Routing techniques in wireless sensor networks: a survey," in IEEE Wireless Communications, vol. 11, no. 6, pp. 6-28, 2004. K. Akkaya, M. Younis, A Survey on Routing Protocols for Wireless Sensor Networks. Ad Hoc Netw. J. 2010.

[8] G. Sklyarenko, "AODV Routing Protocol" in Seminar Technische Informatik Institut fur Informatik, Freie Universitat Berlin, July 2006.

[9] S. Tang, B. Zhang, A robust AODV protocol with local update. In Proceedings of the Joint Conference of the 10th Asia Pacific Conference on Communications (APCC), Beijing, China, 29 August–1 September 2004.

[10] D. Son, B. Krishnamachari, Heidemann, J. Experimental Study of Concurrent Transmission in Wireless Sensor Networks. In Proceedings of the 4th International Conference on Embedded Networked Sensor Systems (SenSys), Boulder, CO, USA, 31 October–3 November 2011.

[11] J. Kang, Y. Zhang, B. Nath, End-to-End Channel Capacity Measurement for Congestion Control in Sensor Networks. In Proceedings of the 2nd International Workshop on Sensor and Actor Network Protocols and Applications (SANPA), Boston, MA, USA, 22 August 2009.

[12] W. Lou, W. Liu, Zhang, Y. Performance Optimization Using Multipath Routing in Mobile Ad Hoc and Wireless Sensor Networks. Combinator. Optim. Commun. Netw. 2012.

[13] A. Woo, T.Tong, D. Culler, Taming the Underlying Challenges of Reliable Multihop Routing in Sensor Networks. In Proceedings of the 1st International Conference on Embedded Networked Sensor Systems, Los Angeles, CA, USA, 5–7 November 2011.

[14] M. Zamalloa, B. Krishnamachari, An Analysis of Unreliability and Asymmetry in Low-Power Wireless Links. ACM Trans. Sens. Netw. 2011.

[15] H.Alwan, A. Agarwal, A Survey on Fault Tolerant Routing Techniques in Wireless Sensor Networks. In Proceedings of the 3th International Conference on Sensor Technologies and Applications (Senosrcomm), Athens, Greece, 18–23 June 2009.

[16] M. Tarique, K. Tepe, Adibi, S.; Erfani, S. Survey of Multipath Routing Protocols for Mobile Ad Hoc Networks. J. Netw. Comput. Appl. 2009.

[17] S. Mueller, R. Tsang, D. Ghosal, Multipath Routing in Mobile Ad Hoc Networks: Issues and Challenges. Lect. Notes Comput. Sci. 2010, 2965, 209–234.

[18] M.K. Marina, S.R. Das, On-Demand multipath distance vector routing in ad hoc networks. In Proceedings of the 9th IEEE International Conference on Network Protocols (ICNP), Riverside, CA, USA, 11–14 November 2001.

[19] H.D. Trung, W. Benjapolakul, P.M. Duc, Performance Evaluation and Comparison of Different ad Hoc Routing Protocols; Department of Electrical Engineering, Chulalongkorn University: Bangkok, Thailand, 2007.

[20] T. Yelemou, New approach to improve the robustness of AOMDV protocol. In Proceedings of the 2013 10th International Multi-Conference on Systems, Signals & Devices (SSD), Hammamet, Tunisia, 18–21 March 2013; pp. 1–6.

[21] N.M. Lima, W.H. da Silva, Santos, D.; A.; Pujolle, G. Survival multipath routing for MANETs. In Proceedings of the Network Operations and Management Symposium (NOMS), Bahia, Brazil, 7–11 April 2008; pp. 425–432.

[22] B. Sharma, S. Chugh, V. Jain, Energy Efficient Load Balancing Approach to Improve AOMDV Routing in MANET. In Proceedings of the Communication Systems and Network Technologies (CSNT), 2014 Fourth International Conference, Bhopal, India, 7–9 April 2014; pp. 187–192.

[23] F. Yang, S. Ling, H. Xu, B. Sun, Network codingbased AOMDV routing in MANET. In Proceedings of the 2012 International Conference on Information Science and Technology (ICIST), Wuhan, China, 23–25 March 2012; pp. 337–340.

[24] M. Tekaya, N. Tabbane, S. Tabbane, Delay Remaining Energy for AOMDV Protocol (DRE-AOMDV). In Proceedings of the 2011 7th International Conference on Wireless Communications, Networking and Mobile Computing (WiCOM), Wuhan, China, 23–25 September 2011; pp. 1–5.

[25] X. Chen, H.M. Jones, D. Jayalath, Channel-aware routing in MANETs with route handoff. IEEE Trans. Mob. Comput. 2011, 10, 108–121.

[26] D. Yoo, G. Jin, B. Jang, S. Ro, A Modified AOMDV Routing Protocol for Maritime Inter-ship Communication. In Proceedings of the ICT Convergence (ICTC), 2011 International Conference, Seoul, Korea, 28–30 September 2011. Doi:10.1109/ICTC.2011.6082694

[27] C. Kanani, A Sinhal. Ant Colony Optimization based Modified AOMDV for Multipath Routing in MANET. Int. J. Comput. Appl. 2013, 82, 14–19. Doi:10.1.1.402.1689

[28] B. Malarkodi, S.K.R Hussain, Venkataramani, B. Performance Evaluation of AOMDV-PAMAC Protocols for Ad Hoc Networks. World Acad. Sci. Eng. Technol. 2010, 38. Doi:10.1.1.310.288.

[29] M. Rantisi, The Development of a Dynamic and Robust Event-Based Routing Protocol in Wireless Sensor Networks for Environmental Monitoring. In Proceedings of the First Global Conference on Communication, Science and Information Engineering (CCSIE), London, UK, 25–27 July 2011.

[30] J. Peral, E. Merlo, R. Labrador, Torralba, A.; Carvajal, R.G.; Gil, M.; Villalba, D.; Grande, A.; Moreno, M.; Viguera, J. Automated meter reading based on IEEE 802.15.4. In Proceedings of the 38th Annual Conference on IEEE Industrial Electronics Society (IECON), Montreal, QC, Canada, 25–28 October 2012; pp. 5996–6001.

[31] Y.W. Lee, S. Eun, S.H. Oh, Wireless digital water meter with low power consumption for automatic meter reading. In Proceedings of the International Conference on Convergence and Hybrid Information Technology (ICHIT), Daejeon, Korea, 28–30 August 2008; Volume 8, pp. 639–645.

[32] W. Wang, Y. Peng, Y. Peng, ZigBee routing algorithm based on energy optimization. Sens. Transducers 2013, 157, 223–228.

[33] A. Prince-Pike, Power Characterization of a ZigBee Wireless Network in a Real Time Monitoring Application. Master's Thesis, Auckland University of Technology, New Zealand, April 2009.

[34] J.A. Gutierrez, M. Naeve, E. Callaway, M.Bourgeois, V. Mitter, B. Heile, IEEE 802.15.4: A developing standard for low power low-cost wireless personal area networks. IEEE Netw. 2001, 15, 12–19.

[35] Y.M.Yussoff, H.Z. Abidin, R.A. Rahman, F.H. Yahaya, Development of a PIC-based wireless sensor node utilizing XBee technology. In Proceedings of the 2nd IEEE International Conference on Information Management and Engineering (ICIME), Chengdu, China, 16–18 April 2010; pp. 116–120

[36] F.P. Correia, M.S. Alencar, F.B.S. Carvalho, B.G. Leal, W.T.A. Lopes, Propagation analysis in Precision Agriculture environment using XBee devices. In Proceedings of the 15th SBMO/IEEE MTTS International Microwave and Optoelectronics Conference (IMOC), Rio de Janeiro, Brazil, 4–7 August 2013; pp. 1–5.

[37] IRROMETER Company. WATERMARK Soil Moisture Sensor MODEL200SS; IRROMETER Company: Riverside, CA, USA, 2010.

[38] Libelium Inc. Weather Stations Comparative—Weather Monitor (Davis) Vs. WS-3000; Libelium Inc.: 2014; Spain; Available online: http://www.libelium.com/weather-stations-comparative-weather-monitor-davis-vs-ws-3000-libelium/

[39] Waspmote Technical Guide; Document version: v6.0-01/2016, Libelium Comunicaciones Distribuidas S.L.: Zaragoza, Spain, 20

Locating Multiple Camera Sensors and Wireless Access Points for a Generalized Indoor Positioning System

Jaime Duque Domingo,
Carlos Cerrada
and J.A. Cerrada

Departamento de Ingeniería de Software y
Sistemas Informáticos
ETSI Informática, UNED,
C/Juan del Rosal, 16. 28040 Madrid, Spain
Email: ccerrada@issi.uned.es

Enrique Valero

School of Energy, Geoscience, Infrastructure and Society,
Heriot-Watt University,
Edinburgh EH14 4AS, United Kingdom
Email: e.valero@hw.ac.uk

Abstract—**This work illustrates the generalization of a previously developed Indoor Positioning System (IPS) based on the combination of WiFi Positioning System (WPS) and depth maps. This generalization extends the use of the proposed system to scenarios containing multiple rooms and several people, in contrast to the more simpler initial version. The combination of both technologies improves the efficiency of existing methods, based uniquely on wireless positioning techniques, for estimating the location of people. Users just require the use of smart-phones, besides the installation of RGB-D devices in the sensing area. But some problems arise when multiple RGB-D sensors and access points must be located in a large area composed of several rooms. The paper exposes how the necessary devices are placed minimizing the total uncovered area. Experimental results for an office space composed by nine differently sized rooms are shown.**

Keywords–indoor positioning; IPS; WPS; RGB-D sensors; Kinect; WiFi; fingerprint; trajectory; skeletons; depth map.

I. INTRODUCTION

Indoor Positioning Systems (IPSs) are used to obtain the position of people or objects inside a building [1]. This work extends a previously developed method for indoor positioning inside a room [2], in which WiFi Positioning System (WPS) and RGB-D sensors are combined. Object recognition can be considered as a part of the core research area of computer vision, and an important number of authors have reported methods and applications for people detection and positioning. The generalization of the previous IPS will deliver the position of users in complete scenarios where there are several people interacting with the environment. Trajectories of users will be obtained by means of the two considered information sources: WPS values and trajectories of the skeletons of users in the *depth map*. While location of wireless sensors does not represent any real problem, special care must be taken in the location of the depth cameras in order to minimize the total uncovered area. In fact, several Kinect v2 sensors should be used simultaneously during experiments to capture the skeletons of users evolving through different rooms. This work shows how coordinates obtained by these sensors placed in different rooms are transformed into a Universal Coordinates System (UCS).

The paper is structured as follows: Section II explores existing solutions concerning positioning, based on WPS, RGB-D sensors, and using both technologies in a joint manner. Section III is devoted to analyze the proposed system and compare it to the previous one. Special attention is given to describe how the multiple cameras should be located in a large area as considered, and how their respective coordinate systems should be related to the universal coordinate system. Section IV presents the layout in which the experiments were performed and analyzes the main obtained results. Finally, Section V states the conclusions of the work.

II. OVERVIEW OF RELATED WORK

WPS is founded on the *fingerprinting* technique [3]. This technique creates a map of the environment recording the *Received Signal Strength Indication* (RSSI) in each point. RSSI is a reference scale used to measure the power level of signals received from a device on a wireless network (usually WiFi or mobile telephony). This map is used to obtain the position of a user in real-time, comparing the values received from the user's portable device to those stored in the map. A recent comparison between WiFi fingerprint-based indoor positioning systems have been presented in [4]. Regarding the use of advanced techniques, authors explain how to make use of temporal or spatial signal patterns, user collaboration, and motion sensors. Also, authors discuss recent advances on reducing offline labor-intensive survey, adapting to fingerprint changes, calibrating heterogeneous devices for signal collection, and achieving energy efficiency for smartphones.

In the field of people and objects detection, other technologies based on computer vision (e.g., RGB-D sensors) have been increasingly used. Authors, in [5], developed a method to detect and identify several people that are occluded by others in a scene. In [6], authors propose a *smart-cane* for the visually impaired that, with the help of a Kinect sensor, facilitates the location of objects. And the method *Kinect Positioning System* (KPS) is analyzed in [7] aiming to obtain the user position. These positioning techniques have also been used in Robotics, such as the work presented in [8], where several *Simultaneous Localization and Mapping* (SLAM) algorithms are proposed for building maps with robots. By means of

SLAM, the environment is built recording the measurements RSSI in each point. Also, in this field of research, the use of different technologies improves positioning systems as shown in [9], where authors analyze how to generate a *fingerprint map* with an RGB-D sensor mounted on a robot.
The work in [10] proposes a hybrid indoor positioning system where WiFi and *Global System for Mobile communication* (GSM) are combined for indoor positioning. Three positioning algorithms from the Nearest Neighbor (NN) family are used for simulations. An architecture for improving indoor positioning, by means of the combination of WiFi and RFID, is presented in [11]. WiFi is used for coordinating the RFID readers when accessing the channel for retrieving tag identifications. This avoids, in the presence of multiple readers, the so-called reader collision problem that RFID suffers from. This problem is caused by the inability for direct communication among them. In [12], a robot is located by using three different systems: a laser rangefinder, a depth camera, and RSSI values. Each system is independently used according to the zone where the robot is located.
The present work extends a previously developed method for indoor positioning inside a room [2], which considers a scenario as represented in Figure 1. That work combined two known technologies: WPS, widely used for indoor positioning, and computer vision by means of RGB-D sensors. However, experiments were carried out just in a room, where the system was set up.

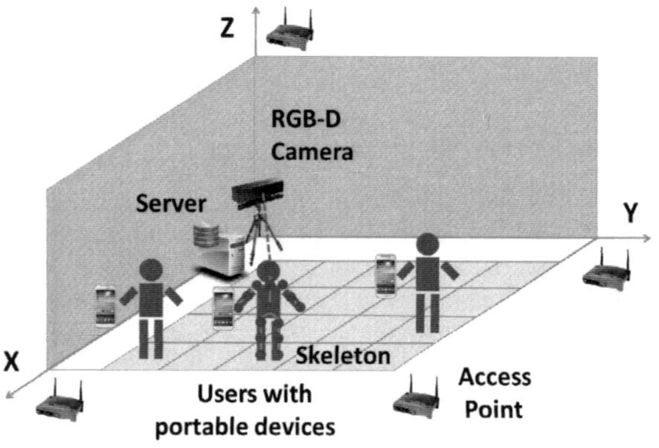

Figure 1. Scenario of the previous work

III. Analysis of the Generalized System

The generalization of the previous IPS will deliver users identification and position in more complex scenarios (i.e. with more rooms) where several users are navigating. This system can be set up in departments or companies where monitoring the position of employees becomes useful to improve the efficiency of business. The trajectories of users will be calculated by combining the two mentioned information sources: WPS data and trajectories of the skeletons of users from the *depth map*. Skeletons are obtained by means of the techniques presented in [13] and [14], where authors propose new algorithms to quickly and accurately predict 3D positions of body joints from depth images. Those methods form a core component of the Kinect gaming platform.

As previously mentioned, the proposed system has been conceived to work in a scenario composed of various rooms (see Figure 2) where there are several people, each of them using a smartphone. Two or more RGB-D sensors are situated in each room to obtain the coordinates of users by means of their skeletons. From these skeletons, neck coordinates are extracted aiming to position people in the environment. This part of the body is chosen because it is less prone to be occluded by elements in the scenario.

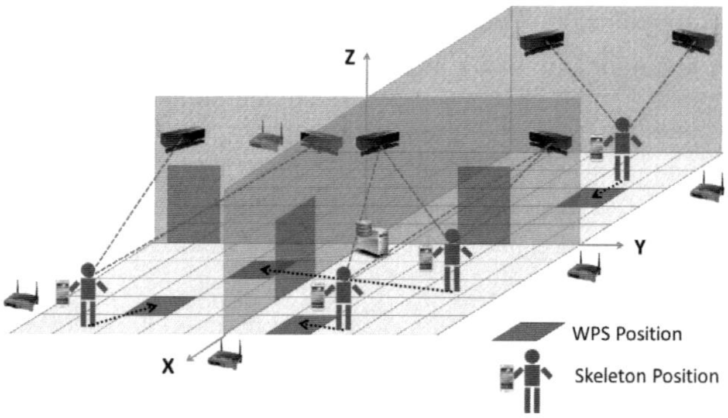

Figure 2. Scenario of the generalized system

The coordinates of the obtained skeletons are considered as illustrated in Figure 3. The distance from the sensor to the skeletons is measured along the Z_{RGB-D} axis, while Y_{RGB-D} axis represents the heights of the users.

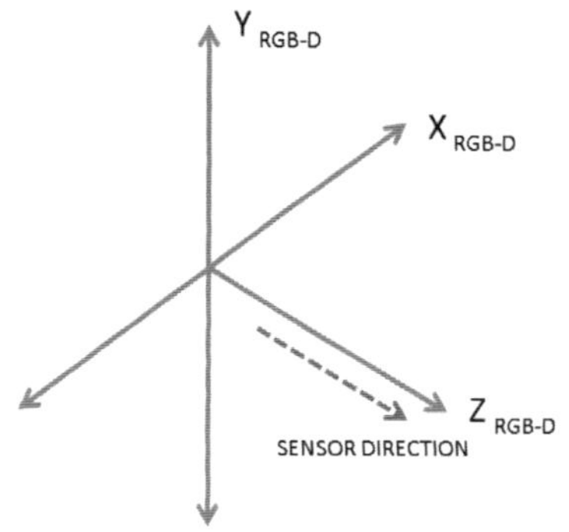

Figure 3. X_{RGB-D}, Y_{RGB-D}, and Z_{RGB-D} axis regarding the RGB-D sensor direction

As one unique Universal Coordinates System (UCS) is considered, the coordinates obtained by the RGB-D sensors are transformed to that this reference system. Only 2D coordinates are considered in this positioning system, as Y_{RGB-D} axis is ignored and Z_{RGB-D} axis corresponds to Y_{POS} axis by means of a transformation.

In order to transform the coordinates obtained by each camera into the UCS, it is necessary to use the angle of the camera and its distance to the universal center point $P(0,0)$.

Each RGB-D sensor has a different angle respect to the UCS and is situated at a different position.
In this work, Kinect sensors have been used as RGB-D sensors. They have a limited angle range (see Figure 4). For this reason, they are turned to obtain a 70° angle from the wall. This implies that it is necessary to calculate the coordinates they deliver into the UCS. These processes are described in the following subsections.

The use of more than one RGB-D sensor reduces the problem of uncovered areas. Since Kinect sensors obtain depth maps with a limited angle of 70°, the proposed system uses two or more Kinect sensors to detect users in all positions. In this manner, the parts which are not covered by a sensor are recorded by another one. In some cases, it is necessary to use more than two sensors because of the geometry of the scene. In addition, the system can discern if two RGB-D sensors are detecting the same user establishing a minimal distance between them. If one Kinect detects a user and this is located at 40cm of another user detected by another Kinect, then both users are considered the same.

A. Position of RGB-D sensors in a room

RGB-D sensors are placed drawing a maximum angle from the walls. As previously mentioned, in the case of Kinect v2, the sensor is able to obtain a 70° angle. To obtain the maximum coverage, the vision line must start at the opposite corner respect the sensor. The values of X_{POS} and Y_{POS} represent the position of the sensor (see Figure 4). Kinect v2 is 25 cm wide. L represents the length of the wall.

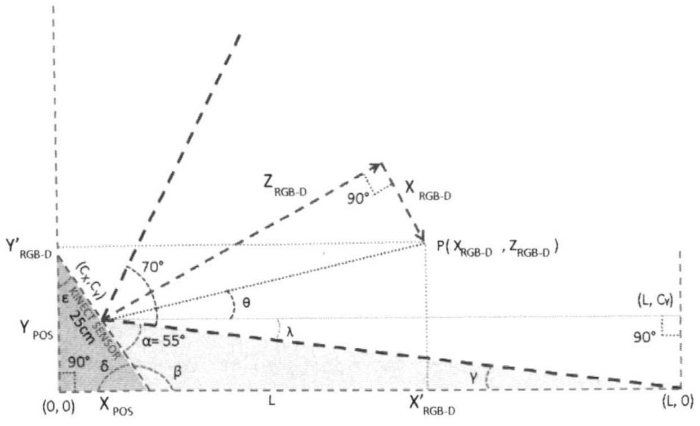

Figure 4. Position of the Kinect v2 sensor

Using the law of sines, it is possible to relate both triangles and obtain the value of X_{POS} with respect to L. The first triangle, the one described between the sensor and the wall, which is represented in light blue, is solved by (1).

$$\frac{25}{\sin 90^\circ} = \frac{X_{POS}}{\sin \varepsilon} \tag{1}$$

where $90^\circ + \varepsilon + \delta = 180^\circ$. Therefore, (1) is simplified in (3).

$$\frac{25}{\sin 90^\circ} = \frac{X_{POS}}{\sin(90^\circ - \delta)} \tag{2}$$

$$X_{POS} = 25 \cdot \sin(90^\circ - \delta) \tag{3}$$

The second triangle is the one formed between the sensor and the opposite corner, represented in light yellow (see Figure 4) and it is solved by (4).

$$\frac{L - X_{POS}}{\sin 55^\circ} = \frac{12,5}{\sin \gamma} \tag{4}$$

where $55^\circ + \beta + \gamma = 180^\circ$ and $\beta + \delta = 180^\circ$. Therefore, $\gamma = \delta - 55^\circ$ and (4) can be modified as (6).

$$\frac{L - X_{POS}}{\sin 55^\circ} = \frac{12,5}{\sin(\delta - 55^\circ)} \tag{5}$$

$$X_{POS} = L - \frac{12,5 \cdot \sin 55^\circ}{\sin(\delta - 55^\circ)} \tag{6}$$

According to (3), it is possible to extract the value of δ (see (7)).

$$\delta = 90^\circ - \arcsin\left[\frac{x}{25}\right] \tag{7}$$

Replacing δ in (6), X_{POS} is related to L (see (8)).

$$L = X_{POS} + \frac{12,5 \cdot \sin 55^\circ}{\sin(35^\circ - \arcsin\left[\frac{X_{POS}}{25}\right])} \tag{8}$$

For example, if a Kinect v2 sensor is placed in a room with 430 cm wide ($L = 430$), X_{POS} will take the value $13,79$ using (8). Y_{POS} is obtained by Pythagoras' Theorem as seen in (9).

$$X_{POS}^2 + Y_{POS}^2 = 25^2 \tag{9}$$

Therefore, $Y_{POS} = 20,85$. So, the Kinect sensor has to be placed at $13,79cm$ from the corner where the 70° angle starts and at $20,85cm$ from the adjacent wall.

B. Position of RGB-D sensors respect to the UCS

The middle point of the Kinect sensor, (C_X, C_Y), has to be considered for the displacements in the UCS. This point is calculated using again the law of sines (see (10)).

$$\frac{25}{\sin 90} = \frac{X_{POS}}{\sin \varepsilon} = \frac{Y_{POS}}{\sin \delta} \tag{10}$$

$$\varepsilon = \arcsin\left(\frac{X_{POS}}{25}\right) \tag{11}$$

$$\delta = \arcsin\left(\frac{Y_{POS}}{25}\right) \tag{12}$$

$$\sin(\delta) = \frac{C_Y}{12,5} \tag{13}$$

$$\sin(\varepsilon) = \frac{C_X}{12,5} \tag{14}$$

Then, (15) is obtained and C_X and C_Y are calculated. Considering $x = 13,79cm$ and $y = 20,85cm$, then $C_X = 10,43$ and $C_Y = 6,90$.

$$\begin{cases} C_X = 12,5 \cdot \sin\left(\arcsin\left(\frac{Y_{POS}}{25}\right)\right) = \frac{Y_{POS}}{2} \\ C_Y = 12,5 \cdot \sin\left(\arcsin\left(\frac{X_{POS}}{25}\right)\right) = \frac{X_{POS}}{2} \end{cases} \tag{15}$$

Since the angle that creates the sensor with the wall is not straight, it is necessary to obtain the deviation λ. Again, this angle can be obtained using the law of sines by means of (16).

$$\frac{\sqrt{(L - C_X)^2 + (0 - C_Y)^2}}{\sin 90^\circ} = \frac{C_Y}{\sin \lambda} \tag{16}$$

Simplifying (16), (17) is obtained, where λ takes the value $1,01^\circ$ in the example.

$$\lambda = \arcsin \frac{C_Y}{\sqrt{(L - C_X)^2 + {C_Y}^2}} \tag{17}$$

Once λ is obtained, it is possible to obtain X'_{RGB-D} and Y'_{RGB-D}. These points represent the position of the skeleton with respect to the corner where the RGB-D sensor is located. The value d_{RGB-D} is obtained by (18). This is used to simplify the rest of expressions.

$$d_{RGB-D} = \sqrt{Z^2_{RGB-D} + X^2_{RGB-D}} \tag{18}$$

Using the law of sines, the θ angle is calculated (see (19) and (20)).

$$\frac{d_{RGB-D}}{\sin 90} = \frac{X_{RGB-D}}{\sin(35 - \lambda - \theta)} \tag{19}$$

$$\theta = 35 - \lambda - \arcsin\left(\frac{X_{RGB-D}}{d_{RGB-D}}\right) \tag{20}$$

X'_{RGB-D} and Y'_{RGB-D} are obtained using the X_{RGB-D} and Z_{RGB-D} coordinates of the skeleton obtained by the sensor (see (21)).

$$\begin{cases} X'_{RGB-D} = C_X + d_{RGB-D} \cdot \cos\theta \\ Y'_{RGB-D} = C_Y + d_{RGB-D} \cdot \sin\theta \end{cases} \tag{21}$$

When the coordinates of the RGB-D sensor with respect to the wall have been obtained, it is necessary to translate the coordinates to the origin of the UCS using the position of the Kinect (X_{CORNER}, Y_{CORNER}). It is also necessary to consider the side of the wall where the sensor is placed in order to select the sign of the X'_{RGB-D} and Y'_{RGB-D} coordinates. If the signs of the coordinates are positive, (22) shows how UCS coordinates are obtained.

$$\begin{cases} X_{UCS} = X_{CORNER} + X'_{RGB-D} \\ Y_{UCS} = Y_{CORNER} + Y'_{RGB-D} \end{cases} \tag{22}$$

IV. EXPERIMENTATION AND RESULTS

Twenty RGB-D sensors based on time-of-flight technology, Kinect v2, have been employed in these experiments. These devices deliver up to 2 MPx images (1920 x 1080) at 30Hz and 0.2 MPx *depth maps* with a resolution of 512 x 424 pixels. All these Kinect are connected to a web server where data are saved and processed. The horizontal field of view of the RGB-D sensor is 70°. This system generalizes our previous work that performed the same activity in a single room with a single RGB-D sensor. The system proposed is valid for a complete department or company where the position of each employee is useful to improve the efficiency of the business.

The experiments have been carried out in an office where twenty RGB-D cameras, Kinect v2, have been deployed (see Figure 5). There are eight different rooms with a central corridor with a total area of $80m^2$. In this corridor, four cameras have been deployed because of the range limitation of the sensor. Each camera is able to obtain skeletons in a 70° angle. The values of the coordinates of each skeleton have to be transformed into a universal coordination system (UCS). The central point of this UCS is situated on the left lower corner of the floor. The experiments have been developed considering the X and Y axis because all rooms are situated in the same floor.

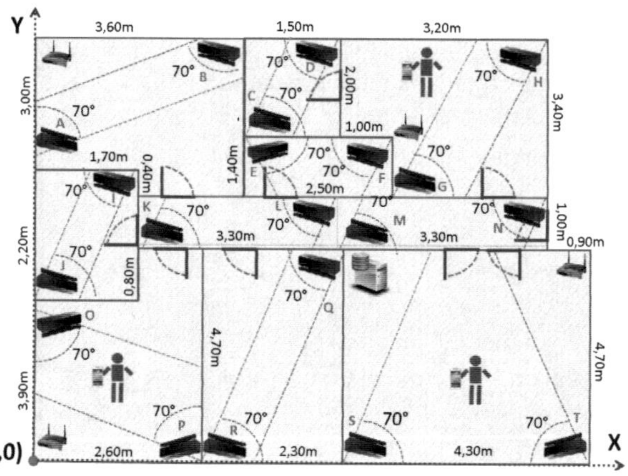

Figure 5. Scenario of the experiments

The Kinect sensors are placed in the corners using the X_{POS} and Y_{POS} displacements obtained by (8) and (9), which represent the distance between the Kinect and the corner. All these values, including the relative angle from the wall λ obtained by (16), are shown in Tables I and II. The distance between the corners, where the sensors are placed, and the origin of the UCS are also shown in Table I: X_{CORNER} and Y_{CORNER}. C_X and C_Y are also taken into account to obtain the displacement of the Kinect sensor in the UCS. These values represent the necessary distance to cover the maximum angle from the wall and are calculated according to (15), as seen previously. X_{UCS} and Y_{UCS} are calculated according to the expression shown in Table II where X'_{RGB-D} and Y'_{RGB-D} are obtained using (20) and (21). For example, the coordinates of a point obtained by the Kinect sensor E in the UCS are determined by (23).

TABLE I. TABLE OF PARAMETERS FOR KINECT PLACEMENT

Kinect RGB-D Camera	*Corner to UCS* X_{CORNER}	*Corner to UCS* Y_{CORNER}	*Sensor to corner* X_{POS}	*Sensor to corner* Y_{POS}	C_X	C_Y
A	0,00	6,10	0,21	0,14	0,07	0,10
B	3,60	9,10	-0,22	-0,13	0,06	0,11
C	3,60	7,10	0,13	0,21	0,06	0,11
D	5,10	9,10	-0,13	-0,21	0,06	0,11
E	3,60	7,10	0,13	-0,21	0,07	0,11
F	6,10	7,10	-0,13	-0,21	0,07	0,11
G	6,10	5,70	0,13	0,21	0,07	0,11
H	8,30	9,10	-0,14	-0,21	0,07	0,10
I	1,70	6,10	-0,13	-0,21	0,06	0,11
J	0,00	3,90	0,13	0,21	0,06	0,11
K	1,70	4,70	0,14	0,21	0,07	0,10
L	5,00	5,70	-0,14	-0,21	0,07	0,10
M	5,00	4,70	0,14	0,21	0,07	0,10
N	8,30	5,70	-0,14	-0,21	0,07	0,10
O	0,00	3,90	0,21	-0,14	0,07	0,10
P	2,60	0,00	-0,21	0,14	0,07	0,10
Q	4,90	4,70	-0,13	-0,21	0,07	0,11
R	2,60	0,00	0,13	0,21	0,07	0,11
S	4,90	0,00	0,14	0,21	0,07	0,10
T	9,20	0,00	-0,14	0,21	0,07	0,10

TABLE II. TABLE OF PARAMETERS FOR KINECT PLACEMENT

Kinect RGB-D Camera	L	λ	X_{UCS}	Y_{UCS}
A	3,00	1,37°	$X_{CORNER} + Y'_{RGB-D}$	$Y_{CORNER} + X'_{RGB-D}$
B	3,40	1,10°	$X_{CORNER} - Y'_{RGB-D}$	$Y_{CORNER} - X'_{RGB-D}$
C	1,50	2,63°	$X_{CORNER} + X'_{RGB-D}$	$Y_{CORNER} + Y'_{RGB-D}$
D	1,50	2,63°	$X_{CORNER} - X'_{RGB-D}$	$Y_{CORNER} - Y'_{RGB-D}$
E	2,50	1,61°	$X_{CORNER} + X'_{RGB-D}$	$Y_{CORNER} - Y'_{RGB-D}$
F	2,50	1,61°	$X_{CORNER} - X'_{RGB-D}$	$Y_{CORNER} - Y'_{RGB-D}$
G	2,20	1,82°	$X_{CORNER} + X'_{RGB-D}$	$Y_{CORNER} + Y'_{RGB-D}$
H	3,20	1,26°	$X_{CORNER} - X'_{RGB-D}$	$Y_{CORNER} - Y'_{RGB-D}$
I	1,70	2,33°	$X_{CORNER} - X'_{RGB-D}$	$Y_{CORNER} - Y'_{RGB-D}$
J	1,70	2,33°	$X_{CORNER} + X'_{RGB-D}$	$Y_{CORNER} + Y'_{RGB-D}$
K	3,30	1,23°	$X_{CORNER} + X'_{RGB-D}$	$Y_{CORNER} + Y'_{RGB-D}$
L	3,30	1,23°	$X_{CORNER} - X'_{RGB-D}$	$Y_{CORNER} - Y'_{RGB-D}$
M	3,30	1,23°	$X_{CORNER} + X'_{RGB-D}$	$Y_{CORNER} + Y'_{RGB-D}$
N	3,30	1,23°	$X_{CORNER} - X'_{RGB-D}$	$Y_{CORNER} - Y'_{RGB-D}$
O	3,90	1,04°	$X_{CORNER} + Y'_{RGB-D}$	$Y_{CORNER} - X'_{RGB-D}$
P	4,70	0,87°	$X_{CORNER} - Y'_{RGB-D}$	$Y_{CORNER} + X'_{RGB-D}$
Q	2,30	1,74°	$X_{CORNER} - X'_{RGB-D}$	$Y_{CORNER} - Y'_{RGB-D}$
R	2,30	1,74°	$X_{CORNER} + X'_{RGB-D}$	$Y_{CORNER} + Y'_{RGB-D}$
S	4,30	0,94°	$X_{CORNER} + X'_{RGB-D}$	$Y_{CORNER} + Y'_{RGB-D}$
T	4,30	0,94°	$X_{CORNER} - X'_{RGB-D}$	$Y_{CORNER} + Y'_{RGB-D}$

$$\begin{cases} X_{E,UCS} = 3,60 + X'_{E,RGB-D} \\ Y_{E,UCS} = 7,10 - Y'_{E,RGB-D} \end{cases} \tag{23}$$

where $X'_{E,RGB-D}$ and $Y'_{E,RGB-D}$ are obtained by (24).

$$\begin{cases} X'_{E,RGB-D} = 0,07 + d_{E,RGB-D} \cdot \cos\theta \\ Y'_{E,RGB-D} = 0,11 + d_{E,RGB-D} \cdot \sin\theta \end{cases} \tag{24}$$

$d_{E,RGB-D}$ and θ are calculated with (25) and (26) respectively.

$$d_{E,RGB-D} = \sqrt{Z^2_{E,RGB-D} + X^2_{E,RGB-D}} \tag{25}$$

$$\theta = 35 - 1,61 - \arcsin\left(\frac{X_{E,RGB-D}}{d_{E,RGB-D}}\right) \tag{26}$$

Finally, (27) shows how to obtain $X_{E,UCS}$ and $Y_{E,UCS}$ coordinates from the Kinect coordinates $X_{E,RGB-D}$ and $Y_{E,RGB-D}$.

$$\begin{cases} X_{E,UCS} = 3,67 + d_{E,RGB-D} \\ \quad \cdot \cos\left(33,39 - \arcsin\left(\frac{X_{E,RGB-D}}{d_{E,RGB-D}}\right)\right) \\ Y_{E,UCS} = 6,99 - d_{E,RGB-D} \\ \quad \cdot \sin\left(33,39 - \arcsin\left(\frac{X_{E,RGB-D}}{d_{E,RGB-D}}\right)\right) \end{cases} \tag{27}$$

The combination of WPS and RGB-D trajectories has been performed using the *Synchronized Euclidean distance* [15], as detailed in [2]. The developed experiments have shown an important advance in terms of indoor positioning. The system is able to locate more than 10 people with a success over 95% (see Figure 6) in a scenario with multiple rooms.

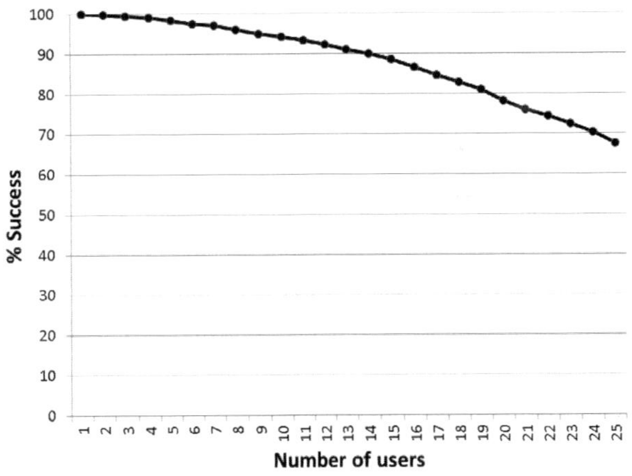

Figure 6. Results for a different number of users

V. CONCLUSIONS

This work presents an extended method for indoor positioning based on a previously developed algorithm, which worked exclusively with one room. This new method allows obtaining indoor positioning inside a complete floor or building. Twenty RGB-D sensors have been used to obtain the *depth maps* and, subsequently, the skeletons of users. The combination of wireless networks with skeletons is a simple and economical method to increase the performance of WPS in interiors. The generalization of the previous IPS allows obtaining the user positions in large areas where there are several users. The trajectories of users can be obtained by combining the two considered information sources: the WPS trajectories and the trajectories of the skeletons of the users in the *depth map*. Although the positioning of the wireless sensors in the complete scenario does not represent a real problem, special attention has been paid to the location of the depth cameras. The purpose of this has been to avoid blind areas, minimizing the total uncovered area. The work has also shown how coordinates obtained from the depth cameras at different rooms are transformed into a universal coordinates system (UCS). At this point, the previous technique can be applied to obtain users positions and trajectories. The position of the sensors is followed by [16], where authors consider the use of this system to obtain the positions of the users in a museum, being this an approach to enrich the indoor users experience.

CONFLICTS OF INTEREST

The authors declare that there is no conflict of interest regarding the publication of this manuscript.

ACKNOWLEDGMENTS

This work has been developed with the help of the research projects DPI2013-44776-R and DPI2016-77677-P of MICINN. It also belongs to the activities carried out within the framework of the research network CAM RoboCity2030 S2013/MIT-2748 of Comunidad de Madrid

REFERENCES

[1] G. Deak, K. Curran, and J. Condell, "A survey of active and passive indoor localisation systems," Computer Communications, vol. 35, no. 16, 2012, pp. 1939–1954.

[2] J. Duque Domingo, C. Cerrada, E. Valero, and J. Cerrada, "Indoor positioning system using depth maps and wireless networks," Journal of Sensors, vol. 2016, 2016.

[3] W. Liu, Y. Chen, Y. Xiong, L. Sun, and H. Zhu, "Optimization of sampling cell size for fingerprint positioning," International Journal of Distributed Sensor Networks, vol. 2014, 2014.

[4] S. He and S.-H. G. Chan, "Wi-fi fingerprint-based indoor positioning: Recent advances and comparisons," IEEE Communications Surveys & Tutorials, vol. 18, no. 1, 2016, pp. 466–490.

[5] G. Ye, Y. Liu, Y. Deng, N. Hasler, X. Ji, Q. Dai, and C. Theobalt, "Free-viewpoint video of human actors using multiple handheld kinects," Cybernetics, IEEE Transactions on, vol. 43, no. 5, 2013, pp. 1370–1382.

[6] H. Takizawa, S. Yamaguchi, M. Aoyagi, N. Ezaki, and S. Mizuno, "Kinect cane: object recognition aids for the visually impaired," in Human System Interaction (HSI), 2013 The 6th International Conference on. IEEE, 2013, pp. 473–478.

[7] Y. Nakano, K. Izutsu, K. Tajitsu, K. Kai, and T. Tatsumi, "Kinect positioning system (kps) and its potential applications," in International Conference on Indoor Positioning and Indoor Navigation, vol. 13, 2012, p. 15th.

[8] C. K. Schindhelm, "Evaluating slam approaches for microsoft kinect," in Proc. 2011 The Eighth International Conference on Wireless and Mobile Communications (ICWMC 2012), Venice, 2012, pp. 402–407.

[9] P. Mirowski, R. Palaniappan, and T. K. Ho, "Depth camera slam on a low-cost wifi mapping robot," in Technologies for Practical Robot Applications (TePRA), 2012 IEEE International Conference on. IEEE, 2012, pp. 1–6.

[10] J. Machaj and P. Brida, "Impact of optimization algorithms on hybrid indoor positioning based on gsm and wi-fi signals," Concurrency and Computation: Practice and Experience, 2016.

[11] A. Papapostolou and H. Chaouchi, "Integrating rfid and wlan for indoor positioning and ip movement detection," Wireless Networks, vol. 18, no. 7, 2012, pp. 861–879.

[12] J. Biswas and M. Veloso, "Multi-sensor mobile robot localization for diverse environments," in RoboCup 2013: Robot World Cup XVII. Springer, 2014, pp. 468–479.

[13] J. Shotton, T. Sharp, A. Kipman, A. Fitzgibbon, M. Finocchio, A. Blake, M. Cook, and R. Moore, "Real-time human pose recognition in parts from single depth images," Communications of the ACM, vol. 56, no. 1, 2013, pp. 116–124.

[14] A. Barmpoutis, "Tensor body: Real-time reconstruction of the human body and avatar synthesis from rgb-d," Cybernetics, IEEE Transactions on, vol. 43, no. 5, 2013, pp. 1347–1356.

[15] C. T. Lawson, S. Ravi, and J.-H. Hwang, "Compression and mining of gps trace data: New techniques and applications," Technical Report. Region II University Transportation Research Center, Tech. Rep., 2011.

[16] J. Duque-Domingo, P. J. Herrera, E. Valero, and C. Cerrada, "Deciphering egyptian hieroglyphs: Towards a new strategy for navigation in museums," Sensors, vol. 17, no. 3, 2017, p. 589.

Delay-Aware Network Optimization in LTE Based High-Speed Railway Wireless Networks

Ali Huseyin Rustem
Department of Electronics and Communications Engineering
Istanbul Technical Univeristy
Istanbul, Turkey
Email: rustom@itu.edu.tr

Selcuk Cevher
Department of Computer Engineering
Karadeniz Technical University
Trabzon, Turkey
Email: cevhers@ktu.edu.tr

Hakan Ali Cirpan
Department of Electronics and Communications Engineering
Istanbul Technical Univeristy
Istanbul, Turkey
Email: cirpanh@itu.edu.tr

***Abstract*—This paper presents an extended joint resource optimization framework for multi-service transmissions in high-speed railway (HSR) wireless networks by introducing the average delay constraint into the dynamic resource management problem. The system utility is maximized under the constraints of average delay, queue stability and average power by formulating a joint stochastic problem, which is transformed into a queue stability problem. Using Lyapunov drift theory, the queue stability problem is decomposed into separate convex subproblems. Golden section search method is used to achieve a globally optimal solution for the resource allocation subproblem. Finally, a distributed dynamic resource management technique is proposed, and its performance is evaluated under realistic conditions for HSR wireless networks. Numerical simulations show that our approach provides an improved throughput performance while satisfying the average delay requirements.**

Keywords*—*High-speed railway wireless networks; Delay requirements.

I. Introduction

High-speed railway (HSR) has been deployed worldwide as the dominant fast public transportation system [1][2]. HSR infrastructure features an increasing amount of control and multimedia transmissions to ensure the safety and efficiency of the transportation, and to support the increasing demand from passengers for the Internet services. Since GSM for railway (GSM-R) offers limited data transmission capabilities and inefficient radio resource usage [3], alternative communication systems should be investigated to support the increasing traffic demand. Therefore, the deployment of wideband wireless communication technologies is an urgent need for the operation of HSR to provide reliable and robust connection with the central control systems, and to offer seamless Internet access for passengers. Long Term Evolution (LTE) is envisioned as the leading candidate to replace GSM-R for the future railway infrastructures due to its packet-switched network architecture with high data transmission capacities and low latency [4].

In a conventional cellular network infrastructure, mobile terminals have a direct communication with the base stations. This type of direct communication fails in HSR environment due to high penetration loss, severe Doppler frequency shift, and high rate of drop calls and handovers [5]. Figure 1 shows an LTE-based HSR network architecture, which avoids the drawbacks of the conventional HSR infrastructure by providing a two-hop communication between the passengers and base stations [1][5]. In this architecture, multiple access points (APs) are placed within the train, and a relay station (RS) with powerful antennas is mounted on top of the train. APs provide the passengers with an indirect communication with a high transmission rate to the RS, which in turn, directly communicates with the LTE-compliant base stations (eNBs) located along the rail line. The evolved packet core (EPC) network of LTE is connected to eNBs via wired lines, and provides a high performance communication between the train and Internet to support the operational and multimedia traffic along the journey. EPC is composed of Mobility Management Entity (MME), Serving Gateway (S-GW) and Packet Data Network Gateway (PDN-GW). The increasing amount of wireless traffic in HSR [6] necessitates the development of radio resource management (RRM) techniques to enable the efficient resource utilization [1]. However, the design of such techniques is quite challenging due to the very dynamic channel conditions between the fast moving train and eNBs, and the operational and passenger services with heterogeneous QoS requirements [7][8]. RRM techniques for HSR wireless networks should jointly optimize the different aspects of resource allocation, admission and power control while observing different network constraints to maximize the

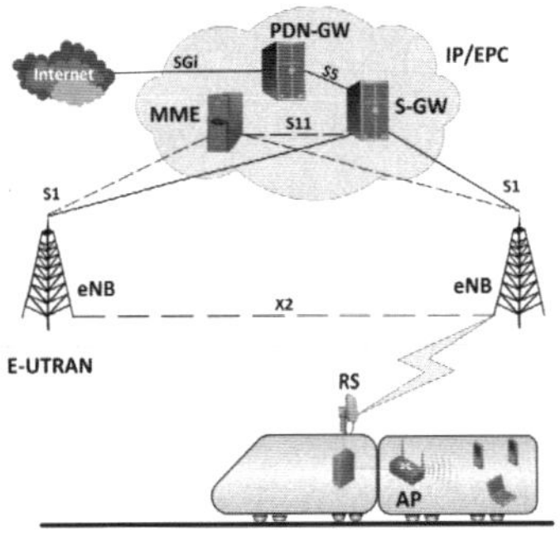

Figure 1. LTE-based HSR network infrastructure

system performance. This optimization should be performed in a cross-layer manner by considering the distinctive parameters of the physical, medium access control (MAC), and application layers. Furthermore, it should manage the inherent trade-offs between these layers in a comprehensive close-to-optimal manner.

The work in [9] investigates the downlink resource allocation in relay-assisted HSR communication systems. It aims to minimize the average end-to-end delay through scheduling actions under the service delivery ratio constraints. In [10], an admission control scheme with the complete-sharing resource allocation model is proposed for LTE-R system to maximize the number of admitted services while guaranteeing their related QoS requirements of each service class. The proposed admission control scheme gives high priority to on-going services and guarantees the full use of system bandwidth resource. The work in [11] studies the utility-based resource allocation problem in HSR wireless networks by jointly considering the power control and packet allocation among services. A joint optimal design of admission control and resource allocation for multimedia service delivery in HSR wireless networks is studied in [12]. A stochastic network optimization problem is formulated to maximize the system utility while stabilizing all transmission queues under the average power constraint. Using the same approach as [12], the work in [13] introduces average delay constraints to the multi-service transmission problem, with a focus only on resource allocation and power control.

In this paper, we combine the cross-layer RRM schemes in [12] and [13] in a more general optimal framework. Thus, we present a delay-aware optimization framework, which jointly optimizes the resource allocation, admission and power control in LTE-based HSR wireless networks. Our framework extends the previous work [12] by introducing an additional delay constraint, inspired by [13], to the dynamic network management of HSR infrastructure, and, hence, maximizing the throughput performance of the network while jointly optimizing the aforementioned aspects. Specifically, we formulate and investigate a cross-layer optimization problem to jointly optimize the network resources under the constraints of average delay, queue stability and power to maximize the system utility. Finally, we propose a dynamic resource management algorithm to guarantee the joint optimization of the studied aspects, and evaluate its performance through numerical simulations showing that our algorithm provides an improved throughput performance while considering the delay requirement.

The rest of this paper is organized as follows. In Section II, HSR network constraints are discussed. In Section III, the stochastic optimization problem is formulated. In Section IV, the application of the Lyapunov drift theory to solve the optimization problem is explained. In Section V, problem decomposition is described, and our dynamic resource management algorithm is presented. In Section VI, our numerical results are reported. In Section VII, our paper is concluded.

II. HSR Network Constraints

In this paper, we aim at improving the throughput performance in HSR wireless networks by dynamically optimizing the management functions. Our optimization framework considers certain constraints whose averages are evaluated over the journey of the train. Assuming that a set $\mathcal{K} \triangleq \{1, 2, ..., K\}$ of services is supported by a slot-based HSR wireless transmission network, and $\bar{x}$ represents the long-term time average expectation for any quantity x, time average constraints are explained below:

A. Average Delay

LTE-based HSR wireless networks are envisioned to offer broadband multimedia services for both passengers and railway operators. These services may be sensitive in varying degrees to the transmission delay so that heterogeneous delay requirements must be taken into account when optimizing the network resources.

Let $\overline{W_k}$ denote the average time that a packet spends in a queue k. According to the Little's law in queuing theory [14], $\overline{W_k} = \overline{Q_k}\ \lambda_k$, where $\overline{Q_k}$ and λ_k represent the average number of packets located in the queue (i.e. average queue backlog), and the average arrival rate of the packets, respectively. Average delay constraint for any queue requires that $\overline{W_k}$ be upper bounded by the maximum time $W_k^{\max}$ during which a packet can stay in any queue. $W_k^{\max}$ depends on the type and QoS requirements of the services. Average delay constraint for any queue k can be expressed as:

$$\overline{Q_k} \leq W_k^{\max} \lambda_k, \quad \forall k \in \mathcal{K}. \tag{1}$$

B. Queue Stability

Since the LTE-based HSR infrastructure has a packet-switched network architecture, buffering is involved at networking devices requiring the stability of the queues to be taken into consideration. According to [14], a queue is strongly stable if it has a bounded time average backlog, $\overline{Q_k} \leq \infty$.

Intuitively, if the inequality (1) holds for any queue, it implies the stability of the queue. Thus, the satisfaction of the average delay constraint implies the satisfaction of the queue stability constraint [13].

C. Average Power

In an LTE-based HSR wireless network, channel conditions dynamically change with respect to the time-varying distance between the eNBs and the train [6][8]. Therefore, the transmit power $P(t)$ should be dynamically adjusted according to this time-varying distance to ensure a reliable communication. However, at any time slot t during the trip, $P(t)$ must be limited between the maximum and average transmit powers, namely, $P_{\max}$ and P_{av}, respectively. The average power constraint can be expressed as:

$$\overline{P} \leq P_{\text{av}}. \tag{2}$$

III. Problem Formulation

The throughput performance of a multi-service stochastic network can be improved by maximizing:

$$\sum_{k\in\mathcal{K}} \phi_k(\overline{r_k}), \quad (3)$$

where ϕ_k is a nondecreasing concave continuous utility function representing the throughput benefit for a service k while $\overline{r_k}$ represents the average throughput. It is difficult to maximize this objective function since it requires the maximization of individual functions of time averages [7]. Therefore, it can be transformed into the following problem to facilitate the maximization process:

$$\begin{aligned} \text{maximize} \quad & \sum_{k\in\mathcal{K}} \overline{\phi_k(\gamma_k)} && (4a)\\ \text{subject to} \quad & \overline{P} \leq P_{\text{av}}, && (4b)\\ & \overline{Q_k} \leq W_k^{\max}\lambda_k, \quad \forall k \in \mathcal{K}, && (4c)\\ & \overline{\gamma_k} \leq \overline{r_k}, \quad \forall k \in \mathcal{K}, && (4d) \end{aligned}$$

where $\gamma_k(t)$ is an auxiliary variable upper bounded by the average throughput [12].

The dynamics of each queue $Q_k(t+1)$, that is, the number of packets located in a queue at time slot $t+1$, are controlled by admission control action $r_k(t)$ and resource allocation action $\mu_k(t)$ as follows:

$$Q_k(t+1) = Q_k(t) - \mu_k(t) + r_k(t), \quad \forall k \in \mathcal{K}, \quad (5)$$

where $r_k(t)$ and $\mu_k(t)$ represents the number of newly arrived packets to be stored into the queue and number of packets removed from the queue for transmission, respectively. These control actions should be jointly decided to maximize the objective function (4a) under the time average constraints.

IV. Lyapunov Optimization

In this section, similar to [12] and [13], Lyapunov optimization theory is used to transform the original problem into a queue stability problem by introducing virtual queues. Then, Lyapunov drift is applied to jointly stabilize these queues. Our Lyaponuv drift is different from [12] and [13] since we use a different combination of virtual queues.

A. *Queue Stability Problem Transformation*

To facilitate the problem transformation and the satisfaction of the time average constraints, the work in [12] and [13] introduces the virtual queues $X_k(t)$, $Y_k(t)$ and $Z_k(t)$ with the following dynamic update equations:

$$X_k(t+1) = \max[X_k(t) - W_k^{\max}\lambda_k, 0] + Q_k(t+1), \quad (6)$$

$$Y_k(t+1) = \max[Y_k(t) - P_{\text{av}}, 0] + P(t), \quad (7)$$

$$Z_k(t+1) = \max[Z_k(t) - r_k(t), 0] + \gamma_k(t). \quad (8)$$

The stabilization of the virtual queues $X_k(t)$, $Y_k(t)$ and $Z_k(t)$ ensures that the respective inequalities (4c), (4b) and (4d) hold [14].

B. *Lyapunov Drift*

Assuming that $\mathbf{X}(t)$, $\mathbf{Y}(t)$ and $\mathbf{Z}(t)$ represent the respective vectors of $X_k(t)$, $Y_k(t)$ and $Z_k(t)$, and $\mathbf{\Theta}(t) \triangleq [\mathbf{X}^T(t), \mathbf{Y}^T(t), \mathbf{Z}^T(t)]^T$ denotes the combined vector, the quadratic Lyapunov function is defined as:

$$L(\mathbf{\Theta}(t)) \triangleq \frac{1}{2}\sum_{k\in\mathcal{K}} (X_k(t)^2 + Y_k(t)^2 + Z_k(t)^2). \quad (9)$$

The one-slot conditional Lyapunov drift $\Delta(\mathbf{\Theta}(t))$ at time t is given by:

$$\Delta(\mathbf{\Theta}(t)) \triangleq \mathbb{E}[L(\mathbf{\Theta}(t+1)) - L(\mathbf{\Theta}(t))|\mathbf{\Theta}(t)]. \quad (10)$$

Minimizing the drift (10) ensures that all virtual queues are jointly stable and the desired constraints are satisfied.

In [12] and [13], the following inequalities are obtained by squaring the equations (6), (7) and (8) to further simplify the drift:

$$\begin{aligned} X_k(t+1)^2 - X_k(t)^2 \leq{}& Q_k(t+1)^2 + (W_k^{\max}\lambda_k)^2 \\ &+ 2X_k(t)(Q_k(t+1) - W_k^{\max}\lambda_k), \quad (11) \end{aligned}$$

$$\begin{aligned} Y_k(t+1)^2 - Y_k(t)^2 \leq{}& P(t)^2 + P_{\text{av}}^2 \\ &+ 2Y_k(t)(P(t) - P_{\text{av}}), \quad (12) \end{aligned}$$

$$\begin{aligned} Z_k(t+1)^2 - Z_k(t)^2 \leq{}& \gamma_k(t)^2 + r_k(t)^2 \\ &+ 2Z_k(t)(\gamma_k(t) - r_k(t)). \quad (13) \end{aligned}$$

Replacing the inequalities (9) and (10), the following inequality is obtained:

$$\Delta(\mathbf{\Theta}(t)) \leq \frac{1}{2}D + \mathbb{E}[G(t)|\mathbf{\Theta}(t)], \quad (14)$$

where D is a finite constant and $G(t)$ is defined to be:

$$\begin{aligned} G(t) \triangleq \sum_{k\in\mathcal{K}} [&X_k(t)(Q_k(t) - \mu_k(t) + r_k(t) - W_k^{\max}\lambda_k) \\ &+ Z_k(t)(\gamma_k(t) - r_k(t)) + Y_k(t)(P(t) - P_{\text{av}})]. \quad (15) \end{aligned}$$

Minimizing the drift (10) can be facilitated by minimizing the upper bound of inequality (14). Since D is constant, it is sufficient to minimize the expectation $\mathbb{E}[G(t)|\mathbf{\Theta}(t)]$, which can be achieved by only minimizing $\mathbb{E}[G(t)]$ [14]. All queues can be stabilized while maximizing the sum of the utility functions by greedily minimizing the following "drift-plus-penalty" expression [12]:

$$\mathbb{E}[G(t) - V\sum_{k\in\mathcal{K}} \phi_k(\gamma_k(t))], \quad (16)$$

where V is a non-negative control parameter that balances between the maximization of the system utility and the satisfaction of the constraints.

V. Our Dynamic Resource Management Algorithm

The objective function (16) can be minimized by jointly optimizing $\mu_k(t)$, $r_k(t)$, $P(t)$ and $\gamma_k(t)$ at each time slot t. By isolating these control variables, the objective function can be easily decomposed into three separated subproblems, namely, utility maximization, admission control, and resource allocation.

In [12], utility maximization subproblem is solved by tracking $Z_k(t)$ to determine the optimum $\gamma_k(t)$, while a simple threshold-based admission control strategy is proposed for solving the admission control subproblem to obtain $r_k(t)$. Since a larger $\mu_k(t)$ demands a larger $P(t)$, a mixed integer programming (MIP) problem with a continuous variable $P(t)$ and an integer variable $\mu_k(t)$ is designed in [13] to jointly optimize $P(t)$ and $\mu_k(t)$. This MIP problem is then transformed into an equivalent single variable problem, and a static resource management algorithm, based on the golden section search method, is proposed to solve the problem with a guaranteed global optimality.

We propose a distributed dynamic resource management algorithm to jointly optimize the network resources by combining the solutions to utility maximization, admission control, and resource allocation subproblems provided in [12] and [13]. Our algorithm aims at improving the system utility under average delay, queue stability, and power constraints.

The distributed algorithm is described in Figure 2. All system parameters and queue vectors are initialized before the beginning of the trip. Then, during the trip, for each time slot t and each service k, the three aforementioned subproblems are solved to obtain the optimal control variables. The auxiliary variable $\gamma_k(t)$ is determined according to [12], while admission control action $r_k(t)$ is decided via a threshold-based admission control strategy by tracking $X_k(t)$. Resource allocation action $\mu_k(t)$ and power control action $P(t)$ are jointly obtained by calling Static Resource Management Algorithm in [13]. At the end of each slot t, each queue vector k is updated according to (5), (6), (7), and (8). This algorithm will be repeated for all time slots, from the origin station to the destination station.

Algorithm 1 Dynamic Resource Management Algorithm

Initialize V, $Q_k(0) = 0$, $X_k(0) = 0$, $Y_k(0) = 0$, $Z_k(0) = 0$ for all $k \in \mathcal{K}$;
while $t \in [0, T]$ **do**
  for $k = 1$ *to* $\mathcal{K}$ **do**
    Obtain the optimal $\gamma_k(t)$ inspired by [12];
    Obtain the optimal $r_k(t)$ by using threshold-based admission control strategy [12];
    Obtain the optimal $P(t)$ and $\mu_k(t)$ by calling Static Resource Management Algorithm [13];
    Update $Q_k(t+1)$, $X_k(t+1)$, $Y_k(t+1)$, and $Z_k(t+1)$ according to (5), (6), (7), and (8), respectively;
  end for
end while

Figure 2. Distributed Dynamic Resource Management Algorithm.

VI. Simulation Results

Our algorithm for dynamic resource management is implemented using MATLAB. Table I summarizes the realistic parameters, according to [7][11][12], used in our simulations. To perform each simulation, our algorithm is executed for 30,000 time slots during which the train moves between the centers of two adjacent cells. In this section, we present comparison results for our scheme and the reference model in [12]; therefore, we use the piecewise linear utility function for all services, namely, $\phi_k(r_k) = \nu_k \min[r_k, \lambda_k]$, where ν_k represents the service priority.

TABLE I. SIMULATION PARAMETERS.

Parameter	Description	Value
P_{av}	Average power constraint	35 W
P_{max}	Maximum transit power	45 W
H	System bandwidth	5 MHz
L	Packet size	240 bits
T_s	Slot duration	1 ms
α	Pathloss exponent	4
λ_k	Packet arrival rate	25 packet/slot
v	Constant moving speed	350 km/h
R	Cell radius	1.5 km
d_0	Distance between BS and rail	50 m
K	Number of services	6

Figure 4 shows the average delay and average power consumption achieved by our algorithm for different values of V. The priority for all services is selected to be $\nu_k = 10$ in this simulation. Figure 4a shows that, in all cases, our algorithm achieves an average delay which increases with respect to V until it reaches a saturation point. However, as shown in the figure, a larger W_k^{max} leads to a higher average delay for a certain value of V. Since the work in [12] does not consider the delay constraint, the average delay achieved by the reference model keeps increasing for all values of V without reaching a saturation point. These results indicate that our algorithm fully satisfies the average delay constraints in our simulations. On the other hand, Figure 4b demonstrates that our scheme will cause a slightly larger average power consumption for the small values of V compared to the reference model while still satisfying the average power constraint.

Figure 3 presents the throughput performances of our scheme and the reference model for varying values of V. W_k^{max} is selected to be 10 in all cases for this simulation. For the small values of V within the range $[0, 15]$, the average throughput for all service priorities (ν_k) increases with respect to V. However, Figure 3a shows that the services of higher priorities achieve a larger throughput performance. On the other hand, for the larger values of V, the average throughput achieved by the services with low priorities has a slightly decreasing trend while continuing to increase for the services with high priorities. The results in Figure 3a indicate that our scheme mostly yields better throughput performance than the reference model for the low values of V. Figure 3b shows that the performance improvement achieved by our algorithm costs a slight increase in the average power consumption within the range of 5 watt. Providing better performance for the low values of V is favorable since high values of V result in more packets to be admitted into the buffers, which necessitates larger buffer size and higher power consumption.

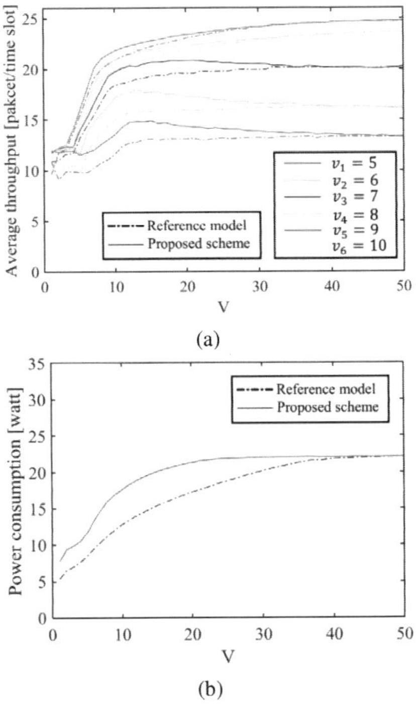

Figure 3. Average throughput and average power consumption achieved by our algorithm for different service priorities.

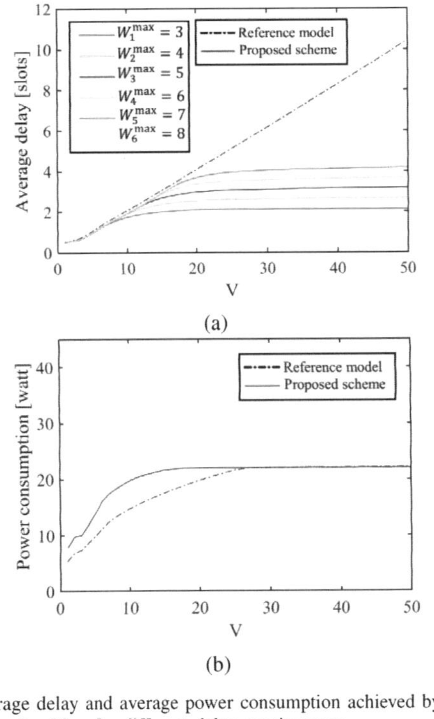

Figure 4. Average delay and average power consumption achieved by our algorithm for different delay requirements.

VII. Conclusion

This paper presents an extended joint resource optimization framework for admission control, power control and resource allocation in LTE-based HSR wireless networks. Our work introduces an average delay constraint to the formulation of dynamic management problem of HSR wireless networks. A joint optimization problem is designed to maximize the system utility under the constraints of average delay, queue stability and average power. The problem is then transformed into a queue stability problem, which is decomposed into the separable convex subproblems using Lyapunov drift theory. Golden section search method is used to solve the resource allocation subproblem, and a dynamic resource management algorithm is proposed to achieve the joint optimization of the network resources. Finally, we perform numerical simulations which show that our proposed model fully satisfies the average delay requirements and significantly improves the throughput performance of HSR wireless networks.

Acknowledgment

This work was supported in part by the Scientific and Technical Research Council of Turkey, TUBITAK, with grant no. TEYDEB-1140093.

References

[1] S. Xu, G. Zhu, B. Ai, and Z. Zhong, "A survey on high-speed railway communications: A radio resource management perspective," Computer Communications, vol. 86, 2016, pp. 12–28.

[2] D. T. Fokum and V. S. Frost, "A survey on methods for broadband internet access on trains," IEEE communications surveys & tutorials, vol. 12, no. 2, 2010, pp. 171–185.

[3] A. Sniady and J. Soler, "An overview of GSM-R technology and its shortcomings," in ITS Telecommunications (ITST), 2012 12th International Conference on. IEEE, 2012, pp. 626–629.

[4] Y. Sun, C.-Y. Lee, J.-m. Jo, J.-h. Lee, and Y.-J. Han, "Study on the effectiveness of high-speed railway communication and signaling system based on 4g lte technology," in Control, Automation and Systems (ICCAS), 2013 13th International Conference on. IEEE, 2013, pp. 402–406.

[5] Y. Zhou, Z. Pan, J. Hu, J. Shi, and X. Mo, "Broadband wireless communications on high speed trains," in Wireless and Optical Communications Conference (WOCC), 2011 20th Annual. IEEE, 2011, pp. 1–6.

[6] L. Liu, et al. "Position-based modeling for wireless channel on high-speed railway under a viaduct at 2.35 GHz," IEEE Journal on Selected Areas in Communications, vol. 30, no. 4, 2012, pp. 834–845.

[7] G. Jung and K. M. Sim, "Location-aware dynamic resource allocation model for cloud computing environment," in International Conference on Information and Computer Applications (ICICA), IACSIT Press, Singapore. Citeseer, 2012

[8] R. He, Z. Zhong, B. Ai, and J. Ding, "An empirical path loss model and fading analysis for high-speed railway viaduct scenarios," IEEE antennas and wireless propagation letters, vol. 10, 2011, pp. 808–812.

[9] S. Xu, G. Zhu, C. Shen, Y. Lei, and Z. Zhong, "Delay-aware online service scheduling in high-speed railway communication systems," Mathematical Problems in Engineering, vol. 2014, 2014.

[10] Q. Xu, X. Li, H. Ji, and L. Yao, "Radio admission control scheme for high-speed railway scenario: An optimal accepted service number approach," in Information and Communications Technology 2013, National Doctoral Academic Forum on. IET, 2013, pp. 1–6.

[11] S. Xu, G. Zhu, C. Shen, Y. Lei, and Z. Zhong, "Utility-based resource allocation in high-speed railway wireless networks," EURASIP Journal on Wireless Communications and Networking, vol. 2014, no. 1, 2014, pp. 1–14.

[12] S. Xu, G. Zhu, C. Shen, Y. Lei, and Z. Zhong, "Analysis and optimization of resource control in high-speed railway wireless networks," Mathematical Problems in Engineering, vol. 2014, 2014.
[13] S. Xu, G. Zhu, C. Shen, S. Li, and Z. Zhong, "Delay-aware dynamic resource management for high-speed railway wireless communications," in Vehicular Technology Conference (VTC Spring), 2016 IEEE 83rd. IEEE, 2016, pp. 1–5.
[14] M. J. Neely, "Stochastic network optimization with application to communication and queueing systems," Synthesis Lectures on Communication Networks, vol. 3, no. 1, 2010, pp. 1–211.

Battery-less Near Field Communication Sensor Tag Energy Study with ContactLess Simulator

David Navarro, Guilherme Migliato-Marega, and Laurent Carrel
Université de Lyon, ECL, INSA Lyon, UCBL, CPE
INL, UMR5270
F-69134, Ecully, France
david.navarro@ec-lyon.fr, guilherme.migliato-marega@ecl15.ec-lyon.fr, laurent.carrel@ec-lyon.fr

***Abstract*—ContactLess Simulator (CLS) was used to simulate a smart tag composed of a Near Field Communication (NFC) circuit, a microcontroller unit and a temperature sensor. More precisely, our study focuses on battery-less electronic systems: sensor and microcontroller are supplied by the NFC circuit. To prove such a system can function, energy budget has to be explored; this is the aim of this simulator. This paper describes the battery-less electronic system we considered, and simulation results prove that each NFC reading of the tag will recharge it for 44 cycles of autonomous functioning (temperature sensing, data logging).**

Keywords-Simulation; Modeling; NFC; Microcontroller; MCU; Energy harvesting.

I. INTRODUCTION

Internet of Things (IoT) is now a well-known ecosystem where physical small and smart objects interact trough communicating networks. These networks are wired or wireless; the trend is the closer to the object, the more often wireless. Small size and wireless communication give faster and easier installation and deployment. Typical architecture of these objects is also composed of several parts from this list: sensors, actuators, central processing unit, communicating device.

Wireless powering systems exist since several years, and are nowadays widespread in powering systems, such as smartphones wireless chargers [1]. Moreover, certain lightweight systems communicate at the same time they power the object. It is the case in RadioFrequency IDentification systems (RFID). They are composed of an emitter and a receiver that is called tag. The emitter sends radiofrequency waves in order to power and communicate at the same time. A classical tag receives radiofrequency waves to power itself, and sends its unique identification number. Near Field Communication (NFC) is based on RFID. It permits very short communications at a high frequency, in a full peer-to-peer mode. NFC inherits characteristics from RFID, network and smart card. It is suitable for secure communications; as an example, smartphone payment is possible with NFC.

This paper focusses on energy study of a NFC battery-less tag. The energy is the major constraint of these systems. A new simulator has been developed in order to study these electronic systems. It is called CLS: ContactLess Simulator. Section II describes the existing simulators in this field. Section III specifies the hardware NFC we consider. Section IV presents the models that are implemented in the simulator. Section V details the test-case results.

II. RELATED WORK

RFID and NFC simulators are numerous. As RFID and NFC systems are electronic and communicating objects, they can be studied at different levels: low-level (hardware, software) or high-level (protocol, network). Many studies involve hardware platforms, like [2]. This study does not consider the so-called "simulation platforms" that are in reality hardware-based measurements system. It is only focused on simulation, with no hardware interaction.

Low-level simulations focus hardware or radiofrequency aspects. For example, Ahn et al. [3] describe a MATLAB-Simulink model of a radiofrequency transceiver in order to provide a quick evaluation of the performances according to noise and non-linearity of each individual block in the transceiver.

Cheng et al. [4] present studies on physical link (emitter, air, receiver) and radiofrequency propagation aspects. Deckmar et al. [5] gives a MATLAB Simulink NFC model for radiofrequency modulation study.

High-level simulations consider protocols, network and communication performance. RFIDSIM is a more complete simulator that considers physical link and protocol [6]. It provides a realistic physical layer and permits a multi-interface and multi-channel analysis. Others higher-level simulators focus on communication protocol and communication performance, such as the well-known NS-3 simulator. NFC models and protocol study have been developed over NS-3 [7].

Thus, RFID or NFC simulators that consider energy aspects are missing. We have developed a graphical simulator for NFC systems. Novelty is that it is focused on energy, and simulations that were done were validated by hardware measurements. We consider energy harvesting from NFC emitter and energy balance according to the tag electrical consumption. The wireless-supplied tag is not only composed of a classical NFC circuit, but of a more complex smart system. It is described in Section III.

III. CONSIDERED NFC SYSTEM

A typical NFC system is composed of an emitter and a tag. It is shown in Fig. 1. The emitter sends energy and data. Tag is supplied at this moment, and it answers requests. The tag is often composed of a NFC circuit that comprises 2 main blocks: energy harvesting block and data decoding block.

The energy harvesting block converts the received electromagnetic field into usable energy in order to supply the circuit. The data decoding block demodulates the signal in order to recover the bit-stream.

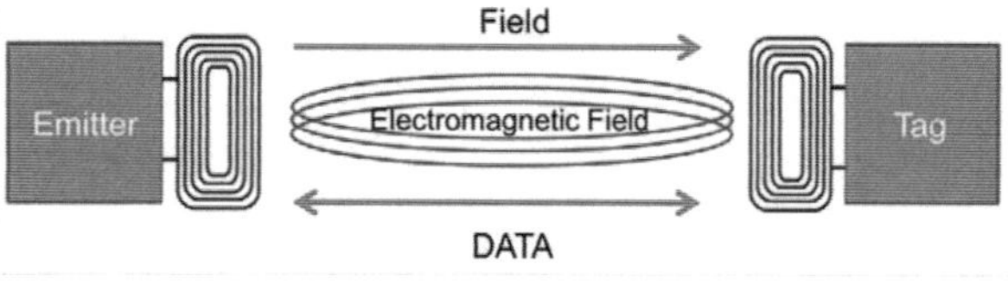

Figure 1. Typical Architecture of NFC system [8].

We consider an active tag (also called dynamic NFC tags) composed of a NFC circuit, a microcontroller unit (MCU) and a temperature sensor. Communication can thus be initiated by the microcontroller, so that communications are event-driven. Neither NFC circuit nor microcontroller nor sensor are externally supplied by a battery as it is classically the case. The only energy source comes from electromagnetic field while NFC communications occur between emitter and tag. To aim this, we choose the ST-Microelectronics M24LR04E chip. It is 13.56 MHz NFC ISO 15693 and ISO 18000-3 mode 1 compatible and it has an energy harvesting analog output that permits to supply other circuits on the board (i.e., microcontroller). The global system is shown in Fig. 2.

IV. SIMULATOR AND MODELS

The CLS simulator has been written in Visual C# in order to be easily portable on Microsoft 64-bit Windows operating systems. It is part of the Visual Studio Community, a free tool for academic research.

Graphical user interface is drawn in a horizontal way, from Emitter on the left towards Load (Electronic system) on the right. Fig. 3 shows the main window of CLS simulator.

As it is shown in Section II, several circuits compose the system, so they have been modeled separately. Models are high-level (at electronic system level), written in C#.

Emitting power and antenna gain permit to calculate radiofrequency output power, in other terms the magnetic field H in mA/m. Frequency and distance between antennas lead to radiofrequency signal attenuation. Emitter model

The emitter is modeled according to:

- emitting power
- frequency of the radiofrequency carrier
- distance between emitter and tag antennas
- emitter antenna gain

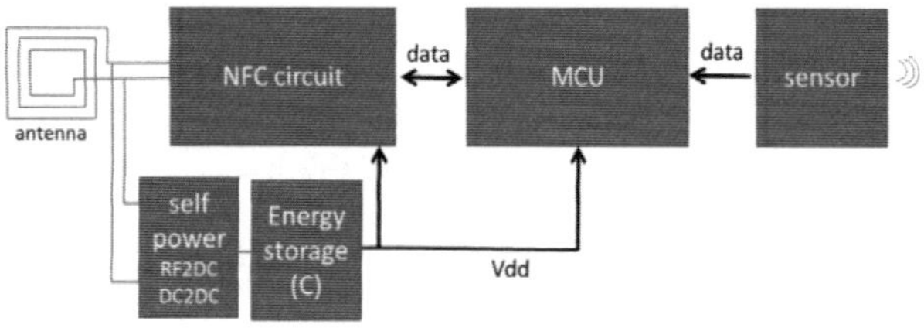

Figure 2. Considered battery-less smart tag.

A. *Tag antenna model*

The emitter and tag antennas are PCB coil antennas in our prototype. Antenna gain is used to calculate propagation losses. According to above calculations, radiofrequency signal strength is known at tag antenna input. Tag antenna gain attenuation thus gives the signal after antenna.

B. *NFC circuit model*

NFC circuit has the task to demodulate the radiofrequency signal. Principle is to extract the low frequency information carried in the high frequency: the carrier. High frequency permits propagation in the medium (air, plastic packages, etc.). Once the information is decoded, an answer can be send toward he emitter. Network-like communications occur in NFC. As this functionality is not the key point of this study, only the electrical consumption of this block is considered.

C. *Self power and energy storage blocks*

Several blocks in NFC circuit are considered. RF2DC block receives the radiofrequency signal and converts it to a DC (voltage and current) signal. The aim is to create a power supply. Conversion goal is to extract the maximum electrical power.

RF2DC is part of the self-power block in Fig. 2. It extracts electrical power from the radiofrequency signal carrier. M24LR04E circuit has been modeled for this power conversion task. The datasheet of this circuit gives H field from radiofrequency strength and output power from H field. Then, the required current at output has to be known in order to calculate the output voltage *Vout* according to the output current *Isink*. These curves are given in datasheet and have been measured.

DC2DC block converts the RF2DC output, in order to create a usable voltage for electronic devices. Electrical power is given according to efficiency of blocks. As power is set, a good balance between voltage and current has to been chosen. It is the role of this DC2DC block.

Energy storage parameters are used to calculate the amount of energy that can be saved in a capacitor. Parameters are capacitance value (in nF) and total losses (leakages in fA) of switches and capacitor. The role of this module is to simulate the energy that can be stored (according to the power input from DC2DC bloc) and the energy that can be used (according to the supplied load and leakages). It will lead to an energy budget analysis.

D. *Microcontroller and sensor models*

Microcontroller is modeled as an electrical load according to its activity. This load can also vary over time. Microcontroller and sensor require a minimal voltage and consume a nominal current. In model, electrical power is calculated according to:

- microcontroller and sensor brand and model
- microcontroller oscillator type
- microcontroller operating frequency

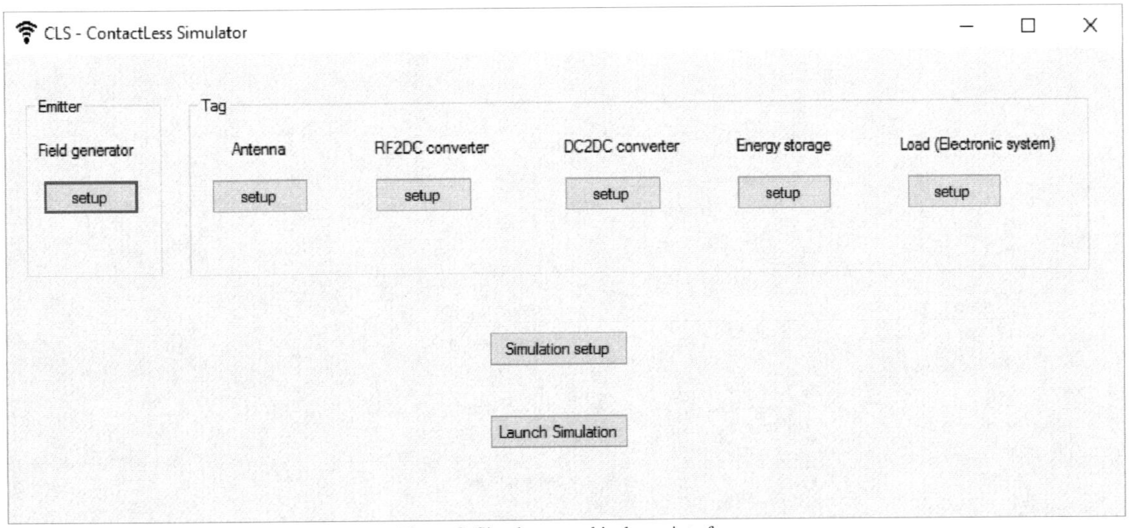

Figure 3. Simulator graphical user interface

Microchip PIC18LF2525 and Maxim MAX6613 are used. MAX6613 analog output is connected to ADC input of microcontroller. MAX6613 is supplied with an output pin of microcontroller. Supply voltage is also the same for both components.

For microcontroller, Microchip PIC18LF2525, oscillator type can be external RC (up to 4 MHz), external XTAL (crystal oscillator, up to 40 MHz), or internal oscillator. For internal oscillator, user can select from the internal 8MHz source down to the INTRC 31KHz source.

Several frequencies are available according to frequency post-scaler in the microcontroller. Frequency (in KHz) is the primary oscillator frequency that must match one possible configuration according to the oscillator type.

Supply voltage is then entered. All the parameters are taken from Microchip PIC18LF2525 (MCU) and MAX6613(temperature sensor) datasheets. Design goal specifies which value is to maximize: voltage or current. Indeed, RF2DC and DC2DC blocks output a given power, and the couple voltage and current can vary. This option also configures the simulation in order to search the maximum current point or the maximum voltage point. The other parameter (for example voltage if current is the design goal) is displayed as a result. Designer has to it take into account in design as a constraint; if the value of this other parameter is unreal, parameters concerning the hardware have to be changed, for example the microcontroller speed.

V. TESTCASE RESULTS

To present how the simulation behaves, the test-case has been simulated. All parameters that are entered in setup windows are sum up in Table II. Results are those in Fig. 4. Simulation time for a static analysis is a few milliseconds. At receiver (tag), magnetic field H is calculated. It depends on emitter power, distance, and antennas gains.

TABLE I. PARAMETERS USED FOR TEST EXAMPLE

Emitting power	50 mW
Frequency	13560 MHz
Distance	5 mm
Duration	5 s
Antennas gain (emitter & tag)	-3 dBi
RF2DC & DC2DC converters	Equations from M24LR04E
Capacitance	1000 nA
Switches leakages	100 fA
Microcontroller brand/model	Microchip / PIC18LF2525
Microcontroller Oscillator	Internal oscillator, 31KHz
Microcontroller Voltage	2V to 5.5V
Sensor Voltage	1.8V to 5.5V
Simulation setup	Design goal = current

The harvesting part gives output of RF2DC and DC2DC parts in the M24LR04E. As design goal of this analysis is the current, the simulator will try to extract nominal current from harvesting part. Nominal current is fixed by the required current from the electrical load (MCU and sensor).

Thus, the simulator firstly calculates the nominal current with the help of the electrical load. Analysis. This current is calculated from MCU and sensor parameters: PIC18LF2525 requires 15.05μA when running from internal oscillator at 31KHz. MAX6613 consumes 7.5μA. Simulator then calculates the harvesting possible voltage output for a sink current of 22.55μA.

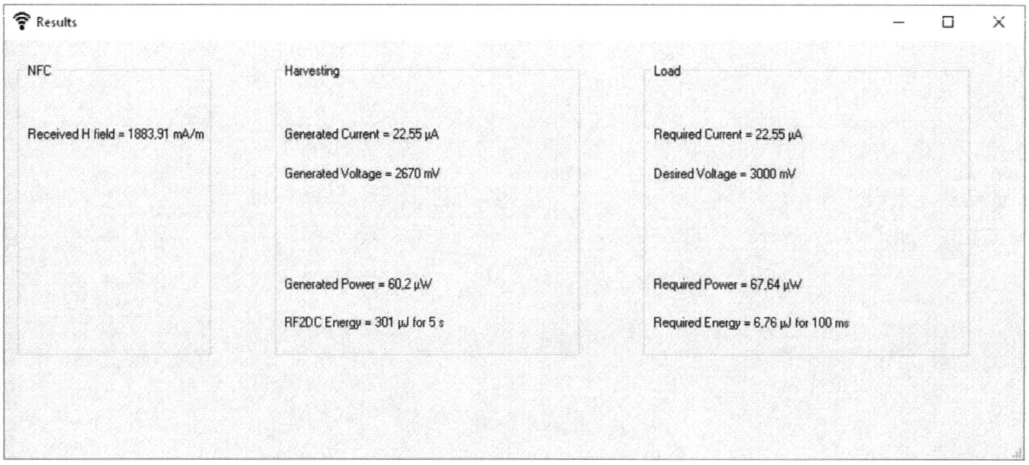

Figure 4. Results Window

From M24LR04E datasheet curves in the model, simulation gives 2.67v. Fig. 4. shows that the required power for load is 67.64µW but the harvester can only provide 60.2µW. As a result, the required voltage 3v is not reached. Designer will have to deal with a 2.67v supply, or decrease the load current consumption in order to increase voltage supply.

Energy calculations have also been implemented in simulator. It considers electrical power consumption and active time. Active time for the emitter is duration of the electromagnetic field. Result window thus displays 301µJ for 5s duration. Active time for the MCU and sensor is the time while MCU and sensor are running. Its energy is then 6.76µJ for 100ms (temperature sensing, analog to digital conversion and data storage in MCU). This result will permit the designer to plan how many cycles this This sensor node could run with a single electromagnetic charge. It is 44 cycles for this example. For this functionality becomes possible, an energy buffer must be used. It will be implemented soon in simulator.

VI. CONCLUSION AND FUTURE WORK

We presented a concrete energy analysis with ContactLess Simulator, that is a novelty. Its graphical interface is fully based on forms where parameters are set. It was used to graphically configure a NFC system composed of an emitter and a smart tag. Tag is battery-less (self-supplied), it thus comprises an energy harvesting module, with a RF2DC and DC2DC converter, a microcontroller unit (MCU) and a sensor. Each hardware block is configured by a setup window form. Simulation can be tuned for one design goal: search maximal voltage or search maximal current. This choice depends on designer priority. A launch button runs the simulation and displays a result window. Several electrical outputs are calculated: electromagnetic field at tag input, harvested power (voltage and current), harvested energy for a single contactless energy intake, required power (voltage and current) for the microcontroller and sensor, required energy for a main program loop. Result analysis on a test-case shows that the harvested power is a bit weak (60.2µW) compared to the required power (67.64µW). According to the design goal, fixed to prioritize current, harvested voltage is 2.67v instead of 3v. Electronic design can thus be refined with this simulator. Energy calculation permits to think about a better use of the energy. Indeed, harvested power is weak, but harvested energy (301µJ) is much bigger that required energy (6.76µJ). Feasibility is also possible with smart energy management; we will detail them soon. Further releases of the simulator will support transient analysis and more electronic circuits in library.

REFERENCES

[1] R. Tseng, B. von Novak, S. Shevde, and K. A. Grajski, "Introduction to the alliance for wireless power loosely-coupled wireless power transfer system specification version 1.0", Wireless Power Transfer (WPT) Conference, pp. 79-83, 2013, doi: 10.1109/WPT.2013.6556887.

[2] C. Angerer, B.Knerr, M.Holzer, A.Adalan, and M. Rupp, "Flexible simulation and prototyping for RFID designs", EURASIP Workshop on RFID Technology, pp.51-54, 2007.

[3] D.K. Ahn, S.G. Bae, and I.C. Hwang, "A Design of Behavioral Simulation Platform for Near Field Communication Transceiver using MATLAB Simulink", The Transactions of The Korean Institute of Electrical Engineers journal, Vol. 59, Issue 10, pp. 1917-1922, 2010.

[4] T. Cheng, and L. Jin, "Analysis and Simulation of RFID Anti-collision Algorithms", International Conference on Advanced Communication Technology, volume 1, pp 697-701, 2007.

[5] J. Deckmar, and A.Perez-Boutavin, "NFC", [Online, retrieved: 13th Feb. 2017]. Available from: https://fr.mathworks.com/matlabcentral/fileexchange/34915-nfc

[6] C. Floerkemeier, and S. Sarma, "RFIDSim—A Physical and Logical Layer Simulation Engine for Passive RFID", IEEE Transactions on Automation Science and Engineering, vol. 6, n. 1, pp. 33-43, 2009.

[7] G. Benigno, O. Briante, and G. Ruggeri, "A sun energy harvester model for the network simulator 3", Sensing, Communication, and Networking - Workshops (SECON), pp. 1-6, 2015, doi: 10.1109/SECONW.2015.7328143.

[8] G. Proehl, "An Introduction to Near Field Communications", ST-Microelectronics, 2013, [Online, retrieved: 28th June 2017]. Available from: http://www.st.com/content/st_com/en/applications/connectivity/near-field-communication-nfc.html

Residential Wireless Interfaces Virtualization: a Feasibility Study

Antonio da Silva Fariña,
Ana Belén García Hernando
Dept. of Telematic and Electronic Engineering
Universidad Politécnica de Madrid
Madrid, Spain

antonio.dasilva@upm.es,anabelen.garcia@upm.es

Mary Luz Mouronte López
Universidad Francisco de Vitoria
Madrid, Spain

maryluz.mouronte@ufv.es

Abstract—**This paper investigates the possibility of virtualizing and distributing the functionality that runs on top of residential wireless communications. Specifically, we propose, describe and test a solution that transports USB communications to remote locations, for scenarios in which the in-home wireless interfaces are consumed at the server side through this type of general-purpose and widely used interfaces. We frame this study in a general architecture by which Software Defined Networking (SDN) and Network Functions Virtualization (NFV) bring economies of scale, flexibility and programmability to residential Internet of Things (IoT) environments. As a result of our tests, we prove the feasibility of the remote presence of the IoT systems through the Universal Serial Bus (USB) tunnels, and we obtain approximate bandwidth measurements that serve as a hint on the type of services that can be offloaded to the cloud. For those functionalities that would need more bandwidth, we propose to embed a lightweight virtualization environment in home and to execute in it part of the virtualized components, something that is in line with the recent fog computing approaches.**

Keywords-IoT virtualization; SDN; NFV; residential wireless communications; USB/IP.

I. Introduction

Nowadays application-layer gateways are needed to provide connectivity to IoT devices in the home. Current gateways mix network connectivity, in-network processing, and user interface functions. We share the view of [1] by which separating these functions would improve the connectivity potential for IoT devices. To help in this separation, two new trends, namely SDN and NFV, can be considered.

In fact, both SDN and NFV [2] are recently beginning to be proposed for the home environment. With SDN the control plane (in which the logical procedures supporting the networking protocols and the most important decisions are carried out) is separated from the data plane (in which the forwarding of packets on the most suitable interface towards the intended destination is carried out). SDN is an excellent mechanism to do Traffic Engineering (TE) and exploit effectively the network resources in an IoT scenario. NFV leverages commodity storage, networking and processing equipment in order to execute, through the use of a virtualization layer (sometimes called hypervisor), sophisticated network functionality on top of a virtualized infrastructure. It may be used to combine the available resources in a network by dividing the available bandwidth into channels or slices, each of which is independent from the others. NFV allows multiple service providers to carry out multiple separate and isolated virtual networks by sharing physical resources.

The main use cases of SDN and NFV in the home deal with pure networking tasks, and more specifically with the virtualization of the Customer Premises Equipment (CPE). There are also some recent proposals to augment the scope of cloud computing, NFV and SDN and integrate some IoT (basically sensing and actuation) capabilities into their frameworks [3] [4].

In our previous work [5], we proposed to leverage the virtualization possibilities of NFV together with the programmability of SDN in order to offer a portfolio of IoT-related functions to the residential users. Specifically, we aimed at the existence of a set of remote and virtualized "Plug-and-Play" (PnP) functions in order to recognize and manage IoT hardware belonging to different manufacturers.

We propose to have a generic and programmable gateway at home, called Home Radio Head (HRH), which does not need to implement any IoT vendor-specific function above the wireless communications provided by USB dongles. USB interfaces would be virtualized and managed remotely thanks to the establishment of tunnels between the HRH and the ISP. At the remote end of these tunnels, a NFV infrastructure hosts the IoT applications and management functionality implemented as a set of Virtual Network Functions (VNFs).

The virtualization of USB interfaces allows reaching economies of scale by offering a reasonably inexpensive customer premises equipment supporting most home wireless communications. In addition, we propose the use of a SDN-programmable data path in order to achieve greater flexibility in the management of the USB tunnels. Furthermore, in order to reduce the necessary bandwidth between home and the ISP, some processing can be carried out inside the customer premises by downloading and running lightweight VM containers. The rest of the paper is organized as follows: Section 2 summarizes the background that forms the basis of our work and some related works. Section 3 describes our proposed architecture and its building blocks. Section 4 explains the experimental setup we have implemented and discusses the results. Finally, in section 5, we provide some conclusions and our foreseen future work.

II. BACKGROUND

In this section we start by describing two technological trends that we leverage for our work (namely, virtualization and remote execution of radio functionality, and lightweight virtualization environments) and continue by summarizing recent work very related to our proposal (virtualization of local wireless smart home functionality).

A. *Virtualization and Remote Execution of Radio Functionality*

The Remote Radio Head (RRH) approach used in cellular wireless access networks aims to move wireless baseband processing to the cloud. This has a high cost in terms of bandwidth and it is solved using dedicated high speed lines connecting the RRH with the Base Band Unit (BBU) at the edge of the core network.

We find that the virtualization of higher level functionality is appealing also for residential environments. However, the specificities of local area protocols, inherently different from cellular wireless, make it necessary to assess to what extent and under what circumstances this externalization of functions is feasible.

B. *Lightweight Virtualization Environments*

The orchestration and maintenance of the software running on the gateways in large-scale deployments is a challenging task. There are studies, such as [8], that evaluate the performance of the container-based approach compared to a hypervisor-based virtualization when running on gateway devices. The comparison between traditional heavy VMs vs Docker containers architecture is shown in Figure 1. Docker containers are a type of lightweight VMs that can be easily deployed in inexpensive common single board computers like Raspberry Pi.

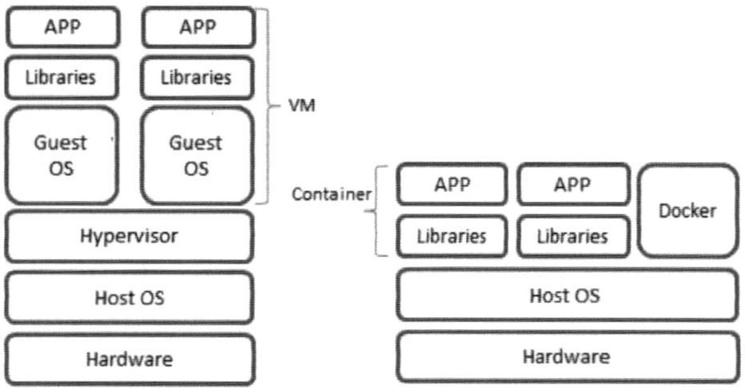

Figure 1. Traditional VM vs Docker architecture.

This Platform-as-a-Service (PaaS) environment is very useful to deploy custom home sensors preprocessing functionality at runtime. In this way, both the necessary bandwidth to the cloud and the round trip delay for those functions are reduced.

The possibility of distributing the resource-intensive functions in intermediate points between the end devices (e.g., sensors and actuators) and the cloud is aligned with the philosophy behind fog computing approaches. This distribution has to be done transparently for the users, and a certain amount of intelligence is needed to manage a fog scenario, preferably in an open and interoperable manner. IoT and 5G are two of the drivers that currently push the activity in fog computing.

C. *Virtualization of Local Wireless Smart Home Functionality*

Building functions that cope with all the diversity that the products in the home present is not feasible, at least currently and at a reasonable cost, for the residential user. However, for an Internet Service Provider (ISP) this would be much easier, especially if these functions are offered as services to its customers and economies of scale can be applied. The ISP should virtualize the actual physical infrastructure of its customers to deliver a set of general and reusable services [5]. In fact, sensing as a service (S2aaS) architectural proposals are specifically concerned with the organizational relationships between the different components and omit details about short range components communications as well as other technical aspects [7].

This is a very active research field. Among the recent works in this area we highlight the following:

In [1], the authors propose an architecture that leverages the increasingly ubiquitous presence of Bluetooth Low Energy radios to connect IoT peripherals to the Internet. The authors propose the use of mobile devices (i.e., Laptops, Smartphones and tablets) as a gateway. The same approach is followed in [8] where the use of smartphones running as a gateway bridges with Bluetooth-enabled devices in a home environment is evaluated.

In [9], a new user-centric management architecture is proposed, to increase the active engagement of residential users in the management tasks of their own networks, improving the usability of the network and facilitating the provision of new services. The proposed architecture combines the SDN and NFV approaches. Additionally, the user-centricity is achieved by implementing interaction and management layers. These layers together constitute a residential network management application. The interaction layer, which can be deployed over different devices, hosts the application that allows the user to configure the network and receive notifications. The interaction layer interacts with the management layer by means of a REST API.

In [2], the authors survey the state of the art on the application of SDN and NFV to IoT. They provide a comprehensive description of the possible implementation aspects for both technologies

In [3], the authors highlight some IoT challenges that the network & IT infrastructure will face. The NFV and SDN benefits are presented from a network operator point of view. The authors present a new multi-layered IoT architecture involving SDN and NFV, and they show how the proposed architecture is able to cope with the identified IoT challenges.

In [4], the authors discuss the usage of NFV technologies and construct a virtual advanced metering infrastructure (AMI) network to transmit energy-related information in a dependable and cost-effective way. The reliability, availability and cost of the new architecture is analyzed and compared to current AMIs.

In [10], the authors review the distributed approach to NFV, discuss phased NFV deployment and present critical factors to take such functionalities into account at the customer edge.

III. Proposed Architecture

In our previous work [5], we described our proposal for an architecture that leverages NFV and SDN to offer residential users a portfolio of IoT services. The virtualization of IoT vendor-specific functionality together with the presence of a cost-effective and generic customer premises equipment called HRH would bring economies of scale, easier updates and faster support for new IoT products, among others. This in-home HRH:

- Would not need to implement IoT vendor-specific functions, since these functions would be virtualized and run on a standard NFV infrastructure.
- Would exhibit the in-home raw layer 1 physical flows to the ISP by using tunnels.
- Would be SDN-manageable to establish and maintain the aforementioned tunnels in a standardized manner.

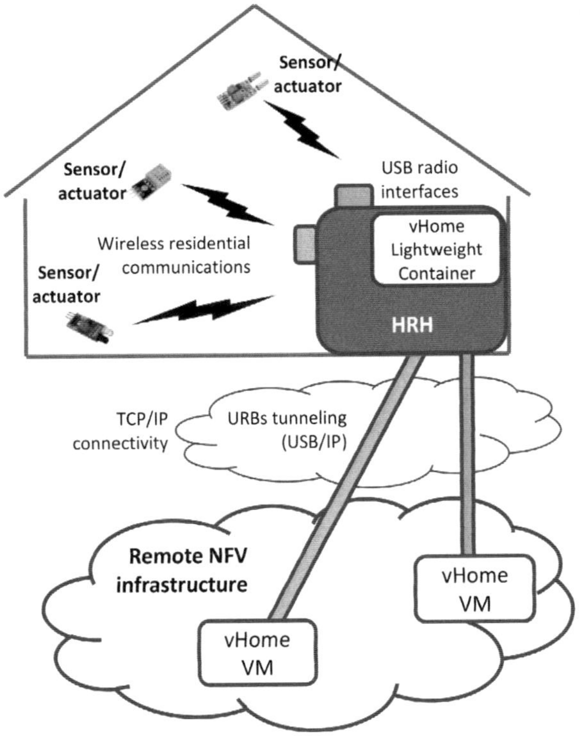

Figure 2. High-level architecture for the remote virtualization of wireless residential communications by means of USB tunneling.

With the work described in this paper we elaborate further on this architecture and decide to establish USB as the vendor-agnostic frontier between the in-home radio flows and the vendor-specific functionality that would be implemented as VNFs. In Figure 2 we show the high-level view of our proposal.

Our architecture is based on the following principles:

- The support of varied short-range wireless interfaces widely used by residential IoT products (e.g., WiFi, Bluetooth or ZigBee). These radio flows are processed locally at low level and exposed to the HRH as standard USB interfaces.
- The establishment of tunnels between the HRH and the virtualization infrastructure at the ISP side, in order to propagate transparently the USB Request Blocks (URBs) that are to be processed by VNFs. The establishment of these tunnels is programmable by using SDN, i.e., the HRH supports Openflow (or any other SDN-compliant southbound interface).
- The vendor-specific functionality, which is realized by means of one or several VNFs (represented as "vHOME" virtual machines in Figure 2), can be distributed if necessary. In this line, the HRH supports a lightweight virtualization environment on which a subset of the VNFs necessary for a service can be downloaded and executed, as commanded by the Virtualized Infrastructure Manager (VIM), see Figure 3.

In the following sub-sections, we elaborate on the implications, advantages and rationale behind each of our main architectural design decisions.

A. *Virtualization of USB Interfaces*

The rationale behind the virtualization of USB interfaces is threefold. Firstly, USB is widely supported by IoT vendors in residential environments. Secondly, the existence of USB dongles at reasonable prices and easily interchangeable is very convenient for the residential market. Lastly, fast prototyping of proof of concepts becomes possible with general purpose equipment (see section IV below).

Moreover, virtualizing the functionality above the USB interface would make various existing IoT products immediately available through our proposed schema. New products also supporting USB would become available to customers almost in a "plug-and-play" manner as long as ISPs supported the adequate virtualized drivers.

Each tunnel would correspond to a new IoT product that utilizes a specific wireless technology (see Figure 2), and the specific drivers and all upper functionality would be placed at the other end of each tunnel, on the ISP side. To implement this idea, we propose to use USB/IP [11], a means of sharing USB devices over a TCP/IP network by encapsulating USB messages between a server (the equipment with the USB device physically connected) and a remote client.

B. *SDN-Programmable Data Path*

In order to provide a flexible configuration, the URB flows must be dynamically provisioned and managed. The HRH would benefit from a generic datapath that is programmable by following the SDN principles. The concrete policies to be applied to the establishment of the tunnels would be implemented and enforced by a SDN controller, and a southbound Openflow-programmable

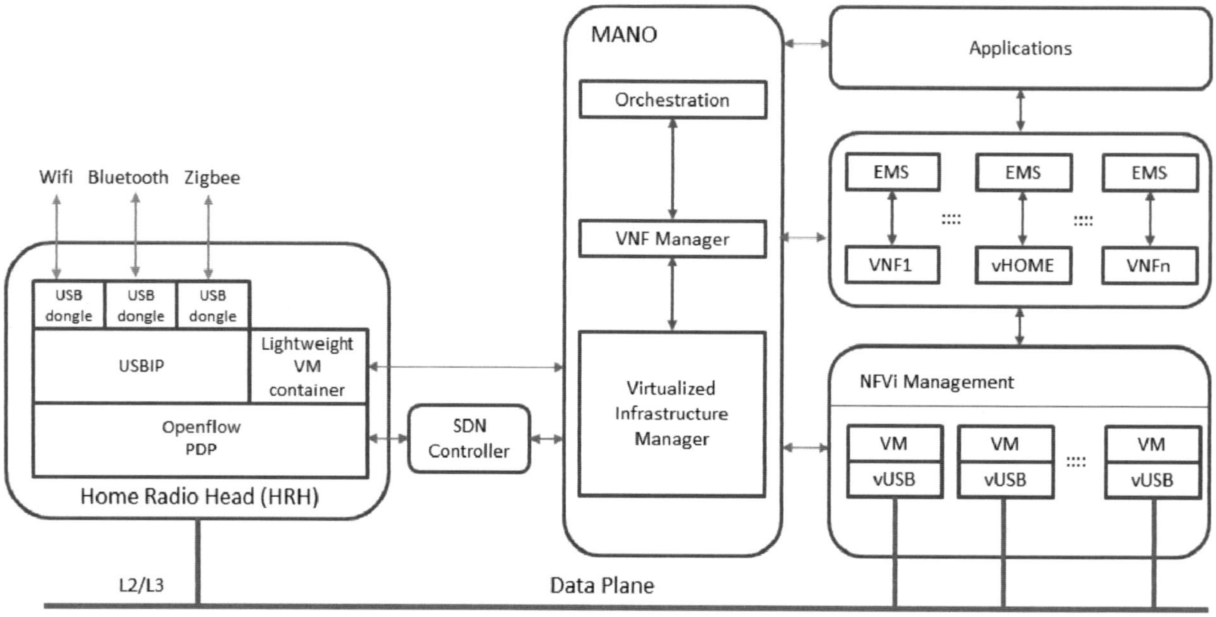

Figure 3. SDN and NFV as considered in our proposal.

datapath has to be supported by the HRH. This way, SDN advantages brought by the software definition of networking configuration are present in our scenario. Also, our HRH would be more easily integrated with a SDN-based residential gateway as proposed in [9].

C. *Lightweight Docker Containers*

Under certain circumstances it might be convenient or even necessary that a subset of the vendor-specific functionality is carried out inside the customer premises. This might be the case for complying with stringent delay requirements or for saving uplink bandwidth. We propose to provide a light virtualization environment, based either on light virtual machines or on Docker containers, inside the HRH, in which specific modules can be downloaded and executed locally when commanded by the NFV management and orchestration layer.

This distribution of functionality has to be done transparently, without the user being aware of the decomposition of the global service into different modules that may be executed at different points.

D. *SDN/NFV Relationship*

Our HRH follows the principles of both SDN and NFV. As such, it contains on one hand a generic and programmable networking datapath, and on the other hand a lightweight virtualization environment. The former offers a standard SDN southbound interface so that the SDN controller can provision the USB tunnels dynamically. The latter is formally part of the virtualized infrastructure that has to be managed by the VIM, as per the NFV architecture.

Figure 3 is an enhanced version of a figure we included in our previous paper [5]. We have completed the modules and technologies inside HRH, and we have also made the virtualization capabilities of HRH explicit. The SDN controller that is functionally located between the VIM and the HRH (see Figure 3) can itself be implemented as another VNF, this way leveraging the existing NFV infrastructure.

IV. EXPERIMENTAL SETUP AND RESULTS

We have implemented the experimental setup shown in Figure 4. To act as HRH, we have equipped a Raspberry Pi 3 with a USB/IP server running on Raspbian OS. This HRH is located inside the Smart Home that the Universidad Politécnica de Madrid has in its South Campus. Both a Bluetooth USB dongle and a USB mass storage device (i.e., a USB pendrive) are connected to the HRH. The ISP side is emulated by means of a Windows PC equipped with a VirtualBox hypervisor. On top of this virtualization infrastructure, a guest OS is run which contains a USB/IP client. This client is in charge of terminating the USB tunnels and offering the virtualized USB dongles as if they were local to the guest OS. On top of these virtualized USB dongles, the concrete specific functionality can be deployed.

The first test we have performed is purely functional. The remote Bluetooth USB dongle is perceived as local at the ISP side. The BT dongle inside the Smart Home receives periodical temperature measurements obtained from a sensor connected to an Arduino board.

These measurements are available at the ISP side thanks to the USB tunneling mechanism. The second test is actually a group of different measurements. The objective of this test is to estimate the bandwidth that would be available through the USB tunneling infrastructure for different local-remote networking scenarios. To perform this estimation, we have run several write and read tests on the regular USB pendrive and have measured the performance of those operations. Four local-remote setups have been considered:

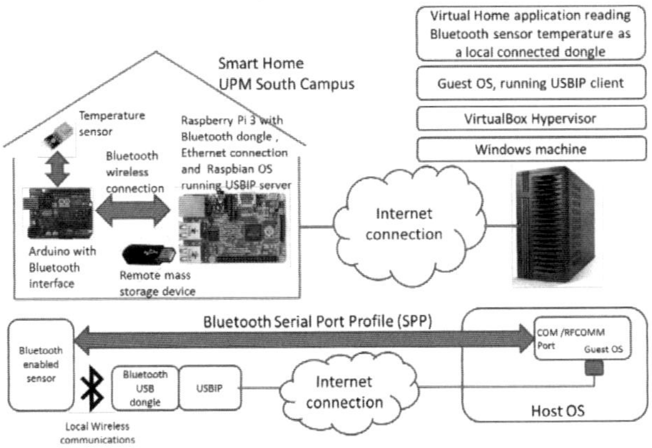

Figure 4. Experimental setup.

- Local connection: This is the baseline that gives us the actual write/read capacity of the device. Both operations are performed with a pendrive connected to the same device.
- Same network: The HRH and the emulated ISP are connected to the same Ethernet network. In this case it is a 100BASE-TX wired Ethernet connection.
- Madrid-Alcalá: The HRH is located inside the Smart Home in the South Campus of UPM, whereas the emulated ISP is connected to a residential network in Alcalá de Henares, a village on the outskirts of Madrid. They are around 30 km. apart from each other. The residential network has a 50 MB/s Hybrid fiber-coaxial (HFC) internet connection.
- Madrid-Galicia: The HRH is located inside the Smart Home in the South Campus of UPM, whereas the emulated ISP is connected through a WIFI access point in a public library in Galicia (North of Spain). They are around 500 km. apart from each other. The internet connection of the library, which is provided by a public ISP, is a 100 MB/s HFC access shared by all users.

These setups are chosen to consider scenarios in which not only the distance but also the expected quality of the networking accesses is varied. We have compiled the obtained results in Table I below.

TABLE I. WRITE / READ PERFORMANCE UNDER SEVERAL LOCAL-REMOTE CONFIGURATIONS

Configuration	*Write*	*Read*
Local conection	7.34 Mb/s	17.5 Mb/s
Same network	4.32 Mb/s	6 Mb/s
Madrid-Alcalá	0.9 Mb/s	1 Mb/s
Madrid-Galicia	0.4 Mb/s	0.5 Mb/s

These bandwidth measures should be taken as a starting point. They have been obtained in controlled environments that implement per-user traffic shaping or bandwidth limits policies in order to control peer to peer communications. Nonetheless, even in the most disadvantageous scenario, the bandwidth estimations show that for sporadic or periodical sensor readings (such as temperature or humidity) and for short actuator orders (such as lights on/off control), it is feasible to execute all virtualized functions remotely. Even low-rate video can be remotely tunneled if necessary: as an example a Youtube video with a resolution of 360p consumes around 0.3/0.4 Mb/s. However, in the case of more intensive multimedia traffic, such as a video camera output with higher resolution, it might be necessary to download and execute some of the processing functionality into the HRH, in order to consume less bandwidth towards the ISP. This decision might be made on the basis of bandwidth or delay measurements with each residential subscriber that could be easily carried out by the ISP.

To better assess the reproducibility of these experiments, we highlight here that all the hardware used is inexpensive and off-the-shelf, and all the software is open source. We have also specified the concrete type of Internet access that is present at each setup location to give a better idea of the influence that this might have on the final perceived figures included in Table I. We are aware that different specific locations would have thrown different numbers, but we consider that the objective of demonstrating the feasibility of virtualizing and executing remotely many of the usual residential functions is reasonably well attained.

V. CONCLUSIONS AND FUTURE WORK

This paper describes a basic implementation which shows that the HRH strategy is feasible through the tunneling of USB blocks. The proposed approach, based on common hardware and open software, has several benefits such as its low-cost, low-complexity, easy programmability and alignment with some of the current networking virtualization trends. However, several important issues need further research in order to improve some aspects, for instance the management of uplink communications bandwidth between the HRH and the remote virtualization infrastructure.

As future work we will aim to implement a complete prototype of the proposed architecture and its seamless integration in an existing SDN/NFV infrastructure including its standardized control plane protocols. As regards the distribution of the virtualized functions, and given the specific QoS requirements of video traffic, we consider video preprocessing an ideal candidate to be runtime deployed in the HRH docker container as a VNF. This way, if the overall composed video processing service can be divided into modules with clear interfaces, it could be easily deployed across the NFVi infrastructure, including the HRH.

In our opinion, the demonstration of this scenario would constitute an interesting proof of concept mixing the service chaining capabilities often mentioned for composite virtualized services and the seamless distribution of components, that is one of the basis of fog computing.

ACKNOWLEDGMENT

This work has been supported by Spanish Ministerio de Economía y Competitividad under the grant TEC2015-67834-R.

REFERENCES

[1] T. Zachariah et al., The Internet of Things Has a Gateway Problem, In Proceedings of the 16th International Workshop on Mobile Computing Systems and Applications (HotMobile '15). ACM, New York, NY, USA, 2015, pp. 27-32.

[2] N. Bizanis and F. A. Kuipers, SDN and Virtualization Solutions for the Internet of Things: A Survey, 2016, 4, IEEE Access pp.5591- 5606.

[3] N. Omnes, M. Bouillon, G. Fromentoux, and O. L. Grand, A programmable and virtualized network & IT infrastructure for the internet of things: How can NFV & SDN help for facing the upcoming challenges, *Intelligence in Next Generation Networks (ICIN), 18th International Conference on*, Paris, 2015, pp. 64-69.

[4] M. Niedermeier and H. De Meer. Constructing Dependable Smart Grid Networks using Network Functions Virtualization, Journal of Network and Systems Management 24, 2016, pp. 449-469.

[5] A. B. García, A. Da Silva, L. Bellido, F .J Ruiz, and D. Fernández. Virtualization of Residential IoT Functionality by Using NFV and SDN, In 2017 International Conference on Consumer Electronics (ICCE), Las Vegas, USA, January, pp. 8-10, 2017.

[6] F. Ramalho and A. Neto, Virtualization at the network edge: A performance comparison, IEEE 17th International Symposium on A World of Wireless, Mobile and Multimedia Networks (WoWMoM), Coimbra, 2016, pp. 1-6.

[7] S. Abdelwahab et al., Cloud of Things for Sensing as a Service: Sensing Resource Discovery and Virtualization, In 2015 IEEE Global Communications Conference (GLOBECOM). IEEE, pp. 1–7.

[8] J. Rossey, I. Moerman, P. Demeester, and J. Hoebeke, Wi-Fi helping out Bluetooth smart for an improved home automation user experience, Symposium on Communications and Vehicular Technologies (SCVT), Mons, 2016, pp. 1-6.

[9] R. Flores, D. Fernández, and L. Bellido, A user-centric SDN management architecture for NFV-based residential networks, Computer Standards & Interfaces, Available online 27 January 2017, ISSN 0920-5489 pp. 279-292.

[10] Y. Gittik. Distributed Network Functions Virtualization (White paper),. March 2014.

[11] T. Hirofuchi, E. Kawai, K. Fujikawa, and H. Sunahara. USB/IP - a Peripheral Bus Extension for Device Sharing over IP Network, 2005 USENIX Annual Technical Conference, pp. 47-60.

Towards a Mobile Enhancement of Glocal Heritage?

Developing user experiences in relation to mobile technologies, geo-localisation and culture

Laurent Antonczak
Auckland University of Technology
AUT
Auckland, New Zealand
email: laurent.antonczak@aut.ac.nz

Catherine Papetti
Université Côte d'Azur
IAE, GRM
Nice, France
email: catherine.papetti@unice.fr

Abstract — **Considering the recent media coverage and online discussions about *Niantic's Pokémon GO*, most academics and professionals would agree that it is the first app to globally popularise mobile locative media (GPS) and augmented reality (AR), raising its potential as a technological medium and as an interface to offer new possibilities for any user. This paper maps technological and user experience changes undertaken through collaboration and professional practices between creative technologists and prosumers (clients and/or users), as they designed digital environments. Based on the notion of augmented space and/or virtual environments, especially in the Tourism sector, the authors analyse how tacit knowledge and service discovery were utilised to facilitate and integrate innovative, engaging and inclusive mobile experiences. Also, whilst proposing a networked model of content creation in augmented space, this paper reflects on some of the mobile characteristics in relation to a *glocal* (term coined by Robertson in the 1990s) approach through two specific collaborative research projects: *Shangri La* and the *Mobile Innovation Network Australasia (MINA)* app.**

Keywords-mobile; locative media; mixed reality; tourism; heritage; user-centred; glocal; innovation; mobiquity.

I. Introduction

Territorial attractiveness and marketing must leave the mechanical conventions of the creation of zones and the competitive race of companies to integrate with the emergence of new area projects. The territory becomes more and more a community composed of individuals participating in its development rather than bounded by managed areas, and the valuation of the region passes through the same community of individuals [28][37]. Furthermore, digital tools, such as mobile devices and social networks allow the co-creation of value and the participation of the community to the attraction of the territory and its heritage. Hence, the new collective environment can be defined as:

"the overlapping of virtual information in real space (…) mixing virtual objects generated by computers with a real environment, generating a mixed environment that can be viewed through any technological device in real time." [10]

Research on Mixed- or Augmented-Reality (MR or AR) has been conducted in various fields including cultural heritage but the majority of studies focus on technical aspects of AR, while others are tailored to specific applications [14]. In this paper, the authors investigate how AR content is created in this theoretical context, and how communities provide one key aspect: a participatory model of creating user presence in mobile environments that ties into Matsuda's hypothetical context. Also, with the smartphone being the "first medium to introduce AR to the mass market which has enormous potential for tourism" [1][17], this paper will specifically focus on mobile AR (m-AR), which allows users to point "the device towards physical objects in *their* surroundings and then *are* able to see additional virtual information overlaid on top of the real-world camera view through virtual annotations" [39]. Furthermore, this paper examines and reflects on two cases of AR projects in order to define a purposeful way to enhance a tourist experience.

This paper investigates how media locative content can be co-created in mobile environments, and is organised into five sections. Section 2 presents the context and some definitions of m-AR and *glocal* heritage, and Section 3 focusses on the methodology, while Section 4 develops the critical analysis of two environmental projects conceived in the early- and mid-mobile technology era. In Section 5, the results are discussed, and Section 6 convenes the conclusion.

II. M-AR, Mobiquity and Glocal Heritage

This section is divided into two parts: the first part aims to define and contextualise AR and the concept of mobiquity, while the second part discusses the connections between technology, content, people and the environment.

A. *Context: mobiquity*

Although many definitions of AR exist, all of them agree that AR refers to any enhancement of the real environment by computer-generated content [14]. AR is a combination of real object and computer-generated data where virtual objects are blended into the real world. It means that user could see virtual and real objects coexisting in the same space. Thus, AR technologies supplement reality rather than completely replacing it [27].

With the huge and rapid adoption of smartphones [1] in the tourism sector, m-AR is the main device used by tourists. Thus m-AR participates in the rapid fostering of mobiquity system. Mobiquity is a word proposed at the beginning of the Internet relating to the mobile phone in the 1990s by Xavier Dalloz. Today, it has become a gateway concept between the real world and the virtual world, rich in new content and services, bringing the convergence between the MOBI-lity of any mobile device and the ubi-QUITY of the Internet [29]. This notion originates from the concept of Any Time, AnyWhere, Any Device (ATAWAD), added later by Any Content, which consists of several elements: the real world tags (tags); the modified reality (increased or decreased); the transmedia (contents adapted to the five screens); a geolocation tool with indication of the different steps to follow; an information tool at every stage that enriches the reality; and an interactive tool through which the tourist-local-user-politician can post a comment, enrich the content, in visual, textual form. This mobile system allows any tourist to become an ambassador of the territory and users to interact with the actual environment while displaying virtual information at the same time [30]. Buxton [5][6] even argues:

"(...) that ubiquitous technologies are enacting a shift in the way that places are encountered and understood. Added to this, places across the planet are increasingly facing 'wicked' problems – issues that are difficult to solve by traditional methods and approaches."

B. m-AR in the context of glocal heritage

In general, the term of heritage refers to the study of everything that is inherited and recovered to remain through the medium of archeology, art, tradition, religious and culture. Cultural heritage is one of the valuable assets that need to be preserved and protected for the future generation.

A wide body of literature identifies that smartphones or AR enabled PC tablets that are applied to cultural heritage can help cultural and urban development in two main ways: by overlaying a map with drawings, graphics, physical models, audio files and digital simulations that helps non-expert users to understand a culturally complex phenomena; and by integrating virtual elements in conjunction with a specific site in order to visualise historical details that helps to increase the awareness of a place on the basis of its uniqueness, as opposed to merely visible. This is a new culture of fulfilling the potential of a place and promoting its tourism industry [2][12].

Digital AR technologies and possibilities (such as bluetooth, wifi and/or geo-location coordinates, gyroscopic information) [7] and pervasive media such as mobile phones [1] in the field of tourism contributes to the "re-enact of historical monuments to reproduce on site historical places as in the golden period" [11]. Tourists can gain many benefits from those mobile technologies, offering them new interactive and highly dynamic experience [31][32]. It opens up a glocal territory [35], in terms of an hybridisation between one local space and a global appropriation by mobile travelers.

III. The Methodology

Due to the complex nature of the technology development and during the early stages of the analysed project, the authors employed a heuristic form of research where "the research process is designed for the exploration and interpretation of experience, which uses the self of the researcher" [16]. After narrowing down areas, the heuristic model evolved into a design-led methodology incorporating "research methods that imbues the full spectrum of innovation activities with a human-centred design ethos" [4]. This was to allow a systematic approach to the practice-led research that utilises a rinse-and-repeat method. The broad framework for all design-led research is analysis and synthesis.

"Analysis relates to the methods of investigation, enquiry and understanding central to the research of a project brief, concept or a particular context. Synthesis, meanwhile, is the means by which a designer is able to draw upon his or her initial analytical work and investigation to produce meaningful solutions or interventions." [26]

However, the collaborative element of the two proposed projects needs to be clearly defined. Then, users' experience of being active members within an authentic professional glocal community of practice can provide new environmental experience for the majority of participants, including professionals or amateurs [8].

Also, ethnography via mainly participant observations, qualitative inquiry conducted via written or oral discussions, and hermeneutic (Heidegger) interpretation methods supports the following analysis of the users presence, actions and interactions in mobile environment in order to draw an adequate but not complete synthesis.

IV. Two examples

Following are two examples of mobile-based collaborative research projects: the first one was conceptualised and developed in 2011, during the very early stages of mobile environment development and the second one was created late 2012.

A. *Shangri La* - an experience in Virtual Reality [2011]. This project was developed by Virtuo Ltd in collaboration with Māori-Samoan artist Lonnie Hutchinson on New Zealand's first outdoor virtual binocular experience in Wellington. The artwork Shangri La is located in Chew Lane, at the heart of Wellington City. The concept is based on historical facts: before the settlement of Wellington, the area of land that Chews Lane occupies was originally the seabed and shoreline. The original bay was surrounded in native bush which was also known for its towering Totara trees. In order to acknowledge the areas Māori cultural and natural history, *Shangri La* was developed as a series of animations that observed and propositioned the physical architecture of the Chews Lane by embedding a conceptual landscape and stories, which weave their way around the lane [21]. In terms of user experience, any *flâneur* is invited to view or gaze the environment through the binocular. The binocular can be rotated left or right approximately 360 degrees and up and down approximately 30 degrees. There are black and white motifs in the canvas image. When the binocular is held stationary over these motifs a crosshair appears (much like the crosshair on a camera when taking a photo), which triggers an animation.

B. Mobile Innovation Network Australasia (MINA) app – New Zealand [2012/2013]

The *MINA* app is a collaboration between *MINA*, an Australasian-based network that creates interactions between people, content and the creative industries, and *Snapr*, which brings together photos/videos from a range of different apps. The joint-creation of the app came initially from a need of the *24 Frames 24 Hours* project, which engages with local communities around the world through mobile-filmmaking workshops. Originally, participants used mobile-filmmaking via their smartphone as a means of cultural expression. However, the process of filming, downloading the footage on a computer and then uploading it online became tedious and frustrating for participants. By using the metadata (i.e., GPS) of each new mobile short video clips created, the app can automatically and systematically upload and place the content on *Google Maps*. Hence, participants are empowered to shape representations about themselves and their communities, while connecting and representing seamlessly a specific place or location, "through a kind of no strings attached virtual proximity and co-presence" [34]. This mobile project focuses on bringing amateur and/or professional filmmakers together via a social geo-locative platform and fostering a community of practice thanks to creative practices [8][18].

V. RESULTS

Both projects are based on most of the key mobile benefits defined by Ahonen [1]: mobile is the first personal mass media; always connected; always carried; available at creative impulse; as most accurate audience info; captures social context of consumption; enables AR; and offers digital interface (to real world).

Shangri La was conceived as an m-AR installation in order to invite any user to merge historical and contemporary realities and events. Unfortunately, due mainly to technical issues in relation to some of the limitation of 2011's technologies and their costs; the project *Shangri-La* needed to scale down some of its ambitions while keeping its first intention as authentic as possible: the choice of 3D animation and pre-rendered VR was prioritised over m-AR and live data [3]. However, collaboration between an artist, some creative technologist and an engineer [20] resulted into a relevant and pertinent locative attraction and community interaction for Wellington City.

The *MINA* app reached its use optimisation and momentum after hurricane Sandy (late 2012, early 2013): a few people contributed to the documentation of the semi-permanent landscape of devastation and reconstruction thanks to their mobile devices and the *MINA* app. The app served as a catalyst for more dialogue between people, local bodies and insurance companies. The *MINA* app development is in hibernation at the moment however it is easy to imagine that the next step of such a project is to get a direct link with *Google Street view* to provide users a live m-AR experience on any site or to outfit participants with an immersive experience thanks to *Google Cardboard,* for instance. In this case, mobile functionality, and mobile capability provides an interfaces between international people and local content by virtue of a global collaborative and creative project.

In both cases, the key attributes and functionality of mobile technologies, although used at its early stage, are about enhancing user experience in relation to their settings, to their spatial coordinates. While there is more and more suspicion and awareness of big data and surveillance, the authors are cognisant of arising ethical questions and concur with Buxton's perspective:

"My work at each of these places was to collaboratively create a mobile based user experience which supported the spirit of that place, and the work of those associated with it." [5][6]

Also, based on Stedman [35], Director of the Human Dimensions Research Unit –Cornell University, who declared that "understanding place in its true complexity is a multidisciplinary exercise", the authors argue that historical, political, sociological and economical meanings highly influence one's perception about a specific location through the lens of a mobile device. The main idea raised from the authors' experiences resides in developing user experiences in relation to mobile technologies, geo-localisation and culture. As Matsuda wrote:

"Like photography, the design of AR environments has been democratized (...) everyone participates in its consumption and creation. The augmented space is truly a spatial expression of the people who live in it." [23].

Furthermore, across various papers or article focusing on emerging mobile technologies [4][9][36][39], Buxton [6] noted that only a few "cite authors such as Rose (2002) or Somerville (2007, 2010) in their work – however many of these themes are the same i.e. embodiment, practice, interconnection and permeability. Today's technologies bridge between worlds using the body and screens (portals) as points of connection."

Referring back to *Pokemon Go* and based on the finding of the *Shangri-La* and *MINA* app projects, the authors concur with Rieser [32] and Haque [15] who highlighted that different forms of 'invisible' technologies and data are shifting people's relationship to spaces and places and that society is evolving from perceiving its surroundings as 'static' and 'dead', to an environment which is rather 'fluid', 'dynamic' and inherently interactive, and where technology has been so integrated into the environment that it is no longer visible [9].

VI. CONCLUSION

In this paper, the authors contextualised and defined the notion of m-AR, mobiquity and glocal heritage in relation to user experience; they discussed their methodological approach based on phenomenology and qualitative data;

they reflected upon two environmental projects conceived using early mobile technologies and capabilities and highlighted the importance of collaboration [20] to facilitate and integrate innovative, engaging and inclusive mobile experiences.

A process-driven creative approach can question the existing linearity of creation and user experience in mobile environment, as well as multiple perspective contributions. Therefore, the authors argue that co-creation and multi-disciplinary collaborations enrich and enhance interactive environments, and enhance the potential of user experience in tourism [25]. Following is a pertinent quote from Holliday, that summarises this position:

"Engineers are efficient problem solvers. Business people think short term. Designers want things to be elegant and beautiful. All three need to create collaboration and harmony, and honor the value each other brings. There needs to be a new kind of 'multi-dimensional' approach to design that is yet to be invented." —Linda Holliday (@lmholliday / CITIA)

Additionally, the concept of a general augmented space could soon be a reality with the development of AR-based technologies, such as *Magic Leap* (2010), *Google's AR* smart lenses (2014), and *Microsoft HoloLens* (2016). Moreover, Cara Kahl [19] argue that:

"Social groups play an integral part in establishing creativity. Their perception and evaluation processes may be hard to decipher in an increasingly networked world, but ignoring this complexity does not necessarily facilitate scientific comprehension of creativity. This notion implies adopting a relational approach to investigating it. And taking the phenomenon for what we make of it: a dynamical construct based on social stimulation and judgment processes".

The critical analysis and the results developed in this paper lead the author to state that the notion of prosumers needs to be addressed in the wider context of tourism, from a political and cultural perspective in order to design a coalition for a new social reality. For instance, mobile AR, VR or MR should allow for more interactive experience, and less passive connection such as traditional in-situ or online content delivery. Beyond mobile AR, MR and VR, shall we start investigating about the *phygital*, a combination of physical and digital?

ACKNOWLEDGMENT

IAE-Nice (France); Maison des Sciences de l'Homme et de la Société Sud Est (MSHS Sud Est), University of Nice Sophia Antipolis; Auckland University of Technology (New Zealand); Dr Maggie Buxton, Dr Thomas Cochrane, Dr Max Schleser, Amanda B. Lees, and Pete Lipponen.

REFERENCES

[1] Ahonen, T. (2011). *Insiders' guide to mobile.* Chicago: TomiAhonen Consulting.

[2] Alba, A. (2014). *Virtual reality moves past gaming to sell travel destinations, hotels.* Retrieved from http://www.nydailynews.com/news/world/virtual-reality-moves-gaming-preview-travel-hotels-article-1.2038240

[3] Bellini, H., Chen, W., et al. (2016). *Virtual & Augmented Reality: Understanding the race for the next computing platform.* Retrieved from https://360.gs.com/gs/portal/home/fdk/?st=1&n=%2Fportal%2Fannouncement%2Fresearch%2

[4] Brown, T. (2008). *Design thinking.* Harvard Business Review.

[5] Buxton, M. (2015). *Practicing place with locative mobile technology*, Whanake: The Pacific Journal of Community Development, 1(1), pp. 29-38.

[6] Buxton, M. (2015). *Tricksters, Technology and Spirit: Practising Place in Aotearoa-New Zealand.* (PhD Thesis / AUT University)

[7] Bystrom, K.-E., Barfield, W., and Hendrix, C. (1999). *A Conceptual Model of the Sense of Presence in Virtual Environments. Presence: Teleoperators and Virtual Environments*, 8(2), pp. 241–244. doi:10.1162/105474699566107

[8] Cochrane, T., Narayan, V. and Antonczak, L. (2015). *Designing Collaborative Learning Environments Using Mobile AR.* In S. Carliner, C. Fulford & N. Ostashewski (Eds.), Proceedings of EdMedia: World Conference on Educational Media and Technology 2015 (pp. 1394-1402). Association for the Advancement of Computing in Education (AACE).

[9] Deuze, M. (2012). *Media life.* Cambridge, UK: Polity.

[10] Fonseca, D., Redondo, E., Puig, J., Villagrasa, S., and Navarro, I. (2014). *Augmented and Geo-located information in architectural educational framework.* 16th International Conference on Human-Computer Interaction in Virtual, Augmented and Mixed Reality, R. Shumaker (Eds.). *Human-Computer Interaction, Part II, HCII 2014, LNCS, 8526*, 15.

[11] Fritz, F., Susperregui, A. and Linaza, M.T. (2005). *Enhancing cultural tourism experiences with augmented reality technologies.* in the 6th International Symposium on Virtual Reality, Archaeology and Cultural Heritage VAST. Retrieved from http://public-repository.epoch-net.org/publications/VAST2005/shortpapers/short2005.pdf

[12] Garau, C. (2014). *From Territory to Smartphone: Smart Fruition of Cultural Heritage for Dynamic Tourism Development*, Planning Practice & Research, 29:3, pp. 238-255.

[13] Govers, M. and Go, F.M. (2005). *Projected destination image online : website content analysis of pictures and text*, Information Technology & Tourism, Vol. 7 pp. 73–89.

[14] Han, D., Jung, T., and Gibson, A. (2014). Dublin AR: *Implementing Augmented Reality (AR) in Tourism*, In Xiang, Z. and Tussyadiah, I. (eds), Information and Communication Technologies in Tourism, Springer International Publishing, Wien, New York, pp. 511-523 (ISBN: 978-3-319-03972-5) DOI: 10.1007/978-3-319-03973-2_37

[15] Haque, U. (2004). *Invisible topographies.* In M. Rieser (Ed.), The mobile audience: Media art and mobile technologies, pp. 245-252. New York, NY: Rodopi.

[16] Hiles, D. (2001). *Heuristic inquiry and transpersonal research.* In proceedings of the CCPE Conference, London - October, 2001. Retrieved from http://www.psy.dmu.ac.uk/drhiles/HIpaper.htm

[17] Höllerer, T. H., and Feiner, S. K. (2004). *Mobile augmented reality.* In K. H & H. A (Eds.), Telegeoinformatics: Location-

Based Computing Services, pp. 1–39. Taylor & Francis Books Ltd.

[18] Jenkins, H., Ford, S., and Green, J. (2013). *Spreadable media: Creating value and meaning in a networked culture postmillennial pop*. New York, NY: NYU Press.

[19] Kahl, C. H., da Fonseca, L. H., and Witte, E. H. (2009). *Revisiting creativity research: An investigation of contemporary approaches*. Creativity Research Journal, 21 (1), pp. 1-5.

[20] Maeda, J. (2016). *#DesignInTech Report 2016*. Kleiner Perkins Caufield & Byers, (2016). Retrieved from http://www.slideshare.net/kleinerperkins/design-in-tech-report-2016

[21] Manovich, L. (2002). *The Poetics of Augmented Space*. Retrieved from http://manovich.net/index.php/projects/the-poetics-of-augmented-space

[22] Matsuda, K. (2010). *Domesti/city: The dislocated home in augmented space*. Master's thesis, University of London, London, United Kingdom. Retrieved from http://km.cx/projects/domesticity-the-dislocated-home-in-augmented-space/

[23] Matsuda, K. (2015, September 23). *Keiichi Matsuda: Future ways of living* [Video file]. Retrieved from https://www.youtube.com/watch?v=8xq5oMwgaug&t=832s

[24] Matsuda, K. (2016, May 19). *Hyperreality* [Video file]. Retrieved from https://www.youtube.com/watch?v=YJg02ivYzSs

[25] Metz, R. (2015). *Four Important Things to Expect in Virtual Reality in 2016*. Retrieved from http://www.technologyreview.com/news/545011/four-important-things-to-expect-in-virtual-reality-in-2016/

[26] Noble, I., Bestley, R. (2011) *Visual Research: An introduction to research methodologies in graphic design*. London, UK: AVA Publishing.

[27] Noh, Z., Sunar, M. and Pan, Z. (2009). *A review on augmented reality for virtual heritage system*, 4th International Confrence on E-Learning and Games: Learning by Playing. Game-based Education System Design and Development, pp. 50-61.

[28] Nonaka, I., and Konno, N. (1998). *The concept of" ba": Building a foundation for knowledge creation*. California management review, 40(3), pp. 40-54.

[29] Papetti, C. and Miranda, S. (2014). *Les nouveaux paradigmes du tourisme mobiquitaire* (The New Paradigms of the Mobiquity Tourism), Hors-série de la revue Mondes du tourisme, décembre.

[30] Petkova, V. I., and Ehrsson, H. H. (2008). *Being There Together: Experiments on Presence in Virtual Environments*. PloS one, 3(12). doi:10.1371/journal.pone.0003832

[31] Rahman, N. H. A., Khalifah, Z., and Ismail, H. N. (2016). *The role of sensory experiences in appreciating the cultural heritage attractions*. Tourism, Leisure and Global Change, 3, TOC-117.

[32] Rieser, M. (2004). *Overview*. In M. Rieser (Ed.), The mobile audience: Media art and mobile technologies. New York, NY: Rodopi.

[33] Robertson, R. (1995). *Glocalization: Time-Space and Homogeneity-Heterogeneity*, in Mike Featherstone, Scott Lash and Roland Robertson (eds.), Global Modernities, pp. 25-44. London: Sage.

[34] Schleser, M. and Turnbridge T. (2013). *24 Frames 24 Hours*. Ubiquity: The Journal of Pervasive Media 2 (1&2).

[35] Stedman, R. C. (2003). *Sense of place and forest science: Toward a program of quantitative research*. Forest Science, 49(6), pp. 822-829.

[36] Sussmann, S., and Vanhegan, H. (2000). *Virtual Reality and the Tourism Product Substitution or Complement?* In Proceedings of the Eighth European Conference on Information Systems (ECIS), pp. 1077–1083. Vienna, Austria: Wirtschaftsuniversität Wien.

[37] Wenger, E. (1998). *Communities of practice: Learning, meaning, and identity*. Cambridge university press.

[38] Witte, E. H., and Kahl, C. H. (2008). *Small Group Performance: reinterpreting proximate evaluations from an ultimate perspective*.

[39] Yovcheva, Z., Buhalis, D., Gatzidis, C. (2012). *Smartphone Augmented Reality Applications for Tourism*, e-Review of Tourism Research (eRTR), Vol. 10, pp 63-66, No. 2, 2012.

Monetizing IoT: Enabled via LTE Broadcast

Rajat Kochhar, Nipun Sharma
Ericsson Global Services India (Pvt.) Ltd.
Gurgaon, India
e-mail: rajat.kumar.kochhar@ericsson.com , nipun.sharma@ericsson.com

Abstract **- This paper proposes the mechanisms for Communication Service Providers (CSP) to boost the M2M/IoT monetization, enabled via upcoming Long Term Evolution (LTE) broadcast technology. LTE Broadcast will play a crucial role in delivering the multimedia services efficiently to smart devices (sensors, connected vehicles, smart phones) for long range communication including mission critical services. Relevant contents can be positioned strategically across different network nodes and accessed in an optimized manner to provide economical delivery model for business to business (B2B) and business to consumer (B2C) ecosystem. This paper further suggests mechanisms by which operators can monetize the cached data in the network by providing economical charging plans to the end customer. LTE broadcast based commercial deployment has already started since 2014 and is gaining traction across different verticals enabling reduced expenditure and providing enhanced customer experience.**

Keywords-LTE Broadcast;Content Caching;Internet of things (IoT);Communication Service Provider;Mission critical services, etc.

I. INTRODUCTION

There has been tremendous growth in data traffic, particularly multimedia contents, over mobile broadband networks in the last couple of years. This growth has been fueled by the increase in the number of users and variety of applications delivering multimedia contents e.g., movies, songs, sports, video on demand etc. In addition, launch of smart devices with higher media capabilities, and advancements in 3G/4G technologies have further complemented this growth.

The mobile networks are constantly evolving to cater to the needs of new business models across different services. For example, LTE Cat-M1 or LTE-M as it is commonly known and Narrow-Band IoT (NB-IoT) emphasize on low bandwidth communication while LTE Broadcast enables high speed multimedia content delivery e.g., live Sport events. LTE network architecture is further evolving to support Machine to Machine e.g., M2M/IoT communication so that billions of new devices can be connected to support IoT specific use cases. While LTE-M/NB-IoT primarily focuses on low power/cost and low bandwidth communication requirements, LTE Broadcast enables delivery of contents to millions of devices in an efficient and cost effective manner.

Multimedia Broadcast Multicast Services (MBMS) is a point-to-multipoint unidirectional service in which data is transmitted from a single source entity to multiple recipients. The MBMS service offers two modes: Broadcast mode and Multicast mode. Broadcast mode is supported for LTE and 3G, and Multicast mode is supported for 3G. The specification is referred to as Evolved Multimedia Broadcast Multicast Services (eMBMS) when transmissions are delivered through an LTE network. eMBMS is also known as LTE Broadcast. This paper will emphasize on LTE broadcast as it is upcoming and will act as a baseline technology for future deployments.

The multicast services can only be received by those users which have subscribed to that specific service and are part of the multicast group associated with the service for 3G subscribers only. Both broadcast and multicast services across 3G/4G technology are unidirectional, point to multipoint transmissions of multimedia content and involve transmission of text, audio, video, pictures, emergency alerts like Tsunami warning, firmware upgrade of sensors/devices associated with smart meters/homes/cities, Live Streaming of sports event etc.

For delivering multimedia content to the multiple users, LTE Broadcast (eMBMS) is technically positioned as more effective and efficient technology than ubiquitously used unicast mode for data communication. This technology further optimizes the network resources to reduce the overall operational expenditure and exploits the network for mission critical activities. Moreover, LTE Broadcast could be instrumental in maximizing the network utilization including radio interfaces. LTE broadcast services enable delivering content in densely and crowded location efficiently and therefore free up the capacity for other services including voice services, proximity services, etc.

LTE broadcast has the potential to lead to commercial pay-per-view TV channels from mobile operators. It could also enable many more use cases, including the delivery of device updates to smartphones and tablets, distributing data to connected cars or broader IoT applications including important emergency alerts. The operators can either create their own services or enable the delivery of third party services via Application servers (as suggested by 3GPP specification in Release 13 or onwards).

In this paper, we will propose new mechanisms that CSPs can use, by leveraging on LTE Broadcast technology along with innovative caching techniques. CSPs can adopt differential charging for their customer based on the location of the content which the customers are accessing. We also suggest in the paper, about the benefits of having a content registry node in the network which can greatly reduce the signaling needed to update all cached data in the network.

The remainder of the paper is organized as follows: Section II describes LTE Broadcast Network Architecture details along with major network nodes in the system. Section III deals with various caching mechanisms used in the network. Each caching mechanism has its own pros and cons. We will have a detailed look on them and propose ways to monetize LTE Broadcast services in the network along with some real-life examples in Section IV. We conclude our paper in Section V.

II. LTE BROADCAST/eMBMS NETWORK ARCHITECTURE

Content via LTE Broadcast is delivered by collaboration of three core network elements. eMBMS is realized by enhancing capabilities of existing functional entities of the 3GPP architecture and by addition of new functional entities like BM-SC node [6].

A. Broadcast Multicast Service Centre (BM-SC)

The BM-SC provides functionality for MBMS related user service provisioning and delivery. Typically, it serves as an entry point for content provider, used to authorize and initiate MBMS Bearer services including schedule and delivery management. Typically, the multimedia content for MBMS is placed outside the core network. The BMSC schedules the MBMS session and is also responsible for monetizing the services enabled via offline and online charging interfaces.

B. Multimedia Broadcast Multicast service Gateway (MBMS GW)

Another new network element is the MBMS-GW, which provides the gateway functionality between the radio and service networks. It forward streams from the BM-SC to all participating eNodeB in the single frequency network (SFN) transmission. MBMS Gateway (MBMS-GW) delivers MBMS traffic using IP multicast to multiple cell sites in single transmission. SFN technology is used to distribute broadcast streams into well-defined areas – where all contributing cells send the same data during the same radio time slots [4].

In general, LTE broadcast can deliver multimedia content to a broad area, ranging from a shopping street to a part of city e.g., in case of sporting events, musical concerts etc. but can also be extended to entire network covering many cities e.g., emergency alerts etc. The size of broadcast area is often decided by the type of content and the intended audience.

C. MCE/MME

Multi-cell/multicast coordination entity (MCE) is responsible for administration of radio resources for MBMS to all radios that are part of the MBMS service area. The same is not explicitly highlighted in the diagram below. The mobility management entity (MME) performs the MBMS session control signaling including session start, update, and stop, as well as delivering additional MBMS information to the MCE including QoS and MBMS service area.

With the wide deployment of Content Distribution Networks (CDNs), delivery of multimedia content to the users has been optimized to some extent. Deployment of CDNs has reduced the backhaul issues faced by Communication service providers. Additionally, with different caching mechanisms, operator can further cache the content from CDN or external servers within the operator's network for enhanced content management. This will further reduce the dependency and latency introduced by accessing content external to the operator's network. Fig. 1 below provides the network architecture for LTE Broadcast network.

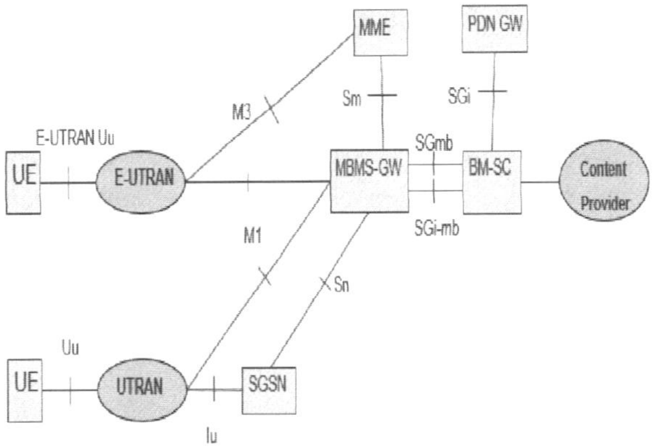

Figure 1. Reference architecture for Evolved Packet System with E-UTRAN and UTRAN (MBMS Broadcast Mode only) 3GPP 23.246

III. CACHING MECHANISMS

Caching is a mechanism to store the content for future or simultaneous requests enabling faster access. Content stored in the cache might be the result of an earlier access or copy of data available in the network.

Caching, in general is extensively used in IP and telecom networks for faster access of relevant content. Typically, the contents were stored and accessed from content providers network which was external to the operator's network. Due to ever growing demand for multimedia content, operators were forced to devise innovative ways to deliver contents which reduces network load and provides superior customer experience. LTE Broadcast services provide an effective method to deliver content to multiple users. LTE Broadcast, complemented by caching techniques could further optimize the network resource utilization, which could be used by other real time services such as Voice over LTE (VoLTE) services.

Deploying caches in mobile networks is regarded as a promising way to improve user experiences and reduce the signaling within the network nodes as data traffic is expected to increase many folds in future. Caching within the network can be done on different network nodes e.g., Radio Access Network (RAN) nodes or core network nodes. Caching on RAN nodes has more advantages in comparison to caching on core network nodes in terms of reduction of back-haul traffic and improvement of user experience, since contents can be retrieved at base stations. Content can also be pushed to the cache of user equipment and the user is provided a preview of the content. Caching reduces the cost of content delivery by optimum usage of radio and network resources, which can be utilized for other critical communications.

There are multiple caching techniques which can be implemented to reduce response time and network latency as described below:

A. *Core Network Caching*

In LTE networks, core network caching is typically deployed at the packet data network gateway or the PGW, within the evolved packet core (EPC). For LTE broadcast, this content can be cached at eMBMS core network nodes e.g., BM-SC and MBMS GW [1]. These cache servers offer huge data storage capacity and store content that is popular among large number of users. Caching at core network nodes reduces the uncertainties of latency and remote server response times towards content provider network, outside operators trusted domain. When a popular content is found in a networks cache, this information is no longer obtained from the content provider. This reduces the traffic between the EPC and the content providers, thus reducing the bandwidth and cost of the Internet connection.

B. *RAN Caching*

RAN caching position the content towards the edge of the network typically at RAN nodes. With caching at core network nodes, multimedia content still need to navigate through the backhaul links of an LTE network. For LTE broadcast RAN caching, the contents are cached at participating eNodeB (enabled by SFN). LTE macro, metro and pico base stations are ideal platforms to incorporate RAN caching because of their all-IP architecture and their proximity to the end user.

By positioning contents at multiple eNodeBs, backend signaling is considerably reduced. Since backend signaling and transport costs are often the largest parts of the LTE network OpEx, the savings can be remarkable [5][9]. Technical artifacts are already available suggesting different cache techniques at RAN level, cache content management (e.g., replicating the cache contents across eNodeBs), etc. and further enhancements are ongoing. One of the well identified use cases in IoT domain includes small amounts of non-critical data transfer to multiple IoT devices. Typically, Firmware updates for connected vehicles, smart meters, etc. are initiated simultaneously which might lead to network and RAN congestion. Connected cars require firmware updates and typically need to be downloaded while the cars have the ignition on typically during morning hours. LTE network can push the firmware updates to participating eNodeB at non-peak time (or night) and same can be broadcasted from eNodeBs to all the participating connected cars simultaneously. RAN caching techniques can support the above and other relevant IoT based use cases efficiently, releasing the bandwidth for LTE network for critical and real-time communication like VoLTE.

C. *User Equipment (UE) Caching*

Content can also be cached in user equipment, thereby providing fast access to popular videos, news, songs etc. When the network is comparatively less utilized, multimedia content is typically pushed into the cache memory of the User Equipment (e.g., Smartphone). User is provided with a preview of the content and the ability to purchase the content, if interested. In case the user does not purchase the content, then the content is purged from the cache memory and the user is not charged for the downloaded multimedia content pushed by the operator [3]. Artificial Intelligence (AI), along with customer experience management, will play a major role in providing the contextual analysis on user's behavior and preferences. Additionally, utilizing the network when it is less loaded will further support operators to monetize existing infrastructure and reduce busy hour spikes in the network. Events relevant to the geography, linguistics or global events like Olympic games highlights are some of the use cases where content can be pushed by operator to multiple users based on machine learning algorithms e.g., historical behavior.

Research is also ongoing on collaborative caching [8] e.g., caching at EPC and RAN to reduce costs and support more requests compared with existing caching schemes when fetching dedicated contents.

Table II gives the main differences between different caching mechanisms as explained in Section III.

TABLE II . TYPES OF CACHING IN NETWORK

	Core Caching	RAN Caching	UE Caching
Content Placement	Content is placed within EPC	Content is placed at eNODEBs	Content is pushed to UEs cache
Size of cache	It's generally tera bytes of cache.	It's few Giga bytes of Cache	The content size could vary from few KB to few MB
Benefits	Bandwidth and cost to ISPs are reduced for the operator	Backhaul signaling and transport cost is reduced	Reduction in busy hour traffic by pushing the content to UE at non-peak period.

IV. MONETIZING LTE BROADCAST SERVICES

Commercial deployment of LTE broadcast had been initiated few years back primarily in 2014. LTE broadcast technology was demonstrated during Global events like XX Commonwealth Games in Glasgow, FA Cup final UK, Super Bowl XLVIII in US. Tier-1 Operators like Verizon have commercially launched their Go90 service including both On-Demand and LiveTV offerings. LTE Broadcast alliance was formed in Apr 2016 include global operators and Vendors like Verizon, KT, Reliance JIO, Ericsson, Netgear, etc.

Operators must leverage upon the caching techniques discussed above and develop methods to boost the monetization of LTE Broadcast offerings to create mutually beneficial business models for operators and end customers. CSPs should enable differential charging mechanisms based on the content location, providing economical offering for (cached) contents to the customers. End customer should be charged based on location of the content and the network resource utilization for offered services from CSPs [2]. Operators can further exploit the content location information indicating the content location, as determined by the requested multimedia content, and sending the charging-related information to the charging node in the network. The charging-related information enables differentiated charging by the charging node.

In LTE Broadcast architecture, BM-SC node is responsible for generating the charging event towards Charging Data Function (offline) and Online Charging System (Online) node depending upon the Rf/Ro Interface [7]. Charging information generated by event produced by BM-SC nodes are S-BMSC-CDR and C-BMSC-CDR for subscriber and content provider charging respectively. For every MBMS bearer, the BM-SC would be aware of the location of multimedia content either through communication with MBMS-GW or a Content Manager. If the content is available in the internal cache or externally, BM-SC sets up the content location to a predefined value for each of the cases representing the logical location of the content cache e.g., device, eNodeB, local network provider, external content provider. Fig. 2 below provides the network architecture for LTE Broadcast network along with content Registry node which will contain the information regarding the cached content in the network.

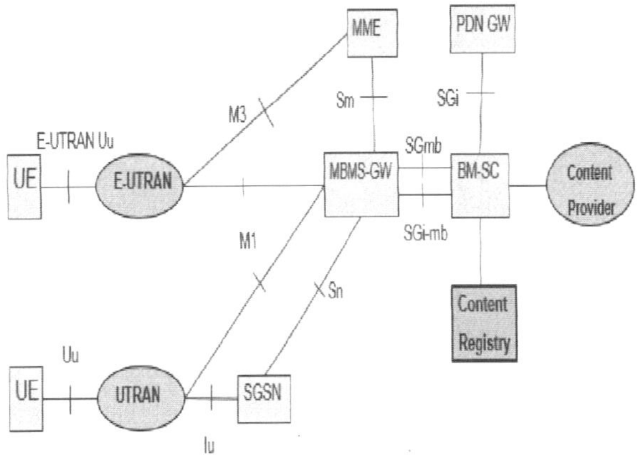

Figure 2. Introduction of new logical entity named Content Registry in LTE Broadcast architecture

We propose that BM-SC node should maintain a content registry (logical entity), that should keep the details of all the content which are cached at different core and RAN nodes. On signaling level, BM-SC would query each eNodeB periodically or eNodeB could send the information on the control plane to BM-SC regarding the content location so that BM-SC has the most updated information available in Content Registry. Information from Content Registry module would further be populated with "Content Location Information" while charging event would be generated from BM-SC towards the charging interface to OCS and CDF module.

Differential charging e.g., charging based on the content location provides CSPs a mechanism to minimize the dependency on content providers for multimedia content. The most watched movies, sports videos, events can be cached locally by the operators thereby offering economical rates to the subscribers.

Content location based charging would encourage the subscribers to use the locally cached content leading to efficient use of the network. This would in-turn result in lower Cap-Ex and Op-ex. Additionally, empowering subscribers with multiple as well as economical options for consuming multimedia content would lower the churn rate.

V. CONCLUSION

IoT's evolution has been closely linked and complemented by the evolution of the mobile communication and Internet to enable a connected world. To enable faster IoT adoption, LTE Broadcast services will further support to monetize service models across B2B and B2C domain. For B2B segments, CSPs will support IoT offerings across multiple domains e.g., firmware/OS upgrades for IoT enabled equipment's like health monitoring devices, smart home devices and sensors. Additionally, LTE broadcast will play a major role in broadcasting public safety communication for emergency as well as routine updates like traffic snarls at highways, extreme weather warnings.

CSPs can further optimize their offering in existing B2C ecosystem by streaming multimedia contents like Live events, next generation TV services, internet radio, video on demand providing enhanced user experience. LTE Broadcast enables the operators to charge premium rates for premium content with guaranteed quality, knowing that they can deliver always, no matter how popular any certain live event or media offering may become. This certainly allows the operators and its media partners to offer new services without the fear of congestion or failure to deliver to its customers. Additionally, the paper suggests innovative delivery model for proactively advertising the information cached at various nodes and promoting economical charging use cases.

The capability and the flexibility enabled by LTE Broadcast is a very powerful tool for operators wishing to embrace and evolve the non-traditional business models spanning across IoT offerings and media content delivery.

ACKNOWLEDGMENT

The authors would like to thank Abhay Vaish - CTO and Head of Network Engineering, Rana Pratap Sircar, Rahul Verma and Srinivas Mylavarapu, all of Ericsson Global Services India Pvt. Ltd. for their valuable feedback, support and guidance.

REFERENCES

[1] S. Nanjunda Swamy Jamadagni, R. Rajadurai and S. Anegundi Ganapathi , Jan 2014 , Patent Pub No. : WO 2014017789 A1

[2] D. Shrader, S. Kumar, T. Lohmar and N. Sharma , June 2016 , Telefonaktiebolaget L M Ericsson (Publ), Patent Pub No.: US 20160182244 A1

[3] E. Lyons Soelberg, M. Austin and J. Fraser Whitehead , June 2013 , At&T Mobility Ii Llc , Patent Pub No. : US 8467773 B1

[4] Ericsson Review - 90th Anniversary 2014, doi:https://www.ericsson.com/assets/local/publications/ericsson-technology-review/docs/2014/ericsson-review-90-years.pdf

[5] H. Sarkissian , The business case for caching in 4G LTE networks, doi:http://www.wireless2020.com/docs/LSI_WP_Content_Cach_Cv3.pdf

[6] 3GPP TS 23.246, "Multimedia Broadcast/Multicast Service (MBMS); Architecture and functional description"

[7] 3GPP TS 32.240, "Telecommunication management; Charging management; Charging architecture and principles"

[8] S. Ren , T. Lin and W. An , "Collaborative EPC and RAN Caching Algorithms for LTE Mobile Networks" , IEEE Explore , Dec 2015 , doi: 10.1109/GLOCOM.2015.7417681

[9] H. Ahlehagh and S. Dey , " Video caching in Radio Access Network: Impact on delay and capacity" , IEEE Explore , April 2012 , doi:10.1109/WCNC.2012.6214173

DISCLAIMER

This paper reflects the authors own opinions and not necessarily those of their employer.

Blockchain for Enterprise: Overview, Opportunities and Challenges

Elyes Ben Hamida*, Kei Leo Brousmiche *, Hugo Levard *† and Eric Thea *
*Institute for Technological Research SystemX, France
Email: elyes.ben-hamida,kei-leo.brousmiche,eric.thea@irt-systemx.fr
†SQLI, France
Email: hlevard@sqli.com

Abstract—**The Blockchain technology has received increased interests in recent years, from both the scientific community and the industry. This technology represents a major paradigm shift in the way smart cities solutions will be built, operated, consumed and marketed in the near future. Even though Blockchains will have a tremendous potential impact on businesses and societies, there are many open challenges that need to be carefully tackled. This article focuses on enterprise Blockchains and provides a detailed analysis on its core components, technologies and applications. Finally, various research challenges and opportunities are discussed.**

Keywords–Blockchain; Distributed Ledger Technology; Smart Contract; Consensus Algorithm; Data Privacy and Security; Scalability.

I. INTRODUCTION

Blockchains have recently attracted increased interests within the governments, businesses and research community, with applications in key industries, such as finance, insurance, logistics, energy and transportation. Indeed, the blockchain technology is foreseen as the core backbone of future smart cities and Internet of Things by enhancing its security, data management and process automation.

A blockchain [1] is essentially a trustless, peer-to-peer and continuously growing database (or ledger) of records, including distributed applications (or smart contracts), that have been executed and shared among the participating entities. It enables applications and systems to operate in a fully decentralized fashion without the need for any third party or trust authority.

This technology per se is not novel, but is rather a combination of well-known building blocks, including peer-to-peer protocols, cryptographic primitives, distributed consensus algorithms and economic incentives mechanisms. A blockchain is more a paradigm shift in the way applications and solutions will be built, deployed, operated, consumed and marketed in the near future, than just a technology. Blockchain is secure by design and relies on well-known cryptographic tools and distributed consensus mechanisms to provide key characteristics, such as persistence, anonymity, fault-tolerance, auditability and resilience. Indeed, each record in the chain is verified by consensus of a majority of the blockchain's participants, and once committed on the ledger, cannot be easily tampered with.

More recently, smart contracts [2] have emerged as a new usage for blockchains to digitize and automate the execution of business workflows (*i.e.,* self-executing contracts or agreements), and whose proper execution is enforced by the consensus mechanism. This makes the blockchain technology particularly suitable for the management of medical records [3], notary services [4], users' identities [5] and reputations [6], data traceability [7], *etc.*

However, several challenges will need to be addressed to unlock the tremendous potential of blockchains, especially before this paradigm shift becomes technically, economically and legally viable in business environments. The first category of these challenges concerns the technical aspects of blockchains, including in terms of governance (*i.e.,* open, private or consortium), scalability, data privacy, and validity of smart contracts. The second set of challenges is related to the development of viable underlying business models and incentives mechanisms. Last but not least, the legal aspects of blockchains represent a challenge, especially in France and Europe, where this technology should be analyzed in the light of upcoming new regulations, such as the General Data Protection Regulation (GDPR) (Regulation (EU) 2016/679 [8]), and whose objective is to strengthen users' data privacy and protection within the European Union.

This article focuses on the technical aspects of blockchains and their potential benefits to enterprises and industrial use cases. The remainder of this article is organized as follows. Section II discusses the technical aspects of blockchains in terms of taxonomy, system architecture, consensus algorithms and technologies. Section III provides a classification of blockchains applications and highlights typical use cases in the finance, energy, mobility and logistics sectors. Section IV draws and discusses various research challenges and opportunities. Finally, Section V concludes the article.

II. PUBLIC AND PRIVATE BLOCKCHAIN TECHNOLOGY

While public blockchains enable parties to make transactions in a secured manner in trust-less environments, they show certain limitations when applied to industrial use cases. Indeed, we believe that aspects, such as controlled data reversibility (1), data privacy (2), transactions volume scalability (3), system responsiveness (4) and ease of protocol updatability (5) that are crucial for the majority of corporate applications are not covered by public blockchain implementations. These shortcomings led industrials to develop alternative blockchain technologies tackling the aforementioned aspects and intended for restricted audience. These technologies can generally be classified into two categories: private and consortium blockchains [9]. The distinction between them comes down to the governance scheme. In private chains, one participant rules the whole system whereas members of consortium blockchains share the authority among them. Nowadays, new terms and concepts are flourishing for categorizing approaches between public and private blockchains such as semi-private or enterprise technologies. However, their differences concerns the application level and not architectural aspects. For the sake of simplicity and clarity, we will assume that the term of private blockchain encompasses these different non-public concepts in the following. In next sections, we overview the architecture of both public and private blockchain and highlight their inherent differences.

A. Blockchain Architecture

a) Data structure: The data structure of a blockchain, whether public or private, corresponds to a linked list of blocks containing transactions. Each element of the list, has a pointer to the previous block. Moreover, each pointer of a block contains the hash of the previous block. This hash is the key element of the blockchain security. Indeed, if an adversary tries to modify the content of a block, anyone can detect it by computing its hash and comparing it to the hash stored in the next block to see the inconsistence. In order to avoid this detection, the adversary could try to change all the hashes from the tampered block to the latest block. However, this is not feasible without the consenting of more than the half of the participants (see Section II-A0c). Therefore, modifying the content of a block is impossible over public chains. On the other hand, private chains members can easily come to an agreement off-line and modify data content (1). Private chains can be seen as append-only databases where the main goal consists in sharing and syncing data within a consortium.

b) Network and privacy: Along with its data structure, a blockchain is based on a peer-to-peer network that ties its participants. Depending on the implementation of the blockchain, the network can be public (*i.e.,* anyone can access it) or private (*i.e.,* only accounts that are allowed can participate). This restricted access to the network assures data privacy (2). Moreover, some private blockchains allows to control data visibility at a more finer grain by enabling data encryption at transaction level (*e.g.,* [10]). Nodes can read data and ask the network to add new data, these pending data are then picked by some special nodes called the miners (also known as block generators or validators).

c) Security and scalability: Miners, or validators, are nodes that are willing to share their computational power to add blocks to the blockchain. The process for selecting the actual node that will add the next block among all the validators is referred as a consensus protocol. In a trust-less public configuration, this consensus is crucial for the integrity and security of the data. Thus, to prove their commitment and prevent malicious activity, miners usually have solve a computationally demanding cryptographic puzzle (*i.e.,* Proof of Work [11]).

On the other hand, in private chains, since miners or rather validators are preliminary known and trusted to some degree, this process of selection can be lowered in terms of computational power. This reduction of complexity in the consensus protocol leads directly to an increased scalability in terms of transactions throughput (3). An overview of the major consensus algorithm is proposed in section II-B.

d) Forks and responsiveness: Once a miner's block has been selected, it is added to the blockchain and the information is broadcast. Due to network effects, there are cases where multiple miners blocks are selected, so there are different versions of the blockchain in different regions of the network. This is called a fork: the blockchain splits into branches. In this case, nodes should somehow converge towards acknowledging a unique and same version of the blockchain. In practice, the Proof of Work consensus achieves this result by requiring miners to work on the longest branch that they see. However, this means that even if a transaction has been validated, we cannot be sure that it will remain on the main chain. In Bitcoin, users usually wait 6 blocks of confirmation before considering a transaction as valid. Thus, there is a correlation between the probability of fork occurrence and the *responsiveness* of the blockchain. On private chains, the use of adapted consensus algorithm lowers the risk of forks and increases the system responsiveness by shrinking waiting time for confirmations (4).

e) Forks and updates: In addition, miners software is sometimes updated to fix bugs or add functionalities. This also can create forks, as different nodes might handle transactions differently depending on their software versions. We usually distinguish:
- soft forks where the transactions considered valid by the new version are also valid for the old version.
- hard forks where the transactions considered invalid by the old version might be valid for the new version.

While it is complicated to synchronize the software over public blockchains due to the huge amount of anonymous participants and potential disagreements among them, it is easily feasible on private chains where members know each other and can quickly come to a mutual agreement (5).

This overview of blockchain architecture components highlighted the main differences between public and private implementations. In the next section, we present major consensus algorithms used in private blockchains that enables high transaction throughput compared to the regular algorithm such as the Proof of Work or the Proof of Stake.

B. Consensus Algorithms

As we saw in the previous section, generating and adding blocks to the linked list is a crucial step in terms of security and scalability. In this section we describe the major consensus algorithms that are used today in private blockchains by which participants choose the block generator node (*i.e.,* miner).

1) Proof of Elapsed Time: At each cycle, miners wait for a given random time. The first miner for which the waiting time has elapsed is selected to validate a block before repeating this process. In other words, the miner with the shortest wait time is elected the leader. For instance, this mechanism is used in Quorum, a permissionned fork of Ethereum [10]. This is one of the least secured consensus protocol aimed for private blockchain with high trust among the block makers since miners can cheat on the random generation.

However, Intel proposed to use Trusted Execution Environment (TEE) such as Software Guard Extensions (Intel SGX) to ensure safety an randomness. The idea is to protect code and data from disclosure or modification through the use of enclaves, which are protected areas of execution [12]. Another way to prevent miners to cheat and monopolize leadership on the network is to add a voting consensus on top of the elapsed time protocol. While this protocol is less secured that its competitors (without using safety protocols), it remains very fast and scalable.

2) Leader based consensus: This category gathers algorithms that attempt to solve the problem of *agreement* in which distributed/asynchronous processes have to agree on a

TABLE I. BENCHMARKING OF ENTERPRISE BLOCKCHAIN PLATFORMS AND TECHNOLOGIES.

Company	Platform	Popularity	Activity (GitHub)	Consensus	Performance	Data Encryption	Smart Contract	Virtual Machine	Oracle	Additional Features
Coin Sciences	Multichain	Medium	Medium	Round robin (diversity)	100-1000/s	No	No	No	No	Assets, streams
J.P. Morgan	Quorum	High	Medium	Time and vote based	12-100/s	Yes	Yes	EVM	-	-
IBM	Hyperledger Fabric	High	High	PBFT	10k-100k/s	Yes	Yes	Chaincode	No	-
Coinprism	OpenChain	Medium	Low	Partitioned	Thousands/s	Yes	No	Yes	-	Assets, side-chains
Chain	Chain Core	High	High	Federated consensus	N/A	Yes	No	Yes	-	Assets
R3	Corda	Medium	High	BFT, etc.	N/A	Yes	Yes	JVM	Yes	Assets, market
Monax	Monax	High	Medium	Tendermint	10k/s	No	Yes	EVM	-	-

leader process believed to be valid. While it is mathematically proven that this problem is impossible to solve [13] (*i.e.*, if one process fails, the termination/validity of election cannot be guaranteed), in practice some algorithms manage to achieve the agreement with a probability close to 1 [14]. This is achieved by using either an oracle that provides random numbers or failure detection (or a combination of these) [15][14].

3) Practical Byzantine Fault Tolerance (PBFT): PBFT is a replication algorithm that is able to tolerate Byzantine faults [16]. To put it simply, this algorithm ensures the consistency of consensus as long as $2/3$ of the network's nodes are safe (*i.e.*, not malicious or faulty). This is enabled by replicating behaviors (*i.e.*, state machines) of generating nodes and applying protocols for choosing a leader among them. However, this method requires that all the generating nodes know each other since they need to communicate. In other words, all the parties have to agree on the exact list of participants.

4) Federated Byzantine Agreement (FBA): The FBA consensus protocol breaks the prerequisite of the unanimously accepted membership list of PBFT by letting any new participants to grow the network [17]. Each participant knows some nodes that are considered as important and waits that the majority of them and the majority of the rest of the network agree on a new transaction before considering it as valid. The main limitation of this protocol remains its performance: it costs a lot of messages (*i.e.*, communication over the network) that come with latency.

5) Tendermint: Tendermint is another byzantine fault tolerant algorithm based on a state machine that enables nodes to propose and vote for the next validator [18]. It makes the assumption that the network is partially synchronized since the time factor is central to this protocol. For each new block, a validator node is selected in a round-robbin manner which has to propose a block. This block is then spread into the network and has to gather more than two third of votes of *members* within a given time period before being added to the blockchain. However, these members are selected based on their stake and thus ties trust to resource ownership.

6) Diversity Mining consensus: The mining diversity consensus approach was proposed by MultiChain [19] to resolve the case where one participant of a private bockchain could monopolize the mining process. The solution consists in limiting the number of blocks that might be created by one specific miner within a given time period. This implicitly enforce a round robin schema where each permitted miner must create blocks in rotation. A *mining diversity* parameter defines the strictness of the rotation, where a value of 1 means that every permitted miner should be included in the rotation, whereas a value of 0 means no restriction at all.

C. Benchmarking Existing Technologies

Blockchain is currently under extensive research and development, leading to a high market fragmentation, with more than 20 different technologies and frameworks, which have been released by companies, open-source communities and universities. Table I compares the key characteristics of some popular blockchain technologies, especially for the context of enterprise and consortium based case studies.

III. APPLICATIONS

A. Classification

Many criteria can be used to classify blockchain applications. We will start here with a technology approach: we will first describe use cases where the blockchain is a self-sufficient technology, and then move on to explore new scenarios, where the combination of blockchain and other technologies/competencies can enable new perspectives.

1) Assets and Data Management: The blockchain can be used as an immutable distributed ledger where transactions are timestamped by block, therefore directly enabling asset tracking, ownership transfert certification and history record. The appearance of Bitcoin and its crytotoken has opened an incredible potentiality: it is now possible to create a digital asset that is unique. Indeed, as opposed to a MP3 file that can be infinitely duplicate without alteration, it is not possible to give away a bitcoin without losing it. So from this perspective, a bitcoin resembles a physical object, except it lives in the digital world, and tying digital asset and difital identity leads to proof of ownership.

2) Market Places: The wish to exchange or sell these digital assets on a peer-to-peer network, *i.e.,* without relying on intermediary, leads to blockchain-based market places. One potential benefit from a decentralized market place could be reduced costs. By removing a trusted third party, and its associated fees, the created value should be better shared between the buyer and the seller. Another benefit is the system resilience, as it is not relying on a central actor that could be a single point of failure. But more importantly, we could foresee that this model generates more end-user empowerment. From an operation perspective, we could rely on peers, for example for conflicts arbitration. From a content perspective, we could imagine that end-users would have better control about which of their data is shared, and with whom. For this market place use case, optimization algorithms and multi-agents simulation could be used to enrich the trading mechanisms.

3) Data Exchanges and Processes Automation: Smart contracts (a.k.a. chaincodes) are programs that can be used to automate company internal processes, or even B2B/B2C services. But in order to be efficient, smart contracts should be combined with Artificial Narrow Intelligence (ANI) so that the workflow is smooth and fast. This requires domain specific data to build up this machine expertise. Then, ANI-driven calls to smart contracts will be possible, making the most of automation and data knowledge. Obviously, this functional layer can sit on top of the marketplaces defined above, therefore creating new opportunities for data monetization in an automatic manner (say between connected objects) or in a permissioned manner (say a marketplace where the end user keeps control of its data and decides who can access them, for how long and to do what).

4) Decentralized Autonomous Organizations (DAOs): A decentralized autonomous organization (DAO) is an organization that relies on rules implemented in smart contracts. This requires yet another level of sophistication, namely artificial general intelligence, to make it fully efficient. One can imagine that this new type of ventures could decide how to invest its money to crowdfund projects for profit, how the eventual benefits from its proceedings should be distributed, how the governance should evolve in case of disagreement and so on. So in this example, the DAO fully replicates in the blockchain world the behavior of a company board. And one can imagine many other life-similar examples.

B. Case Studies

While we described above the blockchain use cases from a technology perspective, we can also use a sectorial approach to map them.

1) Finance and Insurance: The first blockchain application was the cryptocurrency Bitcoin. But many use cases have followed since. As an example, Chaincore implements the distributed ledger technology for clearing and settlement, as a way to lower costs and improve efficiency. It can also be used to issue and trade assets, such as bonds, in a decentralized market place (see the proof-of-concept from Caisse Des Depots in France). The blockchain can also help with processes such as KYC (Know Your Customer), by sharing the proof of identity and not the data itself between banks (see KYC-chain as an implementation example). Finally, crowdsharing an insurance deductible can be a good DAO application in the insurance sector.

2) Energy: With the rise of solar panels and other green sources of energy, the energy production is becoming more decentralized and offers a promising field for blockchain applications. As an example, the distributed ledger technology can be used to certify the source of energy production, therefore guaranteeing that it is green. It can also be used to trade energy at the local grid level, between individual producers and consumers (see the proof-of-concept from LO3 Energy in Brooklyn). We can imagine further benefits in the home where devices can schedule their energy charging to optimize costs and exchange data autonomously between them.

3) Mobility: In this sector, the distributed ledger technology can be used to safely store the car data (for example, its mileage). Another example is arcade city, which is a blockchain-based ridesharing platform that matches passengers and drivers. So this is basically an uber-like service, in a decentralized architecture. One more example would be a decentralized transportation ecosystem, where people can use a same token to ride on a bus, rent a bike or carpool, without any central authority to organize its operation.

4) Logistics: In this sector, the distributed ledger technology can be used to track an asset. For example, Everledger tracks diamonds to ensure their authenticity, Provenance can track food origin to guarantee its sanitary safety. Another example would be using a blockchain to create a collaborative IT system, which matches transporters and customers timetable for efficient delivery.

IV. Research Directions and Opportunities

Blockchain is currently under extensive research and development from both the academia and the industry, however, there are still major challenges to be overcome before mass market penetration and adoption. In this section, we highlight major research directions and opportunities that we believe are important to investigate.

A. Data Analysis and Visualization

A blockchain being no more than a ledger of transactions between accounts, data from a blockchain can be seen as no more than nodes connected by occasionally existing multi-property edges. Under which structural form should they be tackled depends on the aimed the analysis. From a blockchain *network supervision* point of view, crucial in a private companies consortium, the relevant data aggregation level is the block, with a time-series scheme. From the point of view of auditing the *quality of the user activity*, transactions should be considered the atomic level to investigate, under a graph scheme, and more specifically under a time-varying graph (TVG) scheme [20].

The aim of efficiently auditing a blockchain brings several challenges:

1) Real-time analysis: Because of the possibility of forks, there is no such thing as absolute reliability of the data retrieved from the blockchain. It is decreasingly high toward the most recent blocks data, as one only get the version of the ledger stored on a node at a given time, so that a blockchain-specific time-dependent reliability weight has to be determined. This procedure must be highly dependent on the chosen consortium governance scheme.

2) Exploitable visual representation of TVG: From a graph point of view, each edge (transaction) represents a unique and directed communication bridge between nodes, having an infinitesimally narrow timewidth. To be able to graphically analyse a blockchain networks, or to compute common graph indicators such as centrality or community borders, systematic smart ways to define edges weight based on non-Dirac delta function in time have to be conceived.

3) Smart contract internal transactions unravelling: Unless explicitely coded as so, the transactions from and to smart contracts, or from smart contracts to users, are no written down in the ledger, and this can be used for transaction obfuscation allowing token laundering [21], Ponzi scheme [22] or other uses where the blockchain only serves itself. In order to determine whether or not blockchain transactions are related to real-world event, or more generaly what it is used for, studies on specific key quality indicators related to smart contract have to be conducted.

B. Blockchain Audit

Data immutability is generally put forward when referring to Blockchain technologies. However, as already discussed in Sub-section II.A.a, the written data could still be tampered and the blockchain rebuilt as long as the majority of the participants (or miners) have reached a consensus. This is especially true in consortium and private blockchains where the number of miners is generally limited in comparison with public Blockchains.

In this context, it becomes extremely difficult for a regulation authority to audit consortium based Blockchains and to check whether the data and transactions have been tampered with or not. A commonly adopted solution, consists in piggybacking data hashes from the consortium Blockchain into the Bitcoin network, by embedding those hashes inside the OP_RETURN field of Bitcoin transactions. However, this contribute in polluting and increasing the size of the Bitcoin network with nonsense and non-financial data.

More recently, alternatives solutions have been proposed to reduce the impact of piggybacking on public blockchains, including the concepts of side-chains and notary chains whose main objective is to make it extremely hard for malicious users and/or the network participants to alter the blockchain data.

C. Governance

The governance in a private blockchain assigns authority and responsibility among the consortium members. It determines nodes that will be able to create blocks (*i.e.*, miners), to read/write data, to contribute in the consensus mechanism (*e.g.*, voting for a miner) and/or to participate in decisions for the system evolution (*e.g.*, software updates, allow new nodes to join the system etc.). This power distribution has an impact not only within the system but also on the business model of the use case.

Costs linked with the system activity such as the system set-up, its execution or maintenance are shared within the consortium according to the governance scheme. It also affects future incomes or losses at a business level since the governing nodes decide the rules of the system. For example, the majority of governing nodes can decide to allow the membership a of new company into the consortium that is concurrent with a member who has no power over this decision that could jeopardize the viability of the system.

The viability of the system can also be affected by the governance definition. In many cases, to be durable, the consortium has to be able to grow by allowing new members to integrate the system. It is the case for example of new services over blockchain like dematerialized car service books. The more companies join the consortium such as car manufacturers, car repair shops or insurance companies, the more durable and available is the system. On the other hand, the power is dissolved with the growth of consortium.

One should also take into account the impacts on the business model when building the governance scheme as it will be discussed in the next section.

D. Incentives and Business Models

Blockchain solves the issues of trust between actors in situations of exchange where the temptation of cheating is high by *removing* this need of trust. Any business model based on a solution that would not claim to solve a trust issue would inevitably fail, as its solution could be replaced by a less constraining and probably already existing centralized system.

In a blockchain whose users are exclusively individuals, the pecuniary incentives must ensure that, because members either receive additional incomes or just lessen their expenses, they find a financial interest in participating to the process. In a consortium of commercial entities however, it should be pointed out that the simple fact *not to* be part of the consortium might represent a handicap that could lead to loss of turnover or customers attrition, because of the latter attraction to blockchain promises and interest in financial incentives.

E. Data Privacy

Data privacy is an imperative for enterprise blockchains. But lets first distinguish anonymity and privacy. A transaction is considered anonymous if we cannot identify its owner, whereas a transaction is called private if the object and the amount of transaction are unknown.

We have seen many schemes on public blockchains to improve privacy: Stealth Addresses, Pedersen Commitments, Ring signature, Homomorphic encryption, Zero-knowledge-proof. No scheme can hide the sender, the receiver and the amount at the same time, so we see actual implementations mixing these techniques in order to achieve the desired level of privacy. In addition, there are some known drawbacks such as computational time, so further research is needed. But we can expect that these initiatives on public blockchains will drive improvement on enterprise blockchains privacy as well.

F. Security

Guaranteeing End to End security means identifying vulnerabilities and mitigating risks at each element level and at the system level. This goes beyond looking at the blockchain building blocks (consensus, distributed network, cryptographic tools) and includes evaluating the virtual machine, the Smart Contracts, the Oracle, the user client, the hardware component, the keys management and PKI, etc. Some areas of research are the following: Formal verification of smart contracts, Usage of trusted platform modules for key storage, Identification of the different types of attack vectors and their counter strategies (sybil attacks, double spending attacks, distributed denial of service attacks, botnet attacks, storage specific attacks, censorship), Audit (detect issues a priori or a posteriori), Supervision (detect issues during run time).

G. Scalability

As usual, there is always a trade-off between costs, security and performance. Because participants are known in enterprise blockchains, the scalability issue is therefore easier to solve, as compared to public blockchains. Yet, in order to achieve scalability, we first need to keep in mind the usage context and the performance metrics we want to optimize: transactions throughput, validation latency, number of participant nodes, number of validating nodes, energy costs, computation costs, storage costs or other criteria? As always, remember the trade-off principle: A round robin consensus algorithm will scale well, but the participants need to be honest. A PBFT algorithm can recover from malicious behaviors (up to 1/3) but the validating nodes should not be too many (tens of nodes at most) if the system is to work [23]. All in all, scalability is an active area of research and we can mention some initiatives such as: fragmenting the global ledger into smaller sub-ledgers run by sub-groups of nodes, removing old transactions in order to optimize the storage, using a hierarchy of blockchains (transactions are done at a higher level and settled optionally afterwards in the blockchain), and so on.

V. CONCLUSIONS

The Blockchain technology represents a major paradigm shift in the way business applications will be designed, operated, consumed and marketed in the near future. In this paper, we analyzed the technical component of this technology and we provided a taxonomy of applications and use cases. Finally, we highlighted the major research challenges that need to be addressed before achieving mass market penetration, including the issues related to governance, audit, scalability, incentives, data privacy, security and data analytics.

ACKNOWLEDGMENT

This research work has been carried out under the leadership of the Institute for Technological Research SystemX, and therefore granted with public funds within the scope of the French Program Investissements d'Avenir.

REFERENCES

[1] Z. Zheng, S. Xie, H.-N. Dai, and H. Wang, "Blockchain challenges and opportunities: A survey," International Journal of Web and Grid Services, 2017, pp. 1–23.

[2] K. Christidis and M. Devetsikiotis, "Blockchains and smart contracts for the internet of things," IEEE Access, vol. 4, 2016, pp. 2292–2303.

[3] M. Mettler, "Blockchain technology in healthcare: The revolution starts here," in 2016 IEEE 18th International Conference on e-Health Networking, Applications and Services (Healthcom), Sept 2016, pp. 1–3.

[4] "stampd.io: A document blockchain stamping notary app," accessed: 2017-07-01. [Online]. Available: https://stampd.io/

[5] A. Yasin and L. Liu, "An online identity and smart contract management system," in 2016 IEEE 40th Annual Computer Software and Applications Conference (COMPSAC), vol. 2, June 2016, pp. 192–198.

[6] R. Dennis and G. Owen, "Rep on the block: A next generation reputation system based on the blockchain," in 2015 10th International Conference for Internet Technology and Secured Transactions (ICITST), Dec 2015, pp. 131–138.

[7] F. Tian, "An agri-food supply chain traceability system for china based on rfid blockchain technology," in 2016 13th International Conference on Service Systems and Service Management (ICSSSM), June 2016, pp. 1–6.

[8] "Regulation (eu) 2016/679 of the european parliament and of the council of 27 april 2016," accessed: 2017-07-01. [Online]. Available: http://eur-lex.europa.eu/eli/reg/2016/679/oj

[9] V. Buterin, "On Public and Private Blockchains," 2015, accessed: 2017-07-01. [Online]. Available: https://blog.ethereum.org/2015/08/07/on-public-and-private-blockchains/

[10] "Quorum | J.P. Morgan," accessed: 2017-07-01. [Online]. Available: https://www.jpmorgan.com/country/US/EN/Quorum

[11] S. Nakamoto, "Bitcoin: A peer-to-peer electronic cash system," 2008, accessed: 2017-07-01. [Online]. Available: http://www.cryptovest.co.uk/resources/Bitcoin%20paper%20Original.pdf

[12] V. Costan and S. Devadas, "Intel sgx explained." IACR Cryptology ePrint Archive, 2016, p. 86, accessed: 2017-07-01. [Online]. Available: https://pdfs.semanticscholar.org/2d7f/3f4ca3fbb15ae04533456e5031e0d0dc845a.pdf

[13] M. J. Fischer, N. A. Lynch, and M. S. Paterson, "Impossibility of distributed consensus with one faulty process," Journal of the ACM (JACM), vol. 32, no. 2, 1985, pp. 374–382.

[14] A. Mostefaoui and M. Raynal, "Leader-based consensus," Parallel Processing Letters, vol. 11, no. 01, 2001, pp. 95–107.

[15] L. Lamport, "Paxos made simple," ACM Sigact News, vol. 32, no. 4, 2001, pp. 18–25.

[16] M. Castro and B. a. Liskov, "Practical Byzantine fault tolerance," in Third Symposium on Operating Systems Design and Implementation (OSDI), vol. 99, 1999, pp. 173–186.

[17] D. Mazieres, "The stellar consensus protocol: A federated model for internet-level consensus," 2015, accessed: 2017-02-10. [Online]. Available: https://www.stellar.org/papers/stellar-consensus-protocol.pdf

[18] J. Kwon, "Tendermint: Consensus without mining," 2014, accessed: 2017-07-01. [Online]. Available: https://cdn.relayto.com/media/files/LPgoWO18TCeMIggJVakt_tendermint.pdf

[19] "MultiChain | Open source private blockchain platform," accessed: 2017-07-01. [Online]. Available: http://www.multichain.com/

[20] A. Casteigts, P. Flocchini, N. Santoro, and W. Quattrociocchi, "Time-varying graphs ans dynamic networks," International Journal of Parallel, Emergent and Distributed Systems, vol. 27, no. 5, 2012, pp. 387–408.

[21] M. Moser, R. Bohme, and D. Breuker, "An inquiry into money laundering tools in the bitcoin ecosystem," in eCrime Researchers Summit (eCRS), 2013. IEEE, 2013, pp. 1–14.

[22] M. Bartoletti, S. Carta, T. Cimoli, and R. Saia, "Dissecting ponzi schemes on ethereum: identification, analysis, and impact," CoRR, vol. abs/1703.03779, 2017.

[23] M. Vukolic, "The Quest for Scalable Blockchain Fabric: Proof-of-Work vs. BFT Replication," Open Problems in Network Security (iNetSec), 2015, pp. 112–125.

Roadside-Assisted V2V Messaging for Connected Autonomous Vehicle

Manabu Tsukada
Graduate School of Information Science and Technology, The University of Tokyo, 1-1-1,
Yayoi, Bunkyo-ku, Tokyo, 113-8656 Japan
Email: tsukada@hongo.wide.ad.jp

***Abstract*—Vehicle-to-vehicle (V2V) messaging is an indispensable tool for real-time dynamic information sharing in cooperative Intelligent Transportation Systems (ITSs). Although V2V standards are specified in the European Union, United States, and Japan, all such standards suffer from a set of common drawbacks. In this paper, we first analyze these issues and derive a problem statement. We then propose a roadside-assisted V2V messaging scheme in which roadside units construct a database of dynamic information obtained from sensors and transmit data to nearby and remote vehicles. We also design a common solution to the problem of differing regional standards by making the system independent of any specific set of standards. Finally, we analyze the potential requirements for designing a specification of roadside-assisted V2V messaging. The proposed system is designed to be technically compatible with 5G mobile edge computing.**

Keywords*–*Cooperative ITS; Vehicle-to-Vehicle; Standard; VANET; Internet

I. INTRODUCTION

Road transport is an essential infrastructure for supporting human activity; at the same time, it introduces many problems, including traffic accidents and congestion, air pollution, and increased energy consumption. Solving the problems of road transport is therefore a key to making road travel safer, more efficient, and more pleasant. Autonomous vehicles are currently attracting the attention of researchers and engineers; however, stand-alone autonomous vehicles simply replace human perception, decision-making, and maneuvering with computer control. Taking the concept one step further, Intelligent Transportation Systems (ITSs) can, for example, improve perception where there are blind spots in vehicle sensors by connecting vehicles to roadside units.

Road networks are interconnected among countries and, in the many cases where there are insignificant barriers, vehicles can easily cross country borders. To enable interoperability among countries, cooperative ITS need to be developed based on universal architecture, protocols, and technologies. To standardize cooperative ITS, the International Organization for Standardization (ISO) Technical Committee 204 Working Group 16 (TC204 WG16) (also known as Communications Architecture for Land Mobile (CALM)), in coordination with the European Telecommunications Standards Institute (ETSI) TC ITS, is developing a standard architecture for cooperative ITS called the ITS Station reference architecture [5], [4]. In the US, the Institute of Electrical and Electronics Engineers (IEEE) is standardizing a Wireless Access in Vehicular Environments (WAVE) architecture in the IEEE 1609 family of standards [2] as well as an IEEE802.11 variant for vehicular communication, IEEE802.11p [3].

Vehicle-to-vehicle (V2V) messaging is indispensable for implementing cooperative ITS involving real-time information sharing among vehicles of, for example, vehicle position data. As VRV message standards, the Cooperative Awareness Message (CAM) [8], Basic Safety Message (BSM) [1], and Advanced Safety Vehicle (ASV) have been specified in the EU, US, and Japan, respectively. Messages are transmitted by single-hop broadcasting via $5.8 \sim 5.9Ghz$ ITS wireless media (i.e. IEEE802.11p [3]) under the EU and US standards and by 760 Mhz ITS wireless media in Japan.

In theory, connected autonomous vehicles can be made aware via wireless single-hop V2V messaging of other, out-of-sight vehicles. However, the three schema described above have four potential problem areas: 1) mixed environments in which V2V message receivers cannot receive messages from vehicle without V2V transmitters; 2) V2V messages may be lost because of interference and obstacles filtering wireless communication; 3) communication ranges are limited to within the wireless range; and 4) V2V message exchange systems are vulnerable to malfunctions in sender vehicles and to malicious messaging.

In this paper, we first present an analysis of a problem statement on the above issues. To develop a potential solution addressing all the problems, we investigate a roadside-assisted V2V messaging scheme embodying a real-time cyber-physical system (CPS) comprising sensing technology and a V2V and Vehicle-to-Infrastructure (V2I) network. To take advantages of these technologies, we design a system that employs ITS dedicated media, cellular media, and IPv6. As V2V messaging systems under the EU, US, and Japanese share the four problems above, we investigate a common solution for all standards and propose adapting a layer of localization to the standards in each country.

The rest of the paper is organized as follows. Section II describes the problem statement on V2V message exchange. Section III presents details of our potential solution, called roadside-assisted V2V messaging. Section IV analyzes the requirements for the potential solution. Section V introduces related works. Finally, Section VI concludes the paper by summarizing the main discussion and addressing future work.

II. PROBLEM STATEMENT

In this section, we first describe a general scenario using the V2V messaging. Then, we analyse four potential issues arisen in the scenario.

A. Scenarios

In the ITS station reference architecture, neighboring vehicle information obtained by V2V messaging is stored in the Local Dynamic Map (LDM) [6][7] specified in the facilities layer, which provides a set of common functionalities shared by several applications for various tasks. The LDM supports various ITS applications by maintaining information on objects influencing or comprising the traffic, including highly dynamic data such as vehicle, roadside, and traffic conditions and the presence of accidents.

The LDM data, as updated by the V2V messaging, enables a connected autonomous vehicle to be aware of other vehicles out of the line of sight. Figure 1 illustrates a case in which the LDM provides accurate information to vehicles near an intersection. The lower layer of Figure 1 shows the physical space in which the road, vehicles, and a pedestrian are located, while the upper layer represents the parallel cyber space in which networked computers maintaining data that can be modified, exchanged, and shared. In the ITS station architecture, digital data received as CAMs from neighboring vehicles are stored in the LDM. In the following, we describe the protocol used the EU; however, the scenario described below applies in the US and Japan as well.

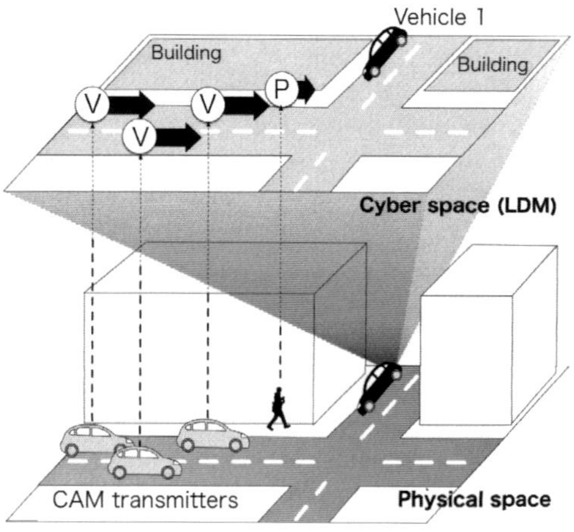

Figure 1. LDM and V2V messaging

In the case shown in Figure 1, vehicle 1 is made aware via a driver assistance alert of other vehicles behind the building. If the LDM provides accurate information that the other vehicles are not on a collision course, vehicle 1 does not need to stop before the intersection.

B. *Issues*

The above scenario assumes that all cyber-physical systems are working correctly, that V2V messages from all of the vehicles and the pedestrian are successfully delivered to vehicle 1, and that the LDM of the vehicle is kept up-to-date with respect to the surrounding environment.

In real situations, however, physical space information is often not projected correctly into cyber space. In the section, we describe the issues of cyber physical projection using V2V messaging.

1) **Mixed Environment:** To detect all vehicles using V2V messaging, all vehicles must be equipped with at least sender-side V2V device functionality. In this regard, the penetration of V2V devices is the key factor to enabling cooperative ITS. The US National Highway Traffic Safety Administration (NHTSA) had studied the possibility of implementing regulation to require V2V devices in new light vehicles [29]. However, regardless of the level of such deployment old vehicles will likely lack V2V devices, and thus we should consider mixed environments in which V2V-enabled vehicles operate among legacy vehicles.

Beyond legacy vehicles, it is important for cooperative ITS to accommodate pedestrians and bicycles, which are also generally not equipped with V2V sender devices. The current assumption of V2V messaging excludes such non-V2V aware nodes and therefore their presence is not projected into cyber space. Again, this strongly suggests that V2V messaging requires adaptation to mixed environments in which V2V-aware vehicles and non-aware nodes (legacy vehicles, pedestrians, and cyclists) coexist.

2) **Interference and Obstacle:** V2V messages are broadcast over ITS-dedicated media (ITS-5G or 760Mhz) within a single-hop distance. Messages may be lost in delivery if there are obstacles between the nodes that screen wireless radio propagation. On the road, such obstacles would include buildings, bridges, tunnels, hills, and heavy vehicles. In the above case that the V2V message does not reach the receiver, the physical information is not reflected accurately to the cyber space. The V2V receiver (Vehicle 1 in Figure 1) is not aware of the other vehicles presence or it is only aware of the old information. V2V messaging needs the solution to ensure message delivery.

3) **Limited wireless range:** V2V messages cannot be delivered beyond the range of wireless radio propagation from the sender vehicle. This range is often described as being from 500 m to 1 km when using ITS-5G in an ideal environment with a clear line of sight; however, the distance often becomes shorter in non-line-of-sight scenarios.

4) **Malfunctioning and malicious message:** In V2V systems, physical information is projected into cyber space based on data obtained from received V2V messages. In such cases, the receiver must be able to trust the sent information. To ensure trust, NHTSA's current research is based on the assumption that V2V systems will use Public Key Infrastructure (PKI) to authenticate messages [29]. However, such V2V systems would still be vulnerable to malfunctions of sender vehicles in which senders broadcast incorrect information (e.g., position, time, or speed). Such situations can be caused by GPS signal loss or metering device hardware problems. Alternatively, senders may broadcast V2V messages with incorrect information generated by software bugs or even false information generated by malicious software.

In the cases above, a receiver will generally not have the capability of validating the information in the V2V messages and incorrect physical data will be projected into cyber space. This underscores the importance of identifying and excluding incorrect or falsified physical information in the V2V message exchange process.

III. On the Design of Roadside-assisted V2V Messaging

To solve the issues of 1) mixed environments and 2) interference and obstacles described in Section II, we previously proposed a roadside assisted V2V messaging scheme called Proxy CAM. The system is compliant with EU V2V message standards (CAM) and can be adapted to the other standards (US and Japan) by adopting their V2V message formats (BSM and ASV, respectively). With some extension, the scheme represents a potential solution to all of the issues raised in Section II.

In this section, we briefly describe our previous work (Proxy CAM [20]) and then propose some extensions to Proxy CAM for a complete solution to all four issues raised in the preceding section.

A. *Proxy Cooperative Awareness Message*

An overview of Proxy CAM [20] is shown in Fig. 2. In the system, roadside sensors detect vehicles and obtain relevant information for each vehicle including position, velocity, and acceleration. The vehicle information obtained from the sensors is then sent to a server located in the system infrastructure and stored in a database. The database generates CAMs from its stored data and broadcasts these from roadside transmitters. CAM-supported vehicles receive the CAMs and store the information in their LDMs following a reception procedure identical to that involved in the baseline CAM process (Proxy CAM), and receiver vehicles ITS applications can access the data from this Proxy CAM.

In the following sections, we describe the system in detail by function.

To test the roadside system, it was implemented on Linux-based systems and evaluated in indoor and field tests.

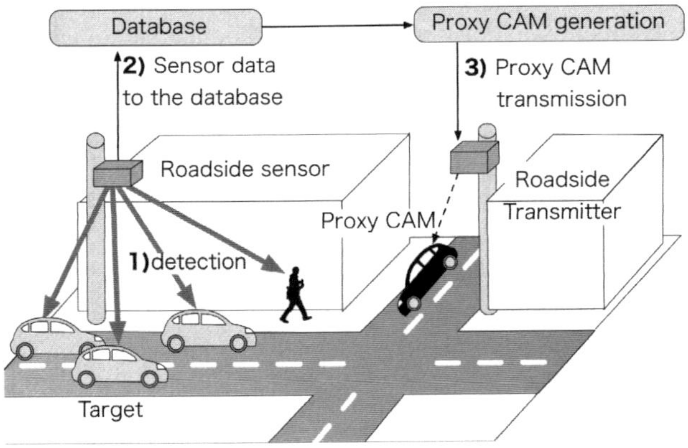

Figure 2. Overview of Proxy CAM

B. *Roadside Station for Proxy V2V Messaging*

Although Proxy CAM solves issues 1) and 2) in section II, issues 3), limited wireless range, and 4), malicious messaging, remain unsolved. In this section, we propose an additional functionality for the Proxy CAM roadside system to solve the all four issues.

1) Overview of proposed system: An overview of the proposed system is shown in Figure 3. In the system, roadside stations are installed at distributed locations, with each station detecting objects (vehicles, pedestrians, and bicycles) in the target area using sensors and wireless message receivers. The detected objects information is stored in real-time in the database (a). Data processing includes malicious message detection through comparisons between sensor data and received V2V messages (b). The roadside station then advertises its proxy V2V messages from its database over ITS-dedicated media, sharing its dynamic information on the target area (c). The remote proxy messaging system delivers this dynamic information on demand using a cellular network such as LTE (d). Receiver vehicles can obtain this dynamic information from a combination of genuine and proxy V2V messaging and remote messaging. In this manner, fresh, dynamic information is available over a wider area.

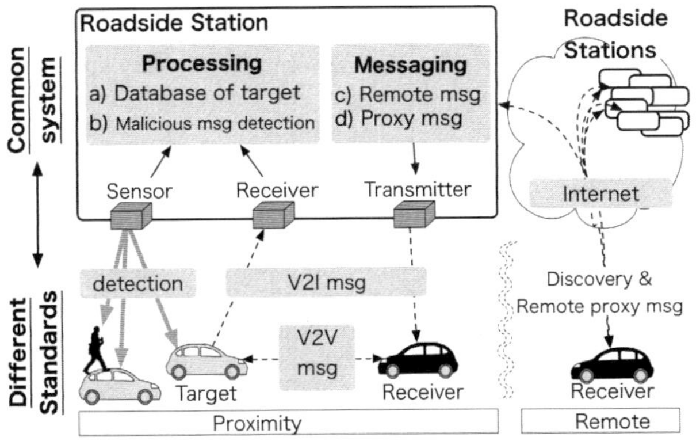

Figure 3. Roadside Station for Proxy V2V Messaging

2) Malicious message detection: Each roadside station detects target objects from both sensors and vehicle-sent V2V messages. The station can therefore check the correctness of received V2V messages by comparing their content with the sensor information during database processing (function b in Figure 3). If the location data (position, speed, direction) of the received message match the sensor data, the roadside sensor can trust that the information is correct and add the corresponding entry to the database. Data mismatching occurrences can follow two cases: 1) there are V2V message data but no sensor data at the location, or; 2) there are no V2V message data but there are sensor data at the location.

In the first case, if an object is in the target position of the sensor but no relevant V2V messages have been received, the system must add the objects information to the database. This is the normal procedure used in cases in which a vehicle is not equipped with a V2V transmitter. In the second case, if there is no object at the position indicated by a V2V message, it is highly likely that the message sender is disseminating false information. The system must therefore not include such data in its database and it must identify the sender as a malicious node. However, the manner in which malicious node alerts are sent to other nodes is outside the focus of this paper because, as mentioned in section IV-H, the dissemination of trusted information must be considered carefully for security reasons.

Conceptually, the roadside station regularly checks the consistency of physical space with cyber space and eliminates incorrect physical information projected to cyber space. To do so, the system must preferentially trust its sensor data over received messages data, following the principle generally used in connected autonomous vehicle systems.

3) Remote Proxy Messaging: A roadside station maintaining a database of dynamic information for its respective area can generate proxy informational V2V messages on behalf of target vehicles. Such messages are disseminated over the ITS media in addition to the flow of genuine V2V messages at, i.e., 760 Mhz in Japan, $5.8 \sim 5.9Ghz$ in the EU and United States. As illustrated in Figure 4, in Japan ASV messages are transmitted directly over ITS media. In the EU and United States, V2V messages are transmitted using transport and network layer technologies, namely, CAM, which is transmitted over the Basic Transport Protocol (BTP), and GeoNetworking (GN). In addition, BSM is transmitted over the WAVE Short Message Protocol (WSMP).

To overcome wireless range limitations, we apply remote proxy V2V messaging via roadside stations, as described above. To assess this scheme, we performed a preliminary evaluation using UDP/IPv6 over LTE in [21].

As shown in Figure 4, we propose remote proxy V2V messaging as a common solution usable by standards in Japan, EU, and the United States. We designed this system to use IPv6 for remote proxy V2V messaging because it fulfils cooperative ITS requirements as a result of its extended address space, embedded security, enhanced mobility support, and ease of configuration. The proposed system also uses UDP because this enables delivery of messages involving real-time data. Using UDP/IPv6, packets can be transmitted over general wireless media such as LTE, 3G, etc., in cases in which the delay is not too long for real-time data transmission.

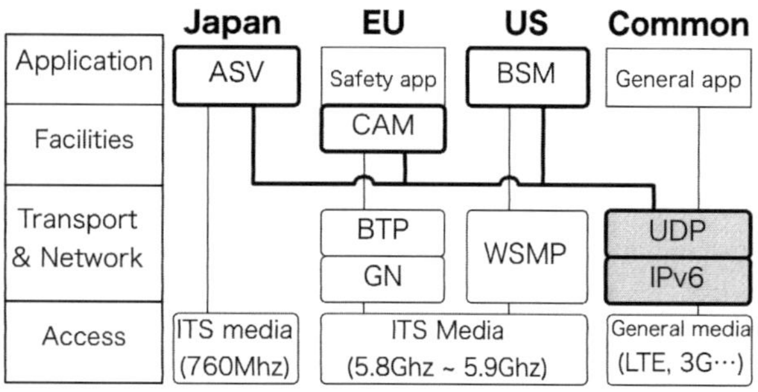

Figure 4. Remote Proxy V2V messaging

Remote proxy V2V messages are sent on-demand from vehicles arriving in a target area, e.g., an intersection, according to the requirements of the ITS application, e.g., a navigation system. The application requests dynamic information regarding future vehicle positions in advance. Note that, although IP address discovery of roadside stations is outside the focus of this paper, possible solutions for discovery include embedding IP addresses into the digital map, downloading static lists of IP addresses, or resolving the IPv6 address from geographical information using a DNS-like system [15], etc.

The remote proxy V2V messaging capability is considered to be an additional feature of the roadside station system. As such, vehicles arriving simultaneously at an intersection receive both proxy messages over the ITS media and remote messages over general media. Depending on the freshness of the data, the receiver side can then decide which data to use.

IV. Requirements for the Solution

In this section, we analyse the design requirements for the roadside-assisted V2V messaging.

A. Coexistence with the CITS Standards

To enable interoperability among countries, a cooperative ITS (CITS) must be developed based on universal architecture, protocols, and technologies. Such a solution must adopt techniques for standardized V2V messages such as CAM in the EU, BSM in the United States, and ASV in Japan. Facilities layer functionalities are of particular importance in ITS Station architecture because applications developed in the architecture access functions via a standard API; correspondingly, any solution for interoperability must not require extensions such as an LDM to the facilities layer.

B. Sensor independence

The solution proposed in this paper uses roadside sensors to obtain vehicle data within the target area with regard to, e.g., position and the velocity. Many types of sensors can be applied in this manner, including image sensors, LiDAR, induction loops, infrared sensors, and microwave radar. However, the implementation should not depend on a particular type of sensor because sensor requirements will vary by environment and purpose, e.g., urban environments or highways and budget or policy drivers. To enable versatility, therefore, roadside assisted V2V platform should support many types of sensors.

C. Distributed sensors

Sensors may be installed in multiple distributed locations to obtain wider coverage depending on need. For example, sensors may be placed to obtain real-time data from many vehicles in an urban scenario or traffic jam. Any implemented solution must have the capacity to handle large real-time data from distributed sensors.

D. Optimized Transmission Coverage

Depending on its configuration, a roadside system must be able to handle installation of multiple transmitters in distributed locations to cover a wider transmission range. It is necessary to consider strategic placement of transmitters, possibly employing message dissemination strategy algorithms for determining, for example, frequency use, message ordering, and area determination, to enable multi-transmitter scenarios. Moreover, the roadside system must be aware of the V2V messaging capabilities of target vehicles to eliminate duplicate message delivery via the genuine and proxy V2V messaging systems. The system must also estimate the original message delivery area and transmit proxy messages to the wider area not reached by the original message transmission.

E. Multi-path Message Delivery

Genuine V2V messaging provides the most accurate real-time dissemination of information on target vehicles; however, it is susceptible to the four problems described in Section II. Proxy V2V messaging is efficient in cases in which the target vehicle does not have V2V sender functionality. However, its wireless coverage is limited. Remote V2V messaging can deliver dynamic messages anywhere, although with deteriorating latency. Correspondingly, the receiver should be able to combine genuine V2V messaging, proxy V2V messaging, and remote V2V messaging functionality into a combined functionality.

F. Real-time delivery of messages

Frequent transmission of V2V messages allows for the tracking of highly dynamic vehicle status information such as position, velocity, and acceleration. Genuine CAMs, for example, are transmitted 110 times per second. A solution should also send dynamic vehicle information frequently. Overall, delays in message sensing and transmission must be minimized.

G. Scalability

In typical urban scenarios or traffic jams, a few hundred vehicles will occupy the target area of a roadside station. The generation of proxy V2V messages to and from hundreds of vehicles ten times per second can cause serious interference, leading to the potential dropping off of several hundred potential remote V2V message receivers with interest in the target area dynamic information. To avoid communication congestion, the solution must transmit dynamic information efficiently to allow for a scalable system.

H. Security Consideration

There are three security considerations relating to the proposed scheme. The first is how to maintain information on vehicles sending incorrect information as detected by the malicious message detection system. A trust model for information dissemination is necessary. Because roadside stations will be operated by public agencies, malicious node information can be shared with the public by such authorities. However, more consideration would be necessary in sharing such information with other administrative domains. Second, the V2V system was designed to send "I am here" messages. However, using proxy messaging changes the scheme to "he is there" messaging. Any potential security concerns arising from this introduction of proxy messaging should therefore be carefully analyzed. Third, the roadside stations send dynamic information via the Internet instead of by V2V single-hop broadcasting. Thus, messages must be encrypted between the roadside station and the requested vehicle to protect their data against tapping and falsification.

V. RELATED WORKS

the Japanese Metropolitan Police Department developed the Driving Safety Support Systems (DSSS) as an infrastructure assisted CITS for accident reduction [9]. DSSS tested three experimental systems: a rear-end collision prevention system for use upon entering traffic jams in which the car is positioned in front of protective obstacles; a collision prevention system for use when turning right at intersections; and a collision prevention system for use at intersections with poor sight lines. Infrastructure-assisted CITS using beacons and FM broadcasting have been implemented on highways across Japan.

It has been shown that the performance of Vehicular Ad-Hoc Networks (VANETs) depends on the transmission power, frequency of transmission, and the V2V and V2I message lifetimes [30]. In turn, it is understood that the performance of V2V and V2I messages depends strongly on the link quality and the propagation conditions [13]. [13] demonstrated that awareness levels for V2I communication are better than those for V2V communication if roadside units are located in an advantageous manner. [13] also explained that transmission power is more important than frequency of transmission in V2X communication.

[24] demonstrated how multi-sensor data fusion can leverage consistency and plausibility checking for perception sensor data. In particular, the contents of CAMs as delivered by connected vehicles with on-board perceptions sensors can be independently validated.

A wide variety of sensing modes can be implemented for use in road traffic. Vision-based vehicle detection and tracking techniques are summarized in [28]. Millimeter-wave radar and cameras are important equipment for sensing vehicles using vision-based systems. Millimeter-wave radar can also be used for measuring target range and speed, as is currently done by police in traffic speed regulation [28]. Furthermore, millimeter-wave radar can be used under poor viewing conditions in bad weather. Stereo cameras are another very effective method for sensing vehicles. Such cameras can sense both a vehicle position and velocity [11].

One approach to creating messages for sharing object perceptions relayed from sensors is Cooperative Perception Messaging (CPM), which is specified in Ko-PER as a method for sharing perceived dynamic objects in equipped vehicle or roadside station environments [26][27]. Environmental Perception Messaging (EPM) uses proprietary messages that contain lists of all perceived objects and carry unique IDs for vehicles registered by local perception sensors [17][16] Sensory Observation Messaging (SOM) is a proposed method for sharing infrastructure sensor information with potentially vulnerable road users [12].

Cloud-based cooperative awareness between vehicles and pedestrians was proposed in [10]. Under the scheme, pedestrians repeatedly send their positions to the cloud from their smartphones, allowing the cloud to alert vehicles to the approach of pedestrians. Vehicle-to-Pedestrian (V2P) communication was also investigated in [23], who proposed a scheme in which pedestrians receive CAMs on their smartphones from vehicles hidden behind obstacles.

In the field of cooperative autonomous driving, [22] introduced a method of occupancy grid map merging dedicated to multivehicle cooperative local mapping purposes in outdoor environments. [18][19] proposed a multimodal cooperative perception system that provides see-through, lifted-seat, satellite, and all-around views to drivers. The features of the system were validated in real-world experiments involving four vehicles sharing a road.

Traffic lights have long been used to coordinate traffic flows at intersections. To update traffic management to the connected autonomous vehicle age, [14] proposed autonomous intersection management in which vehicles coming to an intersection connect to a dedicated intersection controller that schedules transfer through the intersection. [25] extended the priority-based coordination approach at an intersection to support both autonomous and legacy vehicles.

VI. CONCLUSION AND FUTURE WORK

We have found that the V2V messaging standards in the EU, US, and Japan all suffer from four general shortcomings. To overcome these, we proposed a roadside-assisted V2V messaging system. The proposed system is a real-time cyber-physical system that integrates sensing technology with V2V and V2I networks and combines ITS and cellular media with IPv6 to disseminate dynamic, fresh information to a wider area. The proposed system also presents a common solution for differing national and regional standards, such as those in the EU, US, and Japan, as it is independent of any specific standards. We further analyzed the potential requirements for designing a specification for roadside-assisted V2V messaging.

In future work, we will need to fully implement the proposed system and validate it in field operational tests. We are also planning to evaluate the large-scale performance of the system using simulation. In the development of the fifth-generation mobile network (5G), mobile edge computing will play an important role in achieving ultra-low latency between V2V messaging. Because edge stations must be located in positions with good visibility such as intersections if they are to cover wider areas, our aim is to ensure that the proposed roadside system has high technical compatibility needed to co-locate with 5G edge stations. To this end, further study on the integration of 5G systems will be necessary.

ACKNOWLEDGMENT

This work was partly supported by JSPS KAKENHI Grant Number JP17H04678 and JP26730045.

REFERENCES

[1] SAE J2735 Dedicated Short Range Communications (DSRC) Message Set Dictionary, November 2009.

[2] IEEE 1609.0 Draft Standard for Wireless Access in Vehicular Environments (WAVE) - Architecture, April 2010.

[3] IEEE Standard for Information technology - Telecommunications and information exchange between systems - Local and metropolitan area networks - Specific requirement, Part 11: Wireless LAN Medium Access Control (MAC) and Physical Layer (PHY) Specifications, July 2010. IEEE Std 802.11p-2010.

[4] Intelligent Transport Systems (ITS); Communications Architecture, September 2010. ETSI EN 302 665 V1.1.1 (2010-09).

[5] ISO 21217:2010 Intelligent transport systems – Communications access for land mobiles (CALM) – Architecture, April 2010.

[6] Intelligent transport systems – Cooperative systems – Definition of a global concept for Local Dynamic Maps, November 2014. ISO/PRF TS 18750.

[7] Intelligent Transport Systems (ITS); Vehicular Communications; Basic Set of Applications; Local Dynamic Map (LDM), Sept. 2014. ETSI EN 302 895 V1.1.1 (2014-09).

[8] Intelligent Transport Systems (ITS); Vehicular Communications; Basic Set of Applications; Part 2: Specification of Cooperative Awareness Basic Service, Dec. 2014. ETSI EN 302 637-2 V1.3.2 (2014-11).

[9] N. Atsushi, N. Tsuyoshi, and O. Yasukazu. Demonstration Experiments of Driving Safety Support Systems Using Vehicle-to-Infrastructure Communications Systems (Japanese), 2009.

[10] M. Bagheri, M. Siekkinen, and J. K. Nurminen. Cellular-based vehicle to pedestrian (v2p) adaptive communication for collision avoidance. In *Connected Vehicles and Expo (ICCVE), 2014 International Conference on*, pages 450–456, Nov. 2014.

[11] M. Bertozzi, A. Broggi, A. Fascioli, and S. Nichele. Stereo vision-based vehicle detection. In *Intelligent Vehicles Symposium, 2000. IV 2000. Proceedings of the IEEE*, pages 39–44, 2000.

[12] R. Blokpoel and A. Stuiver. Sensory observation message and cam extensions for vru safety.

[13] M. Boban and P. M. d'Orey. Exploring the practical limits of cooperative awareness in vehicular communications. Mar. 2015.

[14] K. Dresner and P. Stone. A multiagent approach to autonomous intersection management. *Journal of artificial intelligence research*, 31:591–656, 2008.

[15] T. Fioreze and G. Heijenk. Extending the domain name system (dns) to provide geographical addressing towards vehicular ad-hoc networks (vanets). In *Vehicular Networking Conference (VNC), 2011 IEEE*, pages 70–77. IEEE, 2011.

[16] H.-J. Günther, B. Mennenga, O. Trauer, R. Riebl, and L. Wolf. Realizing collective perception in a vehicle. In *Vehicular Networking Conference (VNC), 2016 IEEE*, pages 1–8. IEEE, 2016.

[17] H.-j. Gunther, O. Trauer, and L. Wolf. The potential of collective perception in vehicular ad-hoc networks. In *ITS Telecommunications (ITST), 2015 14th International Conference on*, pages 1–5. IEEE, 2015.

[18] S.-W. Kim, Z. J. Chong, B. Qin, X. Shen, Z. Cheng, W. Liu, and M. H. Ang. Cooperative perception for autonomous vehicle control on the road: Motivation and experimental results. In *Intelligent Robots and Systems (IROS), 2013 IEEE/RSJ International Conference on*, pages 5059–5066. IEEE, 2013.

[19] S.-W. Kim, B. Qin, Z. J. Chong, X. Shen, W. Liu, M. H. Ang, E. Frazzoli, and D. Rus. Multivehicle cooperative driving using cooperative perception: Design and experimental validation. *IEEE Transactions on Intelligent Transportation Systems*, 16(2):663–680, 2015.

[20] T. Kitazato, M. Tsukada, H. Ochiai, and H. Esaki. Proxy cooperative awareness message: an infrastructure-assisted v2v messaging. In *2016 Ninth International Conference on Mobile Computing and Ubiquitous Networking (ICMU)*, pages 1–6, Oct 2016.

[21] M. Kitazawa, M. Tsukada, K. Morino, H. Ochiai, and H. Esaki. Remote Proxy V2V Messaging using IPv6 and GeoNetworking. In *Vehicular 2017*, July 2017.

[22] H. Li, M. Tsukada, F. Nashashibi, and M. Parent. Multivehicle Cooperative Local Mapping: A Methodology Based on Occupancy Grid Map Merging. *Intelligent Transportation Systems, IEEE Transactions on*, 15(5):2089–2100, Oct. 2014.

[23] P. Merdrignac, O. Shagdar, I. B. Jemaa, and F. Nashashibi. Study on perception and communication systems for safety of vulnerable road users. In *Intelligent Transportation Systems (ITSC), 2015 IEEE 18th International Conference on*, pages 1876–1881, Sept. 2015.

[24] M. Obst, L. Hobert, and P. Reisdorf. Multi-sensor data fusion for checking plausibility of v2v communications by vision-based multiple-object tracking. In *Vehicular Networking Conference (VNC), 2014 IEEE*, pages 143–150. IEEE, 2014.

[25] X. Qian, J. Gregoire, F. Moutarde, and A. De La Fortelle. Priority-based coordination of autonomous and legacy vehicles at intersection. In *Intelligent Transportation Systems (ITSC), 2014 IEEE 17th International Conference on*, pages 1166–1171. IEEE, 2014.

[26] A. Rauch, F. Klanner, and K. Dietmayer. Analysis of v2x communication parameters for the development of a fusion architecture for cooperative perception systems. In *Intelligent Vehicles Symposium (IV), 2011 IEEE*, pages 685–690. IEEE, 2011.

[27] A. Rauch, S. Maier, F. Klanner, and K. Dietmayer. Inter-vehicle object association for cooperative perception systems. In *Intelligent Transportation Systems-(ITSC), 2013 16th International IEEE Conference on*, pages 893–898. IEEE, 2013.

[28] S. Sivaraman and M. M. Trivedi. Looking at vehicles on the road: A survey of vision-based vehicle detection, tracking, and behavior analysis. 14(4):1773–1795, Dec. 2013.

[29] U.S. Department of Transportation, National Highway Traffic Safety Administration. Vehicle-to-Vehicle Communications: Readiness of V2V Technology for Application. pages 1–327, Aug. 2014.

[30] M. Van Eenennaam, W. K. Wolterink, G. Karagiannis, and G. Heijenk. Exploring the solution space of beaconing in vanets. In *Vehicular Networking Conference (VNC), 2009 IEEE*, pages 1–8. IEEE, 2009.

A Robust Distributed Notch Filtering Algorithm for Frequency Estimation Over Sensor Networks

Wael Bazzi

Electrical and Computer Engineering Department
American University in Dubai
Dubai, UAE
Email: wbazzi@aud.edu

Amir Rastegarnia, Azam Khalili, Mahtab Bahrami

Department of Electrical Engineering
Malayer University
Malayer, Iran
Email: {rastegarnia,khalili,bahrami}@malayeru.ac.ir

Abstract—**In this paper, we consider the distributed frequency estimation problem where nodes of a network collaborate with each other to estimate the frequency of a single-frequency signal from measurements corrupted by impulsive noise. In the proposed algorithm, we reduce the impulsive noise effect by using the maximum correntropy criteria (MCC). The MCC is a robust optimality criterion for non-Gaussian signal processing. In the proposed algorithm, each node employs an adaptive notch filter to filter the input noisy measurements. The nodes collaborate with each other to optimize a cost function (given in terms of the MCC) in such a way that the filter output resembles as closely as possible, the desired signal. To derive the algorithm, we first formulate the distributed frequency estimation problem in terms of the MCC. Next, we use the iterative gradient ascent approach in our solution. The developed approach will be referred to as the diffusion notch filter-MCC (dNF-MCC) algorithm. The effectiveness of the proposed algorithm is demonstrated by computer simulations.**

Keywords–Adaptive networks; frequency estimation; diffusion; notch filter.

I. Introduction

The frequency estimation problem appears in many practical applications, such as biomedical engineering, power systems, radar detection, source localization, and speech processing [1]. Several methods have been introduced in the literature for frequency estimation and tracking. In the absence of measurement noise, Pronys method can be applied [2]. For noisy environments, different algorithms such as linear prediction (LP) methods have been developed [3]. When SNR is low and limited (short data length) is available, the principal eigenvector (PE) method is a proper solution [4]. For the mentioned case, the total least squares (TLS) method can provide better frequency estimation performance [5]. Adaptive notch filtering based methods are also developed for the frequency estimation problem to track the time-varying frequencies.

All mentioned methods have been developed for single processing node. However, in many practical applications, such as radar, power systems, sensor networks we need to solve frequency estimation problems in a fully distributed manner. Recently, distributed estimation has become an important topic in signal processing research due to the developments in wireless networking and computer and sensor technologies. Several useful distributed solutions for the estimation problem have been developed, such as consensus strategies [6]–[8], adaptive networks (i.e., incremental strategies and diffusion strategies). It has been shown in [9] that adaptive networks are more stable than consensus networks and they provide better steady-state error performance. In this paper, we focus on an adaptive network based solution.

We adopt the term adaptive networks from [10] to refer to a collection of nodes that interact with each other and function as a single adaptive entity that is able to track statistical variations of data in real-time. The two major classes of adaptive networks are incremental strategy [11]–[14] and diffusion strategy [15]–[19]. Comparing the two, incremental algorithms require less communication among nodes of the networks while diffusion algorithms are scalable and more robust to link and node failure. In general, diffusion based algorithms consist of two steps including the adaptation step, where the node updates the weight estimate using local measurement data, and the combination step where the information from the neighbors are aggregated. Based on the order of these two steps, diffusion algorithms can be categorized into two classes known as the Combine-then-Adapt and Adapt-then-Combine (ATC).

In [20], a diffusion LMS algorithm for frequency estimation over sensor networks have been introduced. Although the algorithm works well in noisy environments, as we will show in this paper, it performs poorly when the data are disturbed by impulsive noises. To address this issue, we need to move beyond mean squared error (MSE) and exploit higher order moments of the error. To this end, we propose a new ATC diffusion algorithm which relies on the maximum correntropy criteria. MCC is a robust optimality criterion for non-Gaussian signal processing and has recently been successfully applied in adaptive filtering [21]–[23]. In the proposed algorithm, each node employs an adaptive notch filter to filter the input noisy measurements and generate the output signal. The nodes collaborate with each other to optimize a cost function (given in terms of the MCC) in such a way that the filter output resembles as closely as possible, the desired signal. To derive the proposed algorithm, we first formulate the distributed frequency estimation problem in terms of the MCC. Then, we resort to iterative gradient ascent approach to solve it and derive the proposed algorithm, which will be referred to as the diffusion notch filter-MCC (dNF-MCC) algorithm. We also present simulation results to show the effectiveness of the new proposed algorithm.

The remainder of this paper is organized as follows. Section

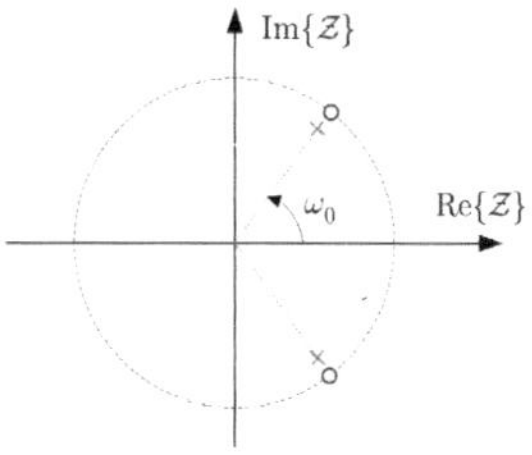

Figure 1. Pole-zero plot for the IIR notch filter with transfer function (2).

II briefly reviews the notch filter and the maximum correntropy criteria. In Section III, the proposed algorithm is introduced. In Section IV, we present simulation results to verify our theoretical analysis, and we conclude in Section V.

II. Preliminary Knowledge

To make the paper self-contained, in this section, we introduce the notch filter and maximum correntropy criteria.

A. Notch Filter

The transfer function for an M order IIR can be expressed as

$$H(z) = \frac{\sum_{i=0}^{M} a_i z^{-i}}{\sum_{i=0}^{P} b_i z^{-i}} = \frac{\prod_{i=1}^{M} (z - z_i)}{\prod_{i=1}^{P} (z - p_i)} \tag{1}$$

where in (1) $\{z_i\}$, $i = 1, 2, \cdots, M$ and $\{p_i\}$, $i = 1, 2, \cdots, P$ denote the zeros and poles of $H(z)$ respectively. As $H(z)$ reaches zero at $\{z_i\}$ and infinity at $\{p_i\}$, then we can obtain the transfer function of a notch filter with desired properties, by the appropriate placement of poles and zeros. In [24], the transfer function for a notch filter has been introduced as follows

$$H(z) = \frac{Y(z)}{X(z)} = \frac{1 + \theta z^{-1} + z^{-2}}{1 + \rho\theta z^{-1} + \rho^2 z^{-2}} \tag{2}$$

where $\theta = -2\cos(\omega_0 T)$ (T is the sampling period used to generate a discrete-time sinusoidal signal from a continuous time signal) and $0 \ll \rho < 1$. The idea is to place constrained pole-zero pairs with their angles equal to ω_0 relative to the horizontal axis on the pole-zero plot [24] (See Figure 1). Taking the inverse $\mathcal{Z}$ transform of (2), we can obtain the input-output relation for the notch filter as

$$y(n) = -\rho\theta y(n-1) - \rho^2 y(n-2]) + x(n) + \theta x(n-1) + x(n-2) \tag{3}$$

In this paper, we consider the given notch filter model in (2) to develop our proposed algorithm.

B. Maximum Correntropy Criteria

For two scalar random variables X and Y the Correntropy is defined by [21]

$$\begin{aligned} C_\sigma(X, Y) &\triangleq \mathbb{E}[\kappa_\sigma(X - Y)] \\ &= \kappa_\sigma(x - y) f_{X,Y}(x, y) dx dy \end{aligned} \tag{4}$$

where $\kappa_\sigma(\cdot)$ is a shift-invariant Mercer kernel, with the kernel width $\sigma > 0$ and $f_{X,Y}(x, y)$ denotes the joint probability distribution function of X and Y. The most widely used kernel in correntropy is the complex Gaussian kernel which is given by

$$\kappa_\sigma(\zeta) = \frac{1}{\sqrt{2\pi}\sigma} \exp\left(\frac{-|\zeta|^2}{2\sigma^2}\right) \tag{5}$$

Comparing correntropy with MSE, we note that Correntropy is a local similarity measure, whereas MSE is global; meaning that all the samples in the joint space contribute appreciably to the value of the similarity metric, while the locality of correntropy means that the value is primarily dictated by the kernel function along the $x = y$ line. Thus, we can use the localization provided by the kernel width to reduce the effects of outliers in the measured data. Note that the metrics, such as MSE that rely only on the second order moment can easily get biased in such conditions.

Remark 1. *It must be noted that in practice, the joint pdf $f_{X,Y}(x, y)$ is unknown and only finite number of samples $\{x_t, y_t\}$, $t = 1, 2, \ldots, L$ from X and Y are available. Thus, a sample estimator for correntropy can be defined as*

$$\hat{C}_\sigma(X, Y) = \frac{1}{L} \sum_{t=1}^{L} \kappa_\sigma(x_t - y_t)^2 \tag{6}$$

Remark 2. *In general, a larger kernel size makes a kernel-based algorithm less robust to the outliers, while a smaller kernel size makes the algorithm stall. Note that as $\sigma \to \infty$ the MCC approximately becomes equivalent to the MSE criterion.*

III. Proposed Algorithm

We consider a connected sensor network with N sensors (nodes) and denote it by a set $\mathcal{N} = \{1, 2, \cdots, N\}$. We denote by $\mathcal{N}_k$ the neighborhood nodes of node k where, by definition, we have $k \in \mathcal{N}_k$. The network is deployed to estimate the frequency of a sinusoidal signal $s(t) = A\sin(\omega_0 t + \phi)$ through the collected measurements by its nodes. We can assume that at any discrete time instant n, the observed discrete measurement by the node can be expressed by

$$x_k(n) = A_k \sin(\omega_0 nT + \phi_k) + \epsilon_k(n) \tag{7}$$

where A_k and ϕ_k are the amplitude and initial phase respectively and $\epsilon_k(n)$ denotes the observation noise term which is modelled as zeros mean Gaussian with variance $\sigma^2_{\varepsilon,k}$. Note that the input-output relation for the notch filter embedded in node k is given by

$$\begin{aligned} y_k(n) = &-\rho\theta_k(n) y_k(n-1) - \rho^2 y_k(n-2) \\ &+ x_k(n) + \theta_k(n) x_k(n-1) + x_k(n-2) \end{aligned} \tag{8}$$

where $\theta_k(n)$ denotes the local estimate of θ at time instant n at node k. We can estimate θ at every node by an adaptive filter algorithm as follows: at time instant n, every node k uses $x_k(n)$ as the filter input and updates $\theta_k(n)$ to generate the output $y_k(n)$ such that as time evolves, $\theta_k(n)$ converges to $-2\cos(\omega_0 T)$. To this end, we need to consider a suitable cost function. Using the MCC, we can formulate the estimation of parameter θ as the following optimization problem:

$$\underset{\theta_k(n)}{\operatorname{argmax}} \; J(\theta_k(n)) \tag{9}$$

with

$$J(\theta_k(n)) = J_0 \sum_{k=1}^{N} \sum_{m=n-L+1}^{n} \exp\left(\frac{-(d_k(n) - y_k(n))^2}{2\sigma^2}\right) \tag{10}$$

where $J_0 = \frac{1}{L\sigma\sqrt{2\pi}}$. Note that once $\theta_k(n) \to -2\cos(\omega_0 T)$, the notch filter will reject the single-frequency signal $\sin(\omega_0 nT + \phi_k)$, so the desired output is $d_k(n) = 0$. Hence, the cost function in (10) will change to

$$J(\theta_k(n)) = \frac{1}{\sigma\sqrt{2\pi}} \sum_{k=1}^{N} \exp\left(\frac{-y_k^2(n)}{2\sigma^2}\right) \tag{11}$$

Obviously the cost function in (11) can be expressed by the following equivalent form

$$J(\theta_k(n)) = \sum_{k=1}^{N} J_k(\theta_k(n)) \tag{12}$$

where

$$J_k(\theta_k(n)) = \frac{1}{\sigma\sqrt{2\pi}} \exp\left(\frac{-y_k^2(n)}{2\sigma^2}\right) \tag{13}$$

Problems of the form in (11) can be solved by diffusion adaptive networks. The general adapt-then-combine (ATC) diffusion strategy solution for (11) is given by

$$\begin{aligned} \phi_k(n) &= \theta_k(n-1) + \mu\left(\nabla_\theta J_k(\theta_k(n-1))\right) \\ \theta_k(n) &= \sum_{\ell=1}^{N} c_{\ell k}\phi_\ell(n) \end{aligned} \tag{14}$$

where $\phi_k(n)$ denotes an intermediate estimate at node k, $\mu > 0$ is the step-size parameter and ∇_θ denotes the gradient $J(\theta_k(n-1)$ with respect to $\theta_k(n-1)$. Moreover, nonnegative coefficients $c_{\ell k}$ satisfy the following conditions

$$\begin{cases} c_{\ell k} = 0, & \ell \notin \mathcal{N}_k \\ \sum\limits_{k=1}^{N} c_{\ell k} = 1 & k \in \mathcal{N}_k \end{cases} \tag{15}$$

Substituting $y_k(n)$ in (11) and taking the gradient with respect to $\theta_k(n-1)$ yields

$$\nabla_\theta J_k(\theta_k(n-1)) = \frac{-y_k(n)}{\sqrt{2\pi\sigma^3}}\Big(-\rho y_k(n-1) + x_k(n-1)\Big)\exp\left(\frac{-y_k^2(n)}{2\sigma^2}\right) \tag{16}$$

Replacing (16) in (14) gives the update equation for our proposed algorithm as follows

$$\begin{aligned} \phi_k(n) &= \theta_k(n-1) \\ &\quad - \frac{\mu}{\sqrt{2\pi\sigma^3}} y_k(n)\Big(-\rho y_k(n-1) + x_k(n-1)\Big) \\ &\qquad \times \exp\left(\frac{-y_k^2(n)}{2\sigma^2}\right) \\ \theta_k(n) &= \sum_{\ell=1}^{N} c_{\ell k}\phi_\ell(n) \end{aligned} \tag{17}$$

The pseudo code for the proposed algorithm is given in Algorithm 1.

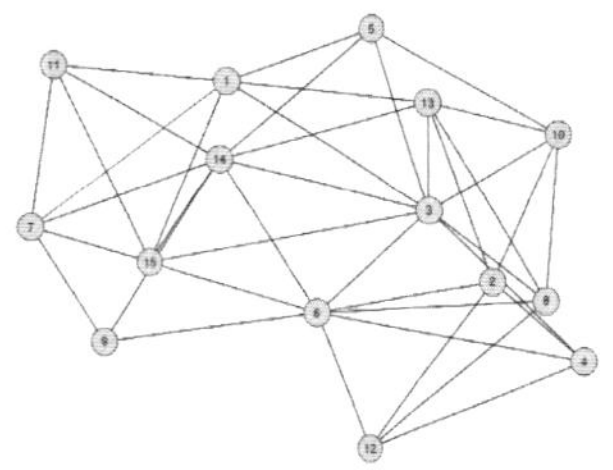

Figure 2. The network topology.

IV. Simulation Results

In this section, we present the simulation results to show the effectiveness of the proposed algorithm. To this end, we consider a network with $N = 15$ nodes as shown in Figure 2. The frequency of the sinusoidal signal is $\omega_0 = 100$ and the sampling rate is 600 Hz. So, the observed signal by every node k can be expressed as

$$x_k(n) = \sin(2\pi 100 nT + \phi_k) + \varepsilon_k(n) \tag{18}$$

where ϕ_k is selected randomly for every node. To generate the impulsive noise at node k, we can assume that the measurement noise term is given by

$$\varepsilon_k(n) = g_{k,1}(n) + b_k(n) g_{k,2}(n) \tag{19}$$

where $g_{k,1}(n)$ and $g_{k,2}(n)$ are independent, zero mean Gaussian noise with variances $\sigma_{g,1}^2$ and $\sigma_{g,2}^2$, respectively, and $b_k(n)$ is a switch sequence of ones and zeros which is modeled as an independent and identically distributed Bernoulli random process with occurrence probabilitiesprob$(b_k(n) = 1) = pr$. Note that the variance of $g_{k,2}(n)$ is chosen to be very much larger than that of $g_{k,1}(n)$ so that when $b_k(n) = 1$, a large amplitude impulse is generated. In our simulations we set $\sigma_{g,1}^2 = 0.001$, $\sigma_{g,2}^2 = 5000\sigma_{g,1}^2$and $pr = 0.02$. For the notch filter, we set $\rho = 0.95$. For the given algorithm in [20], we select the step-size as 0.01, while for the proposed algorithm we set $\mu = 0.2$ and kernel size $\sigma = 1.5$. Note that these parameters are selected for the mentioned algorithms such that when the observation noise is Gaussian, their performance is similar. In Figure 3, the learning curves, in terms of the network mean-square deviation (MSD) metric, for both algorithms are presented. Note that the network MSD is defined as

$$\text{MSD} \triangleq \frac{1}{N} \lim_{n\to\infty} \mathbb{E}\left[|\theta_k(n) - \theta|^2\right]$$

From Figure 3, we can see that the proposed algorithm achieves lower steady-state MSD than the dNF-LMS algorithm. The stead-state frequency for node $k = 4$ for both algorithms are plotted in Figure 4, where it is clear that the proposed algorithm provided more robust estimates than those of the dNF-LMS algorithm.

V. Conclusions

In this paper, we proposed a diffusion MCC-based notch filtering algorithm for the distributed frequency estimation problem. We resorted to iterative gradient ascent approach to derive the proposed algorithm. Simulation results showed that the proposed algorithm outperforms the available dNF-LMS algorithm when data are corrupted by impulsive noise.

Algorithm 1 Proposed Distributed Stackelberg Algorithm

1: **Initialization**
2: **for** $n = 3, 4, \cdots$ **do**
3: For $k \in \mathcal{N}_k$ initialize $\theta_k(1)$, $\theta_k(2)$,$\theta_k(3)$, μ
4: **Adaptation**
5: Every node updates $\phi_k(n)$ as $\phi_k(n) = \theta_k(n-1) - \frac{\mu}{\sqrt{2\pi\sigma^3}} y_k(n) \left(-\rho y_k(n-1) + x_k(n-1)\right) \exp\left(\frac{-y_k^2(n)}{2\sigma^2}\right)$
6: **Combination**
7: Every node updates $\theta_k(n)$ as $\theta_k(n) = \sum_{\ell=1}^{N} c_{\ell k}\phi_\ell(n)$
8: **end for**

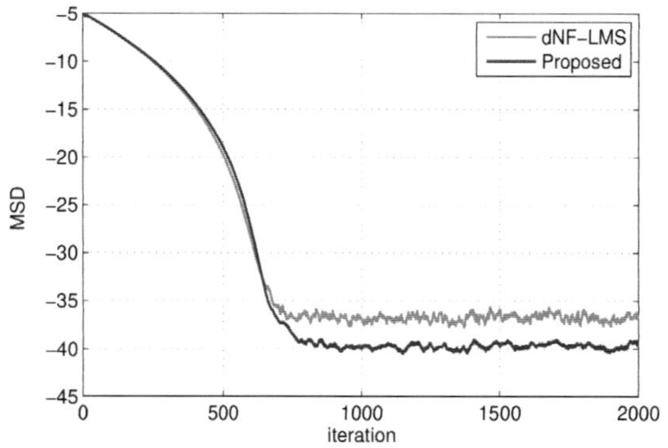

Figure 3. The network MSD learning curves for dNF-LMS and the proposed algorithm.

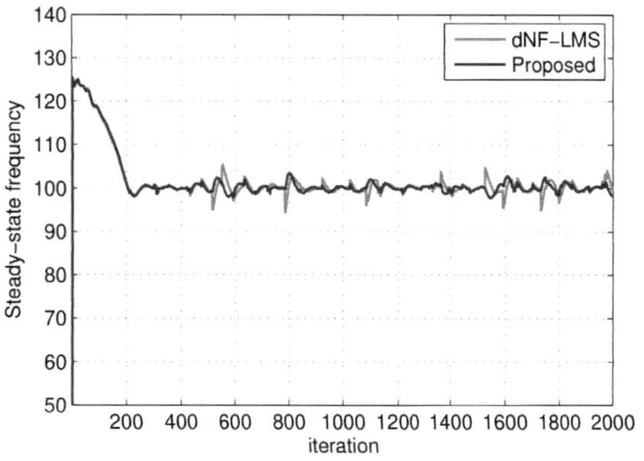

Figure 4. steady-state frequency estimations for dNF-LMS and the proposed algorithm.

REFERENCES

[1] B. G. Quinn and E. J. Hannan, The Estimation and Tracking of Frequency, ser. Cambridge Series in Statistical and Probabilistic Mathematics. Cambridge University Press, 2001.

[2] V. Slivinskas and V. Šimonytė, "Cramér-rao bound for estimates of frequencies and damping factors of real superimposed signals with multiple poles in noise," Acta Applicandae Mathematica, vol. 38, no. 1, 1995, pp. 55–78.

[3] T. J. Ulrych and R. W. Clayton, "Time series modelling and maximum entropy," Physics of the Earth and Planetary Interiors, vol. 12, no. 2, 1976, pp. 188 - 200.

[4] D. Tufts and R. Kumaresan, "Singular value decomposition and improved frequency estimation using linear prediction," IEEE Transactions on Acoustics, Speech, and Signal Processing, vol. 30, no. 4, Aug 1982, pp. 671–675.

[5] M. D. Rahman and K.-B. Yu, "Total least squares approach for frequency estimation using linear prediction," IEEE Transactions on Acoustics, Speech, and Signal Processing, vol. 35, no. 10, Oct 1987, pp. 1440–1454.

[6] R. Olfati-Saber and R. M. Murray, "Consensus problems in networks of agents with switching topology and time-delays," IEEE Transactions on Automatic Control, vol. 49, no. 9, Sept 2004, pp. 1520–1533.

[7] A. Nedic, A. Ozdaglar, and P. A. Parrilo, "Constrained consensus and optimization in multi-agent networks," IEEE Transactions on Automatic Control, vol. 55, no. 4, April 2010, pp. 922–938.

[8] L. Chen and J. Frolik, "Active consensus over sensor networks via selective communication," in 2012 9th Annual IEEE Communications Society Conference on Sensor, Mesh and Ad Hoc Communications and Networks (SECON), June 2012, pp. 389–397.

[9] S. Y. Tu and A. H. Sayed, "Diffusion strategies outperform consensus strategies for distributed estimation over adaptive networks," IEEE Transactions on Signal Processing, vol. 60, no. 12, Dec 2012, pp. 6217–6234.

[10] A. H. Sayed, "Adaptive networks," Proceedings of the IEEE, vol. 102, no. 4, April 2014, pp. 460–497.

[11] C. G. Lopes and A. H. Sayed, "Incremental adaptive strategies over distributed networks," IEEE Transactions on Signal Processing, vol. 55, no. 8, Aug 2007, pp. 4064–4077.

[12] L. Li, J. A. Chambers, C. G. Lopes, and A. H. Sayed, "Distributed estimation over an adaptive incremental network based on the affine projection algorithm," IEEE Transactions on Signal Processing, vol. 58, no. 1, Jan 2010, pp. 151–164.

[13] C. G. Lopes and A. H. Sayed, "Randomized incremental protocols over adaptive networks," in 2010 IEEE International Conference on Acoustics, Speech and Signal Processing, March 2010, pp. 3514–3517.

[14] A. Khalili, M. A. Tinati, and A. Rastegarnia, "An incremental block lms algorithm for distributed adaptive estimation," in 2010 IEEE International Conference on Communication Systems, Nov 2010, pp. 493–496.

[15] C. G. Lopes and A. H. Sayed, "Diffusion least-mean squares over adaptive networks: Formulation and performance analysis," IEEE Transactions on Signal Processing, vol. 56, no. 7, July 2008, pp. 3122–3136.

[16] F. S. Cattivelli, C. G. Lopes, and A. H. Sayed, "Diffusion recursive least-squares for distributed estimation over adaptive networks," IEEE Transactions on Signal Processing, vol. 56, no. 5, May 2008, pp. 1865–1877.

[17] R. Nassif, C. Richard, A. Ferrari, and A. H. Sayed, "Multitask diffusion adaptation over asynchronous networks," IEEE Transactions on Signal Processing, vol. 64, no. 11, June 2016, pp. 2835–2850.

[18] X. Zhao and A. H. Sayed, "Distributed clustering and learning over networks," IEEE Transactions on Signal Processing, vol. 63, no. 13, July 2015, pp. 3285–3300.

[19] Z. J. Towfic and A. H. Sayed, "Stability and performance limits of adaptive primal-dual networks," IEEE Transactions on Signal Processing, vol. 63, no. 11, June 2015, pp. 2888–2903.

[20] C. Li and H. Wang, "Distributed frequency estimation over sensor network," IEEE Sensors Journal, vol. 15, no. 7, July 2015, pp. 3973–3983.

[21] A. Singh and J. C. Principe, "Using correntropy as a cost function in linear adaptive filters," in 2009 International Joint Conference on Neural Networks, June 2009, pp. 2950–2955.

[22] A. Khalili, A. Rastegarnia, M. K. Islam, and T. Y. Rezaii, "Steady-state tracking analysis of adaptive filter with maximum correntropy criterion," Circuits, Systems, and Signal Processing, vol. 36, no. 4, 2017, pp. 1725–1734.

[23] A. Khalili, A. Rastegarnia, and S. Sanei, "Robust frequency estimation in three-phase power systems using correntropy-based adaptive filter," IET Science, Measurement Technology, vol. 9, no. 8, 2015, pp. 928–935.

[24] L. Tan and J. Jiang, "Novel adaptive iir filter for frequency estimation and tracking [dsp tips tricks]," IEEE Signal Processing Magazine, vol. 26, no. 6, November 2009, pp. 186–189.

An Optimal Design of Multiplexer Based Conservative Gate in Quantum-Dot Cellular Automata

Nuriddin Safoev
Department of Computer Engineering
Kumoh National Institute of Technology
Gumi, Korea
nuriddinsafoyev@gmail.com

Jun-Cheol Jeon
Department of Computer Engineering
Kumoh National Institute of Technology
Gumi, Korea
(Corresponding author) jcjeon@kumoh.ac.kr

Abstract—**Nanotechnology based on Quantum-dot Cellular Automata (QCA) is one of the potential alternative technology to CMOS. The design of conservative circuits received significant attention due to error detecting and energy conservation. In this paper, multiplexer based conservative gate (MX-CQCA) is presented. The property of the gate is similar to the Fredkin gate, but MX-CQCA is a conservative gate.**

Keywords-Quantum-dot cellular automata; multiplexer; conservative gate; MX-CQCA.

I. INTRODUCTION

The transistor based complementary metal-oxide-semiconductor (CMOS) technology is reaching its limited point in developing process due to high power consumption, limited physical density and high current leakage. Quantum-dot cellular automata (QCA) is one of the promising nano technologies that has attracted researchers to investigate its reliability constraints. QCA also offers new type of information computation. The basic element of this technology is QCA cell. It is square shape structure that contains four quantum dots positioned at the corners and two free electrons. Electrons can move to any quantum dot in the cell through electron tunneling due to coulombic interaction between them. In that case, polarizations -1 and +1 are encoded as logic binary "0" and "1", respectively [1][2]. QCA standard wire which propagates a logic value can be constructed by placing QCA cells side by side as shown in Fig. 1(a). Moreover, there is an inverter chain that can be constructed using rotated cells, as shown Fig. 1(b). Wire crossing in QCA is usually realized with two ways. Coplanar wire crossing is achieved using inverter chain. Second type of wire crossing is multilayer crossing that uses crossover bridge, like CMOS technology [3].

Fundamental gates of QCA circuits are inverter and majority gates. Any QCA circuits can be built using these gates. Majority gate consists of three inputs and one output as illustrated in Fig. 1(c) and (1). The three-input majority

$$M(A,B,C) = AB + BC + AC; \quad (1)$$

gate performs logic OR operation or logic AND operation by fixing polarization one of the input cells to $P = +1$ or $P = -1$, respectively. The inverter is implemented by placing two cells diagonally.

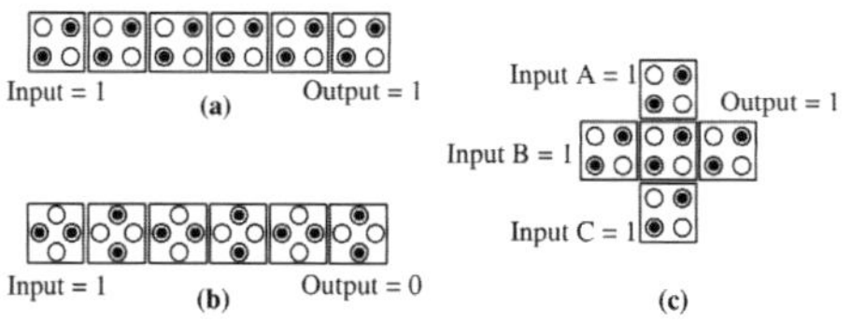

Figure 1. (a) QCA wire, (b) inverter chain, (c) QCA majority gate.

Timing and synchronization of QCA is accomplished by cascaded clocking of four phases. QCA clocking is for providing with power to all part of QCA circuits and regular computation throughout the circuit. The tunneling barrier between two dots of the cell starts to rise in the switch phase. By taking a certain polarization, the cell stores current situation during hold phase. Cell polarization is reduced and eventually lost through release and relax phases [4].

Some defects may occur while positioning cells to surface in QCA circuits. They are divided three major categories: cell misalignment, cell omission and rotation cell defects. In the first category, the defected cell is not properly lined up to its neighboring cells. Sometimes misalignment cells have no effect on functionality of the circuit, but sometimes it may cause the circuit to have unexpected output. Cell omission occur when a cell is missing in its position and becoming defective. A third type of defects occurs when cells are rotated to the other cells [5].

In this paper, multiplexer based conservative logic gate is presented. It can be used to design any majority logic and multiplexer logic based testable nonreversible circuits.

II. RELATED WORK

Conservative logic is a comprehensive model of computation, which explicitly reflects the fundamental principle of thermodynamics. It is multiple-output logic element that the number of 1s (binary 1) at the inputs is equal to its corresponding outputs. Conservative logic network can be reversible if one-to-one mapping is maintained between inputs and outputs. If one-to-one mapping is not preserved, it will be irreversible in nature. There is popular conservative gate called Fredkin gate that has three inputs and three outputs and also it is universal gate in nature.

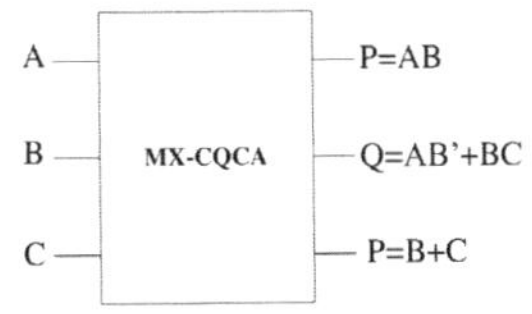

Figure 2. Schematic of MX-CQCA.

Recently, a multiplexer based conservative gate MX-CQCA is proposed, as shown in Fig. 2 [6]. Design of this gate in QCA requires five majority gates and four clocking phases. Conceptually, the target of this work is to improve MX-CQCA conservative gate in terms of complexity, occupied area and delay factors. In the gate, 13-standart functions are represented and these functions are widely used in QCA.

III. DESIGN METHODOLOGY

Commonly conservative gates use to design inverter chain. The existing conservative MX-CQCA gate also has been designed using coplanar wire-crossing. The proposed block diagram is illustrated that one QCA multiplexer and two conventional majority gates are built in the diagram, as shown Fig. 3. R and P outputs are implemented by constructing QCA logic OR and logic AND, respectively.

Construction of 2-1 multiplexer (2-1 MUX) is built based on gate level QCA multiplexer which was proposed in [7]. This structure has achieved significant improvements in terms of complexity and occupied area, as shown in Fig. 4. Moreover, the expected result is correctly simulated without delay. The gate level MUX is more suitable in several conservative structures. Hence, we also will realize this design in our proposed conservative gate for significant achievement.

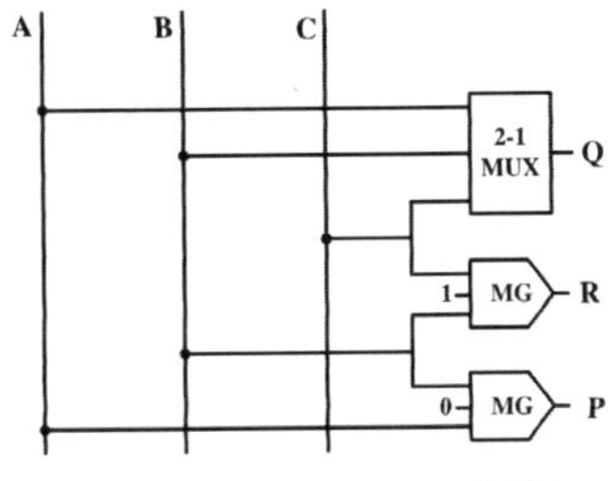

Figure 3. Block diagram of MX-CQCA.

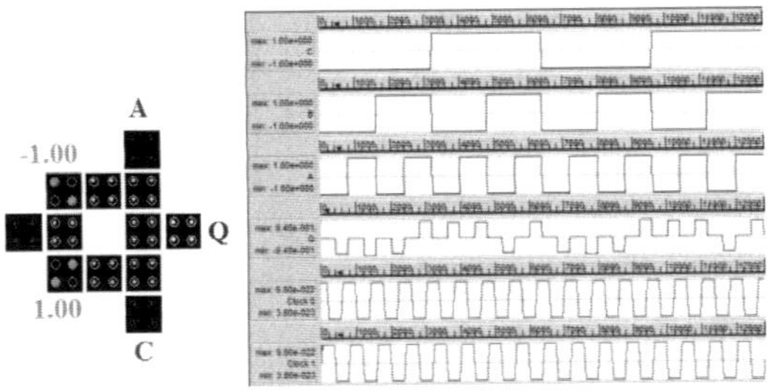

Figure 4. QCA design of MUX.

IV. PROPOSED DESIGN

Based on proposed block diagram, we have designed MX-CQCA conservative circuit in Fig. 5. It is coplanar structure and consists of 128 QCA cells. Occupied total area of the circuit is approximately equal to ($S = 0.1\ \mu m^2$) as well as the output is generated after three clock phases.

The proposed design and previous design [6] have been compared in terms of complexity, area and latency. An improvement of the proposed gate has achieved 41% less cells, 86% less area and also better latency in comparison.

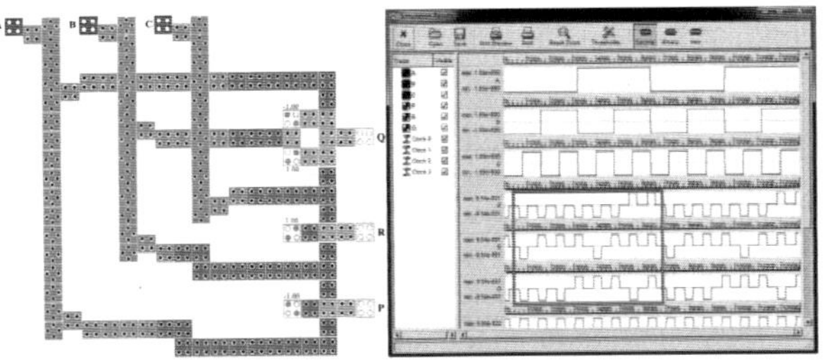

Figure 5. Proposed MX-CQCA design.

V. CONCLUSIONS

In this paper, MUX based conservative gate has been proposed. The sequential circuits can be implemented using this gate. The layout and functionality have been done using QCADesigner tool version 2.0.3 and all features work well. It can be used in testable circuits, as well as in reversible ALU designs.

ACKNOWLEDGMENT

This work was supported by the National Research Foundation of Korea (NRF) grant funded by the Korea government (MSIP) (NO. NRF-2015R1A2A1A15055749).

REFERENCES

[1] P. D. Tougaw and C. S. Lent, "Logical Devices Implemented Using Quantum-Dot Cellular Automata," Appl. Phys, vol. 75, pp. 1818–1824, 1994.

[2] J. C. Jeon, "Low Hardware Complexity QCA Decoding Architecture Using Inverter Chain,", International Journal of Control and Automation, vol. 9, no. 4, pp. 347-358, 2016.

[3] N. Safoev and J. C. Jeon, "Low Area Complexity Demultiplexer Based on Multilayer Quantum-Dot Cellular Automata," International Journal of Control and Automationetism, vol. 9, pp. 165–178, 2016.

[4] J. C. Jeon, "Extendable Quantum-Dot Cellular Automata Decoding Architecture Using 5-Input Majority Gate", International Journal of Control and Automation, vol. 8, no. 12, pp. 107–118, 2015.

[5] R. Farazkish and F. Khodaparast, "Design Characterization of a New Fault-Tolerant Full Adder for Quantum-Dot Cellular Automata," Microprocessors and Microsystems, vol. 39, pp. 426-433, 2015.

[6] H. Thapliyal, N. Ranganathan, and S.Kotiyal, "Design of Testable Reversible Sequential Circuit," IEEE Trans. VLSI, vol. 21, pp. 1201-1209, 2013.

[7] M. N. Asfestani and S. R. Heikalabad, "A Unique Structure for the Multiplexer in Quantum-Dot Cellular Automata to Creat a Revolution in Design of Nanostructures," Physica B, vol. 512, pp. 91-99, 2017

Design of QCA Full Adder for Multiplier Circuit

Young-Won You
Department of Computer Engineering
Kumoh National Institute of Technology
Gumi, Korea
yy6818@naver.com

Jun-Cheol Jeon
Department of Computer Engineering
Kumoh National Institute of Technology
Gumi, Korea
(Corresponding Author) jcjeon@kumoh.ac.kr

***Abstract*—A quantum-dot cellular automata (QCA) is one of the circuit design technology in next generation. It has advantages of nano-sized devices and low power consumption. A multiplier is used in various fields and one of the most important circuits in processor. Multiplier is consisted of AND gates and full adders. In this paper, we design a small-sized 1-bit full adder for an efficient QCA multiplier. The proposed circuit is simulated using QCADesigner tool.**

Keywords-nanotechnology; quantum-dot cellular automata; multiplier; full adder

I. INTRODUCTION

Quantum-dot cellular automata (QCA) refers to quantum computational models that have been devised in the same way as existing models of cellular automata introduced by Von Neumann. QCA is as a candidate to replace complementary metal-oxide-semiconductor (CMOS) technology and it attracts much attention with very small even number molecules or atomic scale and low power consumption [1].

Many circuits have been proposed and simulated [2-5]. One of these circuits, the multiplier receives binary data as input and outputs it. A multiplier is necessary for most processors, and since the circuit configuration is more complex than other operations in the processor, depending on the performance of multiplier circuit, the speed of the system can be affected. A multiplier consists of AND gates and full adders. In QCA, an AND gate can be designed by using a majority gate, but full adders have various circuit design methods. Since the design of an efficient full adder can improve the performance of the multiplier, many full adders have been proposed in the QCA. In this paper, we propose an efficient 1-bit full adder by using a majority gate and a 3-input exclusive-OR (XOR) gate.

II. RELATED WORK

Fig. 1 shows a QCA cell and wire. A QCA circuit consists of quantum cells with four quantum dots. The quantum cell of Fig. 1 (a) has two electrons that can tunnel between the quantum dots, and the electrons are located diagonally from each other by the Coulomb repulsion. The quantum cell has a value of 1 (1) or -1 (0) depending on the position of the electrons. A quantum cell affects adjacent cells by coulomb

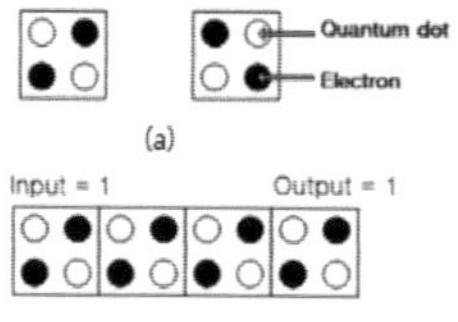

Figure 1. QCA basic concept: (a) QCA cell and (b) QCA wire based cells

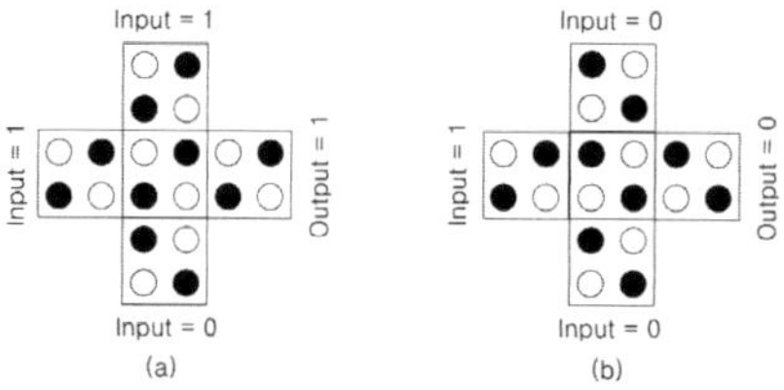

Figure 2. Two types of majority gates: (a) majority gate (output is 1) and (b) majority gate (output is 0)

repulsion. Therefore, the same value propagates along the straight line as shown in Fig. 1 (b). A QCA wire and a majority gate can be designed using the coulomb repulsion between the cells [6]. The majority gate in Fig. 2 is a circuit that determines the output value by majority vote from three inputs. By using this circuit, it is possible to design an AND gate and an OR gate which are the basis of the logic circuit. If one input value is fixed to 1, then the majority gate performs as an OR gate, and if one input value is fixed to 0, then it performs as an AND gate [7]. An AND gate is needed to compose a full adder, and the AND gate computes and outputs with fixed value of 0 and two inputs.

III. PROPOSED QCA FULL ADDER

In this section, we describe a proposed 1-bit full adder. The proposed circuit is 1-bit full adder and is designed using a majority gate and 3-input XOR gate. The majority gate is used as an AND gate and outputs Carry among the outputs of full adders. The 3-input XOR gate is a modified form of the previous 5-input majority gate [8] and outputs Sum.

Figure 3 shows a 1-bit full adder block diagram. Inputs A, B, and C output Carry through the majority gate and Sum through the 3-input XOR gate. Fig. 3 shows a 1-bit full adder

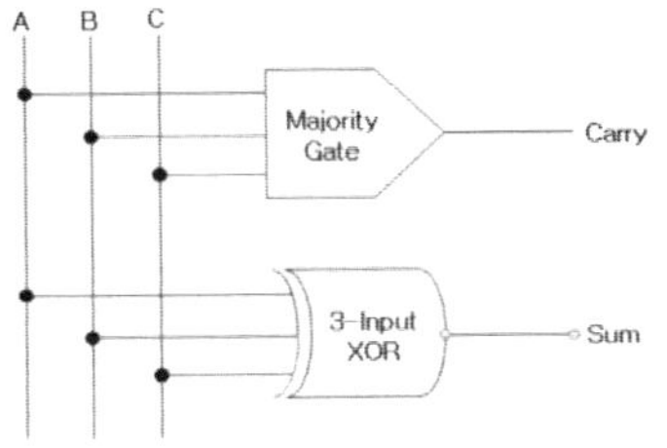

Figure 3. A block diagram of 1-bit full adder

TABLE 1. TRUTH TABLE OF 1-BIT FULL ADDER

Input			Output	
A	**B**	**C**	**Carry**	**Sum**
0	0	0	0	0
0	0	1	0	1
0	1	0	0	1
0	1	1	1	0
1	0	0	0	1
1	0	1	1	0
1	1	0	1	0
1	1	1	1	1

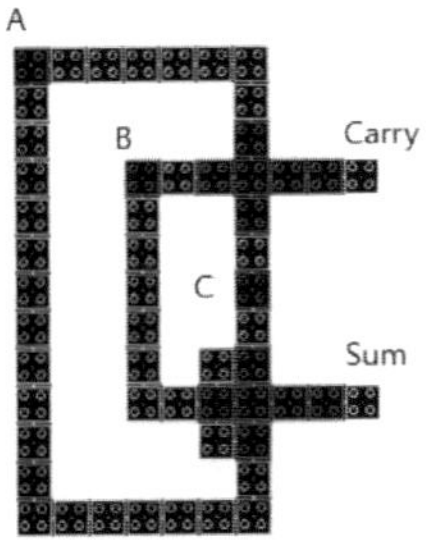

Figure 4. QCA layout of the proposed 1-bit full adder

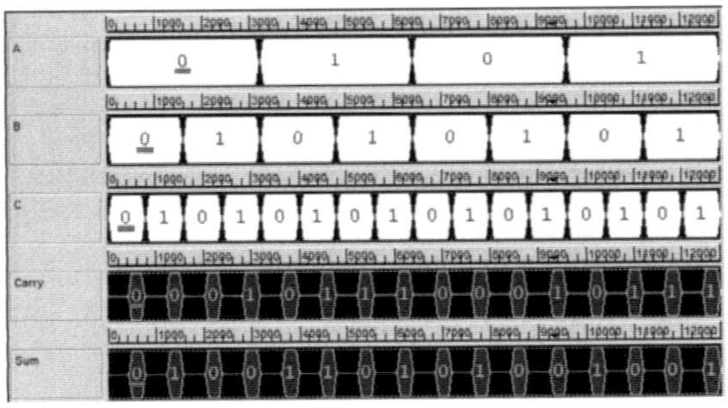

Figure 5. Simulation result of proposed circuit

block diagram. Inputs A, B, and C output Carry through the majority gate and Sum through the 3-input XOR gate. Table 1 is a truth table of 1-bit full adder. The input values are binary bits 000 to 111 and are the same as the simulation result of the proposed QCA full adder.

Fig. 4 shows the circuit layout of the proposed QCA 1-bit full adder. In order to efficiently connect the wiring of the input values on the QCA, the wiring is designed so that one input propagates the signal in both directions respectively. The 3-input XOR gate connected to the output Carry and the 3-input XOR gate connected to Sum are similar in shape, but are modified with the existing 5-input majority gate by adding two cells to the intersection cell diagonal [8]. Fig. 5 shows simulation result of our proposed full adder circuit using QCADesigner tool version 2.0.3. It shows a clear strong signal and the result is consistent with the truth table in Table 1. Three inputs are shown as a blue line on white background and two outputs are as a yellow line on black background in Fig. 5.

IV. CONCLUSIONS

In this paper, we design a new 1-bit full adder with majority gate and 3-input XOR gate in QCA. In the proposed circuit, the wires connected to the input value are designed to propagate in both directions. The proposed circuit is a planar circuit and proposed for the purpose of designing a planar multiplier.

ACKNOWLEDGMENT

This work was supported by the National Research Foundation of Korea(NRF) grant funded by the Korea government(MSIP) (NO. NRF-2015R1A2A1A15055749).

REFERENCES

[1] C. S. Lent, P. D. Tougaw, W. Porod and G. H. Bernstein, "Quantum Cellular Automata," Nanotechnology, vol. 4, no. 1, pp. 49-57, July 1993.

[2] J. S. Lee and J. C. Jeon, "Design of Low Hardware Complexity Multiplexer Using NAND Gates on Quantum-Dot Cellular Automata," International Journal Multimedia and Ubiquitous Engineering, vol. 11, no. 12, pp. 307-318, December 2016.

[3] M. Mohammad, M. Majid, and S. Gorgin, "An Efficient Design of Full Adder in Quantum-Dot Cellular Automata (QCA) Technology," Microelectronics Journal, vol. 50, pp. 35-43, April 2016.

[4] K. Makanda and J. C. Jeon, "Combinational Circuit Design Based on Quantum-Dot Cellular Automata," International Journal of Control and Automation, vol. 7, no. 6, pp. 369-378, June 2014.

[5] Y. W. You and J. C. Jeon, "Design of Extendable BCD-EXCESS 3 Code Converter Using Quantum-Dot Cellular Automata," Journal of Advanced Navigation Technology, vol. 20, no. 1, pp. 65-71, February 2016.

[6] J. C. Jeon, "Low Hardware Complextity QCA Decoding Architecture Using Inverter Chain, International Journal of Control and Automation," vol. 9, no. 4, pp. 347-358, April 2016.

[7] Y. W. You and J. C. Jeon, "Two Dimensional QCA XOR Logic Using NNI Gate," International Journal of Control and Automaton, vol. 10, no. 1, pp. 217-226, January 2017.

[8] F. Ahmad, G. M. Bhat, H. Khademolhosseini, S. Azimi, S. Angizi, and K. Navi, "Towards Single Layer Quantum-Dot Cellular Automata ADDERS based on Explicit Interaction of Cells," Journal of Computational Science, vol. 16, pp. 8-15, September 2016.

A Sensor Networking Architecture for ENTROPY - Energy-Aware Information and Communication Technologies Infrastructure Enabling Smart Building Solutions

Aristotelis Agianniotis, Vincent Schülé, Antonio Jara, Mariam Barque, Dominique Genoud
Institute of Information Systems
HES-SO VS
Sierre, Switzerland
a.agianniotis.in@gmail.com

Abstract—**The ENTROPY project aspires to significantly contribute to (1) the reduction of energy consumption, and (2) the reduction of micro-generated energy losses, in buildings. As part of this ongoing project, we have created a sensor networking infrastructure for the interconnection of heterogeneous smart sensors and devices, and the aggregation and fusion of data from multiple sources. The developed architecture provides the relevant and necessary data for the further development of energy-efficiency solutions for buildings with the aim to reduce the energy consumption and reduce the micro-generated energy losses. The sensor deployment is presented in this article for the two use cases of the HES-SO pilot. Ongoing work envisages to utilize the deployed infrastructure in conjunction with gamification techniques and serious gaming applications to record, and analyze the energy behavior of residents, and train them in order to adopt more energy efficient behaviors.**

Keywords-Wireless sensor networking; Data aggregation and fusion; Smart building; FIWARE platform; Information and communication technologies.

I. INTRODUCTION

The ENTROPY project [1] aims to significantly reduce the energy consumption and the micro-generated energy losses, in buildings. For this to be possible, we have to develop a suitable Information and Communication Technologies infrastructure for the HES-SO Technopole site which will provide the necessary energy-related and behavior-related data. In this article, we present the sensor networking architecture created for the ENTROPY project, and which architecture can be scaled, adapted, and applied to other industrial or residential applications. The deployed infrastructure will serve as a testbed for the ENTROPY project.

II. METHODS AND RESULTS

In order to facilitate the efficient aggregation of data management of smart sensors, we focus on the end-to-end interconnection of heterogeneous set of sensor networking devices, combined with existing monitoring systems and embedded devices, the design and application of efficient routing schemes and the efficient metering and storage of the collected information. We further take into account of Internet of Things (IoT) [2] networking principles for the interconnection of the network nodes. We define the whole functional and technical model of the smart metering process, together with the algorithmic and pilot part. Furthermore, we design and implement mechanisms that support efficient data aggregation and data fusion of the available data from the set of the sensor nodes in the networking infrastructure. We design techniques for information acquisition, learning and managing the associated knowledge to support the aforementioned functionalities, interlinking of collected data with other data sources available in the Linked Open Data cloud [3], and analyze the best data fusion techniques according to the requirements of the project and taking into account Complex Event Processing [4] solutions to correlate data coming from different data streams in different formats. In ENTROPY project, we take advantage of and leverage the tools for different functionalities of the FIWARE platform [5].

Sensor deployment in selected use cases of the HES-SO Technopole site is presented in Fig. 1 for the Institute of Information Systems (IIG) and in Fig. 2 for the restaurant MIKADO, respectively. The figures show the layouts of the two use cases and the specific positions of the installed sensors. Concretely, Fig. 1 shows the layout of the IIG and the position of installed sensors in the different rooms of the IIG (SAP, DUDE, YANN-OFFICE, POLARIS, Cyberlearn). Fig. 2 shows the layout of MIKADO with its different areas (main and secondary dining room, and kitchen) and the sensors currently installed there.

The sensor networking infrastructure in the HES-SO pilot is shown in Fig. 3. The ENTROPY pilot subnetwork infrastructure is centralized in the Access Point Dude-lab. The internal sensors are connected via Ethernet, Wi-Fi and 863.3 MHz radio wave. These different technologies give us a better flexibility on the sensors' placement. The Access Point then routes the connection towards the context broker server. Sensors outside of the network reach, such as the sensors of MIKADO, connect directly to the context broker server. After the data are collected, information is transmitted to the ENTROPY main server outside of our pilot infrastructure.

A minimum of 47 heterogeneous smart sensors and devices are interconnected. The devices and sensors consist of person counters, air thermometers, electric counters, energy meters, luminosity sensors, control valves, windows and door switches, CO_2 detectors. Further, local weather information and weather forecast is integrated into the system. The data aggregation and fusion takes place in almost real-time (adequate for the needs of the project). A frequency of one minute is adopted for all the data sources, with the exception of the weather forecast which occurs on an hourly basis. The data are stored in a MongoDB database and are available and can be queried at any time. A web portal [6] is also developed on which the HES-SO Technopole site manager is able to connect for assigning sensors to rooms, monitoring and visualizing data streams acquired, making queries and exporting data.

III. DISCUSSION

We have created a sensor networking infrastructure for the interconnection of heterogeneous smart sensors and devices, and the aggregation and fusion of data from multiple sources. The collected data include energy-related and behavior-related data. The developed architecture will provide the relevant and necessary data for the further development of energy-efficiency solutions for buildings with the aim to reduce the energy consumption and reduce the micro-generated energy losses. The developed architecture is developed for the HES-SO Technopole site and can be scaled and adapted to other industrial or residential applications. In order to achieve the aim of the ENTROPY project, on-going work envisages to utilize the deployed infrastructure which provides the data in conjunction with gamification techniques and serious gaming applications to record, and analyze the energy behavior of residents, and train them in order to adopt more energy efficient behaviors. To that end, the HES-SO pilot and other pilots are involved within the ENTROPY project and are working closely with academic and industrial partners.

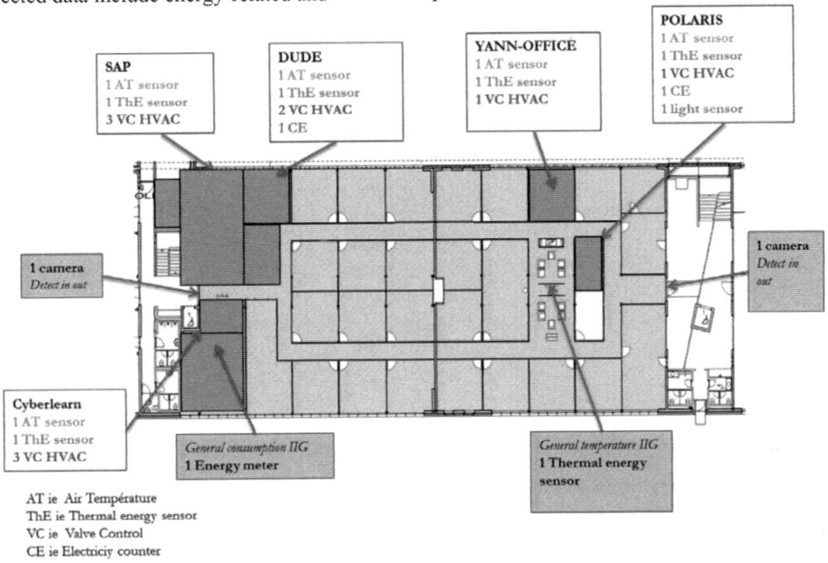

Figure 1. Sensor installation in the use case of the Institute of Information Systems (IIG).

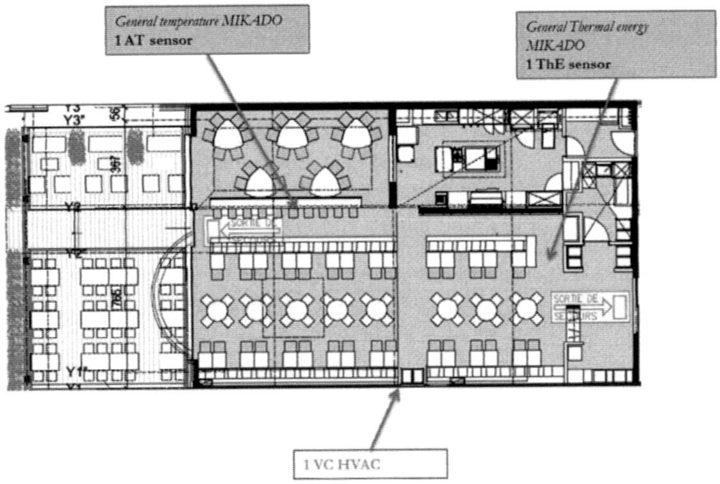

Figure 2. Sensor installation in the use case of the restaurant MIKADO.

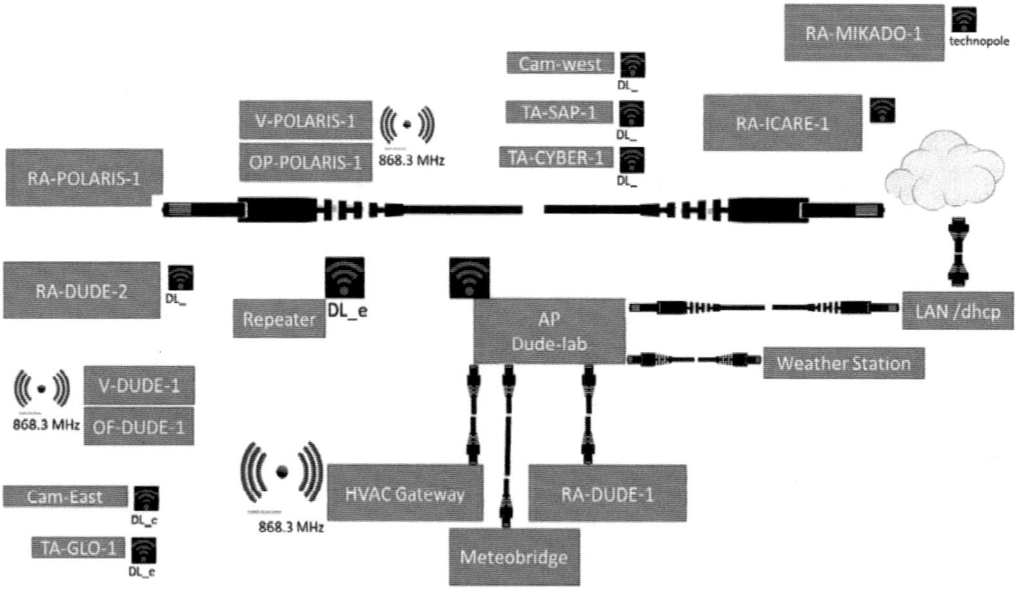

Figure 3. Sensor networking infrastructure in the HES-SO pilot.

REFERENCES

[1] Website of the ENTROPY project: http://entropy-project.eu/ 2017.05.16.

[2] C. Perera, A. Zaslavsky, P. Christen, and D. Georgakopoulos, "Sensing as a service model for smart cities supported by internet of things," Transactions on Emerging Telecommunications Technologies, pp. 81-93, 2014.

[3] V. C. Ostuni, T. Di Noia, R. Mirizzi, and E. Di Sciascio, "Top-N Recommendations from Implicit Feedback Leveraging Linked Open Data," IIR, pp. 20-27, 2014.

[4] D. C. Luckham, "Event Processing for Business: Organizing the Real-Time Enterprise,". Hoboken, New Jersey: John Wiley & Sons, Inc., 2012, ISBN 978-0-470-53485-4.

[5] Website of FIWARE: https://www.fiware.org/ 2017.05.16.

[6] Web portal of the ENTROPY project: http://entropy.euprojects.net/ 2017.05.16.

Accurate Localization Using Augmented UHF RFID System for Internet-of-Things

Jing Wang, Miodrag Bolic
School of Electrical Engineering and Computer Science
University of Ottawa
Ottawa, Canada
Email: jwang226@uottawa.ca, mbolic@uottawa.ca

***Abstract*—This work addresses the problem of accurate indoor localization with an augmented ultra-high-frequency (UHF) radio-frequency-identification (RFID) system. In augmented UHF RFID system, a semi-passive component, called ST (from sense-a-tag), can communicate with the RFID reader as a passive tags, and can also capture the backscattering communication between RFID reader and passive tags within its proximity. The system requires that a grid of passive RFID tags is deployed and ST is attached to object of interest. As such it allows for fine-grained proximity-based localization. ST is localized based on the aggregated binary measurements according to localization algorithms, such as weighted centroid localization (WCL). The aforementioned algorithm assumes that the aggregated binary measurements simply depends on the distance between landmark tags and ST. However, it is not the case for ST-to-tag backscattering communication. To improve the localization accuracy, this paper proposes to use a Monte Carlo-based estimation with the detection probability model of ST-to-tag. The performance of the proposed algorithm is demonstrated by extensive computer simulation.**

Keywords–Internet-of-Things; augmented UHF RFID system; indoor localization; WCL; Monte Carlo estimation.

I. Introduction

The concept of Internet-of-Things (IoT) is simple but powerful, which envisages the infrastructure of ubiquitous wireless sensing and identification of IoT nodes to connect anything from anywhere at anytime [1]. The IoT nodes, such as radio tags, can be embedded into objects, monitoring their status and surrounding environment, as well as acquiring geographical information. Since the popular satellite-based positioning system are restricted to outdoor environment, academic and industrial communities have carried out intense research work to build indoor localization system to realize the vision of IoT [2]. Ultra-high-frequency (UHF) radio-frequency-identification (RFID) has been widely recognized as enabling technology for IoT indoor localization application due to its miniature size, easy deployment, low-cost and ultra-low power consumption [3].

The majority of state-of-art UHF RFID localization approaches is based on the fusion of multiple pieces of relevant information of RF signals, which are either angle-of-arrival (AoA), time-of-arrival (ToA), time-difference-of-arrival (TDoA) or received-signal-strength (RSS) returned to RFID readers from tags [3]. The major problem with the aforementioned methods is that they are easily affected by the non-line-of-sight (NLoS) conditions, severe multi-path distortions and fast temporal change of indoor environment [4]. One direction to resolve this problem is to apply proximity-based method, which is to deploy passive tags at fixed positions as landmarks and attach RFID reader to target of interest [10]–[12], and vice versa [6]. However, these approaches are not realistic solutions for IoT indoor localization application considering size, cost and energy.

The objective of this paper is to analyze and improve a novel augmented UHF RFID system, which includes a semi-passive UHF RFID component, called ST (from sense-a-tag) [5] and off-the-shelf UHF RFID components, reader and tag. The augmented UHF RFID system can be used for fine-grained proximity-based localization for IoT application by keeping both landmark and target tags simple and inexpensive. In the same way as passive tags, ST applies envelope detection to extract the baseband signal in the receiving path, and applies backscattering modulation to talk back in the transmitting path. The difference is that in the receiving path ST does not only capture the RFID reader's command signal, but also passive tag's backscattering signal. ST is fully compatible with EPCGlobal Class 1 Gen 2 RFID protocol. The augmented UHF RFID system requires that RFID reader is installed and a grid of passive tags is deployed as landmarks in the environment. In [7], we showed how to use weighted centroid localization (WCL) to localize ST in augmented UHF RFID system. Strictly speaking, WCL is not fully range-free localization method, since it depends on aggregated binary measurements aside the simple communication link connectivity of ST and landmark tags. However, the aggregated binary measurements of ST-to-tag depends on numerous factors other than the distance between ST and tag, such as the distance from RFID reader antenna, the orientation of antennas and phase cancellation [8]. In this paper, we propose a method where we apply a Monte Carlo estimation based on the probability detection model of ST-to-tag. In Monte Carlo framework, the proposal distribution of ST locations is assumed to be uniformly distributed over a circle area around WCL estimation.

We have calibrated our newly developed UHF RFID simulator PASS based on the real experiment data [8][9]. In PASS, we could simulate various scenarios with all components of the augmented UHF RFID system. The localization algorithms are evaluated in the simulator. The paper is organized as follows: in Section 2, we introduce the background and related work. The localization algorithms are presented in Section 3. In Section 4, we provide the simulation results which show the

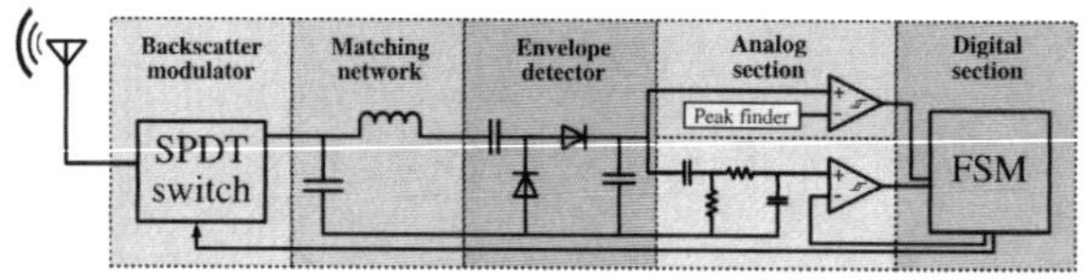

Figure 1. Block diagram of ST hardware.

performance of the proposed localization algorithms, followed by the conclusion with future discussion in Section 5.

II. BACKGROUND AND PRIOR WORK

In this section, we will discuss the state-of-the-art in proximity-based localization approaches, augmented UHF R-FID system, and UHF RFID simulation framework specified for indoor localization research.

A. *Proximity-based localization*

Proximity-based localization techniques exploit symbolic relative location information related to the presence or absence of the target within a small range of reference points [4]. Conventional approaches of proximity-based UHF RFID localization solutions are based on deploying passive tags at fixed locations as landmarks and attaching RFID reader to target and vice versa. Usually, the former approach is referred to as reader-based method while the latter as tag-based method.

In [10], researchers deployed a grid of UHF RFID tags on the ceiling of the building. The read region of each tag is well defined, thus the floor environment is subdivided into a set of cells. When the target equipped with reader enters into the read region of UHF RFID tag, the tag ID or the equivalent tag coordinates are retrieved. Based on the similar fashion, multiple indoor localization systems have been proposed [11][12]. In [6], the area is covered by a mesh grid of a large set of RFID readers and associated antennas, whose locations are known. The objects with attached UHF RFID tags are localized and tracked using particle filter based inference algorithm.

However, these approaches are strictly constrained by energy, cost and size. For example, the former approaches is limited to relatively large and expensive objects that justify carrying the RFID reader, such as human or robot. In the latter approach, it is not cost-efficient to densely deploy RFID readers merely for connectivity information.

B. *Augmented UHF RFID system*

In order to keep both targets and landmarks simple and inexpensive, a novel UHF RFID component, referred to as ST, is developed to augmented the off-the-shelf UHF RFID system [7]. Figure 1 depicts the block diagram of ST hardware. The antenna is followed by a backscatter modulator, a corresponding matching network and a conventional diode envelope detector circuit. The output of envelope detector is fed into the analog section, which can process both reader's pulse-interval-encoding (PIE) command signal and the tag's backscattering signal. The analog section for processing reader's PIE signal is the same as the standard passive tag, which employs a hysteresis comparator to generate digital signal. The processing circuit of tag's backscattering signal is more complex, which consists of a band-pass filter for removing the DC offset, followed by a comparator serving as one-bit A/D converter. The output of analog section is the input of digital section, which runs finite state machine (FSM) for Gen2-based ST locator protocol. As for rapid prototyping, the latest version of digital section is implemented on FPGA Xilinx Spartan 3AN chip.

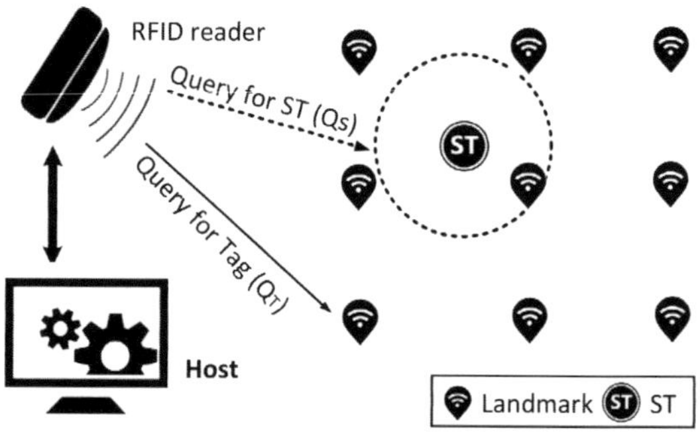

Figure 2. Augmented UHF RFID system.

Figure 2 shows a typical deployment of augmented UHF RFID system for fine-grained proximity-based localization. The system consists of a grid of passive tags as landmarks, ST attached to the target of interest, a standard RFID reader and a computer hosting localization algorithm. The host computer can control RFID reader to send out two distinct query signals, Q_S and Q_T. A query Q_T drives ST to *Listening* state. In this state, ST does not respond but listens to the backscattering communication between RFID reader and passive tags. Upon receiving the tags' ID, ST stores a hash value corresponding to the IDs temporarily. A query Q_S drives ST to *Responding* state. In this state, ST works as a standard passive tag, and backscatters the information of the detected tags' IDs to the RFID reader. Based on such aggregated binary measurements of ST-to-tag, the host determines the location of ST according to the embedded localization algorithm, such as WCL.

C. *PASS simulator*

Proximity-based **A**ugmented UHF RFID **S**ystem **S**imulator (PASS) is a system-level time-domain UHF RFID simulator. PASS simulator inherits the hierarchical software structure, the behavioral model of NXP UCODE G2XM tag and wireless propagation channel from PARIS simulation framework [14]. While PARIS mainly focuses on indoor wireless channel modelling, PASS completes the functionality of RFID reader and tag according to EPCglobal Class1 Gen2 protocol. The behavior model of ST is developed to emulate the specific ST hardware. The channel model consists of large-scale model and statistical model. Besides that, the channel model also includes the virtual transmitter model for the surface reflection. Various characteristics of implemented models can be configured, such as scenario deployment, parameters of wireless channel, tag, reader and ST, etc. With the simulator-provided functions and basic functions, behaviors of implemented components in simulator can be measured, such as wireless signal delay and attenuation. The simulator and user guide are available on GitHub [15].

III. Localization using augmented UHF RFID system

In this section, we will describe our proposed detection probability model of ST-to-tag, as well as the localization algorithm based on Monte Carlo estimation.

A. *The detection probability model of ST-to-tag*

The detection probability of ST-to-tag depends on numerous factors, which include the distance between ST and tag, the distance from RFID reader, antenna orientation and phase cancellation, etc [8]. The existing localization algorithms assume that the detection probability of ST-to-tag simply depends on the distance between ST to tag [7][13]. In order to improve localization accuracy, a more realistic detection probability model of ST-to-tag is developed based on the research on the ST-to-tag backscattering communication link. First, the detection probability model of ST-to-tag is modelled as a function of distance between ST and tag, as well as the distance and orientation from reader to tag. Secondly, while fitting the detection probability model of ST-to-tag, the phase cancellation effect is considered by augmenting phase cancellation-reducing technique to ST.

The proposed probability detection model of ST-to-tag is formulated as a logistic regression model as shown in (1). Figure 3 depicts the model features. D is the distance from RFID reader to passive tag. θ represents the azimuth (the relative orientation between (X, Z) plane with antenna to tag vector), while ϕ represents elevation (the relative orientation between (X, Y) plane with antenna to tag vector). d is the distance between ST with tag. $\{a_i, i = 1, \ldots, 4\}$ are the model parameters.

$$p(D, d, \theta, \phi) = \frac{1}{1 + e^{a_0 + a_1 D + a_2 d + a_3|\theta| + a_4|\phi|}} \quad (1)$$

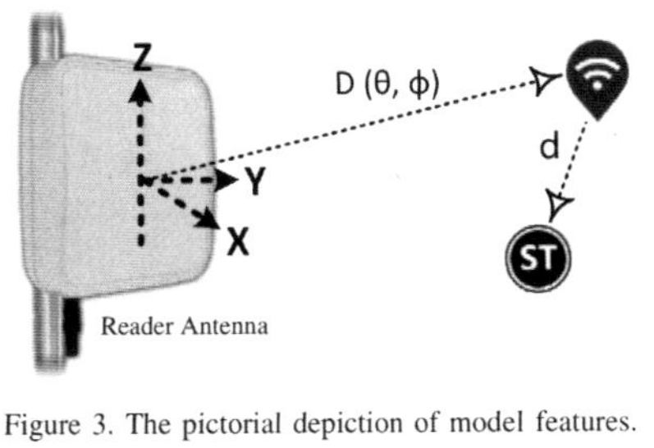

Figure 3. The pictorial depiction of model features.

We fit the detection probability model of ST-to-tag with data obtained from the PASS simulator. In the simulation, the host controls a standard UHF RFID reader to sends out the queries Q_T and Q_S. We use circularly polarized panel antenna RFMAX S9028PCRJ as the reader antenna, whose radiation pattern is shown in Figure 4. The power level of reader antenna is 30 dBm. The channel model is configured as *"room"*. For the scenario setup, the RFID reader antenna is placed at the origin $(0, 0, 0)$. The locations of passive tag are uniformly sampled from the cuboid space of $x \in [1, 8]$, $y \in [-4, 4]$ and $z \in [-4, 4]$. We obtained 3000 samples of tag locations in the space. The locations of ST is uniformly sampled within a sphere space, whose globe is at tag location

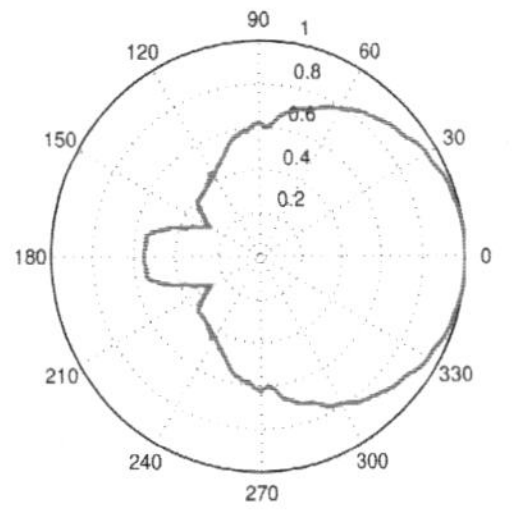

Figure 4. The radiation pattern of reader antenna.

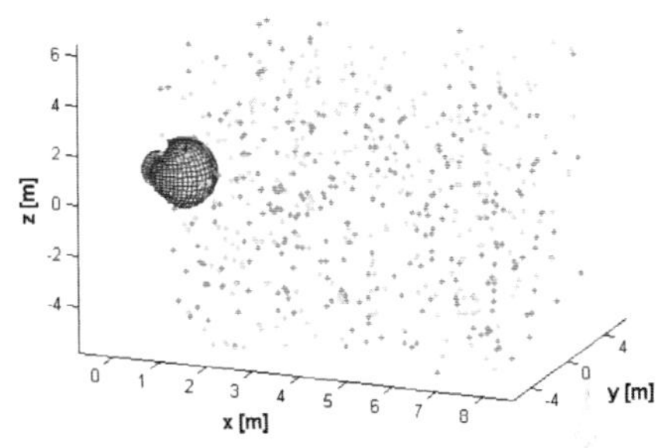

Figure 5. The simulation setup.

with the radius as $2m$. Figure 5 shows the simulation setup, in which the green dots represent tag locations, brown dots represent ST locations.

The logistic regression model is trained with the obtained data set, in which the cost function used is cross-entropy and the optimization method is gradient descent. The parameter estimations are $a_0 = -1.462$, $a_1 = 0.4941$, $a_2 = 2.506$, $a_3 = 0.0126$ and $a_4 = 0.0523$. For comparison, the conventional model, in which the detection probability simply depends on the distance between ST and tag, is presented in (2). With the obtained data set, the parameter estimations are $a_0 = 0.8970$ and $a_1 = 2.4443$. Figure 6 depicts the normalized histogram of the obtained data set, as well as the curves of (1) and (2). Furthermore, we use 1000 newly obtained data set as test data set. The cross entropy cost of (1) 0.1278 is lower than (2) 0.1502. Therefore, (1) possesses higher model accuracy than (2).

$$p(d) = \frac{1}{1 + e^{a_0 + a_1 d}} \quad (2)$$

B. *Monte Carlo estimation*

Let us assume that there are K landmark tags with known location in 2D cartesian coordinate system, $\{LT_k, k = 1, \ldots, K\}$. ST is attached to target of interest with an unknown location x. Here ST is static. RFID reader sends out the number of N rounds of Q_T. A landmark tag k can be detected by ST with probability p_k. In this work, we use (1) to approximate such probability. Let the number of detection of landmark tag k by ST denote by n_k. Then, the probability of n_k is modelled

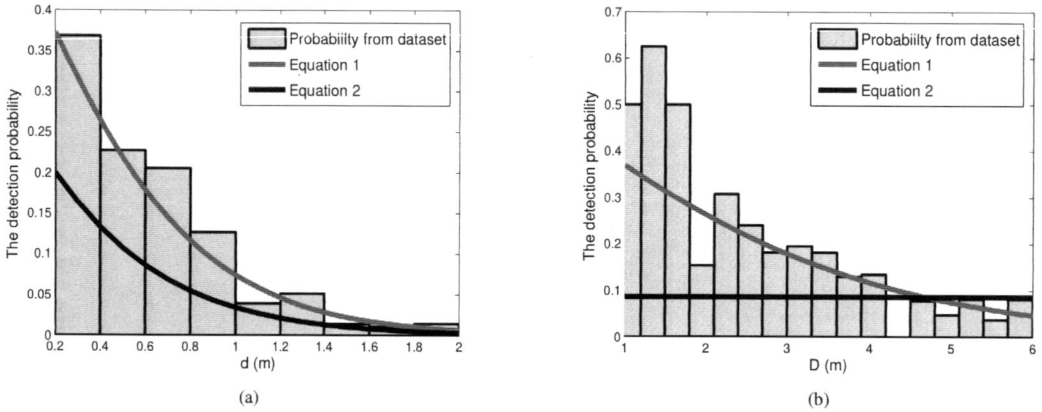

Figure 6. The detection probability histogram versus (a) d with data from the space $D \in [2, 4]$. (b) D with data from the space $d \in [0.4, 1]$. (Since the (2) purely depends on d, the probability is constant along D and the value is based on $d = 0.6$)

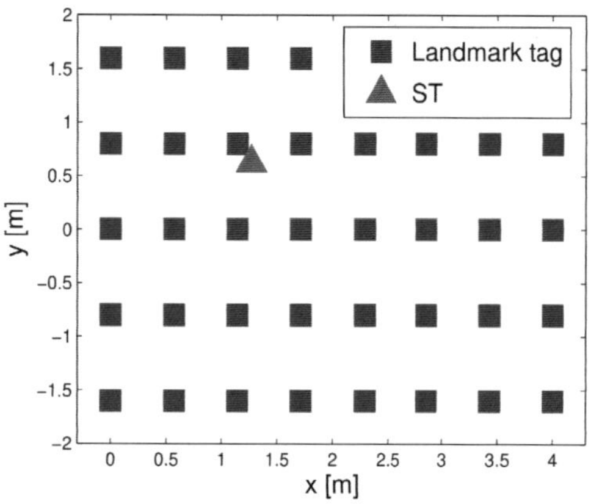

Figure 7. Simulation setup with landmarks tag and ST.

as binomial distribution.

$$P(n_k) = \binom{N}{n_k} p_k^{n_k}(1-p_k)^{N-n_k} \tag{3}$$

where

$$\begin{aligned} p_k &= p(D, d, \theta, \phi) \\ &= \frac{1}{1 + e^{-1.462+0.4941*D+2.506*d+0.0126*|\theta|+0.0523*|\phi|}} \end{aligned} \tag{4}$$

D, d, θ, ϕ are determined by the location of RFID reader, tag and ST as described in Section III-A. After the reader sends out Q_S query, there are K measurements from landmark tags $\mathbf{y} = \{n_k \in \{0, 1, \ldots, N\}, k = 1, 2, \ldots, K\}$. The likelihood function is given by

$$p(\mathbf{y}|x) = \prod_{k=1}^{K} \binom{N}{n_k} p_k^{n_k}(1-p_k)^{N-n_k} \tag{5}$$

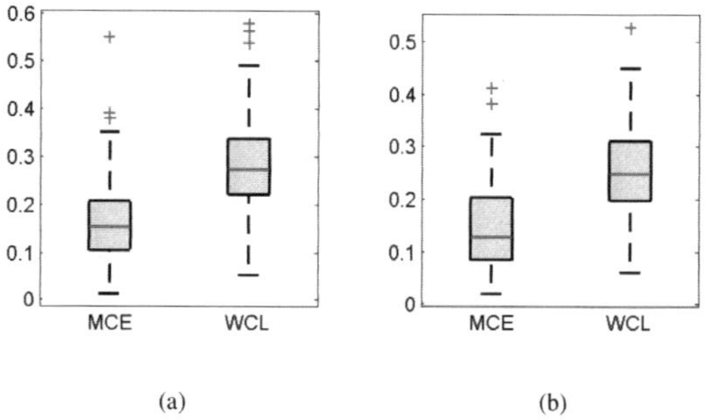

Figure 8. The localization error distribution of Monte Carlo estimation and WCL for two ST locations (a) (3.8804, -0.1470) (b) (1.5443, 0.6334).

Based on Bayes rule, the posterior probability could be written as

$$p(x|\mathbf{y}) = \frac{p(\mathbf{y}|x)p(x)}{p(\mathbf{y})} \tag{6}$$

Therefore, the estimation of ST location x is

$$\hat{x} = \int x p(x|\mathbf{y}) dx \tag{7}$$

However, it is difficult to get a close form solution for (7) based on (4) and (6). According to Monte Carlo method, the distribution can be approximated by discrete random measures defined by particles and associated weights [17].

$$p(x|\mathbf{y}) \approx \sum_{m=1}^{M} w^{(m)} \delta(x - x^{(m)}) \tag{8}$$

where $\{x^{(m)}, m = 1, \ldots, M\}$ is a set of particles and $\{w^{(m)}, m = 1, \ldots, M\}$ is its weights. M is the number of particles in the approximation. However, it is difficult to draw samples from the distribution $p(x|\mathbf{y})$. We could generate sample $x^{(m)}$ from a proposal distribution $q(x)$, which is simple enough to generate random samples from it. And the weight

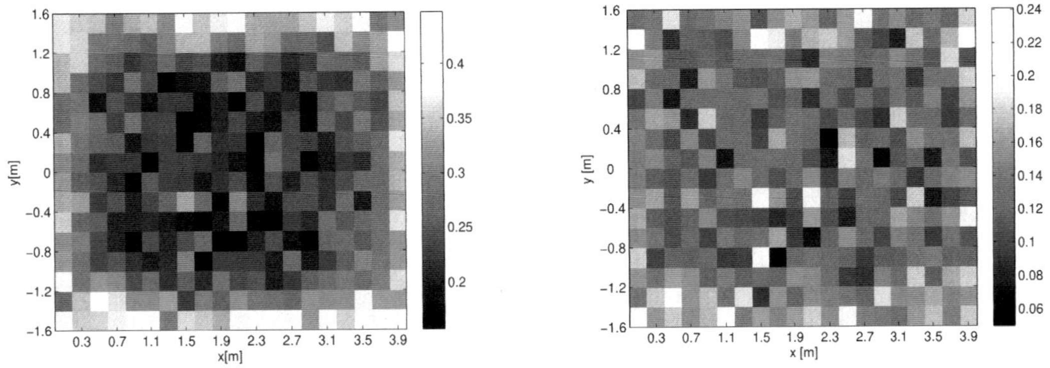

(a) (b)

Figure 9. The heatmap of location estimation error in meters associated with ST true locations applying (a) WCL (b) Monte Carlo estimation (each block is 0.2 m × 0.2 m).

assigned to the particle is

$$w^{(m)} = \frac{p(x^m|\mathbf{y})}{q(x^{(m)})} \tag{9}$$

Then, the weights are normalized by $w^{(m)} = w^{(m)}/\sum_{i=1}^{M} w^{(i)}$.

In this work, the proposal distribution is assumed to be an uniform distribution over the circle region centering WCL estimation. WCL is simple and computationally efficient, the form is as follows

$$x^* = \frac{\sum_{k=1}^{K} n_k * LT_k}{\sum_{k=1}^{K} n_k} \tag{10}$$

Then, a measure $\chi = \{x^{(m)}, m = 1, \ldots, M\}$ is generated from uniform distribution over the region centering at x^* with radius r. The prior distribution $p(x)$ in (6) is assumed as a uniform distribution over the whole target region. $p(\mathbf{y})$ is a constant. Therefore,

$$w^{(m)} \propto p(\mathbf{y}|x^{(m)}) \tag{11}$$

We obtain the estimation of ST location by

$$\hat{x} = \frac{1}{\sum_{m=1}^{M} p(\mathbf{y}|x^{(m)})} \sum_{m=1}^{M} x^{(m)} * p(\mathbf{y}|x^{(m)}) \tag{12}$$

Noteworthily, since the computation task is executed on host computer, the increased computational complexity of Monte Carlo estimation is of little concern.

A pseudo-code description of this algorithm is given by Algorithm 6.

IV. Performance Evaluation

In this section, a number of simulation has been carried out to evaluate the validity of the proposed algorithm. The simulation setup follows the deployment scenario as shown in Figure 7. The area is 4 m × 3.2 m, and covered by 8 × 5 UHF RFID landmark tags. RFID reader's panel antenna is placed at the center of the area facing the ground at the height of 2 m. The PASS simulator is configured as in Section III-A. For the proposed algorithm, the size of particles M is set as 200. The number of query Q_T is set as 10. The radius r of circle region for proposal distribution is set to 0.8 m. The localization performance is measured by average root mean square error (RMSE). The RMSE for one realization is calculated as $||x - \hat{x}||_2$.

ALGORITHM 1: Monte Carlo Estimation

Data: Observations $\mathbf{y} = \{n_k, k = 1, 2, \ldots, K\}$

begin

```
    /* WCL based on observations */
    x* = Σ_{k=1}^K n_k*LT_k / Σ_{k=1}^K n_k , K landmark tags with known
      location {LT_k, k = 1,...,K};
    /* Particle generation */
    Sample generation χ = {x^(m), m = 1,...,M} from
      uniform distribution over the region in circle
      centering x* with radius r;
    /* Weight of particles */
    w^(m) = 1 / (Σ_{m=1}^M p(y|x^(m))) p(y|x^(m)) for all particles;
    /* Location estimation */
    x̂ = Σ_{m=1}^M x^(m) w^(m)
```

end

In the first set of simulations, we place the ST at a fixed location in the region. The location is randomly selected. We conduct 100 independent realizations of simulation with WCL and Monte Carlo estimation. We repeat the aforementioned procedure two times with different ST locations, which are picked randomly. The objective of the simulation is to present the localization performance of WCL and Monte Carlo estimation. Figure 8 shows the localization error distribution of these two scenarios with box-and-whisker plot. In Figure 8a, the ST is placed at $(3.8804, -0.1470)$, the RMSE for Monte Carlo estimation is 0.1641 m, while for WCL the RMSE is 0.2834 m, which is improved by 42.10%. In Figure 8b, the ST is placed at $(1.5443, 0.6334)$, the RMSE for Monte Carlo estimation is 0.1488 m, while for WCL is RMSE is 0.2561 m, which is improved by 41.90%. From the distribution and RMSE, we could conclude that Monte Carlo estimation achieves higher localization accuracy than WCL for these two scenarios.

In the second set of simulations, we randomly sample 3000 locations for ST in the region. We collect the data of the true ST location and the location estimation error for Monte Carlo estimation and WCL. The RMSE of ST location estimation is 0.2673 m for WCL and 0.1330 m for Monte Carlo estimation, which is improved by 50.24%. Figure 9 shows the heatmap of location estimation error associated with ST true locations. Each block of the heatmap is 0.2 m $\times$ 0.2 m, whose value is determined by the RMSE of location estimation while ST resides within the block. The overall localization accuracy of Monte Carlo estimation is higher than WCL. in particular, for the region close to the edge. The reason for such effect is that as ST approaches the edge, the landmark tags within ST's proximity are unequally distributed. Monte Carlo estimation utilizes detection probability model of ST-to-tag, which could alleviate the effect of unequally distributed landmarks. From the figure, we could conclude that Monte Carlo estimation achieves higher localization accuracy than WCL.

V. Conclusion

In this paper, we have investigated the problem of locating static object attached with ST, which can detect the presence of UHF RFID landmark tags with its proximity. Based on a more realistic detection probability model of ST-to-tag, we propose a Monte Carlo-based method for achieving higher localization accuracy. We conduct several sets of simulation in our newly developed PASS simulator, and the simulation results show that Monte Carlo-based method achieves higher localization accuracy than the conventional WCL method.

There are several interesting direction to explore in the future work. First, the detection probability model does not consider shadowing effect, which is important while attaching ST to human or metallic vehicle. Second, this work only considers locating one ST. It would be convenient to localize multiple STs using Monte Carlo estimation method independently. However, we could anticipate that the accuracy and robustness of localization method would be improved with extra ST-to-ST detection information. Third, the landmark deployment does not receive much attention in this work. We simply deploy the landmark tags in square pattern, and distance among neighboring landmarks is constant. However, it is beneficial to investigate the relationship between localization accuracy and the deployment density and pattern of landmark tags.

References

[1] Z. Zou, "Impulse radio UWB for the Internet-of-Things: a study on UHF/UWB hybrid solution," Ph.D thesis, Royal Insititue of Technology (KTH), Stockholm, Sweden, 2011.

[2] R. Mautz, "Indoor Positioning Technologies," PhD thesis, Swiss Federal Institute of Technology in Zurich (ETH Zurich), Zurich, Swiss, 2012.

[3] M. Bolic, D. Simplot-Ryl, and I. Stojmenovic, *RFID systems: research trends and challenges.* John Wiley and Sons, Chichester, West Sussex, UK, 2010.

[4] A. Athalye, V. Savic, M. Boilc, and P. Djuric, "Novel semi-passive RFID system for indoor localization," *IEEE Sensors J.*, vol. 13, no. 2, pp. 528-537, Feb. 2013.

[5] A. Athalye, V. Savic, M. Boilc, and P. Djuric, "A radio frequency identification system for accurate indoor localization," in *Proc. IEEE Int. Conf. Acoust. Speech Signal Process. (ICASSP)*, pp.1777-1780, May 2011.

[6] G. Li, M. Bugallo, A. Athalye, and P. Djuric, "Indoor tracking with RFID systems," *IEEE J. Sel. Topics Signal Process.*, vol. 8, no. 1, pp. 96-105, Feb. 2014.

[7] M. Bolic, M. Rostamian, and P. Djuric, "Proximity detection with RFID: a step toward the Internet of Things," *IEEE Pervasive Comput.*, vol. 14, no. 2, pp. 70-76, June 2015.

[8] J. Wang, and M. Bolic, "Reducing the phase cancellation effect in augmented RFID system," *Int. J. Parallel. Emergent Distrib. Syst.*, vol. 30, no.6, pp. 494-514, Nov. 2015

[9] J. Wang, and M. Bolic, "Exploiting dual-antenna diversity for phase cancellation in augmented RFID system," in *Proc. IEEE Int. Conf. Smart Commun. Netw. Technol. (SaCoNeT)*, pp. 1-6, Jun. 2014

[10] E. DiGiampaolo, "A passive-RFID based indoor navigation system for visually impaired people," in *Proc. IEEE Int. Symp. Appl. Sci. Biomed. Commun. Techno. (ISABEL)*, pp. 1-5, 2010.

[11] L. Yang, J. Cao, W. Zhu, and S. Tang, "Accurate and efficient object tracking based on passive RFID," *IEEE Trans. Mobile Comput.*, vol. 14, no. 11, pp. 2188-2200, 2015.

[12] E. DiGiampaolo, and F. Martinelli, "A passive UHF-RFID system for the localization of an indoor autonomous vehicle," *IEEE Trans. Ind. Electron.*, vol. 59, no. 10, pp. 3961-3970, 2012.

[13] V. Savic, A. Athalye, M. Bolic, and P. Djuric, "Particle filtering for indoor RFID tag tracking," in *Proc. IEEE Statistical Signal Process. Workshop (SSP)*, pp. 193-196, June 2011.

[14] D. Arnitz, U. Muehlmann, T. Gigl, and K. Witrisal, "Wideband system-level simulator for passive UHF RFID," in *IEEE Int. Conf. RFID (RFID)*, pp. 28-33, April 2009.

[15] PASS simulation framework, https://github.com/wacoder/PASS (Rretrieved: June, 2017).

[16] G. James, D. Witten, T. Hastie, and R. Tibshirani. *An introduction to statistical learning*. Springer, New York, USA , 2013.

[17] P. Djuric, J. Kotecha, J. Zhang, Y. Huang, T. Ghirmai, M. Bugallo, and J. Miguez, "Particle filtering," *IEEE Signal Process. Mag.*, vol. 20, no. 5, pp. 19-38, 2003

Channel Estimation and Equalization Algorithm for OFDM-Based Underwater Acoustic Communications Systems

Mhd Tahssin Altabbaa
Department of Electrical and Electronics Engineering
Kadir Has University
34083, Istanbul, Turkey
Email: tahsin.altabbaa@khas.edu.tr

Erdal Panayirci
Department of Electrical and Electronics Engineering
Kadir Has University
34083, Istanbul, Turkey
Email: eepanay@khas.edu.tr

***Abstract*—This paper is concerned with a challenging problem of channel estimation and equalization for orthogonal frequency division multiplexing (OFDM) systems in underwater acoustic (UWA) communications in the presence of Rician fading. The ambient noise is modeled as a correlated Gaussain noise. We combine the matching pursuit (MP), for the Doppler shift and the channel path delays estimation, along with the maximum a posteriori (MAP) estimation for the channel path gains and call the resulting algorithm MP-MAP algorithm. As a prior distribution for the sparse complex-valued channel gains, we choose a Rician distribution with unknown means and variances. They are in turn estimated by the maximum likelihood technique. After the channel equalization, detection of data is implemented at the receiver. Computer simulations show that the UWA channel is estimated very effectively and the proposed algorithm exhibits excellent symbol error rate and channel estimation performance.**

Keywords–Underwater acoustic communications; channel estimation; equalization; detection.

I. Introduction

Due to the importance of underwater acoustic (UWA) wireless communications, numerous proposals that deal with the impairments experienced in such environment have received quite an attention, especially in the last ten years. Several underwater applications such as natural disasters predictors, coastal radars, incoming near-field tsunami waves, and volcanic activity require underwater wireless communication, where acoustic signals are recognized as the best candidate for such implementations [1] [2]. However, UWA communication systems face several challenges such as low speed, long propagation delay, multipath and fading, and time dependent Doppler effects. Deployment of orthogonal frequency division multiplexing (OFDM)-based communication systems for underwater wireless communication is considered to be promising due to its robustness against large multipath spreads [3] [4].

Different related studies on UWA communications have been proposed. Many related studies over different UWA disciplines such as channel and Doppler estimation and noise mitigation algorithms are investigated upon realistic and synthetic data. In [5], the authors model the delay spread of an UWA channel. The proposed study shows a better channel impulse response (CIR) modeling when out-of-plane scattering and reverberation are taken into account. The authors of [6] proposed an algorithm where the receiver can detect the impulsive noise positions using the signal amplitude in the time domain, and the impulsive noise and the Doppler shift estimation are based on the null subcarriers of the OFDM symbol. A channel estimation for relay-based UWA systems is investigated in [7]. The authors considered a sparse CIR and a non-Gaussian channel gains in their channel model. The expectation-maximization (EM) along with the matching pursuit (MP) algorithms were employed for the Doppler shift and the delay estimation. In [8], the authors adopted superposition coding with OFDM for downlink communication in the presence of multiple stations (sensors). Based on statistical representation of each underwater station's channel state information (CSI), a resource allocation mechanism is proposed that obtains the transmitting power of each subcarrier for each user. An adaptive channel estimator based on least squares (LS) and recursive least-squares (RLS) is proposed in [9]. The results show a promising bit error rate (BER) performance and the average mean square error (MSE) can be obtained better than the linear minimum mean square error (LMMSE) or the LS. The authors of [10] investigated different modulation, channel estimation, and channel equalization techniques for OFDM-based and pilot-assisted UWA systems. They assumed in their simulations a channel that follows a Rayleigh distribution. Their results show that QPSK, DPSK, and 16QAM are the most suitable modulation schemes for UWA applications. The authors of [11] proposed a low computational complexity channel estimation algorithm based on fast block-Fourier transform (FFT) and orthogonal matching pursuit (OMP) in the presence of large pilot spacing. In [12], the authors proposed an OMP-based algorithm for channel coefficients estimation with no prior CSI knowledge in the presence of doubly selective channel.

In this paper, we assume a single-transmit and single-receive antennas and a parametric channel model that obeys a Rician distribution, where the CSI is known at the receiver. We model the ambient UWA noise as a correlated Gaussian noise whose correlation function fits well for realistic UWA channels. We then employ the MP algorithm on the oversampled version of the received signal for the estimation of the Doppler shift and the channel path delays of the UWA channel. Finally, we use the maximum *a posteriori* (MAP) technique to estimate the complex-valued sparse channel gains and the maximum likelihood (ML) technique to estimate the unknown mean and variance parameters of the Rician distributed UWA channel.

The remainder of the paper is organized as follows. The underwater channel model is presented in Section II. In Section III, the system model of the proposed OFDM-based UWA communication system is described. The iterative channel estimation algorithm along with the initialization techniques and data detection are described in Section IV. The performance of the proposed approach along with the simulation parameters are investigated in Section V. Finally, conclusions and future work are presented in Section VI.

II. CHANNEL MODEL

In this paper, we consider a sparse multipath channel model parametrized by a time-varying path delays denoted by $\tau_p, p = 0, 1, \cdots, L-1$. The time variations of the path delays can be approximated by a Doppler shift as $\tau_p(t) = \tau_p - \zeta_p t$ [13] [6]. Note that, the Doppler effect experienced at the receiver can be different at each path in underwater environments [14]. However, [15] states that the dominant Doppler shift arose in such environments is due to the motion of the platforms. Consequently, in our paper we assume a constant Doppler shift, that is, $\zeta_p(t) \equiv \zeta$. In addition, we assume the channel path amplitudes do not change over one OFDM symbol duration on each path and vary independently from symbol to symbol, that is, $h_p(t) \approx h_p$. Consequently, the sparse time-varying UWA channel impulse responses (CIRs) with the channel gains can be characterized by

$$h(t, \tau) = \sum_{p=0}^{L-1} h_p \ \delta(\tau - (\tau_p - \zeta t)). \tag{1}$$

The channel taps at the receiver depend on the underwater environmental conditions as well as the sea state where each channel tap can be assumed to obey a different distribution. In our work, the proposed channel path gains h_p follow a Rician fading, and the channel taps are then considered to be complex Gaussian random variables with nonzero means. Define mean μ_p and variance σ_p^2 as the independent real and imaginary parts of the taps such that, $\Omega_p = E\{|h_p|^2\} = 2\mu_p^2 + 2\sigma_p^2$ is the power profile of the proposed channel that follows a Rician fading, where $\sum_{p=0}^{L-1} \Omega_p = 1$. However, we consider the Rician κ-factor for the pth tap as the ratio of the power of the mean component to the power in the diffuse component, that is, $\kappa_p = \mu_p^2/\sigma_p^2$. Consequently, each channel tap can be expressed as [16]

$$h_p = \sqrt{\frac{\kappa_p \Omega_p}{\kappa_p + 1}} \left(\frac{1+j}{\sqrt{2}} \right) + \sqrt{\frac{\Omega_p}{\kappa_p + 1}} \tilde{h}_p \tag{2}$$

where $\tilde{h}_p$ is denoted as a complex Gaussian random variable with zero mean and unit variance. However, a Rayleigh distributed channel model can be considered in (2) when $\kappa = 0$. In addition, we assume that the CIRs remain constant over a period of one block transmission and vary independently from block to block.

III. SYSTEM MODEL

In this work, we consider a direct communication link in an UWA framework where OFDM scheme is chosen for its robustness against long multipath spread experienced in underwater environments, where the derivations and the equations hold only one OFDM symbol at a time. We assume the proposed OFDM symbol is equipped with N subcarriers; K equally spaced subcarriers are modulated by data symbol $d[k]$ along the system bandwidth B, where k represents the subcarrier index of the OFDM symbol, and no data is transmitted over the remaining $N - K$ subacarriers.

After applying a N-point inverse fast Fourier transform (IFFT) of the data sequence, a sufficient guard interval (cyclic prefix) of duration T_g is added. Consequently, the equivalent passband continuous time-domain received signal $y(t) = s(t) \otimes h(t, \tau) + v(t)$ can be expressed as

$$y(t) = \sqrt{2}\mathfrak{Re}\left\{ \left(\sum_{p=0}^{L-1} h_p \ e^{j2\pi f_c \zeta t} S \right) e^{j2\pi f_c t} \right\} + v(t), \tag{3}$$

where $S = s\left((1+\zeta)\, t - \tau_p \right)$, and $v(t) = \sqrt{2}\, \mathfrak{Re}\{\tilde{v}(t) e^{j\omega_c t}\}$ is the passband representation of the additive correlative Gaussian ambient noise $\tilde{v}(t)$.

In order to compensate the dominant Doppler shift, we resample the received signal in (3) with a resampling factor of $(1 + \zeta)$. The resulting signal $y_{RS}(t)$ experiences a residual Doppler shift ϑ on each path around zero in the range of $[-\xi_{max}, \xi_{max}]$ [13]. Define $\xi \triangleq \vartheta f_c$ as the residual carrier frequency offset (CFO), and $\hat{\xi}$ as a finer estimator of ξ. Consequently, we perform another Doppler shift compensation via demodulation process resulting $z_{RS}(t) = y_{RS}(t) e^{-j2\pi \hat{\xi} t}$ [14].

Finally, after applying an A/D conversion, a guard interval removal, and a $N-$point FFT is performed to transform the signal to the frequency domain, the kth subcarrier output of the FFT during any received OFDM symbol can be represented by

$$\begin{aligned} Z_{RS}[k] &= \frac{1}{\sqrt{N}} \sum_{n=0}^{N-1} z_{RS}[n] \ \exp(-j\frac{2\pi n k}{N}) \\ &= \sum_{q=-K/2}^{K/2-1} d_q H[k, q] + V_{RS}[k], \end{aligned} \tag{4}$$

where $k = -K/2, -K/2+1 \cdots, K/2-1$, and

$$H[k, q] = \sum_{p=0}^{L-1} h_p \exp(-j\frac{2\pi q \tilde{\tau}_p}{N}) F_{k,q}(\vartheta), \tag{5}$$

$$F_{k,q}(\vartheta) = \frac{\sin(\Theta_{k,q})}{N \sin(\Theta_{k,q}/N)} \exp\left(-j\frac{N-1}{N} \Theta_{k,q} \right), \tag{6}$$

where $\Theta_{k,q} = \pi\big(q(1+\vartheta) - k\big)$, and the frequency domain noise samples $V_{RS}[k] = (1/\sqrt{N}) \sum_{n=0}^{N-1} v_{RS}[n] \exp(-j\frac{2\pi n k}{N})$. Consequently, substituting (5) in (4), the vector form of (4) is given by

$$\mathbf{Z}_{RS} = \mathbf{H}\ \mathbf{d} + \mathbf{V}_{RS}, \tag{7}$$

where, $\mathbf{Z}_{RS}$, $\mathbf{d}$, and $\mathbf{V}_{RS} \in \mathcal{C}^K$ and the $[k, q]^{th}$ element of $\mathbf{H} \in \mathcal{C}^{K \times K}$ is determined from (5). It can be seen from (4) that the ambient noise vector $\mathbf{V}_{RS}$ is colored and a whitening process has to be carried out in order to proceed to the channel estimation procedure.

Define S as the power spectral density of the ambient noise modeled in the 10 - 100 KHz band as a function of frequency in Hz as

$$S(f) = \frac{f_0 \hat{\sigma}_0^2}{\pi(f^2 + f_0^2)} , \tag{8}$$

where $\hat{\sigma}_0^2$ is the noise variance, f_0 is chosen as a model parameter of the colored noise autocorrelation function ($f_0 T_s = 0.01, 0.05, 0.1, etc.$), and $R_v(t,t') = \hat{\sigma}_0^2 e^{-2\pi|t-t'|f_0 T_s}$ is defined as the autocorrelation function of the ambient noise.

It can be seen easily from (8) that the noise samples in $\mathbf{V}_{RS}$ are complex-valued and correlated Gaussian distributed random variables with zero-means. Hence, the autocorrelation function can be expressed as,

$$R_{v_{RS}}[m] = R_v\left(mT_s/(1+\hat{\zeta})\right)e^{-j\omega_c \frac{\hat{\zeta}}{1+\hat{\zeta}} mT_s}. \tag{9}$$

However, it can be seen that the noise of the resampled observation model in (4) is colored. Therefore, we perform a noise whitening process on the observation model (7) based on the singular value decomposition (SVD) of the noise covariance matrix as $\mathbf{R}_{\mathbf{V}_{RS}} = \mathbf{U}\boldsymbol{\Upsilon}\mathbf{U}^\dagger$, where $\boldsymbol{\Upsilon}$ is a $K \times K$ diagonal matrix with positive real entries, $\mathbf{U} \in \mathcal{C}^{K \times K}$ is a complex valued unitary transformation matrix, and $(\cdot)^\dagger$ denotes the conjugate transpose operator. Hence, the colored noise V_{RS} is transformed into a white Gaussian noise $\mathbf{W}$ vector whose components have zero mean and unit variance.

Define $\boldsymbol{\Psi} = \boldsymbol{\Upsilon}^{-1/2}\mathbf{U}^\dagger \in \mathcal{C}^{K \times K}$ as the whitening matrix, consequently, the observation model in (7) is multiplied by $\boldsymbol{\Psi}$ from the left, and the final form of the observation model can be expressed as

$$\mathbf{Z} = \mathbf{G}\mathbf{d} + \mathbf{W} \in \mathcal{C}^K , \tag{10}$$

where $\mathbf{Z} = \boldsymbol{\Psi}\,\mathbf{Z}_{RS} \in \mathcal{C}^K$, $\mathbf{W} \in \mathcal{C}^K$, and the convolution matrix generated from data symbols $\mathbf{G} = \boldsymbol{\Psi}\,\mathbf{H} \in \mathcal{C}^{K \times K}$.

IV. Sparse Multipath Channel Estimation

In this section, we present the proposed algorithm that aims to estimate the channel path delays, the Doppler spread, and the sparse complex-valued channel gains. From the observation vector $\mathbf{Z}$ in (10), and by means of the pilot data on subcarriers, $\{\mathcal{P} = \{p_1, p_2, \cdots, p_P\} \in \mathcal{K}\}$, the LS estimation technique yields,

$$\hat{G}[p_k, p_k] = \frac{Z[p_k]}{d_{p_k}} = G[p_k, p_k] + V[p_k], \tag{11}$$

where $V[p_k] = \sum_{q \in \mathcal{P}, q \neq p_k} d_q\, G[p_k, q] + W[p_k]$, and $G[p_k, q]$ represents the interference experienced among the subcarriers. Accordingly, using (5) and (6), (11) can be expressed as

$$\mathbf{Z}_P = \mathbf{A}_P \mathbf{h} + \mathbf{V}_P, \tag{12}$$

where $\mathbf{Z}_P = \left[\hat{G}[p_1,p_1], \hat{G}[p_2,p_2], \cdots, \hat{G}[p_P,p_P]\right]^T \in \mathcal{C}^P$, $\mathbf{V}_P = [v(p_1), v(p_2), \cdots, v(p_P)]^T \in \mathcal{C}^P$ and $\mathbf{A}_P \in \mathcal{C}^{P \times L}$ matrix is given by

$$\mathbf{A}_P = \begin{bmatrix} \eta_1(\vartheta)e^{-j2\pi p_1 \tilde{\tau}_0/N} & \cdots & \eta_1(\vartheta)e^{-j2\pi p_1 \tilde{\tau}_{L-1}/N} \\ \eta_2(\vartheta)e^{-j2\pi p_2 \tilde{\tau}_0/N} & \cdots & \eta_2(\vartheta)e^{-j2\pi p_2 \tilde{\tau}_{L-1}/N} \\ \cdot & \cdots & \cdot \\ \cdot & \cdots & \cdot \\ \eta_P(\vartheta)e^{-j2\pi p_P \tilde{\tau}_0/N} & \cdots & \eta_P(\vartheta)e^{-j2\pi p_P \tilde{\tau}_{L-1}/N} \end{bmatrix}, \tag{13}$$

where $\eta_r(\vartheta) = \sum_{k=-K/2}^{K/2-1} \psi_{r+K/2+1,\; k+K/2+1}\, F_{k,r}(\vartheta)$, and $\psi_{m,n}$ is the $(m,n)^{th}$ element of the matrix $\boldsymbol{\Psi}$.

A. Delays, Doppler Shift and Gain Estimation

We perform an oversampling operation on (13) with an oversampling rate $R_s^{(\varrho)} = \varrho/T_s$, where $\varrho = \{1, 2, \cdots\}$, and T_s is the sampling interval [7] [14].

Let $\mathcal{T}_p = \lfloor \varrho\, \tilde{\tau}_p \rfloor$ and $\varphi = \lfloor (\vartheta + \xi_{max})/\Delta\xi \rfloor$ defined as the discretized real-valued normalized path delays and the Doppler spread, respectively. Note that, $\mathcal{T}_p \in \{0, 1, 2, \cdots, N_\tau - 1\}$, $N_\tau = \varrho L_g$, $L_g = T_g/T_s$, $\varphi \in \{0, 1, 2, \cdots, N_\xi - 1\}$, and $N_\xi = (2\xi_{max})/\Delta\xi$. The columns of the oversampled matrix $\mathbf{A}_P^{(\varrho)} \in \mathcal{C}^{P \times N_\tau N_\xi}$ are denoted by $\tilde{\mathbf{a}}_c = \{\, \tilde{\mathbf{a}}_0, \tilde{\mathbf{a}}_1, \cdots, \tilde{\mathbf{a}}_{N_\tau N_\xi - 1} \,\}$ and correspond to different discrete multipath channel taps and Doppler shift positions. The MP algorithm is then applied using the observation at the pilots (11) [17]. Consequently, the received signal in (12) can be rewritten as

$$\mathbf{Z}_P = \mathbf{A}_{c_p}\mathbf{h} + \mathbf{V}_P, \tag{14}$$

where $\mathbf{A}_{c_p} = [\mathbf{a}_{c_0}, \mathbf{a}_{c_1}, \cdots, \mathbf{a}_{c_{L-1}}]$ is the vector holding the $\mathbf{a}_{c_p}$ column vector values taken from the finer resolution matrix $\mathbf{A}_c \in \mathcal{C}^{P \times L}$ that allocates the path delays and the Doppler shifts obtained from MP.

We employ the MAP technique for a better channel path gains $\{h_p\}_{p=0}^{L-1}$ estimation using the reduced dimensional observation model in (14) [7]. For *a priori* information of the channel path gains, we take a Rician distribution in which h_p's are complex Gaussian random variables, having independent real and imaginary parts with mean μ_p and variance σ_p^2 considering a constant Rician factor, $\kappa_p = \mu_p^2/\sigma_p^2$, for each multipath component. Consequently, the parametric form of the prior joint pdf of $\mathbf{h}$ is given by

$$f(\mathbf{h}|\tilde{\boldsymbol{\mu}}, \mathbf{s}) = \prod_{p=0}^{L-1} \frac{1}{\pi s_p} \exp\left(-\frac{1}{s_p} \mid h_p - \tilde{\mu}_p \mid^2 \right), \tag{15}$$

where $\tilde{\mu}_p = \mu_p\ (1+j)$, $s_p = 2\sigma_p^2$ and $\tilde{\boldsymbol{\mu}} = [\tilde{\mu}_0, \tilde{\mu}_1, \cdots, \tilde{\mu}_{L-1}]^T$, $\mathbf{s} = [s_0, s_1, \cdots, s_{L-1}]^T$ are the parameters controlling the prior mean and variance of each channel coefficient h_p. For fixed values of the parameters governing the prior, the posterior density of the channel coefficients vector is complex Gaussian as follows:

$$p(\mathbf{h}|\mathbf{Z}_P, \tilde{\boldsymbol{\mu}}, \mathbf{s}) = \mathcal{CN}(\boldsymbol{\mu}_h, \boldsymbol{\Sigma}_h), \tag{16}$$

with $\boldsymbol{\mu}_h = \boldsymbol{\Sigma}_h(\beta\ \mathbf{A}_c^\dagger\ \mathbf{Z}_P + \boldsymbol{\Gamma}^{-1}\tilde{\boldsymbol{\mu}})$, and $\boldsymbol{\Sigma}_h = \left(\beta\mathbf{A}_c^\dagger\mathbf{A}_c + \boldsymbol{\Gamma}^{-1}\right)^{-1}$, where $\boldsymbol{\Gamma} = \mathrm{diag}(\mathbf{s})$ and $\beta \equiv 1/\sigma_V^2$. Consequently, from (16), the MAP estimator for $\mathbf{h}$ can be expressed as

$$\begin{aligned} \hat{\mathbf{h}}_{MAP} &= \arg\max_{\mathbf{h}} f(\mathbf{h}|\tilde{\boldsymbol{\mu}}, \mathbf{s}) = \boldsymbol{\mu}_h \\ &= (\mathbf{A}_c^\dagger\ \mathbf{A}_c + \frac{1}{\beta}\boldsymbol{\Gamma}^{-1})^{-1}(\mathbf{A}_c^\dagger\ \mathbf{Z}_P + \frac{1}{\beta}\boldsymbol{\Gamma}^{-1}\tilde{\boldsymbol{\mu}}). \end{aligned} \tag{17}$$

However, $\mathbf{A}_c^\dagger\mathbf{A}_c$ is a banded matrix; therefore, it can be approximated as

$$\mathbf{A}_c^\dagger\mathbf{A}_c = \mathrm{diag}\left(\| \mathbf{a}_{c_0} \|^2, \| \mathbf{a}_{c_1} \|^2 \cdots, \| \mathbf{a}_{c_{L-1}} \|^2\right). \tag{18}$$

Consequently, the matrix inversion in (17) can be expressed as,

$$\left(\mathbf{A}_c^\dagger\mathbf{A}_c + \frac{1}{\beta}\boldsymbol{\Gamma}^{-1}\right)^{-1} = \mathrm{diag}(\lambda_0, \lambda_1, \cdots, \lambda_{L-1}), \tag{19}$$

where $\lambda_p = (\beta \parallel \mathbf{a}_{c_p} \parallel^2 + 1/s_p)^{-1}$.

B. ML Estimation of the Parameters $\{\mu_p, \sigma_p^2\}$

In order to obtain the ML estimation of the variance $\boldsymbol{\sigma}^2$ and the mean $\boldsymbol{\mu}$ vectors of $\mathbf{h}$, we use the observation model obtained by MP in (14). Consequently, the mean coefficient can be expressed by

$$\left(\boldsymbol{\mu}_{ML}, \boldsymbol{\sigma}^2{}_{ML}\right) = \arg\max_{\mu,\sigma^2} \log p(\mathbf{Z}_P|\boldsymbol{\mu}, \boldsymbol{\sigma}^2). \quad (20)$$

where $p(\mathbf{Z}_P|\boldsymbol{\sigma}^2, \mu)$ can be evaluated by averaging it over $\mathbf{h}$ as follows,

$$p(\mathbf{Z}_P|\boldsymbol{\mu}, \boldsymbol{\sigma}^2) = \int_{\mathbf{h}} p(\mathbf{Z}_P|\mathbf{h})p(\mathbf{h}|\boldsymbol{\mu}, \boldsymbol{\sigma}^2)d\mathbf{h}, \quad (21)$$

where $p(\mathbf{Z}_P|\mathbf{h}) \backsim \exp\left\{-\beta \parallel \mathbf{Z}_P - \mathbf{A}_c\mathbf{h} \parallel^2\right\}$, and $p(\mathbf{h}|\boldsymbol{\mu}, \sigma^2)$ is given by (15). The integral of (21) with respect to $\mathbf{h}$ is computable and yields

$$p(\mathbf{Z}_P|\boldsymbol{\sigma}^2, \boldsymbol{\mu}) = \pi^{-P} \det\left(\mathbf{C}_z^{-1}\right) \exp\left\{ - (\mathbf{Z}_P - \mathbf{A}_{c0}\boldsymbol{\mu})^\dagger \mathbf{C}_z^{-1}(\mathbf{Z}_P - \mathbf{A}_{c0}\boldsymbol{\mu})\right\}, \quad (22)$$

where, $\mathbf{A}_{c0} \equiv (1+j)\mathbf{A}_c$, $\mathbf{C}_z = \mathbf{A}_c\boldsymbol{\chi}\mathbf{A}_c^\dagger + (1/\beta)\mathbf{I}_P$ and $\boldsymbol{\chi} = \mathrm{diag}\left(2\sigma_0^2, 2\sigma_1^2, \cdots, 2\sigma_{L-1}^2\right)$. Then, the log-likelihood of $\boldsymbol{\mu}$ and σ^2 is given by

$$\log p(\mathbf{Z}_P|\boldsymbol{\mu}, \boldsymbol{\sigma}^2) = (\mathbf{Z}_P - \mathbf{A}_{c0}\boldsymbol{\mu})^\dagger \mathbf{C}_z^{-1}(\mathbf{Z}_P - \mathbf{A}_{c0}\boldsymbol{\mu}) + \log\det(\mathbf{C}_z). \quad (23)$$

Hence, the ML estimate of $\boldsymbol{\mu}$ can be found by minimizing (23) and taking the gradient of $\log p(\mathbf{Z}_P|\boldsymbol{\mu}, \boldsymbol{\sigma}^2)$ with respect to $\boldsymbol{\mu}$ and setting the result to zero. Consequently, $\boldsymbol{\mu}$ can then be expressed as,

$$\hat{\boldsymbol{\mu}}_{\text{ML}} = \left(\mathbf{A}_{c_p0}^\dagger \mathbf{C}_z^{-1}\mathbf{A}_{c0}\right)^{-1} \Re\{\mathbf{A}_{c_p0}^\dagger \mathbf{C}_z^{-1}\mathbf{Z}_P\}, \quad (24)$$

where $\Re\{z\}$ denotes the real part of z. We can express $\mathbf{C}_z^{-1} = \left(\mathbf{A}_c\boldsymbol{\chi}\mathbf{A}_c^\dagger + (1/\beta)\mathbf{I}_P\right)^{-1}$ using the matrix inversion lemma as follows,

$$\mathbf{C}_z^{-1} = \beta\mathbf{I}_P - \beta\mathbf{A}_c(\mathbf{A}_c^\dagger\mathbf{A}_c + (1/\beta)\boldsymbol{\chi})^{-1}\ \mathbf{A}_c^\dagger. \quad (25)$$

Using the property in (18), then (25) can be expressed as,

$$\mathbf{C}_z^{-1} = \beta\mathbf{I}_P - \beta\ \mathbf{A}_c\ \boldsymbol{\Lambda}\ \mathbf{A}_c^\dagger, \quad (26)$$

where $\boldsymbol{\Lambda} = \mathrm{diag}(\lambda_0, \cdots, \lambda_{L-1})$ with $\lambda_p = \left(\parallel \mathbf{a}_{c_p} \parallel^2 + 1/(2\beta\sigma_p^2)\right)^{-1}$. Substituting (26) in (24) and after some algebra, $\hat{\boldsymbol{\mu}}_{\text{ML}}$ takes the form

$$\hat{\boldsymbol{\mu}}_{\text{ML}} = \frac{1}{2}\mathrm{diag}(\parallel \mathbf{a}_{c_0} \parallel^{-2}, \parallel \mathbf{a}_{c_1} \parallel^{-2} \cdots, \parallel \mathbf{a}_{c_{L-1}} \parallel^{-2})\Re\{\mathbf{A}_{c_p}^\dagger\mathbf{Z}_P\}. \quad (27)$$

The ML estimate of $\boldsymbol{\sigma}^2$ can now be found. We substitute the $\hat{\boldsymbol{\mu}}$ obtained in (27) and by maximizing the objective function (23) with respect to $\boldsymbol{\sigma}^2$ as follows,

$$O(\hat{\boldsymbol{\mu}}_{\text{ML}}, \boldsymbol{\sigma}^2) = \arg\max_{\sigma^2} \log p\left(\mathbf{Z}_P|\hat{\boldsymbol{\mu}}_{\text{ML}}, \boldsymbol{\sigma}^2\right), \quad (28)$$

Employing the property obtained from (18) in (25) and by discarding the terms independent of $\boldsymbol{\sigma}^2$, (28) can be expressed as,

$$O(\hat{\boldsymbol{\mu}}_{\text{ML}}, \boldsymbol{\sigma}^2) = \sum_{p=0}^{L-1} \log\left(\parallel \mathbf{a}_{c_p} \parallel^2 \sigma_p^2 + \frac{1}{\beta}\right) - \beta\sum_{p=0}^{L-1}\left(|e_p|^2\lambda_p - \parallel \mathbf{b} \parallel^2\right), \quad (29)$$

where $\mathbf{b} \triangleq \mathbf{Z}_P - \mathbf{A}_{c0}\ \hat{\boldsymbol{\mu}}_{\text{ML}}$ and e_p is the pth component of the vector $\mathbf{e} = \mathbf{A}_{c0}^\dagger\mathbf{b}$. We take the gradient of O with respect to σ_p^2, and we equate it to zero. Consequently, the ML estimate for $\boldsymbol{\sigma}^2$ can be expressed as,

$$\hat{\sigma}_{p,ML}^2 = \left(\frac{|e_p|^2\beta - \parallel \mathbf{a}_{c_p} \parallel^2}{2 \parallel \mathbf{a}_{c_p} \parallel^4 \beta}\right)^+, \quad (30)$$

where $[x]^+ \triangleq \max(0, x)$.

C. Equalization and Data Detection

In this subsection, we demonstrate the data detection technique at the receiver using the observation model presented in (10). The proposed OFDM model contains P known pilot symbols evenly inserted in the K subcarriers, that is, the data symbols $\mathbf{d} = [d_0, d_1, \cdots, d_{K-1}]^T$ denotes the known, $\mathbf{d}_P$, and the the unknown, $\mathbf{d}_D$, data symbols, where the pilot positions vector is denoted by $p_r, r = 1, 2, \cdots, P$. Consequently, (10) can be expressed as

$$\mathbf{Z}_P \triangleq \mathbf{Z} - \mathbf{G}\mathbf{d}_P = \mathbf{G}\mathbf{d}_D + \mathbf{V}_P. \quad (31)$$

Then, the equalized soft data symbols $\tilde{\mathbf{d}}_D$ are recovered at the output of a linear minimum mean square error (MMSE) equalizer as

$$\tilde{\mathbf{d}}_D = \mathbf{G}^\dagger\left(\mathbf{G}\mathbf{G}^\dagger + \gamma^{-1}\mathbf{I}_K\right)^{-1}\mathbf{Z}_P\ , \quad (32)$$

where γ is the signal-to-noise ratio (SNR), $\mathbf{Z}_P^{(r)}$ is calculated from (31) as $\mathbf{Z}_P^{(r)} = \mathbf{Z} - \mathbf{G}^{(r)}\mathbf{d}_P$, and the $[k, q]^{th}$ element of $\mathbf{G}$ is computed from (5) and (6) by replacing the aforementioned channel estimates $\{h_p, (\vartheta, \tilde{\tau}_p)\}_{p=0}^{L-1}$. However, a demodulation process is performed over the equalized data symbols using ML detection technique.

V. Simulation Results

We now present the performance of the proposed approach in this section. The UWA OFDM system specifications along with the UWA channel parameters are summarized in Table-I.

TABLE I. CHANNEL AND SIMULATION PARAMETERS

carrier frequency (f_c)	18 KHz
channel bandwidth (BW)	7 KHz
number of subcarriers (K)	512
OFDM symbol duration (T)	73.15 ms
Subcarrier spacing ($\Delta f := 1/T$)	13.67 Hz
guard interval duration (T_g)	35 ms
number of paths on the link ($L_\times$)	3
maximum Doppler shift (ϑ_{max})	$10^{-2}, 5\times10^{-3}, 10^{-3}$
Doppler spread resolution $\Delta\xi$	10^{-3}
modulation formats	QPSK, 16QAM
pilot spacing (Δ_p)	4
oversampling factor (ϱ)	8

We consider a comb-type pilot structure with equally spaced pilot subcarriers in each OFDM block in order to assess the channel estimator and equalize the channel rapid changes per block. The mean-square error (MSE) and symbol error rate (SER) performance are presented as a function of SNR in Figs. 1 and 2, respectively. The curves show a comparison in performance of the proposed model with the classical MP channel estimation technique in the presence of quadrature phase shift-keying (QPSK) and 16-ary quadrature amplitude modulation (16QAM) signaling formats.

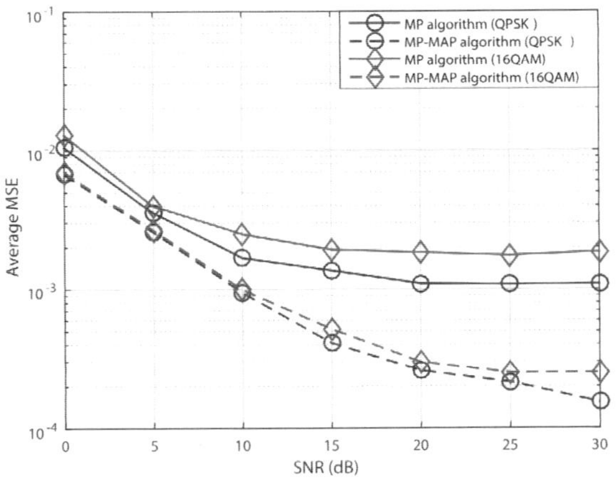

Figure 1. MSE vs. SNR performance comparisons of the MP-MAP and MP algorithms for different constellations: $\varrho = 8$, $\vartheta_{max} = 10^{-3}$

As seen from these two figures, the MP-MAP algorithm yields better channel MSE and SER performance and outperforms the MP estimator in the presence of higher SNR, where the MP curves shown use the linear MMSE equalizer to detect the data symbols.

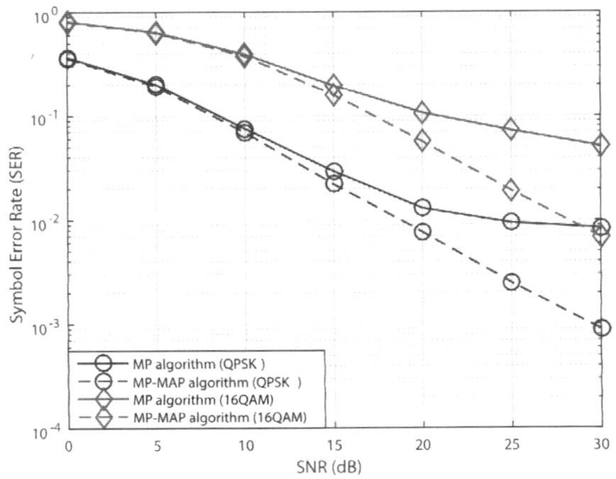

Figure 2. SER vs. SNR performance comparisons of the MP-MAP and MP algorithms for different constellations: $\varrho = 8$, $\vartheta_{max} = 10^{-3}$

Figs. 3 and 4 investigate the residual Doppler effect on the MSE and SER performance of the system as a function of SNR, respectively. It can be seen from these two figures that the performance of the channel estimator degrades with larger residual Doppler effect, whereas the curves of the proposed approach show better robustness compared to the MP algorithm alone against the Doppler shifts up to $\vartheta_{max} = 10^{-3}$, which can be considered as a severe Doppler effect.

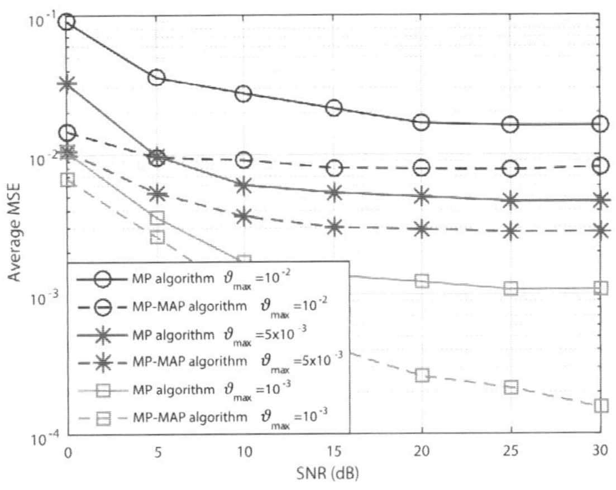

Figure 3. MSE vs. SNR performance of the MP-MAP algorithm for different Doppler shift rates, $\varrho = 8$, QPSK Signaling

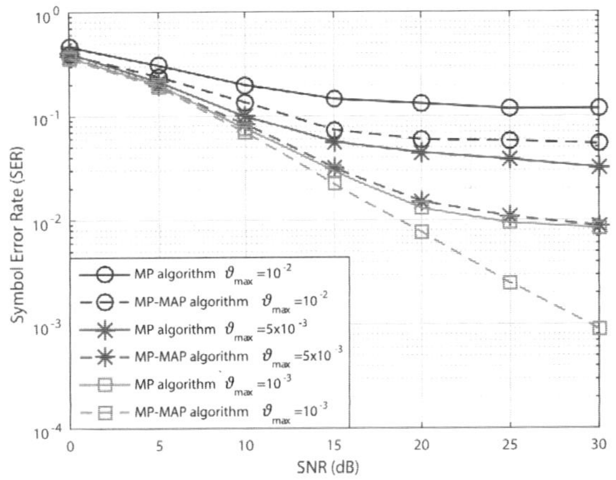

Figure 4. SER vs. SNR performance of the MP-MAP algorithm for different Doppler shift rates, $\varrho = 8$, QPSK Signaling

Note that, the value chosen for the oversampling factor assesses the underwater receiver with a firm Doppler shift and delay estimation and consequently a better MSE and SER performance.

VI. Conclusions and Future Work

In this work, an efficient channel estimation algorithm is proposed, named MP-MAP algorithm, for OFDM-based UWA systems in the presence of an UWA Rician channel with a correlated Gaussain noise. The channel delays and the Doppler shift are estimated by the matching pursuit algorithm, where the unknown parameters of the complex-valued channel gains are estimated by the maximum *a posteriori* algorithm. On the other hand, the variances and the means of the prior pdf of the channel gains are obtained by a ML estimation algorithm. The performance of the proposed approach is presented by means of the minimum mean square estimation of the estimated channel and the symbol error rate for different signaling formats and Doppler shifts. Based on the extensive computer simulations performed, it was concluded that the resulting MP-MAP channel estimation algorithm yields excellent MSE and SER performances as compared to the conventional approaches. For future work, the OFDM UWA communication system can be generalized into MIMO-OFDM-based UWA communication system, and the proposed approach can be extended into an experimental channel model, taking into consideration a real underwater environment and parameters.

ACKNOWLEDGMENT

This research has been supported in part by Suasis as a sub-contract of the Turkish Scientific and Research Council (TUBITAK) under Grant 1140029.

REFERENCES

[1] N. Bahrami, N. H. H. Khamis, and A. B. Baharom, "Study of underwater channel estimation based on different node placement in shallow water," IEEE Sensors J., vol. 16, no. 4, pp. 1095-1102, Feb. 2016.

[2] B. Crosby, A. Rosenberger, and B. Pirenne, "The web-enabled awareness research network (WARN) project," in Proc. OCEANS 2015 - MTS/IEEE Washington, pp. 1-10, 2015

[3] E. V. Zorita and M. Stojanovic, "Space-frequency block coding for underwater acoustic communications," IEEE J. Ocean. Eng., vol. 40, no. 2, pp. 303-314, Apr. 2015.

[4] S. Akada, S. Yoshizawa, H. Tanimoto, and T. Saito, "Experimental evaluation of data selective rake reception for underwater acoustic communication," in Proc. 2015 International Symposium on Intelligent Signal Processing and Communication Systems, pp. 514-519, Nov. 2015.

[5] T. Jenserud and S. Ivansson, "Measurements and modeling of effects of out-of-plane reverberation on the power delay profile for underwater acoustic channels," IEEE J. Ocean. Eng., vol. 40, no. 4, pp. 807-821, Oct. 2015.

[6] X. Kuai, H. Sun, S. Zhou, and E. Cheng, "Impulsive noise mitigation in underwater acoustic OFDM systems," IEEE Trans. Veh. Technol., vol. 65, no. 10, pp. 8190-8202, Oct. 2016.

[7] E. Panayirci, H. Senol, M. Uysal, and V. Poor, "Sparse channel estimation and equalization for OFDM-based underwater cooperative systems with amplify-and-forward relaying," IEEE Trans. Signal Process., vol. 64, no. 1, pp. 214-228, Sept. 2016.

[8] L. Ma, S. Zhou, G. Qiao, S. Liu, and F. Zhou, "Superposition coding for downlink underwater acoustic OFDM," IEEE J. Ocean. Eng., vol. 42, no. 1, pp. 175-187, Jan. 2017.

[9] X. Shi and Y. Yang, "Adaptive sparse channel estimation based on RLS for underwater acoustic OFDM systems," in Proc. Sixth International Conference on Instrumentation and Measurement, Computer, Communication and Control, pp. 266-269, 2016.

[10] M. G. R. Kumar and M. Sarvagya, "Review on enhanced data rate receiver design using efficient modulation techniques for underwater acoustic communication," in Proc. 2016 International Conference on Advanced Communication Control and Computing Technologies, pp. 313-317, 2016.

[11] F. yu, D. Li, Q. Guo, Z. Wang, and W. Xiang, "Block-FFT based OMP for compressed channel estimation in underwater acoustic communications," IEEE Commun. Lett., vol. 19, no. 11, pp. 1937-1940, Nov. 2015.

[12] B. Peng, P. S. Rossi, H. Dong, and K. Kansanen, "Time-domain oversampled OFDM communication in doubly-selective underwater acoustic channels," IEEE Commun. Lett., vol. 19, no. 6, pp. 1081-1084, Jun. 2015.

[13] S. Beygi and U. Mitra, "Multi-scale multi-lag channel estimation using low rank approximation for OFDM," IEEE Trans. Signal Process., vol. 63, no. 18, pp. 4744-4755, Sept. 2015.

[14] S. F. Mason, C. R. Berger, S. Zhou, and P. Willett, "Detection, synchronization, and doppler scale estimation with multicarrier waveforms in underwater acoustic communication," IEEE J. Sel. Areas Commun., vol. 26, no. 9, pp. 1638-1649, Dec. 2008.

[15] Y. Chen, L. Zou, A. Zhao, and J. Yin, "Null subcarriers based Doppler scale estimation for multicarrier communication over underwater acoustic non-uniform Doppler shift channels," in Proc. 2016 IEEE/OES China Ocean Acoustics, pp. 1-6, Jan. 2016.

[16] H. Nouri, M. Uysal and E. Panayirci, "Information theoretical performance analysis and optimisation of cooperative underwater acoustic communication systems," in IET Communications, vol. 10, no. 7, pp. 812-823, 5 5 2016.

[17] L. Zhang, J. Han, J. Huang, and M. Brandt-Pearce, "OFDM transmission over time-varying channel with self interference cancellation," in Proc. IEEE International Conference on Signal Processing, Communications and Computing, pp. 743-746, 2014.

Trust-Based Defence Model Against MAC Unfairness Attacks for IoT

Nabil DJEDJIG
Research Center on Scientific and Technical Information
Abderrahamane MIRA University
ALGIERS, ALGERIA
djedjig_nabil@cerist.dz

Djamel TANDJAOUI
Research Center on Scientific and Technical Information
ALGIERS, ALGERIA
dtandjaoui@cerist.dz

Imed ROMDHANI
Edinburgh Napier University, School of Computing
Edinburgh, UK
I.Romdhani@napier.ac.uk

Faiza MEDJEK
Research Center on Scientific and Technical Information
Abderrahamane MIRA University
ALGIERS, ALGERIA
medjek-f@dtri.cerist.dz

***Abstract*—The vulnerability of Internet of Things (IoT) networks makes channel access security a serious problem. The IEEE 802.15.4 Media Access Control (MAC) layer faces the risk of attacks from malicious nodes which attempts to get a dominating position and hold unfair advantages over the other nodes. In this paper, we address MAC unfairness attacks where attackers attempt to bypass the MAC priority. We propose a MAC-trust-based model to handle unfairness attacks while maintaining channel access to all participating nodes. In our scheme, a Pan Coordinator Manager (PCM) cooperates with PANs and Coordinators to detect malicious behavior, calculate trust values for participating nodes, and maintain a blacklist of malicious nodes. Our model modifies Guaranteed Time Slots (GTS) allocation policies according to nodes' trust values.**

Keywords-Trust; IEEE 802.15.4; Internet of Things; Security; unfairness attack; GTS.

I. INTRODUCTION

The Internet of Things (IoT) is collectively formed of emergent embedded objects, such as smart-phones, tablets, smart watches/glasses, intelligent building devices, and even smart vehicles [1]. These objects are addressable, and have low-power and low-processing capacities. They are interconnected to transfer sensing data to the Internet using compatible and heterogonous radio communications. In such heterogeneous environment, security is among the key issue to overcome.

The research community considers the IEEE 802.15.4 standard as one of enabling technologies for short range, low rate, wireless communications that is most suitable for IoT, which makes it the de-facto standard to define physical and MAC (Media Access Control) layer for IoT networks [2]. Although researches in IoT security have focussed on all security aspects for the different OSI layers, most security solutions are being specifically designed for network and application layers [3]-[6]. Given that, the MAC layer is the basis of interconnecting IoT nodes, it is therefore targeted by several attackers [7]. Yasmin et al. surveyed IEEE 802.15.4 attacks [8]. In this paper, we focus on MAC unfairness attacks, especially Guaranteed Time Slots (GTS) related attacks. In these attacks, malicious node cheats to obtain higher priority than legitimate nodes to maximize the channel access utilization [9]. Most of MAC security solutions proposed in the literature are based on cryptography mechanism to deal with confidentiality and authentication issues. Nevertheless, these solutions cannot handle MAC unfairness attacks. Indeed, embedding minor changes in the IEEE 802.15.4 standard itself will make it more secure against this type of attacks.

In this paper, we introduce a new MAC-trust-based model to solve MAC unfairness attacks. In this model PANs and Coordinators collaborate with a centralized PAN Coordinator Manager to evaluate trust values of participating nodes. Indeed, the allocation of the GTS is based on the evaluated trust values. Each time the trust decreases, the number of slots allocated to the node decreases too until no priority is assigned to the node.

The rest of this paper is structured as follows. Section II presents a background of IEEE 802.15.4 GTS MAC process and related attacks. Section III introduces our proposed model. Finally, Section IV concludes the paper.

II. IEEE 802.15.4 PROTOCOL

A. GTS MAC Background

IEEE 802.15.4 networks can operate on beacon or non-beacon enabled modes. In this paper, we focus on beacon enabled mode. In this mode, a superframe is delimited by two beacons, and is divided into 16 time slots. Each of periodic superframe is divided into a Contention Access Period (CAP) and a Contention Free Period (CFP). Slotted CSMA/CA (Carrier Sense Multiple Access with Collision Avoidance) is used in the CAP, whilst, GTS is used in CFP [10]. The superframe is fully defined using a beacon interval (BI) and a superframe duration (SD). BI refers to the time between two consecutive beacons and is constituted by an active portion and an optional inactive portion, as shown in Figure 1. During the inactive portion, the coordinator enters a low-power mode to conserve its power resources. The active period corresponds to the SD and is divided into 16 time slots, as shown in Figure 2.

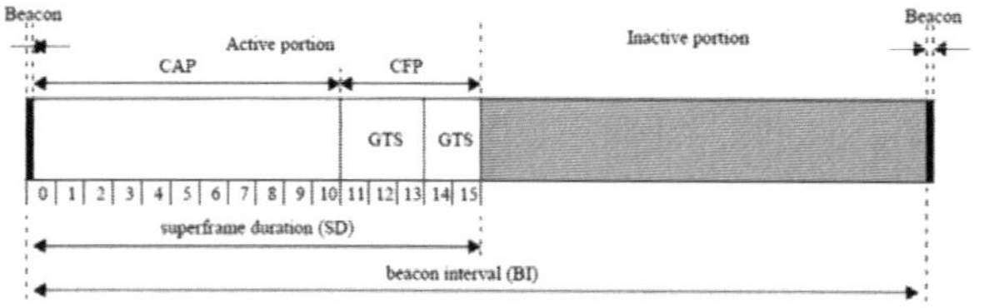

Figure 1. IEEE 802.15.4 superframe structure.

The PAN coordinator reserves GTS within the CFP of each superframe duration in order to provide real-time guaranteed channel access to in-network nodes for delay-sensitive applications. The PAN coordinator allocates and de-allocates GTS on a First-come, First-serve basis [10], as depicted in Figure 3. Indeed, it may allocate up to 7 GTS at the one time. A node requests GTS from the coordinator, by sending a GTS request frame during the CAP. The node waits for the response of the coordinator in the next beacon. The coordinator either accepts or rejects the request based on the current resource capacity available in the superframe. Once a GTS request from a node is granted, the coordinator reserves the GTS for the node during the CFP. Upon receiving beacon transmitted by the PAN coordinator, each node tries to transmit its packet using the superframe. Nodes that do not succeed in accessing the channel discard the packet, and at the next superframe, they generate a new packet.

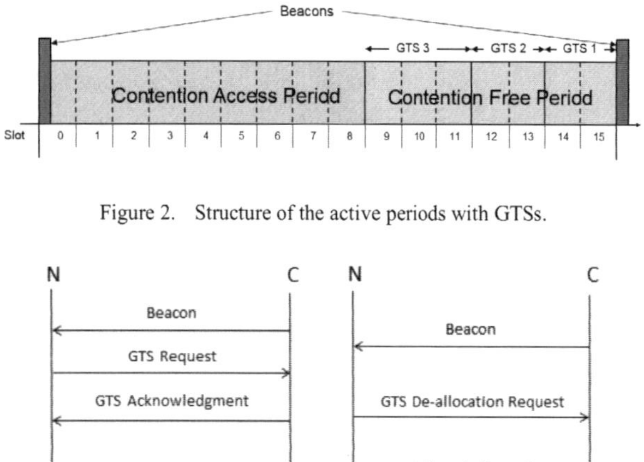

Figure 2. Structure of the active periods with GTSs.

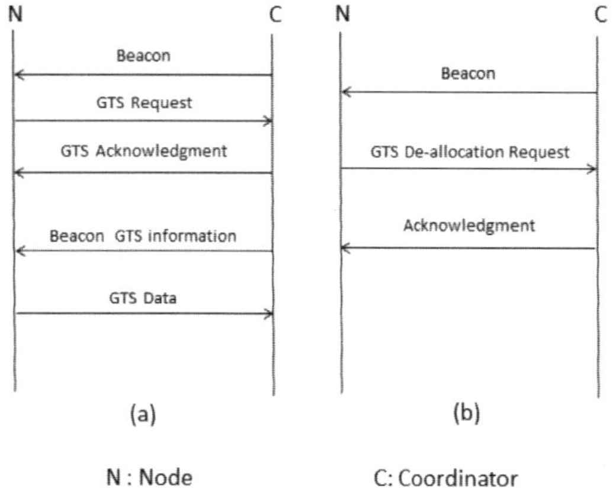

Figure 3. (a) GTS allocation process, (b) GTS de-allocation processes.

B. *GTS MAC Attacks*

The GTS MAC channel sharing mechanisms are vulnerable to malicious nodes that misbehave and break the standard communication rules to capture the channel with higher priority utilization. Indeed, malicious nodes extract slots information from the beacon sent by the PAN/Coordinators to trigger different MAC attacks.

There exist several GTS related attacks that have been defined in the literature. Among them the following:

- Malicious nodes can keep sending several GTS allocation request frames, and thus can allocate a maximum number of GTS and keep the channel busy, omitting legitimate nodes from allocating GTS and transferring data [8] [11] [12].
- A malicious node can spoof unallocated legitimate node identities and send GTS allocation requests on their behalf [13]. The malicious node can then inject false data. Also, the malicious node can use its proper identity or fabricated identities to send GTS allocation requests [14].
- A malicious node can spoof identities of legitimate nodes with allocated GTS. It can then send GTS de-allocation requests on their behalf, which leads to terminate their channel access rights [13].
- One or two attackers can create interference during the GTS allocated to legitimate nodes. This leads to corrupt ongoing transmissions [13] [12].

III. THE PROPOSED MODEL

To enhance MAC security, we propose two algorithms. The first algorithm aims to verify the association process. The second one to allocate GTS dynamically for real time applications based on nodes trustworthiness. The GTS period in the IEEE 802.15.4 is adjustable by beacon parameters (BeaconOrder-BO and SuperframeOrder-RO) [10]. In our model, the GTS period is initially set using BO and RO. After the first GTS request, the GTS period is recalculated and reallocated based on nodes trust values. In the following, we present our model and how to calculate trust values.

Three entities (actors) participate in the proposed model: A Pan Coordinator Manager denoted PCM, at least one PAN Coordinator and Coordinators denoted C_i, and nodes denoted N_j. Coordinators and PANs are full function devices (FFDs), whilst the nodes can be FFDs or reduced function devices (RFDs). The PCM keeps in its table (database) a list of all coordinators and PANs, and a list of all nodes within the network. Indeed, for each Coordinator C_i, PCM maintains the list of nodes associated with it, the trust value, denoted T_{Nj}, of each node N_j, and the number of GTS request frames, denoted NB_{Nj}, for each node N_j. In our model, the PCM monitors GTS across the entire network by keeping the history of all nodes stationary and mobile.

For security consideration, we assume each node N_j is associated to only one C_i at time t.

A. *Controlled Association MAC*

As already said, each node is allowed to be associated to only one PAN/Coordinator at one time t. Thus, each time a node sends an association request to a PAN or a Coordinator, this later sends an association control request to the PCM. The PCM checks in its database the state of the node. Two cases rise: 1) The node does not exist in the database, which means it is not associated to any PAN/Coordinator. 2) The node is already associated to one PAN/Coordinator. In the first case, the PCM sends an Association Control Acknowledgment, and the PAN/Coordinator can associate this node. In the second case, the PCM sends a Request status to the PAN/Coordinator associating the node. Two cases can occur: 1) The node is associated correctly to the PAN/Coordinator. 2) The node became orphan because it lost the connexion with the PAN/Coordinator. In the first case, the PCM blacklists the node and sends an association control notification to all PAN/Coordinators. In the second case, the PCM sends an association control acknowledgment and updates its database. Algorithm 1 (Figure 4) and Figure 5 summarise the controlled association process.

Algorithm 1 Trust-Based Association Algorithm

Input: One PCM; a number of coordinators M; a number of nodes N; each node Nj is associated to only one coordinator $C_i \in M$;
Nj sends Association Request to C_i;
C_i sends Association Control Request (N_j,C_i) to PCM
PCM checks if $N_j \in C_h$ ($h \neq i$)
If $N_j \in C_h$ ($h \neq i$) **do**
  PCM sends Request status to C_h ($h \neq i$)
  If N_j is associated **do**
    $N_j = 0$;
    Blacklists T_{Nj};
    sends Association Control notification (N_j) to C_i;
    sends Disassociation notification (N_j) to C_h;
    C_i sends Disassociation notification to N_j;
  Else If N_j is orphan **do**
    PCM sends Association Control Acknowledgment (N_j) to C_i;
    C_i sends Association Acknowledgment to N_j;
  END If
Else If $N_j \notin C_h$ **do**
  PCM sends Association Control Acknowledgment (N_j) to C_i;
  Ci sends Association Acknowledgment to N_j;
END If

Figure 4. Trust-Based Association Algorithm.

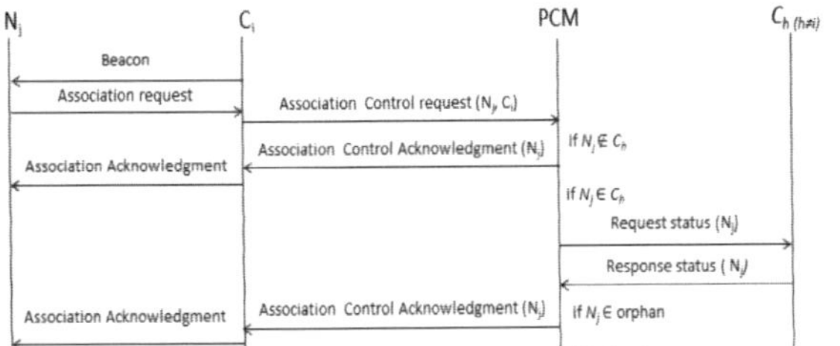

Figure 5. Controlled Association process.

B. *Adaptive Allocation GTS MAC*

Algorithm 2 (Figure 7) and Figure 6 summarise the proposed Adaptive Allocation GTS process.

Initially, at the first association, all nodes are fully trusted, which means trust values of all nodes are set to 1 (i.e. T_{Nj}=1). In addition, the number of GTS request frames for each node is set to 0 (i.e. NB_{Nj}=0). The maximum number of GTS request frames allowed within a period T for each node is set as threshold, denoted TH.

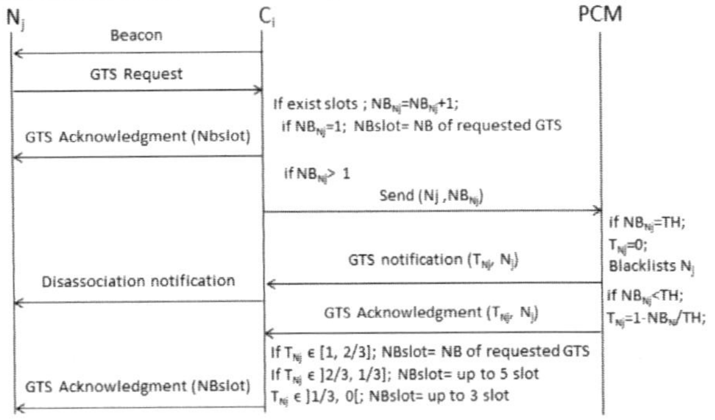

Figure 6. Trust-Based GTS Allocation process.

Algorithm 2 Trust-based GTS Allocation Algorithm

Input: One PCM; a number of coordinators M; a number of nodes N; each node N_j is associated to only one coordinator $C_i \in M$; the trust value of each node $_{Nj} \in N$ is set to T_{Nj} = 1; the number of request to GTS from each node Nj is set to NB_{Nj} = 0; TH= Threshold;(TH : a maximum number of requests to GTS);
While (T) **do**
  N_j sends GTS Request to C_i;
  C_i calculates $NB_{Nj} = NB_{Nj} + 1$;
  If NB_{Nj} = 1 **do**
    NBslots= NB.GTS.Req;
    Sends GTS Acknowledgment (NBslots);
  END If
  If $NB_{Nj} > 1$ **do**
    sends (N_j, NB_{Nj}) to PCM;
    If NB_{Nj}= TH **do**
      T_{Nj}=0;
      Blacklists N_j;
      Sends GTS notification (T_{Nj}, N_j) to C_i;
      C_i sends Disassociation notification to N_j;
    END If
    If NB_{Nj} < TH **do**
      T_{Nj}=1- NB_{Nj}/TH;
      Sends GTS Acknowledgment (T_{Nj},N_j) to C_i;
      If $T_{Nj} \in$ [1, 2/3] **do** NBslots=NB.GTS.Req;
      If $T_{Nj} \in$]2/3, 1/3] **do** NBslots = up to 5 slot of NB.GTS.Req;
      If $T_{Nj} \in$]1/3, 0] **do** NBslots= up to 3 slot of NB.GTS.Req;
      Sends GTS Acknowledgment (NBslots);
    END If
  END If
END While

Figure 7. Trust-based GTS Allocation Algorithm.

After successfully associated with the PAN/coordinator, nodes send GTS request frames through which they ask the PAN/coordinator to assign them a number of GTS (according to BO and RO). Once the PAN/Coordinator receives the request, it increments NB_{Nj} (i.e. NB_{Nj}= NB_{Nj}+1) and sends N_j and NB_{Nj} to the PCM. Upon receiving N_j and NB_{Nj}, the PCM checks if $NB_{Nj} \leq$ TH. If NB_{Nj}=TH, the PCM sets T_{Nj} to 0, blacklists N_j and sends GTS notification to all PAN/Coordinators. If NB_{Nj} < TH, the PCM calculates the new trust value T_{Nj} according to equation 1, and sends GTS Acknowledgment with the node identifier N_j, the number of

GTS request frames NB_{Nj}, and the new trust value T_{Nj} for this node to the PAN/Coordinator.

$$T_{Nj} = 1 - NB_{Nj} / TH \qquad (1)$$

For the first GTS request, the PAN/Coordinator acknowledges the nodes and allocates them a number of GTS equal to the number of requested GTS. After that, the allocation is done according to nodes trust value as follow.

We split GTS to three sub-GTS: GTS1 (2 slots), GTS2 (2 slots) and GTS3 (3 slots) [10]. We split the trust interval onto three sub-intervals: [1, 2/3],]2/3, 1/3], and]1/3, 0[.

- If the new calculated trust value $T_{Nj} \in [1, 2/3]$, the PAN/Coordinator allocates the node a number of GTS equal to the number of requested GTS (Up to 7 slots).
- If $T_{Nj} \in]2/3, 1/3]$, the PAN/Coordinator allocates the node a number of GTS up to 5 slots (GTS3+GTS2). Hence, if the number of requested GTS is greater than 5, the node will be assigned a maximum of 5 slots.
- If $T_{Nj} \in]1/3, 0[$,the PAN/Coordinator allocates the node a number of GTS up to 3 slots (GTS3). Hence, if the number of requested GTS is greater than 3, the node will be assigned a maximum of 3 GTS.

If the PAN/Coordinator receives GTS request from two or more nodes at the same time, instead of allocating GTS on a First-come, First-serve basis, the PAN/Coordinator allocates GTS on trust basis. Which means, the first served is the node with the greatest trust value.

The allocation process is repeated while T not expired. Once T expired, PAN/Coordinators and PCM reset NB_{Nj} to 0 and T_{Nj} to 1.

IV. CONCLUSION

A trust-based defence and dynamic GTS allocation method is introduced in this paper to prevent and detect some MAC unfairness attacks in beacon-enabled IoT 802.15.4 networks. We introduced a new central entity to IEEE 802.15.4 topology to act as a global neighbor discovery proxy. This new entity (PCM), caches the new identity of all nodes and monitor local GTS allocation based on nodes' behavior. This new approach can handle easily mobile nodes.

REFERENCES

[1] C. Shen, H. Choi, S. Chakraborty, and M. Srivastava, "Towards a rich sensing stack for iot devices," in Computer-Aided Design (ICCAD), 2014 IEEE/ACM International Conference on. IEEE, 2014, pp. 424–427.

[2] J. Gubbi, R. Buyya, S. Marusic, and M. Palaniswami, "Internet of things (iot): A vision, architectural elements, and future directions," Future Generation Computer Systems, vol. 29, no. 7, pp. 1645–1660, 2013.

[3] N. Djedjig, D. Tandjaoui, F. Medjek, and I. Romdhani, "New trust metric for the rpl routing protocol," in Information and Communication Systems (ICICS), 2017 8th International Conference on. IEEE, 2017, pp. 328–335.

[4] F. Medjek, D. Tandjaoui, I. Romdhani, and N. Djedjig, "New trust metric for the rpl routing protocoll," in The 10th IEEE International Conference on Internet of Things (iThings-2017). IEEE. IEEE, 2017, in press.

[5] J. Guo, R. Chen, and J. J. Tsai, "A survey of trust computation models for service management in the internet of things systems," Computer Communications, vol. 97, pp. 1–14, 2017.

[6] B. B. Zarpel˜ao, R. S. Miani, C. T. Kawakani, and S. C. de Alvarenga, "A survey of intrusion detection in i nternet of things," Journal of Network and Computer Applications, 2017, pp 25–37.

[7] S. M. Sajjad and M. Yousaf, "Security analysis of ieee 802.15. 4 mac in the context of internet of things (iot)," in Information Assurance and Cyber Security (CIACS), 2014 Conference on. IEEE, 2014, pp. 9–14.

[8] Y. M. Amin and A. T. Abdel-Hamid, "A comprehensive taxonomy and analysis of ieee 802.15. 4 attacks," Journal of Electrical and Computer Engineering, vol. 2016, p. 4, 2016.

[9] C. Balarengadurai and S. Saraswathi, "Comparative analysis of detection of ddos attacks in ieee 802.15. 4 low rate wireless personal area network," Procedia Engineering, vol. 38, pp. 3855–3863, 2012.

[10] IEEE, "Local and metropolitan area networksspecific requirementspart 15.4: wireless medium access control (mac) and physical layer (phy) specifications for low rate wireless personal area networks (wpans)," IEEE Standard for Information Technology, 2006.

[11] B. M. David and T. de Sousa Jr, "A bayesian trust model for the mac layer in ieee 802.15. 4 networks," in I2TS 2010-9th International Information and Telecommunication Technologies Symposium, 2010.

[12] S. Saleem, S. Ullah, and K. S. Kwak, "A study of ieee 802.15.4 security framework for wireless body area networks," Sensors, vol. 11, no. 2, pp. 1383–1395, 2011.

[13] R. Sokullu, O. Dagdeviren, and I. Korkmaz, "On the ieee 802.15.4 mac layer attacks: Gts attack," in Sensor Technologies and Applications, 2008. SENSORCOMM'08. Second International Conference on. IEEE, 2008, pp. 673–678.

[14] C. P. O'Flynn, "Message denial and alteration on ieee 802.15.4 low-power radio networks," in New Technologies, Mobility and Security (NTMS), 2011 4th IFIP International Conference on. IEEE, 2011, pp. 1–5.

Distributed Upstream Data Cleaning in VANET

Mohamed Ben Brahim*†, Hamid Menouar*
*Qatar Mobility Innovations Center (QMIC), Qatar University, Doha, Qatar
†HANA Research Lab, University of Manouba, Manouba, Tunisia
Email: {mohamedb, hamidm }@qmic.com

Abstract—**The mobile road stations in Vehicular Ad hoc NETworks (VANET) are generating huge quantities of traffic-related data over wireless communication medium. For different business purposes, data has to be collected by heterogeneous distributed Road Side Units (RSUs) and pushed to traffic agencies (i.e., back-end) to be processed. Commonly, servers run a heavy processing in schema and data instance levels to ensure data transformation and data cleaning prior to storage in a production data warehouse. In particular, a comprehensive treatment is dedicated to detect and remove data redundancy and filter out or correct outlier instances. In order to alleviate these challenging tasks, a new proposal to delegate part of this data processing to the network edge in the RSUs is going to be investigated. Indeed, the RSUs are subject to potentially capture redundant data as well as defective measurement values from field data sources. Through a cooperative approach, RSUs could perform a near-real-time upstream filtering and cleaning treatment of the gathered data. Hence, an overview to tackle the upstream data cleaning and redundancy removal in a distributed fashion is presented. The proposed approach is expected to reduce the complexity of the data cleaning task and to scale better with the network size and its resulting data.**

Keywords–Distributed data cleaning; data filtering; vehicular ad hoc networks (VANET).

I. Background

The Cyber-Physical Systems (CPSs) are empowering the establishment of future smart cities. Indeed, they cross the borders between physical and computational domains creating a better awareness of the surrounding environment beyond the visual domain. The evolution of sensing, computing, and networking technologies allowed the CPSs to ever increase the data generation causing a deluge of data that need to be managed to serve different business and social applications and services. Intelligent Transportation Systems did not deviate from the general trend and vehicles equipped with communication capabilities are able to measure and share in near-real-time traffic-related data. Similarly to other CPSs, raw data streams generated by mobile road stations might contain faulty values, redundant measurements captured by multiple road side units (RSUs), and differently structured or semi-structures data. These issues have a direct impact on the efficiency of the system as they might falsify the computing of some metrics. Hence, different techniques have been emphasized in the industrial and research communities to mitigate the negative implications of such dirty data and the resulting misleading insights. Zaho et al. [1] investigate the big data challenges resulting from urban mobility as it becomes more available. The raw urban mobility data is usually prone to inaccurate measurements due to physical or computational factors. Hence, a cleaning and pre-processing phase is usually adopted in the urban human mobitiy data mining pipeline through noise filtering, map matching, and/or road matching techniques. Shiyale and Saraf [2] investigate the dirty data cleaning in mobile wireless sensor network to enhance the overall network lifetime. The used technique is in-network and consists of enhancing the data throughput through embedded data re-transmission and leveraging spatio-temporal consistency to clean dirty data and detect outliers. Javed and Wolf [3] present a generic method using spatial and temporal characteristics to derive statistical models of continuous monitored phenomena. These models are exploited to find out defective sensor reports. NADEEF [4] is another system performing data cleaning built on top of big data processing engines like Spark [5]. Bleach [6] is a recently published system for stream data cleaning. It consists of two modules serving respectively for violation detection and violation repair. It addresses mainly real-time and high accuracy requirements. In brief, different

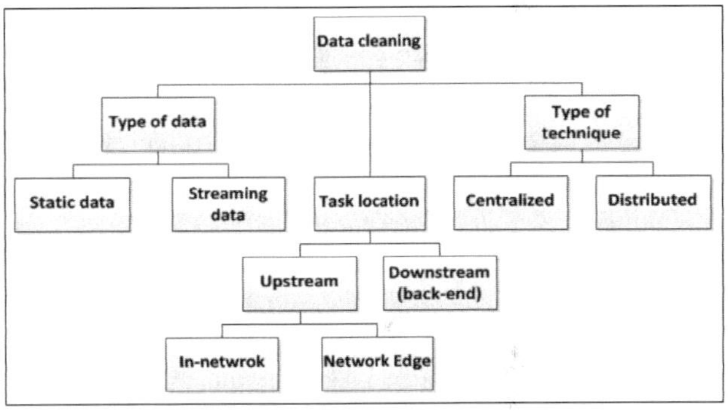

Figure 1. Taxonomy of different data cleaning techniques.

data cleaning approaches are available in the literature. The main difference between the existing solutions is whether they address static or streaming data, they are centralized or distributed systems, and their location in the data pipeline: in-network, in the network edge, or in the central server, as depicted in Figure 1. For datasets already stored in databases, certainly techniques meant for static data, downstream, being either centralized or over cluster of workers are the relevant options. In contrast, online data streams require real-time in-network or network-edge-based methods which are usually performed in a distributed fashion.

In the remainder of this paper, Section II is meant for describing data cleaning within the ETL process. Section III gives an overview of an upwind data cleaning process proposed to alleviate the data management pipeline in the back-end side. The short paper ends with a conclusion in Section IV.

II. Data Cleaning and ETL

The data cleaning process is required to improve data quality in different datasets. It aims at detecting and potentially fixing inconsistencies resulting from operational errors while

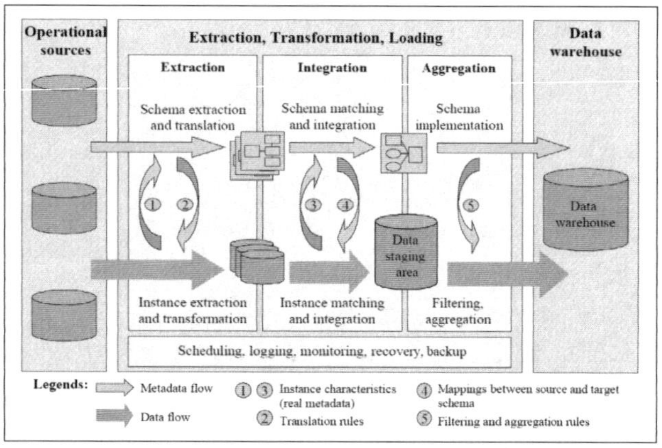

Figure 2. ETL process and data cleaning in data warehouse building [7].

populating the datasets. Data cleaning is largely studied in the well-known Extraction-Transformation-Loading (ETL) process for data warehouses. Indeed, data warehouses are usually meant for decision making and data correctness is therefore a fundamental factor. As illustrated in Figure 2, data undergo several transformation and integration tasks at instance and in schema levels. Afterwards, it is cleaned and filtered in a staging area prior to be loaded to the data warehouse [7]. Regarding the data repair, some fuzzy matching techniques are proposed to measure similarity and potentially fix erroneous data [8]. This technique of data cleaning is located at the end of the data stream for both static or live data. Hence, a considerable time delay is expected, which can reach several hours for big datasets, in order to successfully ingest the incoming data, clean it, and load it to a data warehouse.

III. Upstream Cooperative Data Cleaning

The challenges raised by the downstream data cleaning techniques are obvious. Indeed, with high velocity, high variety, and high volume of collected data, the time-to-value becomes very challenging. Hence, upwind data stream cleaning technique stands as potentially better alternative. In the context of VANET, upstream data cleaning could be performed either in-network similar to the proposed approach in wireless sensor networks [2], or could leverage the computing resources and the spatio-temporal consistency of the distributed road side units, i.e., the network edge. Indeed, as the data volume increasing rate is far exceeding the computing capacity increasing rate, it is wise to divide resources-consuming tasks into lesser complex sub-tasks and to dispatch them to multiple workers. Therefore, RSUs are considered as distributed workers which are able to cooperatively use different data mining and machine learning techniques to learn appropriate models for filtering and cleaning collected data from operational data sources in their neighborhood. As illustrated in Figure 3, mobile nodes might be in the communication range of more than single road side equipment, leading to duplicate data reception of the same packet. In addition, for multi-hop data routing techniques, the multipath scenario might occur which causes the reception of the same message by multiple collection nodes. All these scenarios, along with the inaccuracy of the measured metrics and different data structures will lead to dirty collected data. Hence, the raw collected data is not ready to serve for knowledge discovery and decision making.

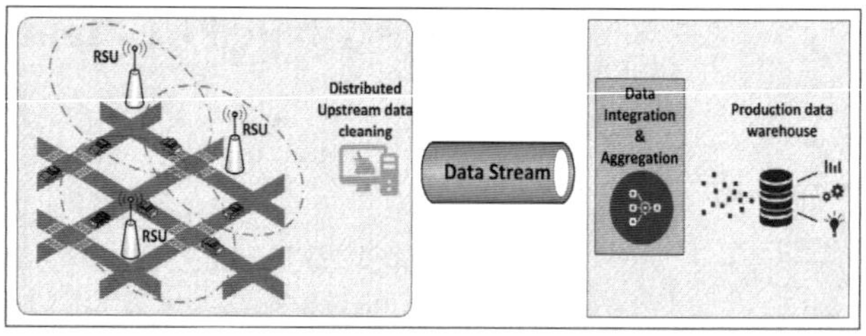

Figure 3. Distributed upstream data cleaning

An RSU could leverage some data characteristics such as spatial and temporal correlation of neighbor nodes to detect outlier values and correct them. Based on the location and time information embedded in the vehicle messages, the RSUs which are likely to receive the same message could perform a cross-check and keep a single copy of the message which solves the data redundancy problem. This could be achieved through exchange of cached messages indexes and willingness to keep a copy of each message based on available buffer size and aptitude to guarantee a data accuracy over short-time periods.

IV. Conclusion and Future Work

Data cleaning is an important task within the data management pipeline for cyber-physical systems. Since the generated data within VANET is often subject to inaccuracy and to redundant occurrences, leveraging spatio-temporal consistency and context-awareness of the distributed road side units to perform cooperative data cleaning and early data filtering is worth investigating. In the extension of this work, we will focus on defining a cooperative technique allowing the RSUs to detect and clean dirty data in the upwind of the data stream, and compare it with legacy downstream and in-network data cleaning systems.

Acknowledgment

This publication was made possible by NPRP grant #NPRP8-2459-1-482 from the Qatar National Research Fund (a member of Qatar Foundation).

References

[1] K. Zhao, S. Tarkoma, S. Liu, and H. Vo, "Urban Human Mobility Data Mining: An Overview," IEEE International Conference on Big Data (Big Data), December 2016, pp. 1–10.

[2] K. V. Shiyale and P. D. Saraf, "Efficient Technique for Network Lifetime Enhancement by Cleaning Dirty Data," International Journal of Science and Research (IJSR), vol. 4, no. 4, April 2015, pp. 2525–2528.

[3] N. Javed and T. Wolf, "Automated Sensor Verification using Outlier Detection in the Internet of Things," 32nd International Conference on Distributed Computing Systems Workshops, June 2012, pp. 1–6.

[4] N. Tang, "Big Data Cleaning," 16th Asia-Pacific Web Conference (APWeb), September 2014, pp. 13–24.

[5] "Apache Spark," http://spark.apache.org/, 2017.06.22.

[6] Y. Tian, P. Michiardi, and M. Vukolić, "Bleach: A Distributed Stream Data Cleaning System," arXiv:1609.05113v1 [cs.DB], September 2016.

[7] E. Rahm and H. H. Do, "Data Cleaning: Problems and Current Approaches," Bulletin of the Technical Committee on Data Engineering, December 2000, pp. 4–13.

[8] S. Chaudhuri, K. Ganjam, V. Ganti, and R. Motwani, "Robust and Efficient Fuzzy Match for Online Data Cleaning," Proceedings of the 2003 ACM SIGMOD international conference on Management of data, June 2003, pp. 313–324.